Beginning ASP.NET 2.0 Databases
Beta Preview

Beginning ASP.NET 2.0 Databases Beta Preview

John Kauffman
with Thiru Thangarathinam

WILEY
Wiley Publishing, Inc.

Beginning ASP.NET 2.0 Databases Beta Preview

Published by
Wiley Publishing, Inc.
10475 Crosspoint Boulevard
Indianapolis, IN 46256
www.wiley.com

Published simultaneously in Canada

ISBN-13 978-0-7645-7081-0

ISBN-10 0-7645-7081-1

Manufactured in the United States of America

10 9 8 7 6 5 4 3 2 1

1B/QS/QT/QW/IN

Library of Congress Cataloging-in-Publication Data is available.

For general information on our other products and services please contact our Customer Care Department within the United States at (800) 762-2974, outside the United States at (317) 572-3993 or fax (317) 572-4002.

About the Author

John Kauffman has written numerous books about ASP and the incorporation of data into ASP pages. Born in Philadelphia and educated at Penn State, he has lived, taught, and programmed on three continents as he follows his wife's diplomatic assignments.

When not writing, he spends his time sailing, teaching electronics to high school groups, and chauffeuring his kids to hockey and music practices.

Credits

Acquisitions Editor
Jim Minatel

Development Editor
Marcia Ellett

Technical Editors
Bradley Millington
Patrick Santry

Copy Editing and Indexing
Publication Services

Proofreader
Jennifer Ashley

Editorial Manager
Mary Beth Wakefield

Vice President & Executive Group Publisher
Richard Swadley

Vice President and Publisher
Joseph B. Wikert

Graphics and Production Specialist
Jennifer Heleine

Quality Control Technician
David Faust

This book is dedicated to my wife's extended family in appreciation for all they have done for me over the last twenty years. Aunt Ethel has been a gracious and generous hostess on so many occasions. Glenn has provided hours of intellectual stimulation in his quest to understand the grandest questions of the universe. Angela provided an open heart and wonderful meals on many extended stays at her home. Stephanie, Diego, Linda, and Dae Gwon have been wonderful hosts during visits to Pittsburgh, Venice, and Sunnyvale, especially when they tolerated our jet-lagged children running around their homes at two in the morning. My thanks to Leigh for his encouragement to our children and patient explanations of his research in the function of the human brain. Tam has generously provided her organizational skills on numerous occasions with travel plans and accommodations, while her daughters have given us another look at the world through children's eyes. And Dave has been so much fun for all of us and is now an inspiration and role model for my son. My thanks to all of you for your generosity, love, and acceptance over the last two decades.

Contents

Foreword

It's hard to imagine a Web site on the Internet today that is without some form of data access. Whether you are building an e-commerce site, a business portal application, a news and information server, a family photo album, or even a personal Web log, all of these sites require some form of data to provide a rich, dynamic experience to viewers and customers. A static Web site simply is no longer an option for most real-world applications. Inevitably, all Web developers from hobbyists to professionals will need to learn dynamic Web programming to stay competitive in today's environment.

Web developers are faced with a wide variety of tools and technologies to choose from when deciding to build dynamic Web sites. Some of the factors to consider when choosing a development framework include ease-of-use, power and flexibility, designer support, maintainability, performance, and security. Of particular importance to building data-driven Web applications is how well the framework integrates with the variety of existing data stores you currently use or intend to use.

Since its introduction in February 2002, ASP.NET, part of Microsoft's .NET Framework technologies, has been adopted by developers everywhere as the platform of choice for building dynamic Web sites. ASP.NET introduced the Web development community to unprecedented simplicity for building dynamic applications, relying on reusable components called server controls to provide rich rendering and behaviors, without requiring developers to manually code complex logic for common scenarios. ASP.NET 1.0 also provided a flexible code separation and event model for programmability, which enabled Web application code to be factored cleanly and maintained easily. The net result was that sites that often required hundreds of lines of code and several weeks of development could be built in ASP.NET with minimal effort.

Of course, it is not in the nature of the ASP.NET team (currently named "Web Platform and Tools" within Microsoft) to rest on its laurels. Since the release of ASP.NET 1.0 (and the subsequent release of 1.1 in 2003), we have been hard at work thinking about how to make the next version even easier and more powerful, to meet the needs and demands of you, our developers. Looking back to ASP.NET 1.0 and 1.1, there were several challenges for developers who wanted to incorporate data into their applications. Specifically, the ASP.NET 1.x data access model required the developer to write code to retrieve the data from an underlying store (such as a database) and then manually bind server controls (like grids) to that data. Often, developers found that they were writing similar code in many different pages in their application, which resulted in a certain amount of "busy work" just to add data to a Web site. In thinking about ASP.NET 2.0, we recognized that these common code patterns could be encapsulated into the framework itself. In ASP.NET 2.0, we designed a data access solution with the following high-level goals in mind:

- **No code required**—Enable a completely declarative (no code) solution for adding data to a Web site and allow all the common data operations such as selecting, filtering, updating, inserting, and deleting data without code.
- **Consistency across different data types**—Allow controls to be bound to different types of data, including SQL databases, XML, and custom objects, in a consistent and transparent way, so that any control can be matched to any data type with no significant difference in the programming experience.

- **Rich designer support**—Provide a design-time tool experience in Visual Studio that enables developers to rapidly add data to their applications without having to manually edit the source code.
- **Flexibility and customizability**—Allow developers to easily add custom code to the processing of data within their application, while still taking advantage of the declarative (no code) model for common operations.
- **Extensibility to other data stores**—Enable a model that third-party developers can extend to support new types of data stores, without requiring changes to existing data-bound controls and application code.
- **Compatibility with version 1.x**—Ensure that applications built using the first version of ASP.NET continue to work without changes.

To achieve those goals, ASP.NET 2.0 introduces a control-based approach to data access that allows developers to add data to a Web site in much the same way as they would add any other server control. Reusable user interface (UI) components such as grids, trees, and lists can easily bind to data through a data source control, which takes care of exposing data from the underlying data store without requiring developers to manually handle the code to retrieve the data. Using controls has the additional advantage of allowing design tools such as Visual Studio to enable a simple drag-and-drop experience for adding data to a Web site. The result of the data control model is that building data-driven Web sites has never been easier. The ASP.NET data controls are a significant leap forward in terms of combining ease-of-use with the power and flexibility required to build real-world applications.

In addition to the new data controls in ASP.NET, Visual Studio 2005 adds a tremendous number of features to enhance developer productivity for common data development tasks. Visual Web Developer, a new member of the Visual Studio 2005 developer suite, is specifically targeted at Web developers and provides the best possible designer experience over ASP.NET. For example, the data controls automatically lead you through configuration wizards that make adding data to your Web site a snap. Visual Studio also comes with SQL Server Express, a lightweight database engine.

Praise for This Book

The book you are holding in your hands provides you with all you need to get started building data-driven Web sites with ASP.NET 2.0, Visual Web Developer Express, and SQL Server Express. Even if you have never built a dynamic Web site or used ASP.NET before, there is no better time to learn. The examples in each chapter guide you through the process of building data-enabled pages step by step, while the surrounding text breaks down the theory to help you understand the fundamental concepts. Simple, straightforward tutorials and a conversational style make this book approachable to the novice developer, while also demonstrating several real-world scenarios and tips that will be appreciated by those already familiar with the basics.

This book covers the data features in ASP.NET in great breadth. You'll learn how to generate rich dynamic data grids that can automatically perform updates, inserts, and deletes against the data. You'll also learn to build dynamic master-details data reports that allow your customers to filter and navigate through related data in your site. A variety of different data sources are considered, from SQL and Access databases to XML and custom business objects. Each topic is covered with an emphasis on the practical applications that you'll use again and again in future projects.

In summary, there is no better time to be a Web developer than right now. The amazing set of features in ASP.NET 2.0 adds a level of productivity and simplicity that no other framework can match. Whether you are a corporate developer, a small business owner, or hobbyist Web site designer, you will appreciate what ASP.NET and this book can do to enhance your development experience. If you are a beginning ASP.NET developer who wants to get started creating data-driven Web applications, this book is for you. I sincerely hope you enjoy it.

Bradley Millington
Program Manager, Web Platform and Tools Team
Microsoft Corporation

Introduction

The ASP.NET 2.0 team has done a tremendous job with the 2.0 version on two fronts. First, it is far easier to use data with ASP now than with any version in the past. Second, site designers can perform more complex tasks with data than at any time in the past. Faster development and expanded capability are two achievements that have made this book a joy to write. I feel privileged to be the bearer of such good news to the ASP community.

Updates

More than any other book that I have written, it is crucial for the reader to get the latest download of support files from `www.wrox.com`. Look for a folder or document of errata and last-minute updates. If you experience problems with the exercises, try redownloading the files to check for updates. This book describes the Beta version of a major upgrade to ASP, so there will be many small changes after the publication deadline. The ASP.NET development team and I will make all revisions needed to the downloads to reflect the current state of the Beta release. Besides changes from the developers, there are bound to be some errors I introduced as changes were incorporated just prior to publication. For these, I apologize and will notify readers with corrections in the download files.

Audience

The target audience for this book remains the same as prior versions. Each chapter and exercise is completely explained, provided the reader has a basic understanding of using ASP without data. The normal prerequisite for this book is an understanding of Beginning ASP.NET 2.0 by the same author. Alternatively, the reader should be comfortable with ASP.NET version 1.x or ASP version 3.0.

Readers should also have some familiarity with databases. This book does not delve into the details of designing or administering a database.

How to Use This Book

This book is presented as a progression from simple to complex topics. In general, I recommend that you start at the beginning and work your way through to the end, doing every exercise. There are several exceptions.

Chapters 2 through 4 describe connections to three sources of data. If you know you will only be using Microsoft SQL Server (or its variants SSE or MSDE) or Oracle, the concepts of Chapter 3 provide your technique. You can skip Chapter 2 and skim Chapter 4.

Conventions

To help you get the most from the text and keep track of what's happening, a number of conventions are used throughout the book.

Try It Out

The *Try It Out* is an exercise you should work through, following the text in the book.

1. They usually consist of a set of steps.
2. Each step has a number.
3. Follow the steps in order.

How It Works

After most *Try It Outs*, the code you've typed is explained in detail.

Boxes like this one hold important, not-to-be-forgotten information that is directly relevant to the surrounding text.

Tips, hints, tricks, and asides to the current discussion are offset and placed in italics like this.

As for styles in the text:

- Important words are *highlighted* when introduced.
- Keyboard strokes are shown like this: Ctrl+A.
- File names, URLs, and code within the text appear like so: `persistence.properties`.
- Code is presented in two different ways:

```
In code examples, new and important code is highlighted with a gray background.
```

```
The gray highlighting is not used for code that's less important in the present
context, or has been shown before.
```

Source Code

As you work through the examples in this book, you may choose either to type in all the code manually or to use the source code files that accompany the book. All of the source code used in this book is available for download at `http://www.wrox.com`. Once at the site, simply locate the book's title (either by using the Search box or by using one of the title lists) and click the Download Code link on the book's detail page to obtain all the source code for the book.

Because many books have similar titles, you may find it easiest to search by ISBN; for this book, the ISBN is 0-7645-7081-1.

Once you download the code, just decompress it with your favorite compression tool. Alternatively, you can go to the main Wrox code download page at `http://www.wrox.com/dynamic/books/download.aspx` to see the code available for this book and all other Wrox books.

Errata

We make every effort to ensure that there are no errors in the text or code. However, no one is perfect, and mistakes do occur. If you find an error in one of our books, like a spelling mistake or faulty piece of code, we would be grateful for your feedback. By sending in errata you may save another reader hours of frustration and you will be helping us provide even higher quality information.

To find the errata page for this book, go to `http://www.wrox.com` and locate the title using the Search box or one of the title lists. Then, on the book details page, click the Book Errata link. On this page, you can view all errata that has been posted for this book. A complete book list, including links to each book's errata, is also available at `www.wrox.com/misc-pages/booklist.shtml`.

If you don't spot "your" error on the Book Errata page, go to `www.wrox.com/contact/techsupport.shtml` and complete the form there to send us the error you have found. We'll check the information and, if appropriate, post a message to the book's errata page and fix the problem in subsequent editions of the book.

p2p.wrox.com

For author and peer discussion, join the P2P forums at `p2p.wrox.com`. The forums are a Web-based system for you to post messages relating to Wrox books and related technologies and interact with other readers and technology users. The forums offer a subscription feature to e-mail you topics of interest of your choosing when new posts are made to the forums. Wrox authors, editors, other industry experts, and your fellow readers are present on these forums.

At `http://p2p.wrox.com`, you will find a number of forums that help you not only as you read this book, but also as you develop your own applications. To join the forums, just follow these steps:

1. Go to `p2p.wrox.com`, click the Register link, read the terms of use, and click Agree.
2. Complete the required information to join, as well as any optional information you wish to provide, and then click Submit.
3. You will receive an e-mail with information describing how to verify your account and complete the joining process.

You can read messages in the forums without joining P2P but to post your own messages, you must join.

Once you join, you can post new messages and respond to messages other users post. You can read messages at any time on the Web. If you would like to have new messages from a particular forum e-mailed to you, click the Subscribe to this Forum icon by the forum name in the forum listing.

For more information on how to use the Wrox P2P, be sure to read the P2P FAQs for answers to questions about how the forum software works and many common questions specific to P2P and Wrox books. To read the FAQs, click the FAQ link on any P2P page.

1

Introduction to ASP.NET 2.0 and ADO.NET

Considering the speed and power that ASP.NET 2.0 and the .NET Framework 2.0 bring to the beginning programmer, it is a joy to write this edition. I believe you will find many moments when you just won't believe the quality of results you can achieve with little effort. I think you will often say, as I did at the first demos, "Wow, this is the way it should be." Hopefully, your managers and clients will be equally impressed by the speed and accuracy with which you produce Web sites.

This chapter presents an introduction to the topic of using data on an ASP.NET 2.0 Web page, how to set up a machine to use ASP.NET 2.0 with software and data for this book, and a set of initial demonstrations of the powerful features you will learn to use. Some of the material will review knowledge covered in the prerequisites (a basic knowledge of ASP.NET and familiarity with basic database tasks). The sections are organized as follows:

- Overview of the .NET Framework, ASP.NET, and ADO.NET
- Introduction to ASP.NET 2.0 and how ASP.NET 2.0 Web pages use data
- Guidance through the setup tasks required for the book
- Demonstration of several ASP.NET 2.0 pages that utilize data

In the middle of this chapter you will find a list of steps to follow to set up the software to do all of the exercises in this book, including the .NET Framework 2.0 (includes ASP.NET), an editor to create pages, database software, and some sample databases.

The last section walks you through three demonstrations, as follows:

Try It Out	Topic
1	GridView Table from XML with Paging and Sorting
2	DataList from Access
3	Tree View from XML

Overview of the Technologies

About a million developers have been creating Web sites using the .NET Framework in its first version. So in the summer of 2003, many ears perked up when rumors came out of Microsoft that a new version was available, which promised to decrease the number of lines of code required to create ASP.NET pages by 70 percent. An increase in productivity of that level does not come often in the world of programming. When samples of ASP.NET 2.0 code were demonstrated in the fall of 2003 at the Microsoft Professional Developer's Conference, the result was at least as good as the expectation. A Web page that warranted a budget of several hours of programmer time in the first version of ASP.NET could easily be built in a few minutes using ASP.NET 2.0. Simply stated, any programmer that continues to create ASP.NET pages in version 1 after the final release of the .NET Framework 2.0 is spending a lot of extra time to accomplish the same results.

Perhaps more than any other area, ASP.NET 2.0 offers advances in the ease of incorporating data into a page. Programmers no longer need to have detailed knowledge of connection, command, and data reader and data adapter objects to implement common data scenarios. ASP.NET 2.0 makes basic data use simple and brings more complex use of data within the grasp of beginners.

Introduction to the .NET Framework

Microsoft developed .NET as a philosophy and set of technologies for computers to work together in the world of the Internet. The overall objective was to provide a smooth flow of information and processes across a wide range of systems and devices. .NET is not a language or a specific product. Rather, it is a set of standards and guidelines that are incorporated into almost all Microsoft products released since about 2002.

.NET embraces a standardized format for the exchange of information using the open-standards XML format. Extensible Markup Language (XML) eliminates the need for a requestor to have any specialized knowledge about how the data store holds information — the data can always come out in the self-describing XML format. Likewise, almost all data stores now have the ability to serve up their information in XML, making them appealing to all .NET data consumers.

.NET supports the Web Services standard for software to request the running of code in remote software using the open-platform standards Simple Object Access Protocol (SOAP) and XML. A .NET Web site can find out from another Web site what services it offers and then consume those services. This makes it possible for a Web site to obtain HTML, calculated results, or sets of data from other Web sites.

As part of its .NET initiative, Microsoft released a runtime and set of programming tools and application program interfaces (APIs), called the .NET Framework, to enable the development community to build .NET-connected applications and XML Web Services. The .NET Framework is composed of the Common Language Runtime (CLR) and a unified set of class libraries.

The CLR provides a fully managed execution environment for running applications, providing several services such as assembly loading and unloading, process and memory management, security enforcement, and just-in-time compilation. What gives the Common Language Runtime its name is the ability to author applications in a wide variety of languages, and compile source code to an intermediate language that the CLR understands and can run regardless of the original source language. This "language independence" is a key feature of the CLR (and also of ASP.NET), and it allows developers to work in their preferred language, such as C#, VB, or Cobol, while still accessing common features in the .NET Framework.

The .NET Framework also includes a set of class libraries that provide common functionality that every application needs. These class libraries can be accessed from any language supported by the .NET Framework. The services (and corresponding namespaces) offered by these class libraries include the following:

- Base Types *(System)*
- Input/Output *(System.IO)*
- Data Access *(System.Data)*
- Security *(System.Security)*
- Data Structures *(System.Collections)*
- Configuration *(System.Configuration)*
- Networking *(System.Net)*
- Reflection *(System.Reflection)*
- Globalization *(System.Globalization)*
- Painting and Drawing *(System.Drawing)*
- Tracing and Diagnostics *(System.Diagnostics)*
- Windows (Client) Application Model *(System.Windows.Forms)*
- Web Application Model *(System.Web)*

Note that the .NET Framework contains two application programming models, one for client applications (System.Windows.Forms) and one for Web-based applications (System.Web). This book is concerned with the latter model. The System.Web namespace in the .NET Framework is the portion of the .NET Framework that provides ASP.NET functionality. In other words, ASP.NET is just one part of the overall .NET Framework for building applications.

Introduction to ASP.NET

ASP.NET is a programming model for building Web-based applications. It is essentially a runtime and set of .NET Framework class libraries that can be used to build dynamic Web pages. It runs within the context of a Web server, such as Microsoft Internet Information Server (IIS), and processes programming instructions on the server to service browser requests. Unlike static HTML, which is served directly from the Web server, ASP.NET pages are actually executed on the server to produce dynamic results. The final rendering of a page might be constructed from a variety of different instructions and/or data sources.

ASP.NET pages are stored under the .aspx extension. Pages are created by a programmer as a combination of text, markup (such as HTML), and ASP.NET server-specific tags and script, and then stored on the Web server. You can think of a stored ASP.NET page as a set of instructions for how to build an HTML page. When the page is requested, the server-side logic is processed to create a page in pure markup that the client browser can understand and render. Because the rendered output is pure markup, any browser can read it; all the dynamic processing happens on the Web server. ASP.NET server-specific tags are very powerful, including the capability to react to user actions, connect to data stores, and automatically build very complex HTML structures.

As previously mentioned, ASP.NET is simply part of the .NET Framework and, consequently, ASP.NET pages can take advantage of all of the services offered by that framework, including networking, data access, security, and much more. The fact that all of these framework services are available to ASP.NET enables you to build much richer Web applications than ever before. You can spend less time reinventing the basic building blocks that all applications need, and spend more time focusing on the specific logic that is unique to your application.

ASP.NET also introduces some unique innovations in Web programming that greatly improve the development model over classic Active Server Pages (ASP):

- **Language-independence** — Because ASP.NET is part of the .NET Framework, ASP.NET applications can be constructed in the language of your choice, for example C#, VB, or J#. Classic ASP, on the other hand, is limited to only JScript or VBScript pages.
- **Compiled instead of interpreted** — Unlike classic ASP, which interprets programming instructions every time the page is requested, ASP.NET dynamically compiles pages on the server into native programming instructions that can be run much, much faster. It is not uncommon to see orders of magnitude difference between the performance of a classic ASP page and the performance of an equivalent ASP.NET page.
- **Event-driven programming model** — In classic ASP, pages are always executed in a top-down linear fashion, and HTML markup is often mixed in with the programming instructions. Anyone with a moderate amount of experience in ASP knows that this can make your pages difficult to read, and even more difficult to maintain. ASP.NET introduces an event-driven model that allows you to separate code from markup content, and factor code into meaningful units for handling specific tasks, such as responding to a button click from the client. This VB-like eventing model greatly improves the readability and maintainability of your pages.
- **Server controls** — Classic ASP requires you to dynamically construct a page rendering by piecing together HTML fragments in code, which often results in writing the same code over and over again across your applications (how many times have you needed to construct a table from a database query?). One of the great advancements that ASP.NET brings to Web programming is the ability to encapsulate common rendering and behavior into *server controls* that can be

easily reused within an application. A server control is created declaratively, just like an HTML tag, but represents a programmable object on the server that can interact with your code and output a custom dynamic HTML rendering. ASP.NET includes 80+ server controls that encapsulate anything from standard form elements to complex controls such as grids and menus.

- **Design time improvements to controls (when used with Visual Web Developer)** — Developers can decrease the time it takes to develop a complex page by using design time interfaces such as smart task panels, tag-level navigation bar, and the wizards that can set control properties.

Introduction to ASP.NET 2.0

The first ASP.NET versions (1.0 and 1.1) rapidly spread throughout the Microsoft-centric developer community from 2001 to 2003. Programmers quickly appreciated that they could spend a lot less time programming using the power and flexibility of the .NET Framework, and CIOs saw that they could devote more resources to high-level improvements to their IT structure when programmers were spending less time troubleshooting custom code. ASP.NET was truly a monumental release that simplified the lives of developers.

However, even prior to the release of version 1, the Microsoft ASP.NET team was already working on ASP.NET 2.0. They set out with the following ambitious design goals:

- Remove 70 percent of the lines of code needed to build a typical Web application.
- Provide a set of extensible application services that provide the building blocks for common application scenarios such as membership, roles, personalization, and navigation.
- Create a rich set of scenario-based server controls that are able to leverage the aforementioned services to deliver complete and customizable user interface (UI) that exposes those services with a minimum of code.
- Improve the performance of IIS when it is serving pages in conjunction with the .NET Framework.
- Provide administration features that enhance the deployment, management, and operations of ASP.NET servers.
- Improve the tools for hosting companies to support multiple sites and to migrate developers' projects to public deployment.
- Enable nearly all features of ASP.NET to be easily extended or replaced with custom implementations for advanced scenarios.

It is worth pausing to reflect on that first goal, namely the removal of 70 percent of the code needed today to write a dynamic Web application. How is this possible? The ASP.NET team at Microsoft looked closely at the variety of common scenarios being implemented in custom code today, and specifically looked for ways to encapsulate those scenarios into building blocks, particularly server controls, that could accomplish those tasks automatically. For example, most Web applications need security or navigation, or personalization services to provide custom experiences for users. In ASP.NET 2.0 these scenarios are exposed as a set of configurable application services, and server controls that talk to those application services, to enable dramatic reductions in the amount of application code required to implement these common scenarios. Among all the common scenarios, however, one stood apart as absolutely essential to every application, and that was data access. Data is the common thread that drives all dynamic Web applications, and so it is no surprise that the ASP.NET team defined some very aggressive goals toward reducing the amount of code and concepts necessary to perform data access in ASP.NET 2.0 applications:

- Enable a declarative (no-code) way to define a source of data in ASP.NET.
- Enable a declarative (no-code) way to display data in UI controls, without having to explicitly data-bind at the right time in the page execution life cycle.
- Enable a declarative (no-code) way to perform common data scenarios such as sorting, paging, filtering, updating, inserting, and deleting data.
- Enable a rich set of UI controls for displaying data, including flexible grid/details controls with the ability to both display and manipulate data.
- Enable an extensible model for building custom data sources to support new types of data.

ASP.NET 2.0 has a specific set of server controls for programmers to add data interactions to a page. The data-specific controls are divided into two groups: data source controls and data-bound controls. Data source controls create the link to the database. The data-bound controls take the information from the data source controls and create a rendering on the page. This simple two-control pattern is available in many variations. There are data source controls for many types of databases and even nonrelational data sources. Likewise, many data-bound controls render to page tables, trees, lists, and other formats of data. The preceding several pages provided an introduction to and theory behind ASP.NET, and we are now at the nuts and bolts of what is covered in the rest of this book: the use of data source controls and data-bound controls. Data source controls include the following, which ship with the product:

- SqlDataSource control to connect to the Microsoft SQL Server and other databases
- AccessDataSource control to connect to MDB files
- ObjectDataSource to connect to middle-tier objects
- XMLDataSource for XML files or data streams
- SiteMapDataSource for XML files in the format of the ASP.NET 2.0 site map

Additional controls are already in development by third parties.

Data-bound controls include many that are familiar from ASP.NET 1.x, as well as some that are completely new for ASP.NET 2.0:

- ListBox, DropDownList and BulletedList, CheckBoxList, RadioButtonList
- AdRotator to provide a data-bound control implementation of an old feature
- DataList and Repeater to provide data in flexible layouts
- DataGrid (same as ASP.NET 1.x) and GridView (new for version 2) for tabular data
- DetailsView and FormView to provide information for one record with easy navigation
- TreeView to display hierarchical data

Taken together, the data source controls and data-bound controls will represent the majority of effort in this book.

Prior to the public beta release of the .NET Framework 2.0, limited groups of programmers were shown working code to solicit early feedback. The uniform response was an enthusiastic "This is great!" followed by "How soon can I replace my ASP.NET 1.x applications with ASP.NET 2.0?" With the beta release now in hand, we need not wait any longer.

Introduction to ADO.NET

ADO.NET is a set of class libraries in the .NET Framework that makes it easier to use data in your applications. Microsoft has gathered the best practices in data connections from the past several decades and written the code to implement those practices. The code is wrapped up into several objects that can be easily used by other software.

The code within ADO.NET handles much of the plumbing and database-specific intricacies so that when ASP.NET page designers want to read or write data they can write fewer lines of code and code that is more standardized. ADO.NET, like ASP.NET, is not a language. It is a collection of objects (classes) that hold code written by Microsoft. You can run that code from outside the object using a programming language such as Visual Basic or C#.

You can think of ADO.NET as a very smart translation layer between the data source and a data consumer. ADO.NET can accept commands from the data consumer's language and turn them into commands that are appropriate to carry out the task in the data source. But, as you will see, ASP.NET 2.0 offers server-side data controls that make it even easier to work with ADO.NET, sometimes eliminating the need to use ADO.NET objects directly at all.

Many readers will already have experience with earlier versions of ASP.NET. This short section recalls that model for the purposes of demonstrating the ADO.NET objects you needed to work with to bring data into a Web page. For those readers who never used earlier versions, view this as a curiosity of history, akin to a study of surgery techniques prior to the discovery of ether. In the past, a typical simple ASP.NET version 1.x page required the following code:

```
<script runat="server">
  Sub Page_Load(ByVal sender As Object, ByVal e As System.EventArgs)
    BulletedList1.DataSource = GetAuthorsByState("CA")
    BulletedList1.DataBind()
  End Sub

  Shared Function GetAuthorsByState(ByVal state As String) As System.Data.DataSet
Dim connectionString As String =
"server=(local);database=pubs;trusted_connection=true"
Dim dbConnection As System.Data.IDbConnection = New
System.Data.SqlClient.SqlConnection(connectionString)

    Dim queryString As String =
"SELECT [authors].[au_id], [authors].[au_fname], [authors].[au_lname],
[authors].[state] FROM [authors] WHERE ([authors].[state] = @state)"
    Dim dbCommand As System.Data.IDbCommand = New System.Data.SqlClient.SqlCommand
    dbCommand.CommandText = queryString
    dbCommand.Connection = dbConnection

    Dim dbParam_state As System.Data.IDataParameter = New
System.Data.SqlClient.SqlParameter
    dbParam_state.ParameterName = "@state"
```

```
        dbParam_state.Value = state
        dbParam_state.DbType = System.Data.DbType.StringFixedLength
        dbCommand.Parameters.Add(dbParam_state)

        Dim dataAdapter As System.Data.IDbDataAdapter = New
System.Data.SqlClient.SqlDataAdapter
        dataAdapter.SelectCommand = dbCommand
        Dim dataSet As System.Data.DataSet = New System.Data.DataSet
        dataAdapter.Fill(dataSet)

        Return dataSet
    End Function
</script>
<html><head runat="server"><title>Untitled Page</title></head>
<body>
        <form id="form1" runat="server"><div>
          <asp:BulletedList ID="BulletedList1"
DataTextField="au_lname" Runat="server" />
        </div></form>
</body></html>
```

The preceding example executes a simple SQL SELECT statement against a database and binds the result to a bulleted list control. The page has a method named GetAuthorsByState that creates several ADO.NET objects to accomplish this task:

- A SqlConnection object represents the connection to the database server.
- A SqlCommand object represents the SQL SELECT command to execute.
- A SqlParameter object represents a value to be substituted for a marker in the command.
- A SqlDataAdapter represents the ability to fill a DataSet object from a command.
- A DataSet represents the command result, which may be bound to the BulletedList.

In the `Page_Load` event, the GetAuthorsByState method is called to retrieve the DataSet result and assign it to the BulletedList's `DataSource` property. We then call DataBind() to force the BulletedList to synchronize itself with the data result. The fact that we need to call DataBind() at the appropriate time in the page execution life cycle is a key step that ASP.NET 2.0 seeks to eliminate in the most common cases. In fact, in most cases, ASP.NET 2.0 completely eliminates the need to interact with ADO.NET. However, it is useful to understand the relationship between the aforementioned ADO.NET objects to discuss how ASP.NET 2.0 improves upon that model.

ASP.NET 2.0 and Data Access

ASP.NET 2.0 gives us an improved model for data access, which eliminates much, if not all, of the code that was required to perform data-binding in ASP.NET 1.x. First, you no longer have to programmatically instantiate, set properties of, and call methods of ADO objects as in the preceding listing. Instead, you can add simple server-side data controls to your page and set their attributes. When the page is rendered, ASP.NET 2.0 will automatically perform all of the object instantiation and method calls to set up and display your data. Compare the following listing in ASP.NET 2.0 to the last listing.

```
<html>
<head runat="server"><title>Demo</title></head>
<body>
    <form id="form1" runat="server">
        <asp:SqlDataSource ID="SqlDataSource1" Runat="server"
   SelectCommand="SELECT au_lname FROM authors WHERE (state = @state)"
   ConnectionString="Server=HPSERV;Integrated Security=True;Database=pubs">
            <SelectParameters>
                <asp:Parameter Type="String" DefaultValue="CA" Name="state" />
            </SelectParameters>
        </asp:SqlDataSource>

<asp:BulletedList ID="BulletedList1" Runat="server"
    DataSourceID="SqlDataSource1"
             DataTextField="Au_lname">
        </asp:BulletedList>
    </form>
</body></html>
```

The second improvement derives from the server-side controls being sensitive to events in the page life cycle. Appropriate actions occur at the right time by the ASP.NET 2.0 server-side controls. Notice that there is no reference in the ASP.NET 2.0 page to any event in the page life cycle. Students of earlier versions of ASP were typically confused by the intricacies of when in a page life to perform various tasks, particularly data-binding. Thus, many ASP.NET 1.x pages suffered from programmers writing code that either called DataBind under the wrong event, or called DataBind duplicate times in multiple events. These timings are now automatic with the ASP.NET 2.0 server-side data controls.

Note in the preceding ASP.NET 2.0 code that two server-side controls are used. The first is a data source control, in this case the SqlDataSource control. Behind the scenes the control sets up all of the ADO connection objects needed for the display of data, including the Connection, Command, and DataReader or Dataset objects. Then, a data-bound control named BulletedList is used to take the data of the data source control and actually render it to the page.

Review of Terminology

To round out the introductory sections, I'll provide a list of some of the terminology used so far and that will continue to be used throughout the book.

- **Dynamic Web Pages** — Files stored on the Web server as code and then converted to HTML at the moment they are requested. When they are converted they can take into account the real-time situation of the user and the owners of the Web site, and thus take different forms for different requests.
- **IIS (Internet Information Server)** — A built-in Web server in Windows that serves Web pages to requestors via TCP/IP. IIS operating on Windows 2000 or Windows XP Professional has the capability to use .NET Framework classes to serve ASP.NET Web pages.
- **.NET Framework** — A group of classes that hold code written by Microsoft to make applications easier and faster to develop and more suitable for operation over the Internet. Various classes are incorporated into a dozen or so Microsoft products that are .NET-enabled.

- **Common Language Runtime** — A feature of the .NET Framework that enables programmers to write in one of many languages, then compile the code to a single, uniform language for deployment.
- **ASP.NET** — A runtime and set of class libraries in the .NET Framework for building dynamic Web applications.
- **Data Store** — A place where data is kept and usually managed. All RDBMS are data stores, but some data stores are not RDBMS because they are not relational.
- **Database or Relational Database Management System (RDMS)** — The software that enables reading and manipulation of data. Most systems include tools to design and test databases as well as tools to optimize sets of procedures. An RDBMS must store data in compliance with some form of normalization (a relational format).
- **DataBase Schema (or Database Metadata)** — The structure of the database, including the design of the tables and relationships. Schema does not include the actual data values.
- **Microsoft™ Access** — An RDMS that is based on the MDB file format, the JET engine, and a series of tools for building and using databases. Access is inexpensive, easy to learn, widely understood, and currently deployed on many machines. However, it does not support more than a few concurrent users.
- **JET** — A database engine that runs in the background and uses MDB (Access) files. JET accepts commands directly from other software (such as .NET or Access) to read or modify MDB files.
- **Structured Query Language (SQL)** — A language used by data consumers to request a read or write from a data provider. For over a decade, SQL has been the standard for communication with a RDBMS.
- **Microsoft™ SQL Server** — An enterprise-strength RDBMS designed to support large amounts of data and many concurrent users.
- **Microsoft™ SQL Server Express (SSE)** — A freely available database engine based on the Microsoft SQL Server database engine. Unlike SQL Server, SSE is limited in the number of simultaneous data connections it can serve and has only a few utilities. This book uses SSE in most examples.
- **Microsoft™ Data Engine (MSDE)** — Similar to SSE, but based on an earlier version of the SQL Server engine. MSDE will work for the exercises in this book.
- **XML** — A standard format for data in which each value is stored and described. XML is not particularly efficient (the space required for the descriptions generally exceeds the size of the data), but it is easily read by many different data management systems.
- **Web Page Editor** — Software that allows pages to be opened and changed. The most basic editor is Notepad. Visual Studio, Visual Web Developer, and ASP.NET Web Matrix bundle an editor with other tools to improve productivity.
- **Integrated Development Environment (IDE)** — A set of tools that assists programmers in developing code. Visual Studio is a very powerful IDE; Web ASP.NET Web Matrix also offers many tools. A typical IDE includes a Web Page Editor.
- **ADO.NET** — A collection of classes (code) written by Microsoft that acts as an intermediary between data stores (such as Access or an XML file) and a data consumer (such as an ASP page).

- **Connection** — An ADO object that represents a unique path between a data consumer and data provider.
- **Command** — An ADO object that represents a SQL statement that can be passed to a database.
- **Parameter** — An ADO object that represents a variable piece of data that can be inserted into the Command Object (SQL statement) just prior to the statement going to the database.
- **DataSet** — An ADO object representing a group of data organized into records and fields.
- **Server Control** — A self-contained set of code (an object) that performs its tasks on the server to contribute to an HTML-compatible page that is sent to the browser. Server-side controls can maintain a sense of state through the ViewState.
- **Data Source Control** — A server-side control that creates a single, unique connection to a database. It provides an abstraction of the ADO objects and makes programming ASP.NET 2.0 pages faster and easier to build. Data source controls are available for Microsoft SQL Server Access, XML, and other sources of data.
- **Data-Bound Control** — A server-side control that takes data from a data source control and renders it on the page. Data-bound controls abstract from the programmer the HTML tags such as `<table>`. Data-bound controls are available to render tables, lists, trees, and other structures.

Setup Requirements for This Book

The installation wizards and packages are one of the last parts of the Beta 2 to be prepared. Therefore, I cannot be sure at the time this book goes to press of the exact steps for install. The following steps will be very close, but be prepared for a few changes. I will post to this book's downloads a section of notes on the final version of the install.

Keep in mind that this edition of the book is published with the release of a beta version of the .NET Framework 2.0. As with all beta software, stability and compatibility are not guaranteed. The safest way to work with beta software is to install it on a non-production machine, freshly formatted and with a newly installed OS. If you expect to do repeated installs, I suggest a machine with a slave drive of at least 10 GB. On the slave drive, make a copy of your install CDs for Windows, .NET Framework 2.0, drivers, Office, and any other software you may want to use. Also, store your user files (databases and ASPX pages) on the slave drive. With each new version of the framework, do a format of the master drive and reinstall the OS from the slave drive. Then install the beta software from the slave drive. Although this procedure takes a few hours (albeit unattended), it is the surest way to have a completely clean install for working with your beta software.

`www.wrox.com` provides all of the demonstration and exercise pages pre-typed for your use. Most of the examples in this book use the Northwind and Pubs databases for three reasons:

- Many readers have already encountered these databases and already have them on their server or hard drive.
- They are available in both Access and SQL versions, which works well for demonstration purposes in this book.
- They provide a wide variety of data types and relationships that you can use to explore several concepts in this book.

The "Install the Sample Databases" section later in this chapter provides installation instructions for both Northwind and Pubs.

We will start with an overview of what must be done to set up for this book in the sections below. Then we will walk through the actual steps back-to-back. The requisites follow:

- Web server
- .NET Framework 2.0
- ASPX page editor
- Database management software
- Sample databases

Install a Web Server

Web pages must be processed by a Web server to be available to a browser. Two options work with the .NET Framework, one for deployment and one for development. Internet Information Server handles the load of a public Web site, but may also be used for development purposes. If you have already turned it on in your development machine, you will find that the .NET Framework automatically registers with IIS and is available for you to create ASP.NET pages. IIS is easy to enable in Windows. First, because it is a good habit to get into, check that you have updated your installation of Windows with the latest service packs and security patches. Then click through Start ➪ Control Panel ➪ Add & Remove Programs. Select Add/Remove Windows Components and add a check mark to IIS to install.

Microsoft also provides a lightweight alternative to IIS for developers, code-named Cassini, that is better suited to developers and students than IIS. The Cassini Web Server comes with Visual Studio and Visual Web Developer and installs automatically. When a page is run from the Visual Web Developer, Cassini will automatically start its Web service on a random port and invoke your browser with a request for your page sent to `http://localhost:xxxx/MySiteName/MyPageName.aspx`. Instead of IIS, Cassini will serve the page, including processing ASP.NET code and server controls. Evidence of the server activity appears as an icon system tray. Note that Cassini is designed for developers and does not scale adequately to support a publicly deployed Web.

For this book either Web server will work. Both servers use the same ASPX pages, so there is no need for any changes in syntax or commands. If you are already using IIS on your development machine, you will not have to take additional steps. If you have not set up and secured IIS, I suggest you use Cassini because it is automatically installed with Visual Studio or Visual Web Developer. Cassini will automatically download and install with VWD Express, so you will not see specific install steps below.

Install the .NET Framework Version 2.0

The .NET Framework version 2.0 is available for download in three ways. The first is the version named .NET Framework 2.0 Redist, which is about 20 MB. The second version includes the Software Development Kit (SDK) that includes the .NET Framework documentation, samples, and several SDK tools. However, the SDK download is significantly larger than the Redist, and this book does not rely on features in the SDK. If you are not in a rush, you can download the .NET Framework and order the SDK on CD for a postage fee, as described on the download page. The third alternative is to use the version that is automatically downloaded and installed with Visual Studio or Visual Web Developer (VWD) Express. That route is both easiest and adequate for this book, and is described in the install of VWD Express that follows.

If you have the .NET Framework version 1 or 1.1 installed, you can upgrade to the .NET Framework 2.0 on the same machine. If you have already installed version 1.0 or 1.1 of the .NET Framework and either of those versions are already registered in IIS, the .NET Framework 2.0 setup will not *automatically* register 2.0 with IIS, since this would potentially upgrade applications to the new version without the user's consent. (This is a change in Beta2 from Beta1, which did in fact upgrade the server.) In order to register .NET Framework 2.0 if version 1.x is installed, run in a command prompt window `aspnet_regiis -i` from the .NET Framework 2.0 installation directory; e.g., `\WINDOWS\Microsoft .NET\Framework\<version>`. This command line utility will upgrade the server and all apps on it to use 2.0. Having said that and because this is beta software, I recommend that you install the version 2.0 of the .NET Framework on a clean machine — that is, without version 1.x of the .NET Framework.

> **Although it is possible to run both 1.x applications and 2.0 applications side by side on the same machine, the steps for doing so are more involved and outside the scope of this book.**

Install an Editor to Create Web Pages

ASP.NET pages must be written using some type of editor. Most readers will select one of three options, depending on their budget and interest in learning to use new software. This book uses VWD Express.

Visual Studio

Visual Studio (VS) provides very powerful tools to design complex Web pages that employ multiple resources from throughout the enterprise. Objectives that require ten or twenty lines of typing in Notepad are performed in VS with a single drag-and-drop or by clicking through a wizard. After the drag-and-drop, VS will type all of the tags, attributes, and code to produce the feature. VS also provides intelligent assistance to typing so that you generally only have to type a character or two and VS will complete the syntax (called "IntelliSense" technology). Debugging features, including trace and immediate windows, are built into the product. For readers of this book, a key VS feature is the ability to read and display database information at design time so you do not need to have Access or a SQL tool open to see the structure and data of your database. Visual Studio includes many tools in multiple programming languages and tools for collaboration of multiple developers at a price starting (as of mid 2004) at around US $500. This book does not discuss the installation of Visual Studio.

Visual Web Developer Express

Visual Web Developer (VWD) Express is a new product from Microsoft that includes most features of Visual Studio needed for Web site development, but at a much lower price (not known at time of writing). All of the exercises in this text can be performed using VWD, as it includes Cassini, the visual design interface, all of the controls I discuss, and the debugging features. VWD does not include some of the large-scale deployment features of the Visual Studio used by teams of developers, but for the purposes of this book you will not need them.

Notepad and Other Editors

Notepad is free with Windows and can be used as a no-frills text editor to create ASP.NET 2.0. Remember that ASPX files are saved as ASCII text files, the same as HTML. Therefore, every exercise in this book can be typed into a Notepad file, saved with an aspx extension (not .txt), and will run fine. On the other hand, Notepad does not offer much assistance other than cut, copy, and paste. If you use Notepad, be prepared to do a lot of typing, look up a lot of syntax, and perform a lot of troubleshooting.

Web ASP.NET Web Matrix is an open-source project that offers a development environment for ASP.NET version 1.x pages. The application is available for free from `www.ASP.NET`. Installation is not difficult, and if you have used Visual Studio or InterDev, the interface looks very familiar. ASP.NET Web Matrix offers clickable property settings, an object browser that allows you to look up syntax, and color-coding. As of this writing, ASP.NET Web Matrix does not support the features of .NET version 2. Therefore, at this point it is ill-suited for the examples of this book.

Because readers will be using various editors, I try to accommodate all. Initial discussions are oriented towards Visual Web Developer because it offers strong drag-and-drop features and wizards at a low price. The resulting code is then presented so typists can enter the page as discussed into Notepad or another editor. All of the files are also available for download from `www.wrox.com`.

Install a Database Management System

This book requires a way to manage data for examples. Several choices are listed here; of those I recommend and use SQL Server Express (SSE) in this book.

- **Microsoft Access** is familiar and already widely deployed, but not recommended for use in a production Web site. It works for learning and development purposes, however.
- **Microsoft SQL Server** is a powerful choice for public deployment but is expensive and more difficult to set up and manage on a development machine.
- **SQL Server Express (SSE)** is a lightweight and free database engine based on the SQL Server Yukon engine (currently in beta release). Because SSE has the same syntax as SQL Server but lower cost and complexity, it greatly simplifies working with local data in a Web application. SSE is used to support this book's examples in most cases.
- **Microsoft Data Engine (MSDE)** is a freely available lightweight version of SQL Server. It is easy to install and stores data in a format that can be directly ported to a full SQL Server installation at time of deployment.
- **Other Relational Databases** such as Oracle or MySQL can be used. However, this book does not discuss their installation or management.

Another option, XML, has emerged as an important format for storing and transferring data. XML and other hierarchical data are addressed in a separate chapter at the end of this book. Other data formats, such as Excel and flat files, can also be used in special cases. They are not covered in this edition of the book.

Microsoft Access

Microsoft Access is sold as part of Microsoft Office Professional or as a separate purchase. When you install Access, you automatically get an install of a sample database named `Northwind.mdb` and the JET database engine. You can also download the `Northwind.mdb` file from the following:

```
www.Microsoft.com/downloads/details.aspx?FamilyID=c6661372-8dbe-422b-8676-
c632d66c529c&DisplayLang=en
```

There are two major problems with using Access as a source of data for Web sites, even in development environments:

- Access was not designed to scale well to significant loads. When loads begin to increase Access uses large amounts of server resources. Therefore, it is unsuitable for deployment in scenarios with more than five or ten users.
- The second problem concerns the syntax of passing information to Access when modifying data. Access relies on a model where the order of the data passed to a parameterized command determines the fields where the data is stored. This creates a number of problems for the page designer, as you will see in later chapters.

Microsoft SQL Server, MSDE, and SQL Server Express use a different model where the parameter values are named; thus, order is unimportant.

For the reasons just described, this book recommends that you not use Access for working with data in ASP.NET; instead, download the SQL Server Express (SSE) database engine described shortly.

Microsoft SQL Server

Microsoft SQL Server is an enterprise-level database management system designed to scale and perform for the needs of entire organizations. It makes an ideal RDMS for public Web sites with high volumes and the need for integration with all other Microsoft products.

Microsoft, to this point, has offered time-limited trial versions of the product at `www.Microsoft.com/sql`. SQL is generally installed by a database administrator, and the steps are outside the scope of this book. If you are installing it yourself, I suggest you select the mixed authentication security model and be sure to install the sample databases. If you are using an existing SQL server installation at your workplace, you may have to ask your administrator to reinstall the Northwind and Pubs sample databases. You will also need to know the name of the server, instance, user ID, and password.

Other Relational Databases

.NET can use other sources of data, including MySQL, Oracle, and any other database for which a provider exists. Those connections are covered in Chapter 4. In theory, you could build Northwind in one of those systems for the purpose of writing the exercises in this text. This book does not cover installation or maintenance of these other sources.

SQL Server Express

The SQL Server Express (SSE) edition provides an engine that holds a database and responds to SQL statement requests. SSE is built from Microsoft SQL Server (in fact, the next generation) and thus responds exactly like the full-scale SQL Server. SSE is the next generation to the Microsoft Data Engine (MSDE), and the upgrade path to SQL Server is seamless. As of this writing, it does not include graphical tools for managing the database, changing the schema, or modifying data, although you will be able to use Visual Studio or Visual Web Developer to perform some of these tasks. I expect to see a basic GUI interface added (perhaps even with the Beta 2), named "Express Manager or XM Tools."

There are several advantages to SSE over other sources of data for readers of this book:

- It is free and installs automatically with VWD
- A developer spends little time acclimating to SSE — it operates as a background service without a visual interface to learn.
- The data format and organization is the same as Microsoft SQL Server, so when you are ready to deploy there are very easy and well-documented solutions. Many Web-hosting companies have extensive experience bringing SSE databases from developers up to SQL Server.

The biggest disadvantage is that in the Beta 2 timeframe, there is no GUI interface for installing or importing a new database. I talk you through the steps of installing your sample databases from the command line.

Setup

Having covered the software needed for running, creating, and testing data-driven ASPX pages, it is time to walk you through the setup. As I mentioned earlier, the final install wizards may be changed at the last minute, so check your download for additional notes. Although you probably will not have problems installing the Beta 2 with the Beta 1 installed, you can be more certain of success by taking the clean-disk approach described in the beginning of the chapter. All elements of .NET 2.0 will harmoniously co-exist with .NET 1.1.

Obtain the download of files specific for this book

First go to `www.wrox.com` and get the download for this book. It will contain notes on install, the sample database setup files, demonstration pages used in the text, and all of the exercises. Read the install notes.

Obtain and install Visual Web Developer (which installs SSE and Cassini)

Visual Web Developer is a one-stop package for most of what is needed in this book. Its wizard will install all of the Microsoft-provided components discussed in the last section: the .NET Framework 2.0, the Visual Web Developer development tools, the Cassini Web server and SQL Server Express.

1. Shut down all applications.
2. Visit the Developer Express page at `http://lab.msdn.microsoft.com/express` and follow the instructions for downloading and installing Visual Web Developer Express. While on that page, check for any notices regarding best practices, security, and changes to the install procedure.
3. Select the Visual Web Developer Express download and run it.

4. When and if prompted, you need to install VWD, SSE, and the Framework. The help library is recommended, and the SDK is optional (it provides sample code and FAQs). If there is a set of quick-start sample applications available, they can be a useful reference. This book does not use the J# component.

5. VWD will give you the option to install SSE. Agree, and (if asked about features) select SQL Server Database Services, SQL Command Line Tools, Connectivity Components, and the Management Tools. The SSE installation may proceed in the background. The default authentication mode will be Windows Authentication. If the install pauses and asks you to specify the authentication, then select Windows Authentication.

6. Finish the install and reboot.

After this step, you can perform two confirmations. Your Start ➪ Programs will now contain Visual Web Developer 2005 Express Edition Beta. Your Start ➪ Control Panel ➪ Administrative Tools ➪ Services will display SQL Server running. Note that your SSE instance will be named (local)\SQLExpress. You can now use SSE as your database management system, but keep in mind that the engine does not yet hold a database

Install the Sample Databases

Install the databases used in this book into SSE by using the provided scripts of SQL statements. These scripts hold several thousand lines of SQL statements that create the entire structure of tables, relationships, queries, and data for Northwind and Pubs.

1. Look within the data folder of the download for this book to find `instPubs.sql` and `instNwind.sql`. Copy the files to `C:\Program Files\Microsoft SQl Server\90\Tools\binn`.

2. Start a command prompt and navigate to the folder mentioned in step 1.

3. Run the following command (do not change the case of any characters). If you are curious about osql, you can see the parameter dictionary with the command `osql -?`.

   ```
   osql -S(local)\SQLExpress -E -i"instNWIND.SQL"
   ```

   You will see thousands of SQL statements scroll by as they execute to create the Northwind database and fill it with data.

4. Repeat for the Pubs database, again making sure not to change case.

   ```
   osql -S(local)\SQLExpress -E -i"instpubs.SQL"
   ```

5. Try testing your installation with the following commands:

   ```
   osql -S(local)\SQLExpress -E -d Northwind -q "SELECT FirstName FROM Employees"
   ```

6. Type **Quit** and press Enter to end the test. Test Pubs as follows:

   ```
   osql -S(local)\SQLExpress -E -d Pubs -q "SELECT Au_LName FROM Authors"
   ```

7. Type **Quit** and press Enter to end the test, then close the command prompt.

Connect VWD to our sample databases

We'll finish our database setup by making the two exercise databases easily available for our pages. VS and VWD can connect to a database and test the connection before using the data on a page. Any database is available, but the following steps give you some GUI management tools from within VWD. Once connected, these IDEs enable some exploration of the database and drag-and-drop creation of data controls on pages.

1. Start VWD and, in the menu, click through View ➪ Data Explorer (or Server Explorer in Visual Studio).
2. Right-click on DataConnections and select Add Connection.
3. On the left panel, click on Providers and select .NET Framework Data Provider for SQL Server.
4. On the left panel, click on Connection. Drop your list of servers and select local or the name of your machine or an alternate server name that you are using.
5. Accept the default logon using Windows NT security and then select a name, in this case, Northwind. Because we are using mixed authentication, check the "save Password" in this dialog box.
6. Click on Test Connection to get a confirmation and then OK to close.
7. Repeat for the Pubs database that you installed.

Note that your Data Explorer (Server Explorer) now has a connection entry for Northwind and Pubs. You can expand the entry to see the tables, and when you right-click on a table you will be offered an option to Show Table Data. You can demonstrate the power of this view by changing some small value, such as the spelling of a person's name. After a database is installed to MSDE using the osql at the command line, you can use VWD as a front end to examine a database.

Demonstrations

To finish off the first chapter, we will create several pages that demonstrate using ASP.NET 2.0 pages with data. I will talk you through creating the pages using the VWD tools. In addition, each of these pages is available in this book's download at `www.wrox.com`. Also, check at that location for the latest updates and warnings to match these exercises to the release version of the beta software.

Try It Out #1 — GridView Table from SQL with Paging and Sorting

In this exercise, we will quickly build a page that uses a GridView control to produce a table of author names that is sortable and supports paging. Then we will add a clickable filtering process to show authors living in just one state. We will finish with a link to a second page that shows more details about one of the authors.

1. Start VWD and Click through File ➪ NewWebSite ➪ General (Other languages/VisualBasic) ASP.NET Web site. Name the site `C:\websites\BegAspNet2Db`.
2. In the solution explorer (use View menu to turn on), right-click on the name of the site and click on New Folder; name it `ch01`.

3. Right-click on ch01 and add a new item of template type Web Form; name it `TIO-1-GridViewSQL`. Set language to Visual Basic and set "Code in Separate Page" to off. Leave other settings at their defaults (select master page = off). Once the nascent page appears on the VWD screen you will see, at the bottom left, tabs for Design and Source views. Switch to Design view.

4. Click through Menu:View ➪ Database Explorer (Server Explorer) to display the explorer of data connections.

5. Expand the Pubs connection, Tables folder, and the Authors table. Using Control+click, select the four fields au_id, au_lname, au_fname, and state. Drag them onto the page. VWD will automatically create a GridView and data source control for you.

6. The Tasks menu automatically opens next to the new control (or open it by selecting the GridView and clicking on the small arrow at the top right of the control). Enable paging and sorting, then click on AutoFormat and select one that you like. Click Apply. Save the page with Ctrl+S and press Ctrl+F5 to run it. When warned about debugging being disabled, select to modify the Web.config file to enable debugging. In ASP.NET 2.0, the first viewing of a page is delayed as the framework compiles and optimizes the code. Subsequent user hits are much faster.

> **Depending on your security settings, you may get a firewall blocked warning; if so, unblock the firewall for the `WebDeveloper.WebExpress.exe`.**

7. Play with the sorting (click header of each column) and paging (numbers at bottom of table). Close the browser so the page is unlocked for improvements back in VWD. Note that we have used drag-and-drop, but no code, to create a sophisticated display of data on the page.

8. As an alternate way to show data using two steps, go back to VWD and stay in Design view. Press Ctrl+Home, press Enter twice, and then Ctrl+Home again to get the insertion bar above the GridView and two lines of space for some working room. You will now add a display of data where you can be more specific about the source. You do this by adding the data source control separately from the data-bound control that displays the data.

9. Display the toolbar by clicking on Menu:View ➪ Toolbox. If the sections of the toolbox are collapsed (you see only the dark gray headings of Standard, Data, Validation. . .), expand the Standard and Data sections. Drag a SqlDataSource control to the top of the page.

10. The smart tasks panel will automatically open; click on Configure Data Source. Click on New connection, for server name enter `(local)\SQLExpress`, and use Windows NT integrated security. Drop the list of databases and select Pubs. Test the connection and then finish with a click on OK. Back in the Configure Data Source dialog, click Next. Do not save this connection string to the application configuration file because you want the string to be more obvious in this first demonstration. Select the table named Authors and click on just one column from the check boxes: State. Turn on Return only unique rows, and click Next. Test the query and then click Finish. You now have a SqlDataSource control named SqlDataSource2, the first step in this two-step method to add data to the page.

11. Display the list of distinct states by dragging a list box from the Standard section of the toolbox to the top of the page. In the list box's smart task panel, click on Choose Data Source and select SqlDataSource2 (the distinct states list). The display and value fields can both remain State. Click OK. Back on the smart task panel, click on Enable AutoPostBack and close the task menu, save, and press Ctrl+F5 to view in your browser. You now have a list control on the page along with an invisible SqlDataSource control. Close the browser before returning to VWD.

12. This step links the list box to the GridView, so only authors from the selected state appear. Select the SqlDataSource1 control (below the GridView—be careful you don't use the #2 control) and open its CommonTasks menu. Click on Configure Data Source, keep the same connection (AppConnectionString1), and click Next. If needed, change the option button to specify columns and check off the same four fields (id, firstname, lastname, and state). Now click on the WHERE button. In this box, you specify which authors to show. You want only those whose State value equals the selection in the States list box. Under the Column list, select State. The operator can stay as equals, and the source should be set to Control. Note the new options to pick a Control ID; you want ListBox1. Set the default value by typing in the string `CA` to start with a view of just authors in California. Click the Add button to append that `WHERE` clause to your SQL statement and then click OK, and Next. In the next page of the wizard, test the query using the default value of CA. Click Finish and then close the CommonTasks menu. If you are asked to refresh the control, click on Yes, save and hit Ctrl+F5 to run. Select various states and note the change in the table. Close the browser when you are done.

13. Now you will create a second page to display details about one author from our GridView. Check that you exited your browser. In VWD, click your Solution explorer tab so it is on top. Right-click on ch01 and add a new item of template type Web Form and name it `TIO-1-GridViewSQL-Details.aspx`. At the bottom left of the screen, select the Design view. Drag and drop a DetailsView control from the toolbar (Data section). Choose a New data source and select the type of (SQL) database. Choose the connection named AppConnectionString1 and click Next. Check on the Specify columns, click on the asterisk (all columns), and click Next. Click on the WHERE button and set the au_id column equal to a source of `querystring` named `au_id`. Set a default value of `213-46-8915`. Click Add and double-check that the SQL expression shows `[au-id]=@au_id`. Click OK, clink Next, test the query, and click Finish. Close the Details view control's CommonTasks menu, save, and press Ctrl+F5 to run. You will only see the details on one author.

14. Now that you have a page to show details about an author, you can finish by giving the user a way to click on the GridView to jump to the details page. Check that you exited your browser; then, in VWB, open `TIO-1-GridViewSql.aspx` in Design view. Select the GridView and expand the little top-right arrow to see the CommonTasks menu. Select Edit columns to see the Fields dialog box. Select Hyperlink in the Available Fields and click Add. Keeping your hyperlink field selected in the lower left, go to the properties on the right and set the following:

```
Text =  ViewDetails...
DataNavigateUrlFields =  au_id
DataNavigateUrlFormatString =  TIO-1-GridViewSQL-Details.aspx?au_id{0}
```

Click OK and close the smart task panel.

15. Save and run. Observe the behavior in the browser. If you are typing outside of Visual Studio or VWD, the finished pages should appear as shown in Figure 1-1:

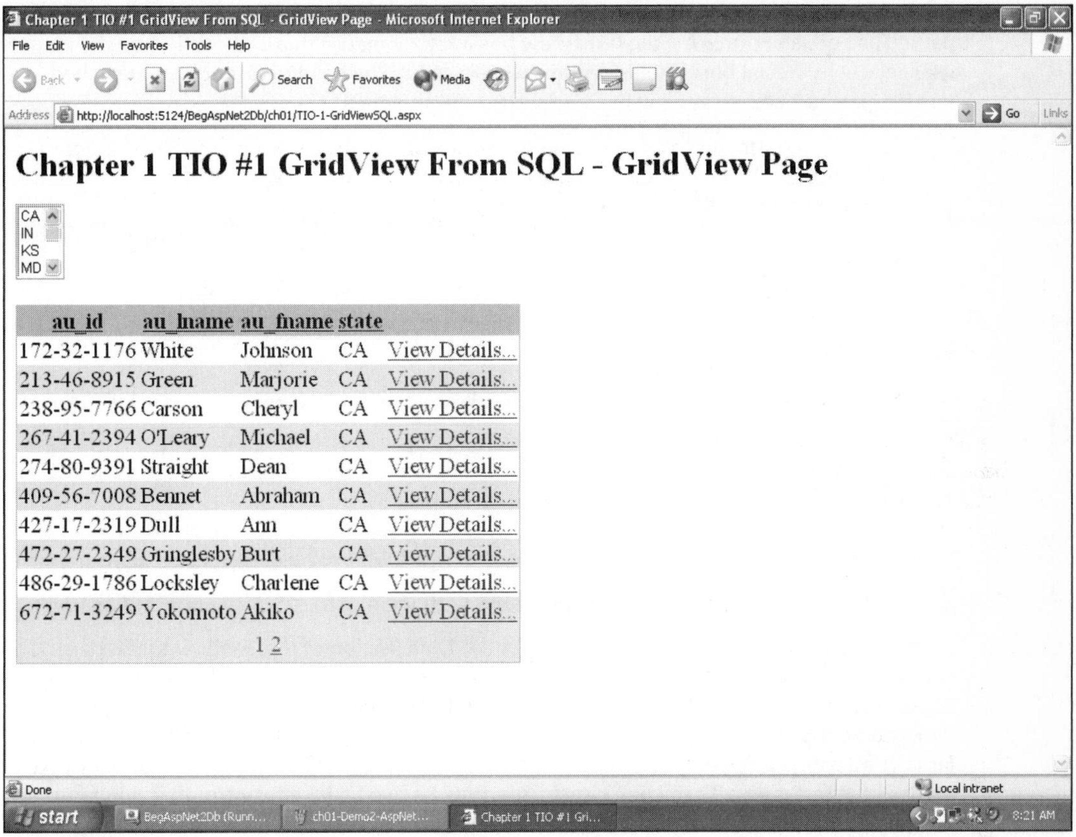

Figure 1-1

How It Works #1 — GridView Table from SQL with Paging and Sorting

This exercise covered a lot of small steps. When finished, you have two pages of medium complexity (similar to the type that will be discussed in detail in the middle chapters of this book). For now, there are five general concepts you should observe:

- All of the steps were performed in the VWD designer interface. You did not write any Visual Basic or C# code, nor did you directly write any HTML tags or set tag attributes.
- Take a look at the code that VWD generated for you by clicking on the Source view of the file `TIO-1-GridViewSQL` (or looking at the preceding code listing). Note that there is nothing in the initial `<script>` tags. All of the characters on the page are in standard HTML syntax with opening and closing tags, hierarchical tags, and attributes within tags.
- Look at the general pattern of the pages. There are pairs of controls: data source controls (SqlDataSource) and data-bound controls (GridView, DetailsView, and Listbox). The first gives you a connection to a database. The second displays data. For example, at the top of the GridView page, you have an `<asp:SqlDataSource>` and then an `<asp:ListBox>` that uses the SqlDataSource as its DataSourceID. You will study this pattern in detail throughout the book.

- Notice how a data source control can have its attributes controlled by another control on the page. The SqlDataSource for the GridView has a `WHERE` clause that is modified by the value the user selects in the list box. The information is passed in the form of @state in a tag called `<SelectParameters>`.
- You can pass a parameter from one page to the next in the querystring, and that parameter can be used to modify the DataSource on the new page. For example, in the `HyperlinkField` tag of the GridView you specified to pass the au_id field. The DataNavigateUrlFormatString added the target page's text to the au_id value. Then on the Details page, you set your SqlDataSource SelectCommand to use the query string value.

Overall, even on a first try, in less than 15 minutes you can produce pages with functionality that would have taken many hours in earlier versions of ASP.

Try It Out #2 — DataList from Access

In this exercise you will use a DataList control to display data with flexibility to arrange your fields within a template space. For variety, use an Access data source.

1. Double-check that a copy of `Northwinds.mdb` is in a folder named `App_Data` of your Web site.
2. Right-click on CH01 and add a Web Form item with the name `TIO-2-DataListAccess.aspx`.
3. In Design view, drag a DataList control from the Data section of the Toolbox to the page. Choose a data source = New Data Source. Select the data source type of Access database and accept the default name of AccessDataSource1. Choose a database file by browsing to `C:\websites\BegAspNet2Db\App_Data\Northwind.mdb`. Click Next and, for the Name (which means of a table or query), select Categories and check the ID, Name, and Description fields. Click Next and run the test query. Then click Finish. You now have a DataList control that points to categories of Northwind and in the background creates an AccessDataSource control.
4. Select the DetailsList, open its smart task panel (small arrow at top right) and click on the property builder to set some overall properties for the details list. Change the columns to 3 in the `RepeatColumns` property and the direction to horizontal for Repeat Direction. Click Apply and OK.
5. Now you will configure the display of each record's data. Continuing with the DataList selected, in its smart task panel click on Edit Templates. You can now add and format controls within the white ItemTemplate space. First select and delete the six controls in the template. Check that your insertion bar is in the editable space, then type the word **Item**. Now click through Menu:Layout ➪ Insert Table. Set the table to be 2 rows by 2 columns with a border of 2, and set the Cell Properties Background Color to a light shade of yellow. Click OK to create the table in the DataList's template.
6. Now we will get some data-bound controls into the template.

   In the top left cell, we will place the Northwind logo. Prepare by copying the `NorthwindLogo.bmp` file from the Images folder of the download into the `ch01` folder of your site (`C:\Websites\BegAspNet2Db`). (You can use any other bmp or gif if you don't have the download). Into the top left cell, drag an image control from the Standard section of the toolbar. Select the image control and in the properties window set the ImageUrl to `NorthWindLogo.bmp`.

Into the top right cell, drag a label from the toolbar and click Edit Data Bindings in the smart task panel. Bind its text to the category ID field and click OK.

Into the bottom left cell, drag a label and bind it to the description field.

Into the bottom right cell, add a label and bind to the category name field.

7 Now that the cells are filled, select the right column by clicking on the arrow that appears when you locate the mouse cursor right at the top of the column. Once selected, in the properties window, set align to center. Finish by opening the smart task panel (arrow at top right of entire DataList control) and clicking on End Template Editing. Save the document (which will appear as follows) and press Ctrl+F5 to run it. Your page should resemble the following code:

```
<%@ Page Language="VB" %>
<!DOCTYPE html PUBLIC "-//W3C//DTD XHTML 1.1//EN"
"http://www.w3.org/TR/xhtml11/DTD/xhtml11.dtd">
<script runat="server"> </script>
<html xmlns="http://www.w3.org/1999/xhtml" >
<head runat="server">
    <title>Chapter 1 TIO #2 DataList From Access</title>
</head>
<body>
    <h2>
Chapter 1 TIO #2 DataList From Access</h2>
    <form id="form1" runat="server">
         <asp:DataList ID="DataList1" Runat="server"
DataSourceID="AccessDataSource1"
            DataKeyField="CategoryID" RepeatColumns="3"
RepeatDirection="Horizontal">
            <ItemTemplate>
                <table><tr>
                        <td style="width: 100px" bgcolor="aqua">
                             <asp:Image ID="Image1" Runat="server" />
                        </td>
                        <td style="width: 100px">
                            <asp:Label ID="Label1" Runat="server"
Text='<%# Eval("CategoryID") %>'></asp:Label>
                        </td>
                    </tr>
                    <tr>
                        <td style="width: 100px" bgcolor="aqua">
                            <asp:Label ID="Label2" Runat="server"
Text='<%# Eval("Description") %>'></asp:Label>
                        </td>
                        <td style="width: 100px">
                            <asp:Label ID="Label3" Runat="server"
Text='<%# Eval("CategoryName") %>'></asp:Label>
                        </td>
                    </tr></table>
                <br />
                <br />
            </ItemTemplate>
        </asp:DataList>
```

```
    <asp:AccessDataSource ID="AccessDataSource1" Runat="server"
                DataFile="~/Data/Northwind.mdb"
                 SelectCommand="SELECT * FROM [Categories]">
        </asp:AccessDataSource>
    </form></body></html>
```

How It Works #2 — DataList from Access

You can see the same patterns here as in the first exercise. You do not write any code, and the page is in HTML format. All of your actions are drag-and-drop or selections, so you build a page in just a few minutes. As before, you added a DataBound control (DataList) and it automatically walked you through setting up its data source control (AccessDataSourceControl).

The DataList control starts the same way as the GridView, by specifying its DataSource control, but to build a less rigid rendering you go into the control's item template. On this template you can add and format controls and bind them to fields in the underlying DataSource control. The templated controls will then display the appropriate value for their record in the DataList. In this case, you started with a table to organize the space in the template and filled the cells with three labels. When the DataList is rendered you see a more flexible layout than you had with a GridView. All of the topics discussed in this demonstration will be fodder for deeper analysis in later chapters of the book.

Try It Out #3 — TreeView from XML

Your sources of data are not limited to relational databases, and your data displays do not have to be in rectangular grids. In this exercise you read data from an XML file and display it in hierarchical fashion in a TreeView control. You will also see how to handle an event on a TreeView control when a selection is made, one of the few cases where you have to write code.

1. Copy the file named `Bookstore.XML` from the downloads into your Data folder. Then create a sister folder to Data named Images and copy in three gifs from the download: `closedbook.gif`, `notepad.gif`, and `folder.gif`.

2. Create a new Web Form page in `ch01` named `TIO-3-TreeViewXML.aspx`. In Design view, drag an XMLDataSource control from the Data section of the toolbox onto the page and then click Configure Data Source from the common tasks menu. You only need to fill in two spaces (double check your syntax).

```
Data File:                    ~/Data/Bookstore.xml
XPath expression:             Bookstore/genre[@name='Fiction']/book
```

3. Now you need to display the data, so drag a TreeView control from the Standard section for the toolbox onto the page and set its Data Source to XMLDataSource1 (the default name for the control you created in the last step). Save and run the page at this point to see a tree of the generic names of the XML nodes (book, chapter), but not the actual values (Tale of Two Cities, London).

4. Exit your browser and go back to the page in Design view. Open the CommonTasks menu for the TreeView and click on EditTreeNode DataBindings. In the available list click Book and click Add. Set three properties for book, as follows:

```
DataMember:      Book
TextField:       Title
ImageURL (careful - NOT ImageUrlField):       ~/Images/closedbook.gif
```

5. Staying in the DataBindings DialogBox, add the chapter node and set its DataMember to chapter, TextField to name, and ImageURL to notepad.gif. Apply and click OK to close. Save the page and view it in your browser.

6. You will add one last feature to demonstrate that you can handle events in a similar fashion to older versions of ASP. Exit your browser and go to VWD. In Design view, select the TreeView control. Display the properties window with F4. At the top of the properties window, click on the lightning bolt and then double-click on `SelectedNodeChanged` event. VWD will automatically type the first and last lines of an event handler. You can now type in the highlighted line below. The first option uses Visual Basic.

```
<%@ Page Language="VB" %>
<script runat="server">
  Sub TreeView_Select(ByVal sender As Object, ByVal e As EventArgs)
    Response.Write("You selected: " & TreeView1.SelectedNode.Value)
  End Sub
</script>
```

Option two employees C#, as follows, if you chose to use C# when you created the page.

```
<%@ Page Language="c#" >
<script runat="server">
    void TreeView_Select(Object sender, EventArgs e)
    {
        Response.Write("You selected: " + TreeView1.SelectedNode.Value);
    }
</script>
```

7. Last, you need to instruct the TreeView to use this event handler when any value of the tree is clicked. Staying in Source view, add the following gray line to the <asp:TreeView> control:

```
<asp:TreeView ID="TreeView1" Runat="server"
       OnSelectedNodeChanged="TreeView_Select"
      DataSourceID="XmlDataSource1">
```

8. Save the file and run it. When you click on any item in the tree the event is triggered and the page displays a small note repeating the value of the text under the click. The finished file looks like the following using Visual Basic:

```
<%@ Page Language="VB" AutoEventWireup="false" ClassName="TIO_3_TreeViewXML_aspx"
%>
<script runat="server">
    Sub TreeView_Select(ByVal sender As Object, ByVal e As EventArgs)
        Response.Write("You selected: " & TreeView1.SelectedNode.Value)
    End Sub
</script>

<!DOCTYPE html PUBLIC "-//W3C//DTD XHTML 1.1//EN"
"http://www.w3.org/TR/xhtml11/DTD/xhtml11.dtd">

<html xmlns="http://www.w3.org/1999/xhtml" >
<head runat="server">
    <title>Chapter 1 TIO #3 TreeView from XML</title>
</head>
<body>
```

```
        <h2>
    Chapter 1 TIO #3 TreeView from XML
        </h2>
        <form id="form1" runat="server">
        <div>
            <asp:XmlDataSource ID="XmlDataSource1" Runat="server"
                DataFile="~/Data/Bookstore.xml"
                XPath="Bookstore/genre[@name='Fiction']/book" />

            <asp:TreeView ID="TreeView1" Runat="server"
                DataSourceID="XmlDataSource1"
                OnSelectedNodeChanged="TreeView_Select" >
                <DataBindings>
                    <asp:TreeNodeBinding ImageUrl="~/Images/closedbook.gif"
    TextField="Title" DataMember="book" />
                    <asp:TreeNodeBinding ImageUrl="~/Images/notepad.gif"
    TextField="name" DataMember="chapter" />
                </DataBindings>
            </asp:TreeView>

        </div>
        </form>
    </body>
    </html>
```

The script part of the finished file looks like the following using C#:

```
<%@ Page Language="c#" AutoEventWireup="false" ClassName="TIO_3_TreeViewXML_aspx"
%>

<script runat="server">
    void TreeView_Select(Object sender, EventArgs e)
    {
        Response.Write("You selected: " + TreeView1.SelectedNode.Value);
    }
</script>
...
```

How It Works #3 — TreeView from XML

The same themes emerge in this third example. You create a data source control (XMLDataSource) and a data-bound control (TreeView). By default, the tree shows the names of the nodes rather than their values. But even at this level, you have achieved an expanding and collapsing tree with just a few clicks. Then, in the Edit TreeNode Bindings dialog box, you determined what values and images to display at each level.

Note two items that you will cover in more depth later. In specifying the XML file, you started the path with a tilde (~). This represents the root of the Web site. If the site is deployed to another physical location on a drive, the link will not be broken. Second, note how the XPath string is used to limit the number of books displayed. There are five titles in the XML file. If you change the central part of the XPath to `[@name='NonFiction']`, you can see the other two books. Last, note that XPath is case-sensitive.

The last exercise ended with a little coding. As in earlier versions of ASP, you can set an event to fire an event handler with custom code. In this case, the TreeView has an `OnSelectedNode` event that will send the value of the node that was selected to the event handler. You can display that with a simple Response.Write.

Summary

This chapter reviewed some basic ASP.NET topics, set up your machine for the book, and walked through three exercises.

Recall from your study of ASP.NET that pages are stored as a combination of text, HTML tags, scripts, and ASP.NET server-side controls. When a page is requested, IIS directs the request to ASP.NET, which processes the page using the ASP.NET controls and scripts to build a pure HTML page. Therefore, you achieve two objectives. First, you can build each page to suit the individual requestor and the current needs of the business (the pages are dynamic). Second, any browser can read the page because it is delivered as pure HMTL.

The .NET Framework is a collection of classes (code) written by Microsoft that enable programmers to quickly, surely, and easily create solutions for their organization. One set of classes, ASP.NET (System.Web), provides very powerful controls for building dynamic Web pages. ASP.NET 2.0 reduces the amount of coding for common data scenarios to near zero. All of the decisions about ADO object parameters and the timing of bindings are handled automatically. The page architecture follows a pattern of having two controls to show data. The first is a data source control that establishes a connection to a database. The second is a data-bound control that displays the data.

This chapter discussed various software options to implement data on ASP.NET 2.0 pages. The .NET Framework 2.0 must be installed. You have two Web server options. Although public deployment would use IIS, development explained in this book uses the lighter-weight Cassini that comes with Visual Web Developer. To create pages you will be using Visual Web Developer Express because it offers many tools in its Integrated Development Environment (IDE) and is available for free. Several alternatives for a database management system were discussed. This book uses SSE because it is free, overcomes the problems of using Access, and easily scales to Microsoft SQL Server at the time of deployment. Last, you installed two databases (Northwind and Pubs) that you will use for examples in this book.

The exercises in this chapter revealed that it takes just a few ASP.NET tags with a half dozen attributes each to display and modify data. You used data source controls (SqlDataSource, AccessDataSource, and XMLDataSource) to create a conduit to the data. Then you used data-bound controls (GridView, DataList, and TreeView) to display the data. You did not have to use any <script> code to perform the data-binding tasks, although you did demonstrate that you could write an event handler as in earlier versions.

One control can have its parameters set by another control, for example, when the data source for the GridView was changed by the selection in the ListBox. Those parameters were passed easily across pages as when you sent a record ID to the details page. Overall, understand that none of these pages would take more than ten minutes to type and troubleshoot using the drag-and-drop tools of Visual Web Developer.

The next few chapters will examine data source controls, starting with Access, moving on to the SQL data source control, and then connecting to other databases. Following that, several chapters will discuss displaying data using various data-bound controls.

Exercises

1. What is the basic pattern for showing data on an ASP.NET 2.0 page?
2. Name several types of data sources that ASP.NET 2.0 supports.
3. Name several ways that ASP.NET 2.0 can display data.
4. What is the difference between the .NET Framework 2.0 and ASP.NET 2.0?
5. Make some observations comparing SQL Server, MSDE, and SSE.

2

Connecting to an Access Database

The first chapter provided an overview of ASP.NET 2.0 and databases. The next few chapters discuss connecting to different types of databases. This chapter discusses how to create and modify DataSource controls that connect to a Microsoft Access database. Chapters following this one cover the same concepts for Microsoft SQL Server and other data sources.

This chapter covers the following topics:

- Introduction to Microsoft Access and the JET Database Engine
- Connecting to a Microsoft Access Database in Visual Studio or Visual Web Developer (VWD)
- Introduction to the AccessDataSource Control
- Handling Different Locations for Access MDF Files
- Variations in SQL Statements for Selecting Data
- Managing File Permissions to Access Databases
- Handling Connection Failures Gracefully
- Pros and Cons of Using Access as a DataSource

These concepts are also applied in four Try It Out exercises, as follows:

Try It Out	Topic
1	Explore an Access MDB File in Visual Web Developer
2	Connecting to an MDB and Displaying with the GridView
3	Alternate Select Statements for an AccessDataSource
4	Handling AccessDataSource Connection Failures

Microsoft Access and the JET Database Engine

Microsoft Access is one of the most common database management systems in use today. Part of the Microsoft Office family of products, Access is readily available to information workers at both work and home. If you are reading this book, chances are good that you have had some experience with Access at one time or another. To understand what is happening in this chapter, you must differentiate between Microsoft Access, MDB files, and the JET engine.

Microsoft Access provides four basic tools: a structure to hold data (tables), a way to read and write to that data (the JET engine), an environment to create a front end for the data (Design view of forms and reports), and tools that can run the front end (Data view of forms and reports).

With Access, you have a complete package for both the front and back ends of handling data. But when working with ASP.NET pages, you don't need all of the tools for the front end (designing and running forms and reports). All you need are the back-end tools: the ability to hold data and to read and write data. The ASP.NET page itself will serve as the front-end form for rendering and interacting with that data.

Microsoft makes it easy to use just the back-end functions of Access in a tool called the JET engine. You can think of JET as Access without forms or reports. JET can open and read or write to tables and queries, while ignoring the form and report objects in the MDB. JET is installed on any machine where you have set up Access or Visual Basic (and some other software). You do not have to do anything to turn JET on. For this book, you can use Microsoft Access to examine or create MDB files, but ASP.NET data sources will use JET to work with Access files on an ASP.NET page.

Connecting to a Microsoft Access Database in Visual Web Developer

Although you can use the Microsoft Access design tools to create and explore the contents of an Access database, Microsoft has also made it easy to use Visual Web Developer (VWD) to explore the contents of an Access database. Once Visual Studio has established a connection to your database, you can browse the schema (tables and columns) of the database and/or change the data content directly from within the IDE. Note that creating an Access database or altering the database schema must still be performed in Microsoft Access, however.

As previously mentioned, the MDB file format is the container that stores data for a Microsoft Access database. When you save a database in Access, this file gets created on your hard disk. To use an Access database in an ASP.NET application, you will need to know the path to the location of this file, for example:

```
C:\Documents and Settings\Owner\Desktop\MyDatabase.mdb
```

Databases generally require a username and password prior to divulging information. Although it is possible to protect the contents of an Access database by requiring these credentials, Microsoft Access databases do not require this information by default. For the sake of the examples in this chapter, the sample database will not require a username or password.

We will save our discussion of how to connect to a password-protected database for Chapter 4, "Connecting to Other Relational Databases" (for reasons that will be made apparent in that chapter).

It is important to understand the structure (schema) of a database before you begin to use it. At a minimum, you must know the names of tables or queries that you want to run as well as the names of their columns (fields). If you intend to write or change data, you should also have an understanding of the relationships so that data dependencies are not broken. This section will demonstrate how to use VWD to connect to an Access MDB file on your disk. From there you can browse the database contents and familiarize yourself with the schema, including the names of tables and the names and data types of columns (fields).

If you are not using VWD (or Visual Studio) you will have to explore the database using Access to open the MDB and examine the tables and queries in Design view. This would be a good time to run a few tests of any SQL statements you plan to use to see if you get the expected results. Remember to close any Design view windows before using the MDB as a source of data in an ASP page (Access objects that are open in Design view are locked from reads and writes).

Because VWD provides powerful tools to see the schema of a database without leaving the IDE, let's walk through them in the first Try It Out.

Try It Out #1 — Explore an Access MDB File in Visual Web Developer

You must be using Visual Studio (VS) or VWD to perform this exercise. VWD uses the term Database Explorer while VS uses Server Explorer (it includes additional features for connecting to more than just databases). However, they provide the same functionality for connecting to databases.

If you are writing your pages in Notepad or another text editor, do only the first two steps (make folders and copy the database), and then explore the Northwind database directly in Access. Close the database prior to using it as a source of data in your ASP pages. Of course, you must have completed the Chapter 1 setup of ASP.NET 2.0 and the .NET Framework to run the sample pages in this text.

In this exercise, you will copy a database into your Web site and then look at its structure using tools in VWD. You won't put data on a Web page until the next Try It Out.

1. If you haven't done so already, set up your software as described in the first chapter, install the .NET Framework 2.0, install VWD, and check that you have Access or the JET engine by looking at Start/Control Panel/Add Programs and searching for Microsoft Office/Access or Microsoft Visual Studio. Check that you have a copy of Northwind.mdb, which you should have downloaded from `www.wrox.com` or the Microsoft site, as described in Chapter 1.
2. If you didn't create a Web site for this book in Chapter 1, do it now as follows: Open VWD and choose New Web Site from the File menu. Then type the path `C:\Websites\BegAspNet2Db` and click OK. Notice that this directory is opened and a App_Data subdirectory is automatically created for you. Now right-click the `C:\Websites\BegAspNet2Db` directory in VWD and choose Add Folder to add another subdirectory named Ch02. Find and copy the Northwind.mdb file, and then paste it to the App_Data directory (you can do this directly in VWD's Solution Explorer).
3. Within VWD, the Solution Explorer should be visible. If not, use Menu: View ⇨ Solution Explorer to display. You may want to make the Solution Explorer about half the screen width for this exercise.

4. Click View ➪ Database Explorer and note how the Database Explorer (called the Server Explorer in the full Visual Studio) now shares a space with (overlays) the Solution Explorer.

5. Note that at the bottom of the Solution Explorer you have tabs to switch between a view of the Web files (Solution Explorer) and a view of the data sources (Database Explorer). Also note that you cannot expand and look into an MDB from the Solution Explorer window (although you can see that the file exists in the App_Data folder and can double-click the file to open it in Access). You must switch to Database Explorer view to delve into the MDB's schema.

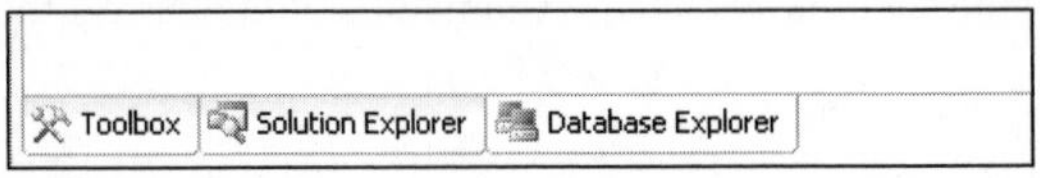

Figure 2-1

6. Click Menu: Tools ➪ Connect to Database (or right-click on the Data Connections item in Server Explorer).

7. Click the Provider button and select the Provider for OLEDB.

8. Click the Connection button and set your OLEDB provider to Microsoft Jet 4.0 OLEDB Provider. Specify a connection to the `C:\Websites\BegAspNet2Db\App_Data\Northwind.mdb` file. You can leave the username — Admin and no password — because there is no security for our sample database. Click on Test Connection and then click OK to exit the dialog box. VWD is now able to see the data and metadata of Northwind.

9. In the Database Explorer, expand the level of Data Connections and then expand your connection to Northwind. You can now view the objects in the MDB. Expand Tables and then expand Employees and Products. At this point, you can see each column name in these tables.

10. Select the ProductID column in the Products table and notice that you can view properties of this column, such as its data type and length, in the VWD Property Grid.

11. Right-click the Access connection and choose New Query to start the VWD QueryBuilder.

12. Select the Products table and click the Add button, and then close the table dialog by clicking the Close button. Inside the QueryBuilder, select the ProductID and ProductName fields by clicking the check box next to each column name.

13. Right-click anywhere in the QueryBuilder and choose Execute SQL to run the command. Notice that the query executes and the results are displayed in the bottom of the dialog. You can also manually edit the SQL statement to write your own queries.

14. Close the QueryBuilder and note that VWD prompts you to save this query as a document you can reopen for future use (you can click Cancel for now to dismiss the prompt).

15. Right-click the Products table node in the Database Explorer and choose Show Table Data. Notice that VWD opens a new document window where you can view and update the data in the Products table directly.

16. Close the Show Table Data document window.

How It Works #1 — Explore an Access MDB File in Visual Web Developer

When you connect to an Access database using the Database Explorer (or Server Explorer), it will open and read the MDB file and display the database schema (tables and columns) in a hierarchical tree. When you click on a node in this tree, you can view the properties of the selected schema object in the Property Grid. You can also right-click to open the QueryBuilder against this database and execute SQL queries. These queries may be saved and reopened for future use, as well. Using the Database Explorer and Query Builder allows you to easily explore database files from within the Visual Web Developer IDE.

Note that when you open a table or query in Design view, Access locks the object for its own exclusive use. So if you are modifying the structure of a table in Access and then switch over to use the new table in VWD or your browser, you may be blocked from even reading the table's values. You must close out of the Design view in Access and then go back to Visual Studio to change your Web page.

Keep in mind that adding a database to the Server Explorer does not add a data source control to an ASP.NET page. Presence in the Data Connections only makes the preview features available in the IDE. In the next section, you actually connect a page to an MDB file using a data source control.

The AccessDataSource Control

ASP.NET 2.0 includes an AccessDataSource control for exposing data from an Access database to an ASP.NET 2.0 (.aspx) page. The control has a very simple set of properties. The most important property of AccessDataSource is the `DataFile` property, which points to the path to the MDB file on disk. The other property that the AccessDataSource must have is the `SelectCommand` property, which assigns a statement that indicates the result set (table and columns) to return. The SelectCommand must be defined using Structured Query Language (SQL) syntax.

In VWD, you can add the AccessDataSource control to your page in one of two ways. If your MDB file is added to your Database Explorer, as demonstrated in the previous example, you can drag and drop column names onto the page and VWD will automatically create an AccessDataSource control and a GridView to display the data for you. If you do not want the GridView or you want to customize the controls, you can add just an AccessDataSource control from the toolbox and walk through its configuration wizard to set it up. The wizard will prompt you to browse for the data file and then allow you to specify the SelectCommand by choosing columns from the tables in your database. If you are typing your pages outside of VWD, you can match the following code:

```
<asp:AccessDataSource
   ID="MySourceName"
   Runat="server"
   DataFile="MyMDBName.mdb"
   SelectCommand="SELECT MyField1, MyField2 FROM MyTable">
</asp:AccessDataSource>
```

Again, note the simplicity. All you provide is an ID, the name of an MDB file, and a SelectCommand.

This chapter is about a data source control, but recall that a data source control does not render anything visible on the page. So to give you a visual way to test your data source controls, the next Try It Out explains the basic steps to display data in a table using the GridView control (an evolution from ASP.NET version 1's DataGrid control). Note that the focus is not on the configuration or customization of the GridView in this chapter; rather, the focus is on the data source control in this case. Later, in Chapter 5, the GridView control will be explored in much more detail.

Try It Out #2 — Connecting to an MDB and Displaying with the GridView

In this exercise, you will display information about products sold by Northwind on your page.

1. Start your page editor and navigate to `C:\Websites\BegAspNet2Db\ch02\`.
2. Add a page named `TIO-ch02-2-DisplayAccessData` from the template Web Form. Change to Design view using the bottom tabs.
3. At the top of the page, type a heading such as "Demonstration of Connection to an MDB Source" and put similar text into the title. Although this step is not discussed in every exercise, we suggest that you include a title and HTML text in each of your pages so that you do not lose track of which page you are viewing.

```
<html>
<head>
    <title>TIO ch02-1 Display MDB Data</title>
</head>
<body>
    <h3>ch02 TIO 2 Demonstration of Connection to an MDB Source </h3>
<body>
</html>
```

4. Display the toolbox (Menu: View ➪ toolbox or Ctrl+Alt+X) and expand the toolbox's Data panel.
5. Drag an AccessDataSource control onto your page.
6. The control's smart task panel should appear automatically, but if not, select the new data source control and then click the top right small arrow to open the smart task panel. Click on Configure Data Source.
7. In the Choose a Database step, click the Browse button and select `C:\Websites\BegAspNet2Db\App_Data\Northwind.mdb`, and note that the designer converts the file spec to a relative reference where the tilde (~) represents the root of the site.
8. In the Configure Select Statement box, select the Specify Columns option and then select the Products table. Check on the asterisk (*) to select all columns. Click Next, Test Query, and Finish.
9. Select the Data control and display the Properties window with F4. Change its ID to NorthwindProducts.
10. Going back to the Data panel of the toolbox, double-click on GridView to add the control to the page and enter its Common Tasks Menu, and then click on Choose Data Source. Choose NorthwindProducts and finish the wizard.

11. Select the GridView and change its ID to NorthwindProducts. Your page should now appear as follows:

```
<%@ page language="VB" %>

<html>
<head><title>ch02 TIO 2 Display MDB Data</title></head>
<body>
    <h3>ch02 TIO 2 Demonstration of Connection to an MDB Source </h3>
    <form runat="server">
        <asp:accessdatasource id="NorthwindProductsAccDataSource" runat="server"
                selectcommand="Select * From Products"
                datafile="~/App_Data/Northwind.mdb">
        </asp:accessdatasource>
        <asp:gridview id="NorthwindProductsGridView" runat="server"
                datasourceid="NorthwindProductsAccDataSource">
</asp:gridview>
    </form></body></html>
```

12. Open your browser and view `C:\Websites\BegAspNet2Db\ch02\ch02_TIO_2_DisplayAccessData.aspx` (see Figure 2-2).

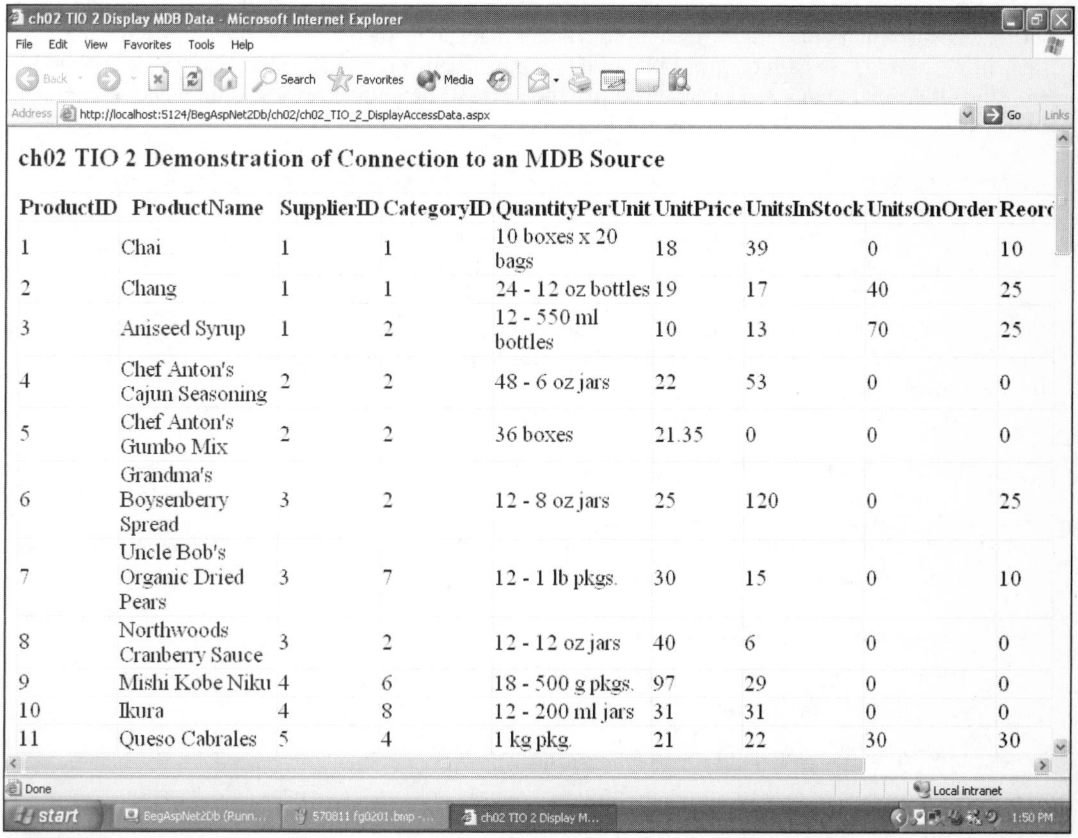

Figure 2-2

13. Finish by displaying data from an MDB Query instead of a table. Close the browser and return to VWD. Save the file with a new name, `ch02_TIO_2_DisplayAccessData-Query.aspx`. Select the GridView and open its Common Task Menu by clicking on the small arrow at the top right of the control. Click on Configure Data Source and Next to pass by the selection of the MDB file. In the screen to Configure Select Statement, change the name to "Sales by Category" and check on the asterisk to get all fields. This query brings together four tables in JOINs, limits the number of records used in one table, and does some grouping and aggregation of data to get totals. Click Next, Test the Query, and Finish. Your data source control will now look like the following

```
<asp:accessdatasource id="NorthwindProductsAccDataSource" runat="server"
        selectcommand="Select * From [Sales by Category]"
        datafile="~/App_Data/Northwind.mdb">
</asp:accessdatasource>
```

14. Open your browser and view the page.

How It Works #2 — Connecting to an MDB and Displaying with the GridView

You have two controls on the page. The first, AccessDataSource, does all of the work of connecting to the ADO.NET objects that talk to the JET engine that communicates with the MDB file. The second, the GridView, takes that data and formats it into HTML that can be displayed on the page. Note that it is very important to give each control a useful ID (name). Then you must be sure that the data-bound control (the GridView) identifies as its data source the AccessDataSource control using its `DataSourceID` property to refer to the ID of the AccessDataSource.

Displaying data from queries is no more difficult; query names can be used instead of table names in Access. There are two caveats. First, if a table or query has spaces in its name, you must enclose the entire name in square brackets. Second, queries that require user input (for example, "sales by year" needs to know which year) require techniques not covered yet in this book.

With the preceding few steps, you can see on your page a display of data from your AccessDataSource control. Later chapters go into great detail about the GridView, but this chapter will continue its focus on the data source controls.

Variations in Select Statements

When you create a data source in VWD, the wizard asks you to specify columns to display or to create a custom SQL statement. In the preceding Try It Out, you simply checked a few columns. You can specify more complex SQL statements in several ways:

- ❑ By the interactive dialog box
- ❑ By typing a custom SQL statement in the AccessDataSource wizard (invoked by the Configure Data Source smart task on the control)
- ❑ By typing the statement into the property grid
- ❑ By typing the statement directly into the tag in the Source view

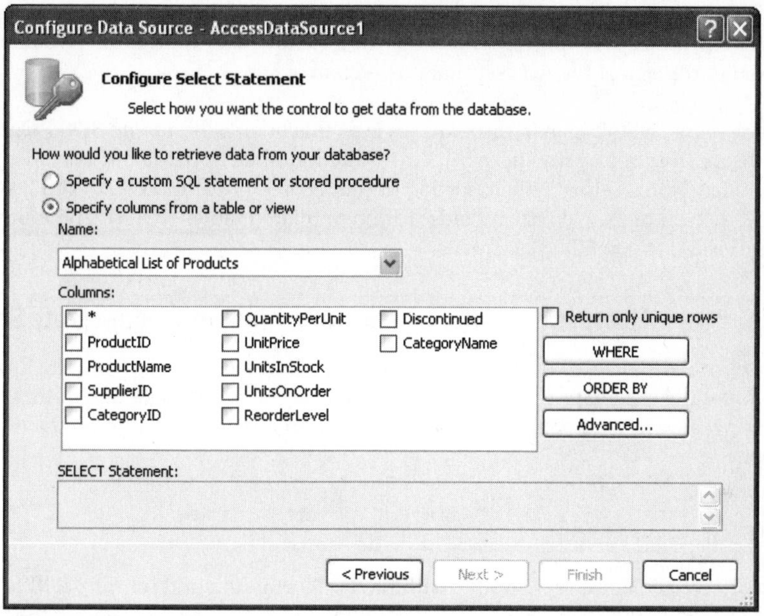

Figure 2-3

For simple queries that return one or more columns from a single table, selecting columns in the AccessDataSource wizard is the preferred technique because it reduces typos and syntax errors (see Figure 2-3). In this wizard, you can select either a table or a query name from the Name drop-down list. You can then select individual columns in the table or query by checking either all of the columns (*) or any set of columns. If you click on the Order By button, you can sort by any column in the source. The field selected in Then By will be used if the first column has a tie. As you choose options from this wizard, notice that the actual SQL syntax of the SelectCommand is being displayed at all times in a read-only textbox.

The WHERE button in this wizard allows you to create parameterized SQL statements, which are discussed in Chapter 9. For now, we will overlook this option, but it is important that before deployment you use parameters as discussed later in the book. In a deployed site, avoid ever directly concatenating user input into a SQL Statement. Skipping the parameterization leaves your site open to SQL injection attacks. This hacking technique uses spurious characters from user input to negate the intended SQL statement then substitute a damaging statement. Using the parameters collection sends (under the hood) the user input through the ADO.NET parameters collection with its ability to reduce SQL injection issues.

Although the Configure Data Source wizard has many options to help you build up an SQL statement quickly, at times you will want to type (or modify) your own SQL statement directly into the tag's SelectCommand. The AccessDataSource wizard allows you to do this. On the wizard page where you can choose tables, queries, and columns, you can choose a radio button option to "Specify a custom SQL statement or stored procedure." Selecting this option and clicking the Next button in the wizard takes you to a separate page where you can define a custom statement by typing it directly in a text area. You can also use the Visual Studio QueryBuilder to visually construct a custom statement here using a tool very similar to the Access QueryBuilder.

If you don't want to use the wizard, you can optionally type a custom SQL statement in the property grid for the AccessDataSource control, or just switch to Source view and type the statement on the `SelectCommand` property of the AccessDataSource control tag.

There are many texts on SQL (one in the same style as this book is *Beginning SQL Programming,* ISBN 1-861001-80-0), and this book provides a brief introduction in an appendix. If you study an SQL text, start with commands that return only a portion of the records (TOP and DISTINCT), syntax to rename a field (AS), and the techniques to return fields from two related tables (JOIN). The following exercise explores a few variations on SQL statements.

Try It Out #3—Alternate Select Statements for an AccessDataSource

In this exercise, you will display only certain columns and certain records from the Products table of Northwind. You will also create a page to display data from a query. Note that in this exercise the criteria for the selection reside in your source code. At this point in the book, you do not have user input to make selections.

1. Create a file in `C:\Websites\BegAspNet2Db\ch02\` named `ch02_TIO_3_AlternateSelectCommands.aspx`.
2. Add an AccessDataSource control with the ID Northwind and set the MDB to your `\App_Data\Northwind.mdb`. As you walk through the dialog boxes, set the Select command to retrieve all fields from the Products table ("name" = Products). Take a look in the Source view and observe the statement you created, as follows:

```
SELECT * FROM Products
```

3. Add a GridView, give it an ID of Northwind, and set its source to Northwind. Following is the entire page as it should be at this point:

```
<%@ page language="VB" %>
<html>
<head runat="server">
    <title>ch02 TIO 3 Alternate Select Commands</title>
</head>
<body>
<h3>ch02 TIO 3 Alternate Select Commands</h3>
    <form runat="server">
        <asp:accessdatasource id="NorthwindAccDataSource" runat="server"
            selectcommand="SELECT * FROM Products"
            datafile="~/App_Data/Northwind.mdb">
        </asp:accessdatasource>

        <asp:gridview id="GridView1" runat="server"
            datasourceid="NorthwindAccDataSource">
        </asp:gridview>
    </form>
</body>
</html> >
```

4. Now open the page in your browser and observe the screen shown in Figure 2-4 (not all columns are shown in the screenshot).

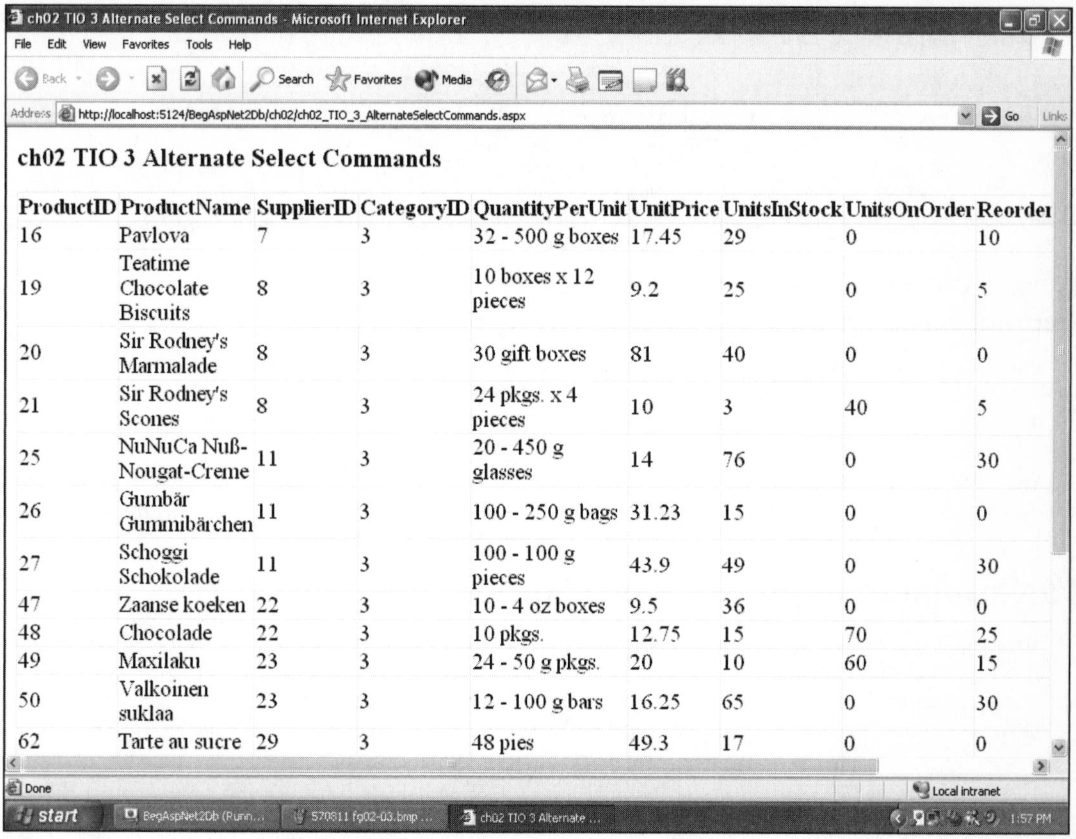

ProductID	ProductName	SupplierID	CategoryID	QuantityPerUnit	UnitPrice	UnitsInStock	UnitsOnOrder	Reorde
16	Pavlova	7	3	32 - 500 g boxes	17.45	29	0	10
19	Teatime Chocolate Biscuits	8	3	10 boxes x 12 pieces	9.2	25	0	5
20	Sir Rodney's Marmalade	8	3	30 gift boxes	81	40	0	0
21	Sir Rodney's Scones	8	3	24 pkgs. x 4 pieces	10	3	40	5
25	NuNuCa Nuß-Nougat-Creme	11	3	20 - 450 g glasses	14	76	0	30
26	Gumbär Gummibärchen	11	3	100 - 250 g bags	31.23	15	0	0
27	Schoggi Schokolade	11	3	100 - 100 g pieces	43.9	49	0	30
47	Zaanse koeken	22	3	10 - 4 oz boxes	9.5	36	0	0
48	Chocolade	22	3	10 pkgs.	12.75	15	70	25
49	Maxilaku	23	3	24 - 50 g pkgs.	20	10	60	15
50	Valkoinen suklaa	23	3	12 - 100 g bars	16.25	65	0	30
62	Tarte au sucre	29	3	48 pies	49.3	17	0	0

Figure 2-4

5. Go back to the Design view and select the AccessDataSource (not the GridView). Open its smart task panel and click on Configure Data Source. In the Configure Select Statement window, select "Specify a custom SQL statement" and then click Next. Modify the SQL statement in the editor, as follows:

```
SELECT * FROM [Products] WHERE (CategoryID = 3)
```

6. Click Next and test query. Click OK and finish out the dialog boxes. Take a look at the page in Source view and focus on the following:

```
<asp:accessdatasource id="NorthwindAccDataSource" runat="server"
    selectcommand="
        SELECT *
        FROM [Products]
        WHERE (CategoryID = 3)"
    datafile="~/App_Data/Northwind.mdb">
</asp:accessdatasource>
```

7. Try building some of the following Select commands using the dialog box, typing in the Source view, or using a combination.

```
SELECT * FROM Products WHERE ProductID = 12
SELECT * FROM Products WHERE ProductName = 'Northwoods Cranberry Sauce'
SELECT * FROM Products WHERE ProductID < 11
SELECT * FROM Products WHERE ProductID <11 ORDER BY ProductName Ascending
SELECT * FROM Products WHERE SupplierID = 6 OR SupplierID = 8
SELECT * FROM Products WHERE SupplierID = 24 AND UnitPrice > 10
```

How It Works #3—Alternate Select Statements for an AccessDataSource

In the first steps, you set up an AccessDataSource control as previously and a GridView. But then you began experimenting with the Select command. Adding and removing columns with the check boxes is intuitive. You can also directly type (or edit) SQL statements in the editor window.

You added `WHERE` clauses that limit which records are returned from the MDB file. If your column names do not have spaces, you can omit the [ ]. If there are spaces in the names, you must use those brackets.

Variations in MDB File Location

Your MDB file may be stored in various physical places on your disk: the same folder as the Web page, a subfolder beneath the Web page, or any other folder on the machine. In Visual Web Developer, you can often just browse for the file in the designer, and the correct path to the MDB file will be typed for you. However, if you are typing your code, you will need to follow the syntax presented in this section.

The `DataFile` property of the AccessDataSource control can contain a path that is either fully qualified (starting with the drive letter, for example) or is specified relative to the location of the page that contains the AccessDataSource. The path may also be application-relative, which uses a URL syntax to refer to the path. This syntax substitutes the tilde (~) character for the application root directory, for example `~/App_Data/products.mdb`. Using application-relative paths enables you to easily move the page from one location to another without breaking the reference to the database, and it is recommended that you use them whenever possible.

First, observe the fully qualified path syntax, which contains the entire path to the MDB file starting at the root of the computer drive where the file is located:

```
<asp:accessdatasource ...
datafile="C:\WebSites\WebApplication1\App_Data\MyMdb.mdb">
```

Although this syntax works, it has the disadvantage of making your application less portable. If you move this application to another machine, the drive or full path to the file may be different, and you would potentially need to modify the `DataFile` property every time you moved the page.

An improvement on the fully qualified syntax uses relative-path syntax, which specifies only the portion of the path that is different from the full path to the page containing the AccessDataSource. Here is the syntax for a database file in the same folder as the page, specified as a relative path:

```
<asp:accessdatasource ... datafile="MyMdb.mdb">
```

Because the page and the MDB file are in the same directory, there is no difference between the paths to these files; hence, you need to specify only the file name itself. This next relative-path syntax is very similar to the preceding one if the MDB is in a folder down one or more levels. In this case, you need to specify only the subfolder name, followed by a slash and the MDF file name:

```
<asp:accessdatasource ... datafile="MyDaughterFolder/MyMdb.mdb">
```

If the MDB file were located in a directory above the page, you could also use the double-period syntax to specify one level up from the current location:

```
<asp:accessdatasource ... datafile="../MyMdb.mdb">
```

Using relative-path syntax, you can easily move the application from location to location without breaking the paths to your MDB file. Because the page and MDB file always travel together (provided the MDB file is part of the application), the relative location between these files always stays the same. However, what happens when you want to move the path around inside of the application, for example, moving the page into a subdirectory? In this case, the relative location between the page and MDB file changes, and the relative-path syntax is then incorrect.

The application-relative syntax alleviates this problem. In this case, the path is always specified relative to the application root directory, instead of relative to the page itself. The root is represented by a tilde (~):

```
<asp:accessdatasource ... datafile="~/App_Data/MyMdb.mdb">
```

Now you can easily move around the application, or move around pages within the application, without breaking your reference to the database. For this reason, you should use application-relative paths whenever possible.

Handling File Permissions

An MDB database is just another file on your disk, and as such, it is subject to all the same file access permissions issues that would apply to any other file. This means that to read (and write, as you will see later in this book) a database file, the application in which your page runs must be given appropriate permission to read (and write) to the file itself in Windows.

The reason why our pages have "just worked" in the examples so far is that you are using the VWD Web Server, a lightweight process that runs under the identity of the user running VWD. That is, the VWD Web Server runs as *you*, and you already have permission to read and write the MDB file to which your page connects.

When running pages under IIS, however, the situation gets a little more complicated. In this case, ASP.NET pages run under the identity of a special limited-privilege user account on your machine. Under IIS 5.1, this account is named "ASPNET." Under IIS 6 or later, this account is named "Network Service," which belongs to a Windows group named IIS_WPG ("worker process group"). To use Access databases under IIS, these accounts need to be given permission to read and optionally write to the directory containing the MDB file.

VWD goes an extra step toward helping you establish these permissions by automatically granting this permission to the ASPNET or Network Service accounts when the database is located under the App_Data subdirectory under the application root. This special directory is always granted the correct permissions, provided you are using VWD to develop pages on the local machine. The App_Data directory has additional benefits, as well — for example, preventing any files from being served to requesting Web browsers. This means that by placing your MDB files in the application's local App_Data directory, you protect those files from inadvertent or deliberate download by your application's clients. For this reason, using the App_Data directory for storing your MDB files is highly recommended.

If you must store your MDB files elsewhere, or if you just need to specify the permissions to the database directory manually (for example, if you are working against a remote Web server), you can use Windows to configure permissions for the ASP.NET and/or Network Service accounts.

To set permissions manually, follow these steps:

1. Navigate to the folder where the MDB file is located using Windows Explorer.
2. Right-click this directory and choose Properties.
3. Select the Security tab and click the Add button.
4. Add either the local ASP.NET account (IIS 5.1) or IIS_WPG group (IIS 6).
5. Click OK; then apply the appropriate permissions to this directory.

For more information, refer to the white paper entitled "Running ASP.NET 1.1 and IIS 6.0" available on the ASP.NET Web site: `http://www.asp.net/faq/AspNetAndIIS6.aspx`.

Handling Access Connection Failures

Errors and failures inevitably happen from time to time in an application. What happens when someone "improves" your server's tree by adding a new level of folders above your MDB? What if the name of your MDB has been changed? What if the MDB has been corrupted? Each of these problems will prevent a successful connection to the data and cause a page failure. Good coding practice dictates that you try to make any failure as graceful as possible.

Before discussing the actual commands, understand that the AccessDataSource control is derived from the SqlDataSource control. In most cases, this is only a background issue. But when handling exceptions, you must use objects that actually reside (and are thus named) in the underlying SQL data source object.

The technique for a soft landing uses code that is triggered when the AccessDataSource control undergoes its `OnSelected event`. That event is triggered internally when the GridView requests data from the data source control. The code to handle a connection error checks an exception argument that the data source control passes. The AccessDataSource control does not have its own name for this argument; you have to use the name SqlDataSourceStatusEventArguments. If the exception argument is null, nothing happens. If the exception argument has a value, the value is checked. If the argument is of an OLEDB Exception type, a warning label on the page can have its text set to a message. Again, note the terminology. It would be clearer if there was an "AccessException" type, but there isn't. You use the more generic object OleDbException and finish the script with a command that the exception was handled. That allows the GridView to continue rendering, albeit without data, and prevents the beige-background general ASP.NET 2.0 failure page. Because the GridView did not get any data, it will display an alternate table, one with a single cell that shows the message in the `EmptyDataText` property.

Don't despair if you have difficulty following these steps; the next exercise will demonstrate. For now, you can just cut and paste the code into your pages to see it work. Later in the book, I will discuss the details of how to create an alternate rendering of the GridView in case of connection failure and more details on handling an error event.

Try It Out #4 — Handling AccessDataSource Connection Failures

1. In your `ch02` folder, create a file named `TIO-4-ConnectionFailure-CS.aspx`. In Design view, add to the page an AccessDataSource control pointing to Northwind that selects all columns from the shippers table.
2. Add a GridView that displays the information from the data source control. Also, add a label control and name it "Message."
3. Now switch to Source view and make a few changes to the tags, as highlighted in the following code. If there is a section of `<columns>` tags, remove them. You should be left with a very simple page, as follows:

```
<html>
<head id="Head1" runat="server">
    <title>Chapter 2 TIO #4 Connection Failure to Access in C#</title>
</head>
<body>
<h3>Chapter 2 TIO #4 Connection Failure to Access in C#</h3>

    <form id="form1" runat="server">

        <asp:label ID="Message" runat="server"/><br/><br/>

        <asp:gridview id="GridView1"  runat="server"
            datasourceid="AccessDataSource1"
            AutoGenerateColumns="true"
            EmptyDataText="No data records were returned" />

        <asp:AccessDataSource ID="AccessDataSource1" Runat="server"
            selectcommand="Select * From Products"
            datafile="~/App_Data/Northwind.mdb"
            OnSelected="AccessDataSource1_Selected"
            />
    </form>
</body></html>
```

4. Check your page; there should be no problems seeing the products sold by Northwind.

5. Now you will add code to deal with a connection problem. Go to the top of the page and enter the following script. The first example is in C# and the second in VB. Enter only one.

```
<%@ page language="C#" %>
<script runat="server">
    void AccessDataSource1_Selected(object sender, SqlDataSourceStatusEventArgs e)
    {
        if (e.Exception != null)
        {
            if (e.Exception.GetType() == typeof(System.Data.OleDb.OleDbException))
            {
                Message.Text = "There was a problem opening a connection to the
database.  Please contact the system administrator for this site.";
                //Optionally set GridView1.Visible = false;
                e.ExceptionHandled = true;
            }
        }
    }
</script>
<html> ...
```

An alternate script in VB follows.

```
<%@ Page Language="VB" %>
<!DOCTYPE html PUBLIC "-//W3C//DTD XHTML 1.1//EN"
"http://www.w3.org/TR/xhtml11/DTD/xhtml11.dtd">
<script runat="server">

    Sub AccessDataSource1_Selected(ByVal sender As Object, ByVal e As
SqlDataSourceStatusEventArgs)
        If (Not e.Exception Is Nothing) Then
            If TypeOf e.Exception Is System.Data.OleDb.OleDbException Then
                Message.Text = "There was a problem opening a connection to the
database. Please contact the system administrator for this site."
                ' Optionally set GridView1.Visible = false
                e.ExceptionHandled = True
            End If
        End If
    End Sub

</script>
<html> ...
```

6. Save and run the page. Since our actual connection remains intact, there should still be no problems. Close the browser.

7. Now move the Northwind MDB file out of `\App_Data` and into your `C:\Temp` folder so that the connection will fail. Alternatively, you can change your code to attempt to connect to Southwind.mdb. Run the page and observe that your browser shows a more elegant failure message.

8. If you moved Northwind.mdb, return it to `C:\BegAspNetDb\App_Data`.

How It Works #4 — Handling AccessDataSource Connection Failures

First, recall that the AccessDataSource control is a derivative of the SqlDataSource control and uses the set of exceptions applicable for all OLEDB data sources, so don't be surprised when objects with SQL or OLEDB names rather than Access names are referred to.

Observe that three modifications were made to the page to handle connection failures. First, you added a property to the GridView data source control to display a message if the GridView did not get any data from the data source control. Second, you added a property to the data source control that invokes the Data_Selected event handler when the `OnSelected` event occurs. Note that this is located in the `DataSource` event. Although the user does not directly select the AccessDataSource control (there isn't even a rendering to the user), the selection occurs internally when the GridView requests data from the data source control. Third, you wrote the script.

The script will receive several arguments, one of which will be exceptions. There is no object named AccessDataSourceStatusEventArgs. Instead, you reach down to the underlying object from which the AccessDataSource is internally derived: the SQL DataSource. The SqlDataSource object has status arguments that bubble up to the AccessDataSource object. If no problems exist, the exception list will be empty. If there is an exception, the code will test to see what kind of exception was thrown. Again, there is no such object as an Access Exception. Instead, AccessDataSource holds its exception in the more generic object named OleDbException. Assume that any exception in this collection is caused by a failure to connect. Our code reacts by putting some friendly failure notification text into the label named Message.

The biggest trick to this code is keeping straight the objects with three different names. You are using an Access file (MDB) for your data source and thus use the AccessDataSource control. But you are using the underlying SqlDataSource for your event arguments. Last, you are using the generic OLEDB set of exceptions. Most mistakes derive from trying to use ASP.NET 2.0 objects named Access at all of these points in the syntax.

A Few Notes on Using Access in Web Applications

Access works very well as a desktop database. The interface is familiar to many readers, many small offices have resources already stored in Access MDB files, and it is easy to open up the database and examine it using the Access tools. However, Access does not scale to support more than a few users simultaneously.

The problem with Access is that it was never designed to handle execution in a fast-paced multithreaded environment such as a Web server. It was designed and intended as a single- or few-user desktop database. When used in a Web server environment, Access simply does not provide enough performance to run a public Web site effectively and may actually produce unpredictable results under these conditions. For this reason, you will have difficulty finding a host that is willing to run Access to support a Web site on their hosting machines.

Access can also provide challenges to development when using parameterized SQL statements such as those required to perform database updates, inserts, and deletes. When using parameters, Access correlates the values to fields based on the order in which the values are presented. This is sometimes difficult to manage if the order of fields in your form does not match the order of fields in your SQL statement. Using named parameters available in other database systems is much, much easier and less prone to errors. Furthermore, parameters provide a higher level of security.

Although Microsoft Access is a reasonable database for learning ASP.NET and performing initial development, it is almost never the right solution for running a production Web site. We suggest that you read on to the next chapter and switch your focus to using SQL Server or SQL Server Express. Either one of these database systems will eliminate the performance problems associated with Access and provide a cleaner path to deployment

Common Mistakes with AccessDataSource Controls

The following list provides a record of the most common errors made by students in a lab setting and is a good place to start if you are having problems:

- **Incorrect name or path for the MDB file**—Recheck the exact name of the MDB and the path. To avoid errors in the pathnames, you can use the Browse button in the Configure Data Source wizard for AccessDataSource.
- **Incorrect permissions to access the MDB file**—If a UserID and password are required by the MDB file, you must use the techniques explained in Chapter 4.
- **Trying to use a data-bound control when there is no data source control**—A data-bound control must have a source of data, that is, a data source control, specified by its `DataSourceID` property.
- **Setting the data-bound control to the wrong data source**—If you are using more than one data source control, be extra careful to accurately name each control. Then double-check which data source you are using in the `DataSourceID` property for each data-bound control.
- **Attempting to use an MDB when JET is not installed on the machine**—Although rare, check that the server has JET available. It is easy to copy the MDB file, but you also must have installed the Access software or the JET engine.
- **Errors in table or column names**—This mistake usually arises when typing; it is less problematic when using the designer wizards or drag-and-drop in Visual Studio and VWD.
- **Incorrect SQL statement syntax**—Make sure you spell the keywords correctly. There must be a comma between each item in a list (such as a group of field names). Literal strings must be in single quotes, but numbers are not. Whenever possible, build your statements using the data source control's Configure Data Source dialog box. You can also test SQL statements directly in the Access Query Design tool or Visual Studio QueryBuilder.

- **Trying to use an MDB object that is locked** — An MDB table or query that is currently open in Access in Design mode is locked to all reads and writes. Close the object before attempting to use it in an ASP.NET page, either at design time or at runtime.
- **Attempting to change a locked page** — VWD Design view is unavailable for a page that is still open in a browser. To use Design view, you must first close the browser. (You can edit in Source view, save, and refresh your browser to see changes.)

Summary

This chapter discussed techniques for connecting an ASP.NET 2.0 Web page to a Microsoft Access database. It covered some general ideas and then focused on the theme and variations of using the AccessDataSource control to read from an Access MDB file. The values in our database are now available for a data-bound control to display. To see the data in this chapter, we used a GridView data-bound control with default settings.

Successful page designers spend time preparing to use data. It is important to know the file's path and be familiar with the tables, queries, and columns within the MDB file. Ensure that you have a login that has been assigned the permissions you will need. You may want to use VWD or Access to open and explore the MDB to understand its structure and constraints before you design the ASPX page.

You can modify the SelectCommand to contain any SELECT statement allowable by Structured Query Language (SQL). The Configure Data Source wizard for AccessDataSource contains very effective tools to build a statement by clicking within the designer.

When using an MDB, you must allow permissions for the MDB file for two cases, VWD (mostly design time) and IIS (at deployment). If you create your Web site using VWD Menu, File ➪ New ➪ Website, VWD automatically creates a folder named Data within which there are permissions for files for the developer based on the Windows login. But at the time of deployment, it will not be the developer requesting use of the files. Rather, permission must be granted to the IIS process. Again, if you created the Web site in VWD, these permissions were automatically set up for you. If you created the Web site in folders created outside of VWD, you must create the IIS permissions by hand, as described in the chapter.

Connections may occasionally fail, particularly if security or location of the MDB changes. The small amount of code demonstrated can modify the page so that it handles failure gracefully. The code runs whenever the GridView is created or refreshed. The code checks whether there were exceptions from the source of data and renders a failure message to the screen.

Last, we discussed the fact that while Access MDB files and the JET engine are useful tools for students or small offices, a public Web site will overwhelm the ability of JET to handle multiple simultaneous users. Furthermore, JET has a model for changing data that creates additional problems for programmers. For these reasons, try using Access for learning or development, and use a dedicated SQL Server or MSDE for your production applications.

Now that you are comfortable reading from an MDB file, the next chapter moves on to the technique of connecting with more robust sources of information — the Microsoft SQL Server and MSDE.

Exercises

1. Describe the difference between the terms Access, JET, and MDB file.
2. What two basic ASP.NET 2.0 server-side controls are required to display data from an MDB file?
3. Explain the advantage of using syntax a instead of syntax b, which follow.
    a. `C:\Websites\MySite\App_Data\MyFile.mdb`
    b. `~\App_Data\MyFile.mdb`
4. List disadvantages to using Access as a source of data for Web sites.
5. If you want to write more sophisticated SelectCommands, what language should you study?
6. When handling an Access connection failure, you will use objects with three names. Fill in the following table:

Purpose	Object Name
Connection with the MDB file	
Transfer arguments to the event handler	
Hold the exceptions raised by the connection	

3

Connecting to SQL Server and SQL Server Express

The topic of this chapter, the SqlDataSource control, will be your workhorse for the rest of the book. For the past 30 years, most organized data has been stored in some form of relational database such as Microsoft SQL Server. These systems feature the kind of scalability, robustness, and management features that can support even the largest and busiest Web sites. The SqlDataSource control is designed to connect between these databases and data-bound controls on your page. This chapter focuses on using the SqlDataSource control with two Microsoft products: SQL Server and the new SQL Server Express (SSE) database engine.

This chapter is divided into seven sections (plus our usual list of common mistakes to help with troubleshooting and a summary):

- Introduction to SQL Server and Connection Strings
- Using the SqlDataSource Control
- Understanding Security in SQL Server
- Storing the Connection String in the Web.config File
- Choosing between DataSet and DataReader
- Discovering the Structure of an Unfamiliar Database
- Handling Connection Failures with the SqlDataSource

This chapter walks you through the following Try It Out exercises:

Try It Out	Topic
1	SqlDataSource Simple Example
2	Storing the Connection String in Web.config
3	SqlDataSource Using a DataReader
4	Determining Database Structure
5	Handling Connection Failures

Introduction to SQL Server and Connection Strings

A site that expects to have more than a few simultaneous users will have to employ a more scalable data source than Access, which isn't really intended for high-performance applications. This chapter explains how to use data from Microsoft SQL Server, an enterprise-strength Relational Database Management System (RDMS).

The full version of SQL Server includes three main parts. First is the engine that actually organizes the data and reads or writes in response to commands. Second is a suite of developer's tools to work with the database, such as Query Analyzer and Data Transformation Services. Last are the tools for managing data, ranging from backup utilities to replication schemes.

Although the full version has invaluable benefits to large-scale enterprises, many developers don't need this entire suite of tools. Fortunately, Microsoft makes available a free version of the SQL Server engine called SQL Server Express (SSE). Although it comes with a command-line tool (osql.exe) for importing schema and data using T-SQL commands, it does not yet include the rich graphical tools included with the full version of SQL Server (keep posted—it probably will by mid-2005). However, you can easily use Visual Studio or Visual Web Developer to develop databases using SSE. SSE enforces a restriction that only local connections are served (it is not possible to run SSE on a different machine than the Web server. For many hobbyist-level or student Web sites, SSE is a perfectly suitable option. You may have worked with an older incarnation named MSDE, which was based on SQL Server 2000; SSE is based on the Yukon version of SQL Server. SSE is used throughout this book; the instructions for downloading it are explained in Chapter 1.

> *Unless specifically denoted otherwise, all of the techniques presented here apply for all three forms of SQL Server (full product, SSE and the older MSDE); thus, the generic term* SQL Server *encompasses all three.*

Because SSE is only an engine and does not come with built-in developer tools (as of 2004), you must use other tools to create, change, or populate a database. The primary tool we will use for this purpose is Visual Studio or Visual Web Developer, which provides a Database Explorer as part of its interface. Note that the Database Explorer can change data and schema in local databases, but it can change only the data in remote databases (not the structure). In Visual Studio, the Database Explorer is called the Server Explorer because it includes some additional capabilities for working against non-database servers. We also use the osql.exe command-line tool briefly in the beginning of this book to import the initial databases we will employ throughout this book. A third alternative for database structure modification is to open Access and link to an external table in your SSE database.

Working with SQL Server requires familiarity with some vocabulary. SQL Server is installed on a machine that becomes a *server* and can be referenced by its machine name. If SQL Server is on the same machine as the requesting software, the machine can be referred to as (local). The engine can be installed more than once on a machine, and each installation is called an *instance*. SSE installs as an instance named `(local)\SQLExpress`. Within an instance, you can create *databases*. Databases have *tables* with *fields* and *records*. Databases can also have *views* that are a set of tables, fields, and constraints available to data consumers. *Stored procedures* (*SPROCs*) can carry out tasks on the data. A SQL Server instance automatically installs one account for a user named "sa" that has rights to all actions on all objects when using SQL Server authentication for users. When using Windows authentication (also called mixed authentication, the user logged on to Windows is also logged on to SSE. More information on authentication follows later in the chapter.

Preparing to Use a SQL Server Database

Time spent up front studying your database will reduce mistakes when you design pages to use the data. Check that you have the following kinds of information in hand before writing a page that uses SQL Server:

- **Server, instance, and database names** — Confirm the exact spelling of the server name, instance, and database name. If there is only one instance of the full SQL Server on a server, you do not need to use an instance name. But even if there is only one instance of SSE on the server, you must refer to it explicitly as MyServer\SQLExpress. Clarify whether you will be testing against live data or a development copy of the database.
- **Security information** — You will need to know your user ID and password to authenticate access to the database for development. Also, check whether the SSE uses Windows or SQL authentication. (The Chapter 1 install specified that SSE should use Windows authentication.)
- **Database schema** — Understand the schema of the database. Obtain the exact spelling of tables and field names, autogenerated or locked fields, dependencies, and constraints. Carefully note the presence of underscore characters and spaces in object names. Find out from the administrator whether you will be using tables directly or whether you will be using views and stored procedures (SPROCs). The latter may require parameters of specific data types. The SQL syntax to check these metadata appears later in this chapter.
- **Test your SQL statements (optional)** — You may have doubts about the syntax or logic of your SQL statements. You will find it more efficient to test the statements using a development tool such as SQL's Query Analyzer rather than checking them for the first time in an ASPX page.

Connection Strings

The major difference between the syntax of the AccessDataSource control (discussed in the last chapter) and the SqlDataSource control lies in the way the database to use is specified. For an MDB, we merely provide the file's name and pathname. The SqlDataSource uses a *connection string* to hold the name of the server, database, and login information. A connection string has different syntax than we are accustomed to in Visual Basic or C# and is the source of mistakes for many students. A typical connection string follows.

```
ConnectionString="Server=MyServer;Database=MyDatabase;User ID=MyID;Password=MyPass"
```

Alternate formatting on multiple lines improves readability, as in the following:

```
ConnectionString="
    Server=MyServer;
    Database=MyDatabase;
    User ID=MyID;
    Password=MyPass"
```

First, note the syntax. The entire string resides within double quotation marks in the source code. When specifying the string in the property window of VWD, you do not need the quotes; VWD will add them. Inside the quotes are a series of pairs in the format `Criteria=value`. Semicolons separate these pairs. Note that quotes are not used around the values. Also note that even though there are spaces in some of the criteria (for example, `User ID`), they are not encased in quotes or brackets. This syntax is not difficult to understand, but because it is different from the VB, C#, and SQL languages, mistakes are common. Let us take a moment to dissect the component parts of this string.

Within this connection string are two kinds of values: database identifiers (server, instance, and database) and security values (user ID, password, and security settings). The database identifiers start with a server value that is the network name of the machine hosting SQL Server. (The machine name is available in XP at Start ➪ My Computer; right-click and select Properties ➪ Computer Name tab ➪ Full Computer Name. For Windows 2000, right-click My Computer on the desktop ➪ Properties ➪ Network Identification.) If you know that the database server will be running on the same machine as the Web server where ASP.NET will run, you can also specify the server name as "(local)" to indicate that the server is the local machine on which the ASP.NET page is running. The instance can be added with `Instance=MyInstance`. More commonly, the instance is appended to the server name as `MyServer\MyInstance` or `(local)\MyInstance`. You may also see code that uses a period (full stop) to represent the local machine, as in `.\SQLExpress`.

SSE, by default, installs with its own instance. Referring to `(local)` alone will fail. You must refer to your SSE as `(local)\SQLExpress`.

Security settings are discussed later in this chapter. For now, understand that for Windows Authentication, use the attribute `IntegratedTrusted_connection=true` instead of the user ID and password attributes. SQL authentication requires two values: `user=MyUserName; password=MyPassword`, where `MyUserName` and `MyPassword` would be replaced with your own credentials. This text uses Windows authentication.

If you are familiar with earlier versions of ASP, you may be wondering about the provider. The default provider for the SqlDataSource control is the .NET Framework Data Provider for SQL Server. So you do not need to specify a provider in this chapter. The next chapter will discuss specifying nondefault providers for other databases.

Using the SqlDataSource Control

When you use the SqlDataSource control to select data, you can start with just two properties, the ConnectionString and SelectCommand, as follows.

```
<asp:SqlDataSource ID="MySourceControlName" Runat="server"
     ConnectionString="
        Server=MyServer;
        Database=Northwind"
     SelectCommand="SELECT Field1, [Field With Space] FROM MyTable">
</asp:SqlDataSource>
```

When using Windows authentication, you add the two authentication data.

```
<asp:SqlDataSource ID="MySourceControlName" Runat="server"
     ConnectionString="
        Server=MyServer;
        User ID=MyID;
        Password=MyPass;
        Database=Northwind"
     SelectCommand="SELECT Field1, [Field With Space] FROM MyTable">
</asp:SqlDataSource>
```

First is the connection string, as previously discussed, and second is the SelectCommand to determine what information is extracted from the SQL Server database. Within the SelectCommand, you can use almost any legitimate SQL SELECT statement, including those discussed in the last chapter or in Appendix A. Many SQL Server administrators will not allow users to directly access tables. Instead, the database administrator sets up limited permissions on SPROCs. Alternatively, views of tables can be created that present only parts of tables or tables with restrictions on what data can be modified. The syntax to connect to a view follows:

```
SelectCommand="SELECT * from MyView">
```

If the table, query, SPROC, or view has a space in its name, enclose the entire name in brackets, as follows:

```
SelectCommand="SELECT * from [My View]"
```

You may have noticed the `Filter` *property in the GridView and wonder how it compares to using a* `WHERE` *clause in the data source SelectCommand. Filter is used only in certain caching scenarios, which are covered in Chapter 15.*

With a connection string and a SelectCommand, you can create a page to use data from a SQL Server.

Try It Out #1—SqlDataSource Simple Example

In this exercise, you want to display a GridView of the products from the SQL version of Northwind in a grid (table) format. You will start with the technique of adding a DataSource control and a data-bound control so that you create the simplest source code. Then you will use a more rapid development technique (drag and drop column names).

1. Ensure that you have installed SSE (as explained in Chapter 1), including the sample database `Northwind`. This exercise will also work with SQL Server or MSDE.

2. Create a folder `ch03` and, within it, a file named `TIO-1-SqlSimple-1.ASPX`. Display the toolbox with Menu: View ➪ Toolbox (Ctrl+Alt+X). Note that the toolbox has a Data section that can be expanded.

3. In Design view, drag a SqlDataSource control from the Data section of the toolbar onto the page. In the smart task panel, configure the data source to a new connection. Type a server name of `(local)\SQLExpress` and use Windows NT authentication. Select the database named `Northwind` and test the connection. Click OK to finish. You will automatically return to the Data Source Configuration dialog; click Next. For this example, do not save the connection string in the configuration file; click Next. Choose "Specify columns from a table" and then select the table name of Products. In the Columns list, click on the ID, Name, and Unit Price. Click Next and Test Query, and then click Finish. That completes your DataSource control.

4. Add a GridView data-bound control. In the smart task panel, choose the SqlDataSource1 and close the smart task panel. That creates the data-bound control. Save and run your page, which appears as follows:

```
<%@ Page Language="VB" %>
<!DOCTYPE html PUBLIC "-//W3C//DTD XHTML 1.1//EN"
"http://www.w3.org/TR/xhtml11/DTD/xhtml11.dtd">
<script runat="server">
</script>
<html xmlns="http://www.w3.org/1999/xhtml" >
<head runat="server">
    <title>Ch03-Tio#1-SqlSimple-ver1</title>
</head>
<body>
    <h2>
        Chapter 3 TIO #1 SqlSimple ver1
    </h2>
    <form id="form1" runat="server">
    <div>
        <asp:SqlDataSource ID="SqlDataSource1" Runat="server"
            ProviderName="System.Data.SqlClient"
            ConnectionString="Server=(local)\SQLExpress;
                Integrated Security=True;
                Database=Northwind;
                Persist Security Info=True"
            SelectCommand="SELECT [ProductID], [ProductName], [UnitPrice] FROM
[Products]">
        </asp:SqlDataSource>

        <asp:GridView ID="GridView1" Runat="server"
            DataSourceID="SqlDataSource1"
            DataKeyNames="ProductID"
            AutoGenerateColumns="False">
            <Columns>
                <asp:BoundField ReadOnly="True" HeaderText="ProductID"
                    InsertVisible="False" DataField="ProductID"
                    SortExpression="ProductID"></asp:BoundField>
```

```
                <asp:BoundField HeaderText="ProductName" DataField="ProductName"
                    SortExpression="ProductName"></asp:BoundField>
                <asp:BoundField HeaderText="UnitPrice" DataField="UnitPrice"
                    SortExpression="UnitPrice"></asp:BoundField>
            </Columns>
        </asp:GridView>
    </div>
    </form>
</body>
</html>
```

5. Close the browser and take a look at the page in Source view. Notice that within the `<form>` of the page, there are two controls. The SqlDataSource has a ConnectionString and SelectCommand. The GridView has several columns bound to the SqlDataSource control's fields.

6. Now you will add a second table using a faster technique. Save the page as `TIO-1-SqlSimple-2.ASPX`. Change to Design view. In the menu, click through View ➪ Database Explorer. Right-click on Data Connections and select Add Connection. As in the previous step, you will go through the connection properties dialogs. Type in the server name of `(local)\SQLExpress`, use Windows NT security, and select the database named Northwind. Test your connection and click OK to close the dialog. Notice the new entry in your database explorer window.

7. Expand the new `(local)\SqlExpress.Northwind.dbo` connection and then expand its tables. Expand the Categories table. Use Ctrl+click to select CategoryID, CategoryName, and Description fields and drag them to the bottom of your page. Although the smart task panel will open for your new GridView, you can just close it. Run the page by striking F5. Scroll down to admire the table you created with a mere drag-and-drop of column names from the Category table. The source code for the additions of version 2 follows. Notice that when you drag and drop a column name you get a larger set of code, including a set of parameters in the SqlDataSource control.

```
...
        <asp:SqlDataSource ID="SqlDataSource1" Runat="server"
        <asp:GridView ID="GridView1" Runat="server"
...

        <asp:GridView ID="GridView2" Runat="server"
            DataSourceID="SqlDataSource2" DataKeyNames="CategoryID"
            AutoGenerateColumns="False"
            EmptyDataText="There are no data records to display.">
            <Columns>
                <asp:BoundField ReadOnly="True" HeaderText="CategoryID"
                    DataField="CategoryID"
SortExpression="CategoryID"></asp:BoundField>
                <asp:BoundField HeaderText="CategoryName" DataField="CategoryName"
                    SortExpression="CategoryName"></asp:BoundField>
                <asp:BoundField
                    HeaderText="Description" DataField="Description"
                    SortExpression="Description"></asp:BoundField>
            </Columns>
        </asp:GridView>
```

```
        <asp:SqlDataSource ID="SqlDataSource2" Runat="server"
            ProviderName="<%$ ConnectionStrings:AppConnectionString2.ProviderName %>"
            ConnectionString="<%$ ConnectionStrings:AppConnectionString2 %>"
            SelectCommand="SELECT [CategoryID], [CategoryName], [Description] FROM
[Categories]"
            UpdateCommand="UPDATE [Categories] SET [CategoryName] = @CategoryName,
[Description] = @Description WHERE [CategoryID] = @original_CategoryID"
            InsertCommand="INSERT INTO [Categories] ([CategoryName], [Description])
VALUES (@CategoryName, @Description)"
            DeleteCommand="DELETE FROM [Categories] WHERE [CategoryID] =
@original_CategoryID">
            <DeleteParameters>
                <asp:Parameter Type="Int32" Name="CategoryID"></asp:Parameter>
            </DeleteParameters>
            <InsertParameters>
                <asp:Parameter Type="String" Name="CategoryName"></asp:Parameter>
                <asp:Parameter Type="String" Name="Description"></asp:Parameter>
            </InsertParameters>
            <UpdateParameters>
                <asp:Parameter Type="String" Name="CategoryName"></asp:Parameter>
                <asp:Parameter Type="String" Name="Description"></asp:Parameter>
                <asp:Parameter Type="Int32" Name="CategoryID"></asp:Parameter>
            </UpdateParameters>
        </asp:SqlDataSource>
```

How It Works #1 — SqlDataSource Simple Example

When it comes to syntax, the SqlDataSource varies little from the AccessDataSource used in Chapter 2. The big difference is the use of a connection string (instead of specifying a data file). This similarity means that your knowledge of one control will help you understand the other data source controls.

The connection string passes three values to the SqlDataSource:

- ❑ The name of the SQL Server
- ❑ The name of the database or view that you want to use
- ❑ Direction to persist the Windows authentication through subsequent SSE logons

For either tables or views, if there are spaces in the name, you must enclose the name within brackets. The second parameter supplies a select command with standard SQL syntax.

When we moved to version 2, we used the full power of the VWD. By adding a connection to our Database Explorer, we make VWD aware of the schema of the database. VWD will display the table and column names. When you drag and drop a column name onto the page, VWD will build a GridView for you including the supporting DataSource control.

Understanding Security in SQL Server

An installation of SQL Server has two options for security schemes. They differ by which software performs the authentication. Authentication is the process of verifying the identity of the user that wishes to connect to SQL Server. Once authentication has been performed, SQL Server can verify whether that user has permission to connect to a requested resource such as a database. If the user has permission to connect to the database, SQL Server allows the connection request to succeed. Otherwise, it fails. This process of verifying permission for a user is sometimes called *authorization*.

- **Windows Authentication** (also called Trusted Authentication or Integrated Security) uses the Windows user identity of the process making the connection request to perform authorization against the database. In this case, the connection string does not provide an explicit username or password. The ASP.NET process runs as a local user named "ASPNET" (or on IIS 6.0 as a user named "Network Service"), so when using Windows Authentication, SQL checks whether this user has permission to use the database. In this case, all ASP.NET applications run as this same user, so this security scheme does not provide isolation between applications. Although it is possible to run each application in a unique ASP.NET process (each as a separate user) or to impersonate the Windows user identity of the browser client making the connection request, these topics are outside the scope of this book. The client impersonation scenario, however, is the most common usage for Windows Authentication in a Web application.
- **SQL Authentication** checks an explicitly provided username and password against a set of known users configured within SQL Server (without any reference to the operating system). In this case, it is easily possible for each application running in the ASP.NET process to connect to a database with a unique set of credentials, providing reasonable isolation between applications (application A cannot connect to application B's database without application B's username and password). This is the most common authentication scheme used for deployed Web applications, especially in shared hosting scenarios. Its one minor drawback is that it requires the application to retain the password of the user account used to connect, and there is always a risk that the security of your database could be compromised if a malicious person obtained this password. However, as you will see later in this book, ASP.NET provides a safe way to store the SQL Authentication password in the Web.config file in an encrypted format, which mitigates the risk that the password will be obtained.
- **Mixed Mode** is a configuration of SQL Server that allows either Windows Authentication or SQL Authentication.

You select which mode of authentication to use when you install SQL Server or SSE. In SQL Server, there is a wizard to assist in the security setup. For SSE, you will get Windows Authentication by default. To install with SQL Authentication, you must configure it explicitly. This text uses Windows Authentication.

If your SQL Server or SSE is already installed, you can figure out which authentication scheme was specified by opening RegEdit (back it up, of course) and looking in `HKey_Local_Machine/Software/Microsoft/Microsoft SQL Server` and searching for LoginMode. A Registry subkey value of 1 means Windows Authentication, and a value of 2 means Mixed Authentication mode.

The differences are summarized in the following table.\

	Windows Authentication	SQL Authentication (Used in This Text)
Alternate Name	Trusted Authentication Integrated Security	None, but Mixed Mode Authentication allows Windows or SQL Authentication
Typical Environment	Intranet	Internet
Location of List of Users and Authentication Process	Windows	SQL Server
SSE Install	Default	Requires special setup

Connection String	`Trusted_connection=true`
	`Or`
	`Integrated Security=true`
		`user=username;`
		`password=password`

User for ASP.NET Web Apps	ASP.NET process, either ASPNET (IIS5.x) or Network Service (IIS6)	SQL User
Strength	Generally better security; activity of a user can be traced across both SQL events and Windows events	Deploys to host without creating new account; independent from operating system Normal technique for hosted intranet sites More flexibility for applications to use different credentials to connect to each of their databases
Weakness	A Windows credential for a Web app is more likely to accidentally give rights to more in the OS than necessary.	Passwords are stored in the Web app (in Windows authentication they are not). Be sure your passwords are stored in the Web.config file and encrypted. Allows poor practice of a Web app using `sa` credentials. Always create a new credential for the ASP.NET Web app and give it only those rights needed.

Now, with the way SQL employs security, consider how the data consumer (our DataSource control) will meet the requirements. First, there is the use of data from VWD and VWD Web Server (Cassini), mainly during design time and testing. Second, you will want to access the data from IIS after deployment.

These two data consumers have different usernames. VWD and VWD Web Server use the name of the person logged on to Windows. The IIS process uses the name ASPNET.

If your SQL Server uses Windows authentication, your SqlDataSource control needs to include the following in its connection string: `Integrated Security=true (or, synonomously, Trusted_connection=true)`. This parameter will instruct SQL Server to authenticate the request for data based on the requestor's Windows login. If you were the user logged in when you installed SSE, your credentials were given access rights to SSE. Using VWD and VWD Web Server will work fine because the user of VW Web Server is considered the programmer that logged on to Windows and thus has an account on SSE. However, even though your application works inside of VWD, it may not work when the site is moved to IIS. IIS operates under an explicit user account named ASPNET (or Network Services in IIS6/Windows 2003 Server). Therefore, the administrator of the machine that hosts IIS must add ASP.NET as a user and give it permissions. That procedure is beyond the scope of this book but is explained in detail in most manuals for IIS administrators. In summary, if your SQL Server is using Windows authentication, you can do this book's exercises with VWD and VWD Web Server. Your pages will work on IIS only after granting the ASP.NET process account permission to your database.

If your SQL Server uses SQL authentication, SQL will do its own authentication. There is no dependence on Windows' list of users. Include in your connection string the two parameters `user=username; password=password`. Now you can use your page from VWD, VWD Web Server, or IIS, because there is no requirement for setting up user accounts in Windows. However, we need to use an account in SQL Server. The only default account is `sa`. Prior to deployment, you should create another account in SQL Server that has only the rights needed to execute your ASPX pages. Failure to create an alternate account to `sa` (and password protect `sa`) will expose your site to one of the most widely known and easily exploited security failures. Any hacker knows to try a log-in of userID='sa' with an empty password.

For both authentication schemes, when you use the connection strings previously mentioned, a user is logged in to SQL Server to the only initial account. It is named `sa`, which stands for systems administrator, and, as the name implies, it has all rights to all objects. With current versions of SQL Server, you cannot install the service with an `sa` having a NULL password. For SSE, you must install with the parameter `SAPWD="`*`MyStrongPassword`*`"`. Strong password in this case means a minimum of not NULL. Better, use at least seven characters and ensure a mix of letters, numbers, and symbols. In most situations beyond a student exercise, you will want a specific account for each database and application. Avoid an application having rights to the data of any other application.

Storing the Connection String in the Web.Config File

Older versions of ASP.NET have stored the connection string right in the ASPX page. Recall that the connection string holds information about the data server name and the user account, sometimes even including the password. Having that information in the code is bad practice for two reasons. First, the information can be seen by every programmer on the design team (however, it cannot be seen on a browser by site visitors). Second, it must be maintained or updated in every place throughout the Web site that has a connection. Updating passwords becomes an onerous job.

ASP.NET 2.0 gives you the option to move the connection string to a connections section of the Web.config file, give the string a name, and encrypt it. Then ASP.NET 2.0 pages just refer to the connection string by name. The steps required to store a connection string to Web.config are not difficult. Open the Web.config file located in the root of your site. Find the section delimited by `<connectionStrings>` (or add it yourself if it is not there) and type in an `<Add>` tag, as follows. There are three attributes to the tag: `name`, `connectionString`, and `providerName`. The `name` is just an ordinary name for the connection string that you will use within your pages. The `connectionString` attribute should be set to the full connection string value for connecting to your database, as previously described. The `providerName` attribute is discussed later in this book, and for now we will leave it blank. The first example is for Windows authentication as we use in this book.

```
<configuration>
<connectionStrings>
  <add
          name="MyConnectionStringName"
          ConnectionString="Server=MyServer;
                Database=MyDatabase" />

  <add
          name="AnotherConnectionStringName"
          ... />

</connectionStrings>
</configuration>
```

When using SQL Authentication, you will need to also present the credentials as follows:

```
<configuration>
<connectionStrings>
  <add
          name="MyConnectionStringName"
          ConnectionString="Server=MyServer;
                User ID=MyUserID;
                Password=MyPassword,
                Database=MyDatabase"/>

  <add
          name="AnotherConnectionStringName"
          ... />

</connectionStrings>
</configuration>
```

Then in our ASPX page, use the following syntax. Note how the syntax is written to execute a single statement `<%$     %>` that returns a string. The `<%$ ... %>` syntax is called an *expression* in ASP.NET 2.0, and in this case we use a `connectionString` expression to evaluate a connection string value. There are other expressions available in ASP.NET 2.0 that are outside the scope of this book.

```
<asp:sqldatasource
    ID="MySmartDataSource"
    ConnectionString="<%$ connectionsStrings:MyConnectionStringName %>"
    Select Command "..."
/>
```

The statement reads the connection string from the set of connection strings in the Web.config file. The Web.config file is the default location and does not have to be specified.

When you use VWD's Design view to create data source controls, your connection strings are automatically stored in the Web.config file. The designer performs this service when you drag a data source control to the page and when you drag a data-bound control (which invokes an option to create a new data source control). VWD will provide a name for your connection, which you can modify if you so choose.

Using a command, you can encrypt the connection string section of the Web.config file. The information will be automatically decrypted by ASP.NET when the connection string is requested by an ASPX page. Encryption must be performed from the command line as follows. Click through Start/Run/cmd and change to the `C:\WINDOWS\Microsoft.net\Framework\v2.0.xxxx`, where `xxxx` is your version. Then enter the following line if `C:\Websites\BegAspNet2Db` is the root of your site:

```
aspnet_regiis -pef connectionStrings c:\Websites\BegAspNet2Db
```

The command-line tool for encrypting connection strings can also take a virtual path syntax (the path in IIS metabase) instead of specifying the fully qualified path to the Web.config file, as follows:

```
aspnet_regiis -pe connectionStrings -app /BegAspNet2Db
```

Once this encryption has been performed, the Web.config file can be opened, but the connection strings will be garbled. They will decrypt automatically when needed by ASP.NET or you can decrypt them by hand with the following line if you need to make modifications such as changing the password.

```
aspnet_regiis -pdf connectionStrings c:\Websites\BegAspNet2Db
```

Note that, by default, the encryption process employs a key that is based on the machine where the encryption algorithm is executed. The process of decryption (either by hand or in the process of serving a page) must occur on the same machine as the encryption. Moving a Web.config to another machine, for example as part of an XCOPY deployment, will render the Web.config undecryptable, so it is recommended that you encrypt your connection strings after you deploy your Web site to its final destination machine

Keep in mind that VWD is a tool for development. The VWD testing Web server was never designed to support public sites. So although you can encrypt a Web.config when using VWD, it is not the typical case. The typical pattern is to create and test pages in VWD that use an unencrypted connection stored in the Web.config. You then use XCOPY to deploy the site to your host machine that runs IIS. Prior to going public, you would run the encryption on the hosting machine. Examples in this book, starting with the following, keep the connection string in the Web.config file. Future exercises will assume that you have done the following exercise.

Try It Out #2 — Storing the Connection String in Web.Config

Like the last exercise, this exercise displays a GridView of the products from the SQL version of Northwind. However, this exercise uses the better practice of storing the connection string in the Web.config file.

1. Create a new file named `TIO-2-ConnectionStringInWebConfig-1.ASPX`. In VWD Design view, drag a GridView onto the page. Step through the common tasks panel to display the first and last names of employees of Northwind, as follows. In the smart tasks panel, drop the list of data sources and select New. Select a type of (SQL) database. Accept the default name of SqlDataSource1 and click OK. Choose a new data connection and enter `(local)/SQLExpress` as the server name. Select Windows NT Integrated security and drop down the list of databases to select Northwind. Test the connection and click OK. Click Next and, this time, keep on the option to save the connection in the application configuration file (recall that in the last exercise you turned this off, so the connection string remained in the ASPX page). Give it the name LocalSqlNorthwind; then click Next. In the window to configure the data source, select the table name Products and click on the asterisk (*) to gather data from all columns. Click Next, Test Query, and then Finish.

2. Run the page to see that it works. Close your browser and, back in VWD, look at the page in Source view. Whereas in the last exercise you saw a connection string with server name, you now see only a reference, as follows:

```
<asp:SqlDataSource ID="SqlDataSource1" Runat="server"
    SelectCommand="SELECT * FROM [Products]"
    ConnectionString="<%$ ConnectionStrings:LocalSqlNorthwind %>">
</asp:SqlDataSource>
```

3. Still in VWD, open in the root of your Web application the file named `Web.Config`. Search for the tag `<connectionStrings>` and observe that the connection information is now in the Web.config.

```
<?xml version="1.0"?>
<configuration>

<connectionStrings>
        <add name="LocalSqlNorthwind"
        connectionString="Server=(local)\SQLExpress;
Integrated Security=True;
Database=Northwind;Persist Security Info = True;
        ProviderName="System.Data.SqlClient" />


</connectionStrings>
```

4. Return to Web.config and add a connection for the Pubs database that will be used later in the book.

```
<?xml version="1.0"?>
<configuration>

<connectionStrings>
        <add name="LocalSqlPubs"
        connectionString="Server=(local)\SQLExpress;
Integrated Security=True;
Database=Pubs;
Persist Security Info=True"
        providerName="System.Data.SqlClient" />
</connectionStrings>
```

How It Works #2 — Storing the Connection String in Web.Config

First, you create a new page with data in the most automated way — by dragging a GridView onto the page and walking through the wizard. The wizard routed you into the steps to create a new SqlDataSource control and then offered the option to store the string in the "application file," meaning Web.config. When this option is turned on, you will store in the page only a reference to a connection, not the actual string. Because the connection string can hold a user ID and password, you want to keep it as secure as possible, that is, off of the ASPX page.

You then looked in the Web.config file. There is a section named `<connectionstrings>` within which VWD created for you an `<add>` holding the name (`LocalSqlNorthwind`) and the connection string. This connection will be available to all pages within the application (including in the root folder and all subfolders like `ch03`).

Choosing between DataSet and DataReader

The SqlDataSource control will communicate with the database in one of two ways according to the setting of the `DataSourceMode` property: DataReader or DataSet. A DataReader streams the information to the data-bound control once, without holding the information in memory for reuse. The information is available just once, going through the values from beginning to end. The other option, the data set, will hold the values in memory and allow the data-bound control to perform tasks such as sorting and paging. The trade-off is performance. There are many variables, but in common scenarios, a data reader will be many times as fast as a data set and will use significantly less memory on the IIS server. As a general rule, you should consider using a DataReader when your page calls for fast, forward-only enumeration of data, such as populating a list or grid, where dynamic sorting or paging of the data is not required. If you need sorting and paging capabilities, consider using DataSet (the default when DataSourceMode is not explicitly set). For more information about paging and sorting behavior, refer to Chapter 7.

Try It Out #3 — SqlDataSource Using a DataReader

Paging in the GridView will fail if its DataSource control is changed from DataSet (default) to DataReader mode.

1. Create a page named `TIO-3-SqlDataSourceDataMode.aspx`. In Design view, drag and drop a SqlDataSource control on the page and configure the Data Source to your `LocalSqlNorthwind` connection. Select the table named Products and just the ProductID and Name fields. By default, the SqlDataSource control will be in DataSet mode. Add a GridView and, in the common tasks panel, set the data source to SqlDataSource1 and enable paging. Save, run, and observe in your browser that the page loads without problems and that paging in the GridView works fine.
2. Go back to the page in VWD Design mode. Select the SqlDataSource control and look in the Properties window (if not visible, click through Menu: View ➪ Properties Window or press F4). Find the DataSourceMode (under the Designer group) and double-click it to change the option to DataReader. Save the page as version 2, and when you view it in the browser, note the error.

How It Works #3 — SqlDataSource Using a DataReader

The DataReader is faster and uses less IIS server memory. However, the SqlDataSource does not support paging or sorting when using the DataReader mode. You saw in step 1 that the default data mode is a data set. When you switched to DataReader, the paging failed. Note that there are many cases when using a DataReader makes sense, such as quickly populating a ListBox or BulletedList.

Discovering the Structure of an Unfamiliar Database

It is important to understand the structure (schema) of a database before you begin to use it. At a minimum, you must know the names of tables or queries that you want to use, as well as the names of their columns (fields). If you intend to write or change data, you should also have an understanding of the relationships so that data dependencies are not broken. Note that if this is the first time you have looked at the structure of a database, you will see more information than you could have imagined. However, it is easy to ignore the extraneous information. Human minds have been separating the wheat from the chaff for tens of thousands of years; they convert well from grain to code.

First, consider tools other than ASP.NET 2.0 pages that might be available to you that can help with discovery. For example, if you are using the full SQL Server, you have the SQL Enterprise Manager that can display and navigate across the components of a database. The full Visual Studio also has the QueryBuilder (and in Beta 2, a database schema designer). Microsoft expects to add to SQL Express a tool named XM (Express Manager) as a Web download. Even in our VWD we have practiced how to use the Data Explorer to add a connection and discover a database's tables and columns. But if you don't have any of these tools available, or want to dig deeper, you can discover the schema using SQL commands. Programmers usually do this on some temporary pages; in the end, this is not part of deployment. These statements are a little tricky to start, but they do follow a logical pattern. This topic is covered in depth, including all of the nomenclature, in Chapter 16 of *Beginning SQL Programming* by Kauffman et al., ISBN 1-861001-80-0.

SQL Server contains schema tables that describe the structure of the data they hold. Schema tables can be read like other data once you know their table and column names. The following list gives those most commonly used.

Schema Table Name (all schema names begin with INFORMATION_SCHEMA)	Most Useful Columns
.SCHEMATA	Catalog_Name (database name)
.TABLES	Table_Name Table_Catalog (which database holds the table) Table_Type (base table or a view)
.COLUMNS (shows all columns of all tables)	Column_Name Table_Name (location of the column) Data_Type Column_Default
.VIEWS	Table_Name (actually this is the View Name) View_Definition
.ROUTINES (stored procedures)	Routine_Name Routine_Definition

The basic syntax to explore a database structure follows.

```
<asp:SqlDataSource ID="SchemaDataSource" Runat="server"
    ConnectionString="  ...   "
    SelectCommand="SELECT Table_Name, Table_Catalog
            FROM INFORMATION_SCHEMA.Tables">
</asp:SqlDataSource>

<asp:GridView ID="SchemaGridView" Runat="server"
DataSourceID="SchemaDataSource"
AutoGenerateColumns="true">
</asp:GridView>
```

You can refine your search by using a `WHERE` clause in the Select command, as explored in the next exercise.

Try It Out #4 — Determining Database Structure

Imagine that Northwind will be hiring people in China and Canada. You are wondering if you can accommodate postal codes with six digits and a mix of numbers and letters. In this Try It Out, your objective will be to learn the data type and size of the postal codes for employees in Northwind stored on your SQL Server. Assume you have no information about Northwind other than what a vague colleague scribbled on a scrap of paper: server = (local)\SQLExpress and database name = Northwind.

1. Create in your folder `ch03` a file named `TIO-4-DatabaseStructure.aspx`. Start with trying to get the largest level of schema, a list of databases on the server, as follows. Because this type of discovery is outside the normal objectives of the VWD, you will work in Source view. Drag a SqlDataSource onto the page between the `<div>` tags. Type the following properties into the SqlDataSource control or step through the SqlDataSource Wizard. Finish by adding a GridView that displays the data from SchemaDataSource.

```
<%@ Page Language="VB" %>
<!DOCTYPE html PUBLIC "-//W3C//DTD XHTML 1.1//EN"
"http://www.w3.org/TR/xhtml11/DTD/xhtml11.dtd">
<html xmlns="http://www.w3.org/1999/xhtml" >
<head runat="server">
    <title>Ch03-TIO4-DatabaseStructure-ver01</title>
</head>
<body>
Chapter 03 TIO #4 DatabaseStructure ver 1
    <form id="form1" runat="server">
    <div>

        <asp:GridView ID="GridView1" Runat="server"
            DataSourceID="SqlDataSource1"
            AutoGenerateColumns="true">
        </asp:GridView>

        <asp:SqlDataSource ID="SqlDataSource1" Runat="server"
             ConnectionString="<%$ ConnectionStrings:LocalSqlNorthwind %>"
            SelectCommand="Select * from INFORMATION_SCHEMA.Tables">
        </asp:SqlDataSource>

    </div></form></body></html>
```

2. View the results in a browser. Note that you are seeing a list of views as well as tables. Restrict the records returned as follows (only the value for the Select command is shown).

```
SELECT * from INFORMATION_SCHEMA.Tables WHERE Table_Type='Base Table'
```

3. Now you can see "Employees" as an obvious candidate table that holds the Postal Codes column you are seeking. Try showing a list of columns.

```
SELECT * from INFORMATION_SCHEMA.Columns
```

4. The information is there, but you see the columns of all the tables. Restrict the result to just columns in the Employees table, as follows:

```
SELECT * from INFORMATION_SCHEMA.Columns WHERE Table_Name='Employees'
```

5. Now you can easily see that the data type is nVarChar (Unicode string that allows numbers and letters) and the size a maximum of 10 characters. You now know that your database can support employee zip codes from China (for example, 1000600) and Canada (for example, J5K S1K).

How It Works #4 — Determining Database Structure

Once you have a guide to the names of objects in the RDMS schema, you can display all of the metadata that you need to work with the database on a developmental ASPX page. Start with a SELECT that shows the databases, for which you do not need to specify a database in the ConnectionString. Then use the object names from the table provided before Try It Out #4 to obtain records about the database. Keeping the GridView `Autogenerate=true` avoids having to know anything about the column schema when you create the ASPX page.

Handling Connection Failures with the SqlDataSource

In spite of taking precautions, there will be times when the SqlDataSource fails to connect to its database. Rather than return a nondescript failed page, you want to present the user with a more graceful and informative failure notice. The strategy is very similar to our discussion for the AccessDataSource in the last chapter. When the GridView is created or refreshed, it requests a set of data from the DataSource control. The DataSource control executes the select command. After the select command has been executed, the DataSource control fires the `Selected` event and sends any exceptions (errors). You write a procedure to be executed on the `Selected` event in which you check for exceptions and then check whether they are from SQL. If yes, then you provide an informative error message to the user. Note that the `Selected` event here means that the DataSource control has executed the select command. This use of the term *select* has nothing to do with the user clicking on (selecting) a control in the browser. I will go into depth about writing event handlers in the last chapter of the book. Feel free to preread that now if you want.

Try It Out #5 — Handling Connection Failures

You'll display a GridView of shippers used by Northwind. Then you will create an error in our connection string and observe a graceful failure. You can write this page using either C# or VB; samples of both are provided. This exercise is very similar to the one for connection failures with the AccessDataSource control.

1. Create in your folder `ch03` a file named `TIO-5-ConnectionFailure.aspx`. In Design view, drag a GridView to the page, and in the smart task panel, choose a data source of New. Select SqlDatabase and name it `NwShipperDataSource`. Add a GridView control named `NwShipperGridView` to show all the fields and all the records from Northwind's Shippers table. If you are unsure of the technique, review the first exercise of this chapter. Check the page in your browser.
2. Close the page in the browser and add a label named `ConnFailMessage` with an empty string for the default `Text` value. Select the GridView and look in the Properties window for `EmptyDataText` and give it a value such as "No records to display" (more details on this property when the GridView is discussed in Chapter 5). Last, switch to Source view and add the following highlighted line to the SqlDataSource control. You will build that procedure in a minute (more details on handling events in general in Chapter 16).

```
<%@ Page Language="C#" %>
<script runat="server"></script>
<html xmlns="http://www.w3.org/1999/xhtml" >
<head runat="server"><title>Ch03-TIO-5-Sql Connection Failure</title></head>
<body>
<h3>Chapter 3 Tio #5 Handling a Connection Failure of a SqlDataSource</h3>
<form id="form1" runat="server">
    <div>

        <asp:Label ID="ConnFailMessage" Runat="server" Text="" />

        <asp:SqlDataSource ID="NwShipperDataSource" Runat="server"
            ConnectionString="<%$ ConnectionStrings:LocalSqlNorthwind %>"

            SelectCommand="Select * FROM Shippers"
            OnSelected="NwShipperDataSource_OnSelected"/>

        <asp:GridView ID="NwShipperGridView" Runat="server"
            DataSourceID="NwShipperDataSource"
            EmptyDataText= "No records available to display"/>
    </div>
    </form>
</body>
</html>
```

3. Now add the procedure in either C# (as follows) or Visual Basic (further below).

```
<script runat="server">
 void NwShipperDataSource_OnSelected(object sender, SqlDataSourceStatusEventArgs e)
    {
        if (e.Exception != null)
        {
```

```
            if (e.Exception.GetType() == typeof(System.Data.SqlClient.SqlException))
             {
                 ConnFailMessage.Text = "There was a problem opening a connection.";
                 //Optionally set GridView1.Visible = false;
                 e.ExceptionHandled = true;
             }
        }
    }
</script>
```

Use the following for Visual Basic:

```
<script runat="server">
Sub NwShipperDataSource_Selected(ByVal sender As Object, ByVal e As
SqlDataSourceStatusEventArgs)
 If (Not e.Exception Is Nothing) Then
         If TypeOf e.Exception Is System.Data.SqlClient.SqlException Then
               Message.Text = "There was a problem opening a connection to the
database. Please contact the system administrator for this site."
         ' Optionally set GridView1.Visible = false
         e.ExceptionHandled = True
         End If
 End If
End Sub
</script>
```

How It Works #5 — Handling Connection Failures

At the moment the GridView is created or refreshed, it requests data from the DataSource control. The request triggers in the DataSource control execution of the select command. Immediately after the select command is executed, an event occurs called `Selected`. At that point, you will know if there was a failure in running the select command. So you specify in the SqlDataSource control an event handler named `SqlDataSource1_Selected`, as follows:

```
<asp:sqldatasource
 . . .
onselected="NwShipperDataSource_OnSelected"/>
```

In the event handler, you will receive several pieces of information, including a set of event arguments passed as the type `SqlDataSourceStatusEventArgs` under a variable named `e`.

```
void NwShipperDataSource_OnSelected(object sender, SqlDataSourceStatusEventArgs e)
```

One property of `SqlDataSourceStatusEventArgs` is named `Exceptions`. It contains an object that represents a description of any problems that were encountered when the data source's select command was executed. Looking into the script, our code checks for the existence of exceptions, as follows:

```
        if (e.Exception != null)
```

If an exception exists, check whether it is of a SQL exception type, as follows:

```
if (e.Exception.GetType() == typeof(System.Data.SqlClient.SqlException))
```

If the exception is from SQL Server, you perform two or three tasks. First is to put an error message into the `ConnFailMessage` label. Second, you have the option not to display the GridView at all.

```
ConnFailMessage.Text = "There was a problem opening a connection.";
//Optionally set GridView1.Visible = false;
```

Third, you set a variable that states you have handled the exception and the page should finish loading.

```
e.ExceptionHandled = true;
```

If `ExceptionHandled` was not set to `true`, the page would throw an unhandled exception and revert to the ASP.NET 2 error page, and you would not have achieved your graceful connection failure.

Common Mistakes

Following are mistakes commonly made in trying to accomplish the tasks described in this chapter:

- Mistaking the syntax connection string. The entire string is placed within double quotation marks. Data is presented in `name=value` pairs, which are separated by semicolons. Quotes are not used around values.
- Putting the ConnectionString into the wrong Web.config file. The string must be in the Web.config file in the root of the Web site that will use the string.
- Attempting to use sorting and paging when SqlDataSource is in DataReader mode.
- Forgetting to grant permission to the ASP.NET Windows user when using Windows authentication in the connection string.
- Attempting to use data with the wrong user ID or password for the RDMS.
- Attempting to use data in an RDMS that is not properly configured and running. Check that your login information and select commands work with another interface to the RDMS, such as SQL Server's Query Analyzer.
- Making syntax errors or typos in select commands.
- Forgetting to set `ExceptionHandled = true` in a connection handler event.

Summary

If your Web site will have more than a few visitors or if it will be hosted outside of a simple network, avoid using Access. An alternative with a logical upgrade path is Microsoft SQL Server, an enterprise-strength relational database management system. For development, you can use a free product called SQL Server Express (SSE) that contains just the database engine from SQL Server. Pages written to use SSE are the exact same in syntax as those for SQL Server, so deployment is seamless. However, SSE does not include tools for development or management of data. All of the techniques discussed and pages written for SQL Server in this chapter work fine against the full SQL Server, SSE, or MSDE (the older version of SSE).

The SqlDataSource control has one major variation from the AccessDataSource control of the last chapter. The SQL version needs a connection string to provide information about the target database and the security information for authentication. Be careful of the syntax because it is different from other languages used in this book. You specify the database in values for the SQL Server, instance, and database. There is no need to specify a provider because the default provider is for SQL Server. Prior to deployment, the connection string should be stored in the Web.config file and encrypted as described.

SQL Server installs with one of two security schemes. Windows Authentication (Trusted Authentication) lets Windows keep the list of users and perform the task of checking prospective users against the list. Examples in this book use Windows Authentication SQL Authentication requires the connection string to include the user ID and password. The `sa` account is used by default, but that should be changed prior to deployment. For Windows authentication, we use `Integrated Security=true` (or `Trusted_Connection=True`) in the connection string, whereas for SQL Authentication we use `User ID=MyUserID;password=MyPassword`.

The SqlDataSource will deliver data in one of two modes: DataReader or DataSet. The former is read-only and forward-reading only. With these constraints, the data reader can execute very fast and with a minimum use of server memory. However, if you want to use a data-bound control with paging, sorting, or editing of data, you must switch to the slower DataSet mode and accept the slight performance penalty. As you will see later in the book, using DataSet mode also enables you to perform caching, which in some cases can greatly improve performance, even exceeding the performance of DataReader.

There are several ways to discover the structure (schema) of a database. GUI tools include SQL Server Enterprise Manager, the Visual Studio QueryBuilder, and the VWD Database Explorer. But if these are not available, the SQL language offers a way to discover the structure of an unfamiliar database by using SQL statements. These are of the general form `SELECT * FROM Information_Schema.MyObject`, where `MyObject` can be databases, tables, columns, or other structures. Many of these commands return large amounts of information about the minutiae of the database, but commonly needed information, such as the exact spelling of column names, is also in the report.

Although you take care to avoid the possibility of a SqlDataSource control failing to connect, it may happen. Instead of the default failure page, you can handle the error. Start by setting the `OnSelected` property of the source control to a procedure. When the data-bound control asks for values, the DataSource control will execute the select command and then fire the `Selected` event and pass to it any exceptions (errors). In the procedure, we check for the existence of errors, and if they exist, we check to see whether they are of a SQL type. If there was a connection error, we give the user a message and inform the DataSource control that we have handled the error so that ASP.NET delivers our error-modified page instead of the default failure page.

The next chapter takes a look at connections to other databases that may be found in the enterprise. Then I move on to several chapters that drill down into the techniques to display data.

Exercises

1. List differences in the connection string for AccessDataSource and SqlDataSource.
2. What is the difference between SQL Server, MSDE, and SSE?
3. What is the syntax to refer to an SSE instance on your local machine?
4. What are the benefits of storing the connection string in the Web.config file?
5. What event is of interest when detecting and responding to a connection failure?
6. What arguments are of interest when detecting and responding to a connection failure?

4

Connecting to Other Relational Databases

So far, you have studied an easy scenario in Chapter 2 (connecting to Microsoft Access databases with no password security) and a very common scenario in Chapter 3 (Microsoft SQL Server and SQL Server Express). Of course, there are many other databases from which you might want to read data, and this chapter explores how ASP.NET 2.0 enables you to connect to those databases. This chapter also looks at the case of using Access with a security scheme.

The concepts presented in this chapter are practiced in three Try It Out exercises:

Try It Out	Topic
1	Connecting to an Access MDB with a Password
2	Connecting to an MDB File with Workgroup Security
3	Connecting to a MySQL Database

Introduction to Connections with Providers

Chapters 1 and 2 discussed two types of connections:

- **Using the AccessDataSource control** — Recall that there is no requirement for a connection string; only the name and path of an MDB file are required. You cannot use this technique on an MDB with a security scheme installed.
- **Using the SqlDataSource control to connect to Microsoft SQL Server, SSE or MSDE** — This control requires a connection string to pass the name of the server, the name of the database, and the user's ID and password. There is no need to designate a provider because the SqlDataSource control uses the provider for SQL Server as its default.

Now we move on to more complex examples. You will need to supply more exact specifications for how to connect to the database, primarily by naming a provider.

The terminology in this chapter can be confusing. In particular, the terms *SQL* and *provider* are used by more than one layer and not always with the exact same meaning. The SQL language is widely used throughout the database world. Therefore, the term "sql" shows up in many places and names. The definition is not always the same and causes problems for many students. Keep in mind that the "sql" in SqlDataSource control is not specific for Microsoft SQL Server. It means that the control is usable with any data source that can understand the SQL language. More specifically, it can connect to any database that is represented by an ADO.NET managed data provider. A provider in ADO.NET is a set of APIs that enable connecting to a specific type of database back end. This chapter demonstrates using that control with Access, Oracle, and MySQL.

This chapter is not a guide to installing or using databases. It assumes that if you are connecting to Oracle, MySQL, or another database, you already have it installed and are familiar with its specific procedures and terminology. Most readers will not do all of the exercises. We suggest that you do only those exercises that connect to databases you have installed. We do not recommend that readers set up these databases just for the exercises.

Relationship between Layers of Connectivity Software

Before looking at new kinds of connections, consider some theory. It would be wonderful if Microsoft and third parties offered sets of data source controls that automatically connected directly to each kind of database, with no other intermediate software. Unfortunately, we are not there yet for technical, business, and historical reasons. Instead, we have a stack of several layers of software. The commands and data pass through these layers between the data store and the ASP.NET 2.0 page.

The essence here is to understand the layers of software between your rendered ASPX page and the tables in the database through which requests or values are passed. When reading data, requests will be passed down from the ASPX page to the database. Values will be passed up from the database to the ASPX page. The topmost layer (the ASPX page) is the highest level and most abstracted. The lowest layer (last in the following list) represents the values in the database.

- **ASP.NET ASPX page** — The highest level, this layer is the template to build the HTML sent to the browser.
- **ASP.NET ASPX data-bound controls** — Server-side controls on the ASPX page that are dynamically rendered on the server. They display to the user the values that come from the data-bound control.
- **ASP.NET ASPX data source controls** — Server-side controls on the ASPX page that can create and connect to back-end sources of data. In the case of SqlDataSource, it connects to ADO.NET providers.
- **ADO.NET Managed Providers** — ADO.NET is a collection of classes that create objects representing connection and commands with a database as well as sets of data derived from the database. Code is *managed* when it is built on top of the Common Language Runtime and supports the built-in management by the CLR of memory allocation/deallocation, pointers, garbage collection, and application isolation. Code is said to be unmanaged in the old world of Win32 (native) code. Managed code talks to unmanaged code using the COM Interoperability

features of the CLR. The data source controls (managed) can instantiate and use unmanaged code such as Object Linking and Embedding for DataBases (OLEDB) or Open DataBase Connectivity (ODBC) connections.

- **OLEDB providers** — A set of code to connect a data consumer (such as an ADO.NET provider) to an ODBC data source. The software, called a provider, is specific for each database management system. OLEDB offers an easier programming interface than ODBC. Modern providers connect directly to the database without ODBC. Older providers connect to the database through ODBC.
- **ODBC Drivers** — An older system to standardize communication between a front end and a database. The software, called a driver, is specific for each database system.

> **OLEDB uses providers; ODBC used drivers.**

- **Database Management System (DBMS)** — Software that manages and holds data, generally in a relational format. Almost all DBMS can respond to requests in the SQL language. Examples include Microsoft SQL Server, Access, Oracle, and many others.
- **Database** — A set of information within the DBMS that is related to a single topic. The information is organized into tables containing rows (records) and columns (fields). Tables are generally related to each other through a set of rules.

When an ASPX page requests data, the request flows from the data-bound control through the data source control to an ADO.NET object and then down to the database management system (possibly going through additional OLEDB and/or ODBC layers). The data is then gathered by the DBMS and passed up through the ODBC and/or OLEDB layers, through the ADO.NET layer, and through the data source control and then is displayed on the page by the data-bound control.

This chapter focuses on the OLEDB provider and ODBC driver layers of the stack. The provider translates between the specific protocol of the DBMS and the general protocol of the ODBC or OLEDB layers.

Supported ADO.NET Providers

Microsoft wrote four managed ADO.NET providers and included them with the .NET Framework 2.0. Microsoft may support additional providers in the future, as will third parties. These providers can be divided into two groups:

- **Native fully managed providers** contain managed code optimized for one data source. They connect directly to the database.
    - **SqlClient Provider** is optimized for the Microsoft SQL Server. This is the default provider for the SqlDataSource, so we did not have to specify it in our examples of Chapter 2.
    - **Oracle Provider**, written by Microsoft, is optimized for the Oracle database. Note that other parties may publish their own versions of an Oracle provider in the future.

- **Partially managed providers** contain managed code that delegates control to an unmanaged (native) provider or driver to do the actual work of connecting to the database. A partially managed provider can't function on its own; there must also be a native provider or driver installed on the machine. The native provider can come from the vendor of the database (such as `www.MySQL.com` or `www.SAP.com`), from Microsoft, or from third parties.
    - **OLEDB Provider** is a provider that delegates to a native OLEDB provider.
    - **ODBC Provider** is a provider that delegates control to an ODBC driver.

The preceding two providers do not actually contain all the code for connecting to the database directly. Rather, they pass requests for data through to a native provider that must be installed on the server and specified in the connection string.

Even though they have similar names, do not confuse the providers (for example, SqlClient) with the data source controls (for example, SqlDataSource). Data source controls read from the ADO.NET object at a higher level in the information stack. Also, not all data source controls connect to their data using ADO.NET.

Using Providers in ASP.NET 2.0

All of the code for using providers can be contained within the data source control on the ASPX page. The `ProviderName` property of a data source control specifies an ADO.NET provider that is registered under the <DbProviderFactories> config section in machine.config. The syntax is a bit tricky for three reasons:

- These properties have defaults, which means in some cases the properties do not have to be used at all (as in Chapter 3 examples).
- Terms such as *SQL* are used at different levels with different meanings.
- The syntax varies for different providers.

Keeping in mind these pitfalls, we will organize the syntax in ways that are easy to remember.

When connecting to a data source through a provider, you need to perform three or five steps (the extra two are for the OLEDB and ODBC providers).

1. If using the OLEDB or ODBC providers, install the native provider or driver for the database you are using.
2. On the page, add a SqlDataSource control.
3. Set the `ProviderName` property of the SqlDataSource to one of the four providers previously listed (`System.Data.SqlClient`, `System.Data.OracleClient`, `System.Data.OleDb`, or `System.Data.Odbc`).
4. Create the connection string with values such as `Server`, `Database`, `UserID`, and so on.
5. If using the OLEDB or ODBC provider, add to the connection string the name of the native provider or driver to use. The syntax for each native provider or driver is slightly different. Consult the documentation for your specific native provider.

The VWD makes these steps easier when you configure a data source control using the Connection Dialog/Provider tab. Providers that can be used in this dialog are registered in the `machine.config` file under `<system.data><DbProviderFactories>`. We will look at the resulting specific syntax momentarily.

To review from Chapter 3, the syntax for connecting to a Microsoft SQL Server database follows. Note that we are using the `System.Data.SqlClient` provider, which is the default ProviderName in the SqlDataSource control, so there is no reference to providers.

```
<asp:SqlDataSource ID="NorthwindProductsSqlDataSource"  Runat="server"
 ConnectionString=        "Server=HPServ;
        User ID=MyUserId;
        Password=MyPassword;
        Database=Northwind"
 SelectCommand="Select * FROM [Sales Totals By Amount]"/>
```

The preceding code, using a default, is the same as the following code, which is explicit for the provider.

```
<asp:SqlDataSource ID="NorthwindProductsSqlDataSource"  Runat="server"
 ProviderName=System.Data.SqlClient
 ConnectionString=
        "Server=HPServ;
        User ID=MyUserId;
        Password=MyPassword;
        Database=Northwind"
 SelectCommand="SELECT * FROM MyTable"/>
```

If you want to use the Oracle managed provider supplied with the framework, you have to specify the ProviderName, as follows. Note here that the “sql” in SqlDataSource refers to connecting to a database that can understand the SQL language. It does not necessarily mean a connection to a Microsoft SQL Server (or MSDE or SSE).

```
<asp:SqlDataSource ID="MyOracleSqlDataSource"  Runat="server"
 ProviderName=System.Data.OracleClient
     ConnectionString=
       "Data Source=MyOracleServer;
       User ID=MyID;
       Password=MyPassword;
        Integrated Security=SSPI"
 SelectCommand="SELECT * FROM MyTable"/>
```

Note that the preceding two cases used fully managed providers (SqlClient and Oracle), so providing the name of another native provider in the connection string wasn’t necessary.

When using the OLEDB or Oracle providers, you must specify a native provider that will actually do the work, because these providers just delegate the provider tasks to a native provider. For example, if you wanted to use a native provider for Microsoft SQL Server from a third party, say AcmeDev, you would specify your ProviderName as the generic OLEDB, and then in the connection string, you would provide the name of the native provider from AcmeDev, as follows:

```
<asp:SqlDataSource ID="MyAcmeSqlDataSource"  Runat="server"
 ProviderName=System.Data.OleDb
 ConnectionString=
```

```
        "Provider=AcmeDev.MsSqlServerProvider.OLEDB.1.2.3;
        Server=MySqlServer;
        User ID=MyUSer;
        Password=MyPass;"
  SelectCommand="SELECT * FROM MyTable"/>
```

The same two-part syntax is used for an ODBC driver from a third party, as follows. Suppose you have an ODBC driver for Excel from AcmeDev. You would specify your ProviderName as the generic ODBC, and then in the connection string, you would provide the name of the native driver from AcmeDev, as follows. Note the peculiarity here in that you use the same `ProviderName` property even though you end up using an ODBC *driver*.

```
<asp:SqlDataSource ID="MyBonzoExcelDataSource"  Runat="server"
  ProviderName=System.Data.ODBC
  ConnectionString=
        "Provider=AcmeDev.ExcelProvider.ODBC.4.5.6;
        FieldName=MySheet.xls;"
  SelectCommand="JanuaryRange "/>
```

Overall, keep the following points in mind. The SqlDataSource can connect to any managed ADO.NET provider that is registered in `machine.config` under the section `<system.data><DbProviderFactories>`. The .NET Framework includes four built-in ADO.NET providers: SqlClient, OLEDB, ODBC, and Oracle. You can specify which provider the SqlDataSource uses by setting the `ProviderName` property to the fully qualified name of the provider, for example, `System.Data.SqlClient` or `System.Data.OleDb`. Note that these names are case-sensitive and must be typed exactly as they appear in `machine.config`. The SqlClient provider is the default provider used by SqlDataSource when the `ProviderName` property is not specified. When using the OLEDB or ODBC providers, the connection string must contain an additional specification of the underlying native provider to use for connecting to your specific database system. Additionally, the native provider or driver must be installed on the machine.

Connecting to Access When a Password Is Used

We used Access in many examples in Chapter 2. Recall that we did not have to get involved in connection strings or providers; we just used the AccessDataSource control and gave the path and name of the MDB file. But also recall that we left you with the caveat that this would not work with an Access installation that had a security scheme. The problem is simple: when using the AccessDataSource control, there is no property (or underlying mechanism) for sending a user ID or password. The reason is that Microsoft wants to encourage storing sensitive data (such as usernames and passwords) in the Web.config file, where it can be properly secured and/or encrypted. This option is enabled by using the SqlDataSource control (with the OLEDB provider) to connect to secured Access database files. The credentials can be specified as part of the connection string, and this connection string can be stored in Web.config.

This is not a book on Access. Make sure that you thoroughly understand Access security before installing a security scheme. It would be wise to make a backup of the unsecured MDB until you know that your security protocol is working. Security rules applied in Access can be irreversible and might even require a reinstall of the software.

Connecting to an MDB with a Security Scheme

If an Access security scheme has been established, you must use a connection technique that allows relaying login information in the connection string. As of the Beta2, the ODBC generic provider is the best option (by the final version of the software, expect an OLEDB solution as well). There are four differences from the technique used in Chapter 2 to connect to an MDB file:

- You use a SqlDataSource control.
- You use the generic OLEDB provider and the native JET provider.
- You include the UserID and Password attributes in the connection string.
- In some cases, you include the name of the workgroup security file.

There are two types of security for Access. One is a simple database password that is global for all users, which can be specified using Tools ➪ Security ➪ Set Database Password in Access. For this configuration, simply include the Database Password attribute in the connection string and keep the connection string in the Web.config file as follows. The property to go on the ASPX page follows further.

```
<add name="NorthwindConnectionString"
connectionString="Provider=Microsoft.Jet.OLEDB.4.0;
Data Source=~\App_Data\MyFile.mdb;
Persist Security Info=True;
Database Password=MyPasswordForTheDatabase;
providerName="System.Data.OleDb" />
```

Access also offers user-level security, which allows the definition of users and assigns to them permissions to specific objects in the database. To configure this type of security, run through the User-Level Security Wizard in MS Access to create a workgroup information file. This file defines the users and permissions that are valid for a given database (or optionally all databases). Once this workgroup file has been created in Access, switch to VWD and specify the path to the workgroup file as a Jet OLEDB:System Database attribute in the connection string, along with the specific credentials (user ID, password) used to connect to the database, as follows (again, this is for the Web.config file). Note that both the data MDB file and the associated security file extended with .MDW are defined in the string.

```
<add name="NorthwindConnectionString"
connectionString="Provider=Microsoft.Jet.OLEDB.4.0;
Data Source=~\App_Data\MyFileWithPassword.mdb;
Persist Security Info=True;
User ID=MyUserId;
Password=MyPassword;
Jet OLEDB:System Database=~\Data\Security.mdw
providerName="System.Data.OleDb" />
```

As a review from Chapter 3, recall that you then use the following syntax in the ASPX page:

```
<asp:SqlDataSource ID="SqlDataSource1" Runat="server"
    ConnectionString="<%$ ConnectionStrings:NorthWindConnectionString %>"
    SelectCommand=" ... ">
</asp:SqlDataSource>
```

> **Again, this is not a text on setting up a security scheme in Access, but if a scheme exists, you can connect to the file as described in the preceding paragraphs.**

Try It Out #1—Connecting to an Access MDB with a Password

Prior to adding a security scheme to Access, you should understand the database security theory. A security scheme can prevent you from using data in an MDB file or even opening any MDB file from Access. The consequences of a mistake are reduced if you use an installation of Access on a separate machine that is not used for a production MDB.

1. In your `C:\Websites\BegAspNEt2Db\App_Data` folder, create a copy of Northwind named `NorthwindPass.mdb`. In Access 2003, open NorthWindPass for exclusive use, as follows. Click through File ➪ Open and navigate to the `C:\Websites\BegAspNet2Db\App_Data` folder. Single-click on NorthWindPass. Observe in the lower right corner that the Open button now has a drop-down option. Expand the Open button and click on Open Exclusive. Add a password by clicking through Tools ➪ Security ➪ Set Database Password. We will use `north56wind`. Close the MDB file and reopen it to check that the password is required. Close `NorthWindPass.MDB` and close Access.
2. Next, add a connection string to our Web.config file, as follows:

```
<connectionStrings>
     <add name="AccessNorthwindPassword"
               providerName="System.Data.OleDb"
               connectionString="Provider=Microsoft.Jet.OLEDB.4.0;
               Data Source=~\App_Data\NorthWindPass.mdb;
               Persist Security Info=True;
               Database Password=north56wind"
     />
 </connectionStrings>
```

3. Create a folder named `C:\Websites\BegASpNet2DB\ch04` and therein a page named `TIO-1-AccessPassword.ASPX`. In Source view, add a SqlData Source control (not an AccessDataSource) and connect it to the nascent connection string in the Web.config. Set the select command to read the customer ID and name from the Customers table. Add a GridView that displays the values. Save the page, which should be similar to the following, and view in your browser.

```
<body>
    <form id="form1" runat="server">
    <div>
        <asp:SqlDataSource ID="SqlDataSource1" Runat="server"
         ConnectionString="<%$ connectionStrings:NorthwindConnectionString %>"
```

```
        SelectCommand="SELECT  CustomerID, Name FROM Customers">
        </asp:SqlDataSource>

        <asp:GridView ID="GridView1" Runat="server"
        DataSourceID="SqlDataSource1"
        AutoGenerateColumns=true
        >
        </asp:GridView>
    </div>
    </form>
</body>
```

How It Works #1 — Connecting to an Access MDB with a Password

You have four key changes in the data source control compared to the no-password examples of Chapter 2. The first is in the ASPX page. Use the SqlDataSource instead of the AccessDataSource because the AccessDataSource cannot accept a connection string (only a path and file name). The connection string is needed to submit login information.

```
<asp:SqlDataSource . . .
```

Now switch focus to the Web.config file. Second, the default provider for the SqlDataSource is for Microsoft SQL Server, so you must override the default. Specify an alternate provider, in this case the generic OLEDB provider.

```
ProviderName="System.Data.OleDb"
```

Third, you are using a generic provider (OLEDB). That means it just delegates the work to a native provider. Therefore, in the connection string, you must specify which native provider will actually do the work.

```
ConnectionString="
  Provider=Microsoft.Jet.OLEDB.4.0;
```

Last, you provide the usual values needed for a connection string, including the path and name of the MDB, the user ID, and password.

```
  Data Source=c:\websites\begaspnet2db\App_Data\NorthwindPass.mdb;
  User ID=MyID;
  Password=MyPassword;"
```

Other than those four points of syntax, the connection is the same as in Chapter 2.

Try It Out #2 — Connecting to an MDB File with Workgroup Security

Now we will set up an Access database that employs user-level security and connect to it with an ASPX page.

1. Start in Windows Explorer where you make a copy of `C:\Websites\BegAspNet2Db\App_Data\Northwind.mdb` and name it `NorthwindWorkgroup.mdb`. Open the new file in

Access 2003. Click on Tools ➪ Security ➪ User-Level Security Wizard and go through the steps, as follows:

a. Create a new workgroup file, click Next, make it the default workgroup file, and click Next again.

b. Allow verification of all objects, click Next, add the Full Data Users group to your file, and click Next again.

c. Do not grant rights to the Users group and click Next. Add a new user named "aspx-page" with the password "north78wind" and be sure to click the "Add this user to list" button, and then click Next.

d. Drop down the list to select `Select aspxpage` and assign to the Full Data Users group; click Next and Finish.

You can save and/or print the security setup report, but it is not needed for this exercise. Test your security scheme by closing the MDB and closing Access and then opening NorthwindWorkgroup and supplying the `aspxpage` and `north78wind` credentials.

2. Switch to VWD and add a connection string to the Web.config file, as follows:

```
<add name="AccessNorthwindWorkgroup"
connectionString="Provider=&quot;Microsoft.Jet.OLEDB.4.0&quot;;
 Data Source=&quot;C:\WebSites\BegAspNet2Db\App_Data\NorthwindWorkGroup.mdb&quot;;
 Persist Security Info=True;
 User ID=aspxpage;
 Password=north78wind;
 Jet OLEDB:System Database=C:\WebSites\BegAspNet2Db\App_Data\Security.mdw"
providerName="System.Data.OleDb" />
```

3. Create a file named `TIO-2-AccessWorkgroup.aspx`. Add a SqlDataSource that uses the AccessNorthwindWorkgroup connection string from the Web.config file. Add a GridView that displays the information, as follows. Save and test in your browser.

```
<%@ Page Language="VB" %>
<!DOCTYPE html PUBLIC "-//W3C//DTD XHTML 1.1//EN"
"http://www.w3.org/TR/xhtml11/DTD/xhtml11.dtd">
<script runat="server">
</script>
<html xmlns="http://www.w3.org/1999/xhtml" >
<head runat="server">
    <title>Ch04-Tio2-AccessWithWorkgroup</title>
</head>
<body>
    <h2>Chapter 04 Tio #2 Access With Workgroup</h2>
    <form id="form1" runat="server">
    <div>
        <asp:SqlDataSource ID="SqlDataSource1" runat="server"
            ConnectionString="<%$ ConnectionStrings:AccessNorthwindWorkgroup %>"
            ProviderName="<%$
ConnectionStrings:AccessNorthwindWorkgroup.ProviderName %>"
            SelectCommand="SELECT [ProductID], [ProductName] FROM [Alphabetical
List of Products]">
        </asp:SqlDataSource>
```

```
        <asp:GridView ID="GridView1" Runat="server"
        DataSourceID="SqlDataSource1"
        AutoGenerateColumns=true
        >
        </asp:GridView>
    </div></form></body></html>
```

How It Works #2—Connecting to an MDB File with Workgroup Security

Access 2003 supports two types of security schemes. The last exercise demonstrated the simple password. This exercise employs the scheme where users and groups are created and then given specific rights. These credentials are stored (encrypted, of course) in a file named `Security.mdw`. After making a working copy of Northwind named NorthWindWorkgroup, you went through the security wizard. This is not a text on Access security, but if you follow the preceding steps, you will end up with a new user named *aspxpage* with the password *north78wind* that is in the group of Full Data Users.

You added a connection string in the Web.config that was different from the last exercise in three ways. First, you specified the username. Second, the property of Password now refers to the specific user's password, not the general database password as in the last exercise. Third, you specified the location of the security file.

Back in the ASPX page, you have little to do. Recall that you use a SqlDataSource instead of the AccessDataSource so that you can specify the OLEDB provider that can pass credentials. Then you just specify the correct connection string from the Web.config file.

Connecting to Oracle

Oracle is one of the most widely used databases in business. It is designed from the ground up to be highly scalable and reliable, and thus it is frequently chosen as the backbone of enterprise IT. If you work in a medium- to large-size organization, you will probably have to obtain at least some of your site's data from Oracle.

Theory and Syntax

Oracle can understand the SQL language, so you can connect with the SqlDataSource control. That control's provider, by default, is for Microsoft SQL Server, so you will have to override the default with one of the three other providers that ship with ASP.NET 2.0. Although you could use the generic OLEDB provider, it is more efficient to use the native Oracle provider.

Keep in mind four points when writing up the code or clicking through the VWD designer:

1. Use a SqlDataSource control because Oracle understands the SQL language.
2. In the data source control, set the ProviderName to `System.Data.OracleClient`.
3. Within the connection string, you do not need to specify a native provider because the Oracle provider is already native.
4. In the connection string, use `Data Source=Oracle8i;Integrated Security=SSPI`.

A typical generic connection to Oracle follows.

```
<asp:SqlDataSource ID="SqlDataSource1"
ProviderName="System.Data.OracleClient"
ConnectionString="
  Data Source=Oracle8i;
  User ID=MyID;
  Password=MyPassword;
  Integrated Security=SSPI"
SelectCommand=" ... "
Runat="server" />
```

Connecting to MySQL

MySQL is a database management system popular with open source Web sites. Implementations are available to run on several operating systems, including Windows. The software is free for most uses from the `www.MySQL.com` site.

Theory of a Connection to MySQL

There are two ways to connect to a MySQL database. Third parties can supply an ODBC driver now, and an OLEDB will probably be available by the final version of ASP.NET 2.0. For the latest in developments for MySQL connections, search `www.dev.mysql.com`, `www.ByteFX.com`, and `www.CrLab.com`. Both OLEDB and ODBC use the ASP.NET 2.0 SqlDataSource control.

Syntax for an ODBC Connection to MySQL

The ODBC technique requires the SqlDataSource to specify a `ProviderName=System.Data.Odbc` and a connection string, as follows. Notice that because we set the ProviderName to ODBC, we now use a `Driver = . . .` in the connection string (OLEDB uses a `Provider = . . .`).

```
<asp:SqlDataSource ID=...>
ProviderName="System.Data.Odbc"
ConnectionString=
 "Driver={MySQL ODBC 3.51 Driver};
 server=MyServer;
 database=MyDatabase;
 uid=MyUserName;
 password=MyPassword;
 option=3"
```

The option setting is a sum value of various aspects of ODBC that are not implemented in this driver. A value of 3 denotes possible errors in the width of a column and the value for number of affected rows.

You can add a MySQL connection to your Database Explorer window to view the names of tables and fields. However, drag-and-drop of fields from a MySQL source in the Database Explorer to the ASPX page is not yet implemented. To add the MySQL connection, click on Add to Database, click on the Provider icon, and select the .NET Framework Data Provider for ODBC. Staying in the Connection

Properties dialog box, click the Connection icon and select "Use Connection String" and enter the following:

```
Driver={MySQL ODBC 3.51 Driver}; server=localhost; option=3
```

Then enter the UserID and Password in the provided textboxes. Where asked to type the initial catalog, type the name of the database to use within the MySQL install.

You can also use the VWD to guide you through the setup, albeit with a couple of catches. Drag a GridView to the page and for Choose Data Source select `<new data source>`. Select the SQL Database and give it an ID. At the Choose Connection dialog box, click New. Click the Provider icon and select ODBC; then click the Connection icon, and enter the same connection string as the last paragraph, the user ID, password, and initial catalog (database). Test if desired, and then click OK to see that your connection is now `ODBC.localhost via TCP/IP.mysql`. Click Next and give the connection a name for the Web.config file. Be prepared for some error messages at this time. The third-party driver for SQL does not support display of tables at this point. You can click on Specify a Custom SQL and click Next to get a textbox to type your SQL statement. In the test query dialog, you may get several error messages from the beta software, but the test results will appear. Click Finish and the properties of the GridView and SqlDataSource will be built by VWD.

Try It Out #3 — Connecting to a MySQL Database

This exercise is optional and should be done only by readers intending to work with MySQL. We do not recommend installing MySQL if it is only for the purpose of this exercise. We do not lead you through the steps of creating a database in MySQL; we assume you have a MySQL installation named `localhost` *with a user named* `root` *with the password* `my99sql`.

1. Download `MySQL ODBC Driver-MyODBC 3.51` from `http://dev.mysql.com/downloads/connector/odbc/3.51.html`. Unzip the download and execute the `MyODBC-<version>.exe` file. Accept the license agreement and click OK to finish.
2. Create a new page in `C:\Websites\BegAspNet2Db\ch04` named `TIO-3-Connection-MySql.aspx`. Add a SqlDataSource that uses the .NET2 ODBC provider and the MySQL ODBC 3.512 Driver. Set the SQL Select command to `SELECT Host, User,Password,Create_priv FROM User`.
3. Add a GridView that displays the values with `AutogenerateFields=true`. Save and view in the browser. You should see four data for the single user in the MySQL administrative database.

```
<%@ Page Language="VB" %>
<!DOCTYPE html PUBLIC "-//W3C//DTD XHTML 1.1//EN"
"http://www.w3.org/TR/xhtml11/DTD/xhtml11.dtd">
<script runat="server">
</script>
<html xmlns="http://www.w3.org/1999/xhtml" >
<head runat="server">
    <title>Ch04-TIO-3-ConnectionToMySql</title>
</head>
<body>
Chapter 04 TIO #3 Connection to mySql
    <form id="form1" runat="server">
    <div>
```

```
        <asp:GridView ID="GridView1" Runat="server"
            DataSourceID="SqlDataSource1">
        </asp:GridView>

        <asp:SqlDataSource ID="SqlDataSource1" Runat="server"
         ProviderName="System.Data.Odbc"
         ConnectionString= "DRIVER={MySQL ODBC 3.51 Driver};
                          SERVER=localhost;
                          DATABASE=mysql;
                          UID=root;
                          PASSWORD=my99sql;
                          OPTION=3"
      SelectCommand="SELECT host, user, create_priv, password FROM user"
     >
        </asp:SqlDataSource>
    </div>
    </form>
</body>
</html>
```

How It Works #3 — Connecting to a MySQL Database

This technique starts with installing a special ODBC driver for MySQL. Then, on the page, you can employ the SqlDataSource with the specification of a ProviderName (the generic ODBC provider) and a connection string. In the connection string, you specify the driver you installed for MySQL. The other connection string values are similar to those used with SSE in Chapter 3. The exception is the `Option=3` setting that warns the programmer of shortcomings in this combination of driver and client.

Connecting to Other Databases

Many additional databases can serve as a source of values for ASPX pages. In general, you can connect to them using either ODBC (older and slower) or OLEDB (faster and more robust). Currently, almost every source of data has an ODBC driver that can be used with the SqlDataSource control. OLEDB providers will enter the market when the final version of .NET 2.0 is ready for release.

ODBC is strong when a single application needs to use data from different sources (ODBC is the most universal of data access techniques). But ODBC involves the most layers and thus provides lower performance.

OLEDB (native .NET provider) is much faster. The native code takes care of memory management and security. It is also easier to use syntax specific to your database management system. The disadvantage is that OLEDB is less widely used and may not work for all data sources for your site. You also have to wait until the final version of ASP.NET 2.0 when third-party providers will be supported.

Searching the Web will yield information on new drivers and providers. For example, software developer Carl Prothman maintains many permutations of connection strings and links to drivers and providers at `http://www.able-consulting.com/ADO_Conn.htm`. I hope he will be expanding his samples to include connections for .NET 2.0.

Common Mistakes

Following are some common mistakes made when trying to connect to other relational databases not covered in previous chapters.

- Confusing the "sql" part of various names. For the SqlDataSource control, the term means that the control works with any database that understands the SQL language.
- Attempting to use the AccessDataSource control for an MDB with a security scheme.
- Specifying a fully qualified path to an Access database in the connection string. This prohibits deployment to another machine that may have a different drive or folder path structure.
- Using a generic provider (OLEDB or ODBC) without including a native provider in the connection string.
- Reversing the names of the providers. The generic provider (OLEDB or ODBC) goes in the SqlDataSource control's `ProviderName` property. The name of the native provider (for example, `Microsoft.Jet.OLEDB.4.0`) goes in the connection string's `Provider` setting.
- Not having the correct native provider installed for an OLEDB or ODBC connection.
- Not typing the name of the provider exactly as it appears in the Framework. Provider names are case-sensitive — for example, `System.Data.OleDb`, *not* `System.Data.OLEDB` or just `OLEDB`.
- Attempting to use a provider that is not registered in `machine.config` under `<system.data><DbProviderFactories>`.
- Using a syntax error when specifying the `Provider` attribute in an OLEDB or ODBC connection string. The syntax for each native provider differs slightly, so consult the provider documentation to be sure of the required format.
- Using terminology from one DBMS in another, for example, confusing how the term *database* differs between Microsoft SQL Server and Oracle.
- Not using the correct SQL syntax for the particular database system you are using.

Summary

For connection to simple databases (Access with no password, Chapter 2) or default databases (Microsoft SQL Server, Chapter 3), you did not have to worry about providers. But for other connections, you must have a better understanding of the layers of software and know how to use providers. At the highest level of the stack sits the ASPX page that holds the data-bound controls and the DataSource controls. The data source controls create and use ADO.NET objects, which in turn talk to OLEDB providers and/or ODBC drivers. Providers and drivers translate from the standard OLEDB or ODBC protocol to the specific internals of the database management system.

Four providers come with the .NET Framework 2.0. Two are written in managed code and are specific for the Microsoft SQL Server DBMS and for the Oracle DBMS. The other two are partially managed providers for generic data sources that have their own providers or drivers. The generics merely delegate the tasks to the native providers. For example, you can download a native provider for MySQL.

When you use a native provider, you have to declare it in the ProviderName of the SqlDataSource control. If you are using a generic provider, you also have to specify the native provider to use in the connection string.

When using an Access MDB file with a security scheme, you must understand the Access security model. If there is only a file password, you can simply add that to the connection string. If there is user-level security, you must specify the name and location of the security file as well as a username and password.

Third parties can be expected to develop managed code providers for various data sources during the beta testing period of .NET2.

Exercises

1. Describe the major differences between connecting to an unsecured MDB file and a password-protected MDB file.
2. Name the two files specified in a connection string to an MDB with user-level security.
3. When setting up a MySQL, you are asked for the initial catalog. What does that mean in MySQL terminology?
4. Why didn't we specify a provider in Chapter 3 when connecting to Microsoft SQL Server?
5. Which data source is used to connect to MySQL and Oracle?
6. In earlier versions of ASP, it was necessary to instantiate ADO objects. Why is this not necessary in ASP.NET 2.0?
7. What additional piece of software must be obtained to connect to a MySQL database?
8. Contrast the `Password` property of the connection string when used with an Access database password security scheme and an Access workgroup security scheme.

5

Displaying Data in Tables

The last several chapters focused on creating a conduit for information between our page and a source of data. We have glossed over the display of that data, using the same GridView of Northwind products in almost every example. You now enter a new section of the book (Chapters 5 to 10), wherein the focus is on how to make the display of data as effective as possible for your business goals. The GridView control remains the core of interest in this chapter; it is the most powerful of the data-bound controls in ASP.NET 2.0. You'll also look at its sibling, the DetailsView, which presents data from one record at a time.

This chapter covers the following:

- Displaying Data in ASP.NET 2.0
- Introduction to the GridView Control
- Connecting a GridView to Data
- Customizing the GridView's Columns
- The DetailsView Control
- Common Mistakes

You will work on eight Try It Out exercises:

Try It Out	Topic
1	Basic GridView
2	Bound Field and CheckBox Field Columns
3	Hyperlink Field Columns
4	Command Field Columns
5	Button Field Columns
6	Template Field Columns
7	Handling Null Values
8	DetailsView Control

Displaying Data in ASP.NET 2.0

We start with a review of the general plan of how to display data in ASP.NET 2.0 and then examine the GridView data-bound control.

Review of Data-Bound and Data Source Controls

As previously discussed, the use of data in ASP.NET 2.0 pages relies on two types of controls: data source controls provide a conduit for data between the page and source, and data-bound controls display the data on the page. This entire section (Chapters 5 to 10) covers displaying data; modifying data (adding, changing, and deleting) is covered in the next block of chapters.

There are many ways to display data on the printed page. A Web page provides fewer options, but they include tables, charts, lists, trees, and arrays of radio buttons and check boxes. ASP.NET 2.0 has controls for each of these formats as well as the ability for them to work with each other so that a selection in a list can change the records displayed in a table. Some data-bound controls can automatically take advantage of capabilities of the data source controls, including paging, sorting, editing, deleting, and inserting. In ASP.NET 2.0 these controls are the GridView, FormView, and DetailsView. If you are using Visual Web Developer (VWD) or Visual Studio (VS), most of the formatting and behavior can be set with drag-and-drop or property choices. But even if you are typing in Notepad, the tasks are easy.

Types of Data-Bound Controls

ASP.NET 2.0 offers a number of types of data-bound controls:

- **GridView** — A tabular representation of multiple records and multiple fields that also offers the capacity to page, sort, change, and delete data. The GridView as a whole is covered in this chapter, and formatting the GridView is covered in Chapter 6. Chapter 7 explains the techniques of paging and sorting in a GridView. Additional material is covered in Chapter 9 on Filtering and Master-Details.

- **DetailsView** — A tabular representation of multiple fields from one record. Allows record navigation (paging), editing, deleting, and creating new records. The DetailsView control is discussed at the end of this chapter and further in Chapter 9.
- **FormView** — A control that renders a single data item at a time as a custom user-defined template (optionally containing other controls). Like DetailsView, FormView also allows record navigation (paging), editing, deleting, and creating new records. FormViews are covered in Chapter 10.
- **DataList and Repeater** — Controls that enumerate over data items and render each data item (row) as a custom user-defined template (optionally containing other controls). This topic is covered in Chapter 8.
- **TreeView and Menu** — Hierarchical presentations of data in an expandable/collapsible tree or menu. Hierarchical data source and data-bound controls are discussed in Chapter 14.
- **List Controls** — Controls for rendering lists of data values, usually displaying one data field and using another field for the underlying value of the list item. These include DropDownList, BulletedList, CheckBoxList, and RadioButtonList. This topic is covered in Chapter 8.

It may come as a surprise not to see controls such as Label and TextBox, as used in earlier versions of ASP. These are still available but are added into the template portions of one of the preceding controls. The concept and practice of templating is discussed in detail in Chapter 10.

Introduction to the GridView Control

The GridView control provides the most flexibility and power for displaying tabular data. If you are familiar with ASP.NET 1.x, the GridView control is the successor to the DataGrid control. The object model for GridView is essentially the same, but its principle advantage over DataGrid is the ability to automatically bind to a data source control and take advantage of sorting, paging, and modifying data through that control. As with other ASP.NET 2.0 controls, these tasks can be achieved with almost zero scripted code.

Capabilities of the GridView Control

Before delving into the details of using the GridView, let's quickly cover its capabilities. Each of these is discussed in detail over the next few chapters.

- **Displaying data** — The GridView will perform all tasks necessary to create an HTML table on the page.
- **Formatting data** — The GridView supports formatting at the level of the entire grid, a column, row, or even cells. Furthermore, the GridView can display buttons, check boxes, links, or images depending on the underlying data.
- **Paging data** — The GridView can automatically divide the entire set of records into smaller sets called pages. A page of records can be displayed along with navigation tools to move from page to page.
- **Sorting data** — The GridView can sort data initially and then re-sort data, as requested by the user, through a click on a column heading.

- **Updating data** — The GridView supports changing data by entering into an update mode. Changes from the user are sent back to modify the data in the underlying database.
- **Deleting data** — The GridView can directly delete an entire record through a simple user interface.
- **Row selection** — The GridView allows the user to select a row. That selection then becomes a parameter available to define the display of other controls.
- **Row navigation** — The GridView can display links for each row that navigate to a separate page, with the option to pass information in the querystring.

Note that the GridView does not directly support the creation of new records (Inserting), but it can be used in conjunction with the DetailsView control to add a record to the grid.

When you consider the amount of coding it took to produce a similar set of functions in classic ASP (or even ASP.NET version 1.x), you can understand our enthusiasm about the GridView in ASP.NET 2.0.

GridView Rendering Elements

A GridView renders with seven kinds of rows, as described in the following table. They will appear from top to bottom in the GridView, the same as in the table. Note that Selected Row and Edit Row are special designations assigned to one of the data (or alternate data) rows.

Row	Description
Header Row	Single row that generally holds the name of each field as column headers
Data Row	Repeated rows holding field values with the basic formatting
Alternate Data Row	Every other data row with an alternate formatting
Selected Row	The one data row that has been selected
Edit Row	The one data row that currently is having its values edited
Footer Row	Single row that generally holds the name of each field as column footers. Useful in a tall table, where column headers may be scrolled out of view. This column can also be used to render column totals (requires custom code).
Pager Row	Single row without column dividers that holds page navigation tools
Empty Data Row	A single cell shown as an alternative to the GridView if there are no records provided by the data source control

Connecting a GridView to Data

The key property of a GridView (beyond its own ID and runat) is the `DataSourceID` property, which can be set to the ID of a data source control. The GridView retrieves data from the data source and automatically generates a table on the page to display the values. You've already seen examples of the basic syntax in earlier chapters. The following code sample is available in the download as `ch05/ Example01 GridView Simple.aspx`.

```
<%@ Page Language="VB" %>
<html>
<head><title>Displaying Data in a GridView</title></head>
<body>
    <form id="form1" runat="server">

        <asp:GridView ID="GridView1" Runat="server"
          DataSourceID="SqlDataSource1" />

        <asp:SqlDataSource ID="SqlDataSource1" Runat="server"
          ConnectionString= '<%$ ConnectionStrings:LocalSqlNorthwind %>'
          SelectCommand="select * from Products"/>
      </form>
</body></html>
```

In this example, the GridView is automatically generating its columns at runtime based on the fields returned from the data source control. An `AutoGenerateColumns` property is set, by default, to `true`. You can exercise much more control over how the data is displayed by setting additional properties of the GridView.

Drag-and-Drop Fields from Data Explorer

The VWD designer greatly accelerates the addition of GridView controls to the page. Recall from Chapter 1 that you can add a database to your Data Explorer window (Server Explorer in Visual Studio). You can then expand that database's tables to see the field names. Those field names can be selected and dragged to the page; then VWD will do all of the work to create a data source control and GridView to display the values. Depending on the type of connection, the data source is either a SqlDataSource or AccessDataSource. Drag-and-drop generates a lot of properties on the GridView and data source to enable column reordering, automatic updates, inserts, and deletes (topics that are covered later). This chapter primarily focuses on displaying data, so in the following sections we'll create a GridView manually by dragging and dropping from the toolbox and setting only the properties under discussion.

Drag-and-Drop Controls from Toolbox

When you drag a GridView from the toolbox, the control starts out with only ID and runat properties. You can then customize additional properties of the GridView using the property grid, Source view, or the GridView's smart task panel.

Try It Out #1 — Basic GridView

In this exercise, you will add a GridView to the page and then use the smart task panel to create a data source control.

First, here is a reminder about the location of connection strings. Starting with Chapter 3 of this book, we have been using connections named `LocalSqlNorthwind` and `LocalSqlPubs` stored in the Web.config file in the root of the application. If you did not create those connections, return to Chapter 3 and step through Try It Out #2. Alternatively, there is a sample Web.config file in the downloads for this text. Your Web.config file should contain the following code lines:

```
<connectionStrings>
    <add name="LocalSqlNorthwind"
         connectionString="Server=(local)\SQLExpress;
         Integrated Security=True; Database=Northwind;
         ProviderName="System.Data.SqlClient" />
    <add name="LocalSqlPubs"
         connectionString="Server=(local)\SQLExpress;
         Integrated Security=True;Database=pubs"
         providerName="System.Data.SqlClient" />
</connectionStrings>
```

1. Create a new folder named `ch05` and, within it, a new page named `TIO-1-GridViewSimple.aspx`.
2. In Design view, drag and drop a GridView control from the toolbox. Note that the smart task panel automatically opens. Drop down the list for "Choose Data Source" and select `<New Data Source>`.
3. VWD will walk you through the configuration for a data source control. In this case, you will select the SQL database type of source and choose the data connection named `LocalSqlNorthwind`. Select all columns from the Products table to display and then click Next, Test Query, and Finish.
4. Save and test the page in your browser. Note that you did not have to create a data source control first; VWD helped through the smart task panel.

   Source code for your page will resemble the following:

```
<%@ Page Language="VB" %>
<html>
<head>
    <title>Displaying Data in a GridView - BoundField</title>
</head>
<body>
    <form id="form1" runat="server">
      <asp:GridView ID="GridView1"  Runat="server"
        DataSourceID="SqlDataSource1"
        AutoGenerateColumns="False" DataKeyNames="ProductID">
        <Columns>
            <asp:BoundField ReadOnly="True" HeaderText="ProductID"
InsertVisible="False" DataField="ProductID"
                SortExpression="ProductID"></asp:BoundField>
            <asp:BoundField HeaderText="ProductName" DataField="ProductName"
SortExpression="ProductName"></asp:BoundField>
            <asp:BoundField HeaderText="SupplierID" DataField="SupplierID"
SortExpression="SupplierID"></asp:BoundField>
            <asp:BoundField HeaderText="CategoryID" DataField="CategoryID"
SortExpression="CategoryID"></asp:BoundField>
            <asp:BoundField HeaderText="QuantityPerUnit"
DataField="QuantityPerUnit" SortExpression="QuantityPerUnit"></asp:BoundField>
            <asp:BoundField HeaderText="UnitPrice" DataField="UnitPrice"
SortExpression="UnitPrice"></asp:BoundField>
            <asp:BoundField HeaderText="UnitsInStock" DataField="UnitsInStock"
SortExpression="UnitsInStock"></asp:BoundField>
```

```
            <asp:BoundField HeaderText="UnitsOnOrder" DataField="UnitsOnOrder"
SortExpression="UnitsOnOrder"></asp:BoundField>
            <asp:BoundField HeaderText="ReorderLevel" DataField="ReorderLevel"
SortExpression="ReorderLevel"></asp:BoundField>
            <asp:CheckBoxField HeaderText="Discontinued"
SortExpression="Discontinued" DataField="Discontinued"></asp:CheckBoxField>
        </Columns>
      </asp:GridView>

      <asp:SqlDataSource ID="SqlDataSource1" Runat="server"
      ConnectionString="<%$ ConnectionStrings:LocalSqlNorthwind %>"
      SelectCommand="SELECT * FROM [Products]"/>
    </form>
</body>
</html>
```

5. Try creating the same page in an even easier way. Create a page named `TIO-1-GridVIewBasic-ver2.aspx`. Switch to Design view, if needed. View the Database Explorer window. Expand `(local)\SQLExpress\Northwind` and then Tables. Drag the name of the Products table onto the page. Ignore the open smart task panel and just run the page. VWD automatically created the correct SqlDataSource control with a pointer to the connection string in the Web.config file. Although this technique is very fast, it does introduce additional tags (see the Source view) that are not covered until later in the text.

How It Works #1 — Basic GridView

The Choose Data Source task of the GridView's smart task panel creates the data source control on the page and sets the DataSourceID property of the GridView control. The data source in this example has two properties set: `ConnectionString` and `SelectCommand`. The GridView creates `asp:BoundField` objects in its Columns collection, matching the fields selected by the data source. Unlike the first example, where the GridView automatically generated its columns at runtime using the fields from the data source, in this case, the GridView uses the bound fields to determine which of the fields from the data source to display. Notice that the `AutoGenerateColumns` property is set to `False`, which means that only fields defined in the Columns collection will be displayed.

Customizing the GridView's Columns

The preceding example showed how the GridView can define explicit columns in its Columns collection instead of automatically generating columns at runtime. This section demonstrates the variety of column types that the GridView can display. The GridView displays columns in the order they are defined in the collection within the `<Columns>` tags.

Selecting Columns in the Edit Columns Dialog

VWD offers a handy tool for adding, moving, and deleting columns from a GridView. On the control's smart task panel, click on Edit Columns. In the lower left, there is a check box to turn on or off the AutoGenerateColumns feature. When defining column fields in this dialog, the AutoGenerateColumns feature should usually be turned off. At the top left are types of columns, discussed shortly. Simply select a type and click Add. Then, on the right, you can set properties for the selected column. Note the up and down arrows to change a column's position as well as the X button to remove a column.

Types of Column Fields

ASP.NET 2.0 supports seven types of columns, as follows:

- **Bound columns** — Show values from the DataSource
- **CheckBox columns** — Display a Boolean value as a checked or not checked icon
- **Button columns** — Give the user a clickable interface to run code the programmer writes
- **Command columns** — Allow the user to invoke methods of the GridView to edit, delete, or select records
- **Hyperlink columns** — Allow the user to navigate to another page
- **Image columns** — Display a jpg, gif, or other image file and can react to a user click with a hyperlink
- **Template columns** — Can contain one or more controls within each cell designed by the programmer in regards to layout, format, and data binding (covered in Chapter 10)

Bound Field

Bound columns will show data from a field delivered by the data source control. Which field to display is determined by the `DataField` property. Keep in mind that if an alias was assigned to a field in the data source control's SelectCommand, you must use that alias in the BoundColumn.DataField.

A tricky but useful attribute is the DataFormatString. To format a number, you must enclose your specification within braces. Additional quotes are not required. Within the braces, you start with a zero and a colon. This represents the first datum within the field. Because you will show only one datum per field, there is no need to use any value other than zero. After the colon, place a letter code for the format of the display followed by a number to set the number of decimal places. For example, a number with three decimal places could be formatted as follows:

```
<asp:BoundColumn ... DataFormatString={0:F3} ... >
```

The following table lists numeric data format options.

Letter Code	Format	Example	Result If Value Is 3.1416 and Windows Is Set to USA Conventions
C	Currency with currency sign	{0:C2}	$3.14 note rounding
E	Exponential	{0:E4}	3.1416E+000
F	Fixed	{0:F3}	3.142 note rounding
G	General	{0:G3}	3.14 like currency but without symbol
P	Percent	{0:P0}	%314 (value must be 0.0314 to get %3.14)

For dates and times, you can use the values listed in the following table:

Letter Code	Format Pattern (Picked Up from Windows Regional Options)	Example	Result If Value Is 14:23:45 on 13 January 2006 and Windows Is Set to USA Conventions
Lowercase d	Short date pattern	{0:d}	1/13/2006
Uppercase D	Long date pattern	{0:D}	Friday, January 13, 2006
Lowercase t	Short time pattern	{0:t}	2:23 PM
Uppercase T	Long time pattern and date	{0:T}	2:23:45 PM
Uppercase F 2:23:45 PM	Short time pattern and date	{0:F}	Friday, January 13, 2006
Either case M	Month and day pattern	{0:m}	January 13
Either case Y	Year and month pattern	{0:y}	January 2006

Other options are available and described when you search in Help for "Formatting Overview," "Formatting Types," "Date and Time Format Strings," and "Numeric Format Strings."

Literal text can also be added to the format, as follows:

```
<asp:BoundColumn ... DataFormatString="My prefix {0:x} My suffix"
```

CheckBox Field

A CheckBox Field binds to Boolean data and then automatically formats the results as a check box icon. The most important attribute is the DataField that determines the linked field of the GridView's DataSource. You must use a data source that is a Boolean or Bit data type. The `CheckBoxField.HeaderText` property can display a short text to the right of the check box. Note the `ReadOnly` property to protect data.

```
<asp:GridView ID="GridView1" Runat="server"
   DataSourceID="SqlDataSource1"
  AutoGenerateColumns="False" >
  <Columns>
   ...
   <asp:CheckBoxField HeaderText="Discontinued"
   DataField="Discontinued" />
   ...
  </Columns>
</asp:GridView>
```

Try It Out #2 — Bound Field and CheckBox Field Columns

In this exercise, you will display some fields from the Northwind Products table.

1. Start with a new page named `TIO-2-BoundAndCheckBoxColumns.aspx`. Add a data source control named `NwProductsDataSource` connecting to the Northwind Products table and returning all fields. Your connection can be through the string saved as `LocalSqlNorthwind` in your Web.config.
2. Drag a GridView to the page and, on the smart task panel, set the data source to `NwProductsDataSource`. Continuing in the smart task panel, click on Edit Columns. Turn off Auto-Generate Fields, and then add a Bound Field and set its ProductID. Repeat for ProductName. Close the smart task panel, save the page, and check in your browser.
3. Close the file in the browser and go back to editing columns in the VWD. Add a bound column for UnitPrice and set its DataFormatString to show currency with three decimal places with the designator `{0,c3}`. Close the smart task panel, save, and view in the browser.
4. This time, add a bound field for UnitsInStock and have the words "on hand" appear after the number by using a suffix in the DataFormatString.
5. To finish, go back to the Edit Columns dialog and add a CheckBox Field with its DataField set to `discontinued`. In the end, your page should resemble the following:

```
<%@ Page Language="VB" %>
<html>
<head>
    <title>Displaying Data in a GridView - BoundField</title>
</head>
<body>
    <form id="form1" runat="server">
      <asp:GridView ID="GridView1" DataSourceID="SqlDataSource1"
AutoGenerateColumns="False" Runat="server">
        <Columns>
          <asp:BoundField HeaderText="Product ID" DataField="ProductID" />
          <asp:BoundField HeaderText="Product Name" DataField="ProductName" />
          <asp:BoundField HeaderText="Unit Price"
                DataField="UnitPrice"
                DataFormatString="{0:c3}" />
          <asp:BoundField HeaderText="Units In Stock"
                DataField="UnitsInStock"
                DataFormatString="{0:c3}" />
          <asp:CheckBoxField DataField="discontinued" />
        </Columns>
      </asp:GridView>

      <asp:SqlDataSource ID="SqlDataSource1"
      ConnectionString="<%$ ConnectionStrings:LocalSqlNorthwind %>"

      SelectCommand="SELECT * FROM Products"
      Runat="server" />

    </form>
</body>
</html>
```

How It Works #2 — Bound Field and CheckBox Field Columns

Bound columns will make up the majority of your GridView columns; they display values from the database. You can add them using the Edit Columns task in the GridView's smart task panel or by editing the `Columns` property in the property grid. Data field values can be formatted using the `DataStringFormat` property set to a valid .NET Framework format string (examples given in the preceding text). If your table has a Boolean value, you can display it using the CheckBox Field, which is a derivative of the Bound Field.

HyperLink Field

A hyperlink column allows the grid to render a hyperlink for one of the columns in the grid. It allows you to redirect the user on a click on the link, with the target of redirection dependent on which record the user clicks. For example, in a GridView of employees, each record could have a hyperlink and each could automatically be linked to the home page of that employee.

You set two properties for a hyperlink column that dictate the text and the URL for the link. Each of those properties can be hard-coded to a literal static value for all rows, or it can come from a field of your data source. First, you must set the hyperlink's text that will appear in the hyperlink column. The `Text` property will hard-code the same literal string for all records, as follows:

```
<asp:HyperLinkField ... Text="Click here for this Employee's home page" ...>
```

An alternative is to pick up a value from the database using the `DataTextField` property, as follows. You can optionally format this field value using the `DataTextFormatString` property.

```
<asp:HyperLinkField ... DataTextField="EmployeeHomePageName" ...>
```

The second setting is the target URL of the hyperlink. Again, this can be hard-coded with the `NavigateUrl` property, but that would not be very useful because all records would hyperlink to the same target. More useful is the `DataNavigateUrlFields` property that allows you to target a page saved in the database, as follows (note that the syntax for the property ends in an "s," the reason for which is described in the following text):

```
<asp:HyperLinkField ... DataNavigateUrlFields="EmployeeHomePage" ...>
```

Assuming that the `EmployeeHomePage` field in the preceding example contains a simple page name such as `JohnsPage.aspx`, you might want to prepend to this field value a full page to the location where the employee home pages are stored. You can do this using the `DataNavigateUrlFormatString` property, as follows:

```
<asp:HyperLinkField ... DataNavigateFormatString="..\EmployeeWebs\{0}"
```

To navigate outside your Web site, you must use a literal `http` designation, as follows:

```
<asp:HyperLinkField ... DataNavigateFormatString="http://{0}"
```

Note that this format string property works the same way as the `DataFormatString` property of BoundField previously described. The `{0}` marker in the format string is a placeholder for the actual field value that is substituted when the page runs.

So why does DataNavigateUrlFields end with an "s" (plural), when we are assigning it only a single field name? The answer is, as you might have guessed, this property can contain multiple field names. The reason you might want to do this is to pass field values along the querystring to a single-page URL, instead of requiring a unique target page for each row in the grid. For example, instead of navigating to JohnsPage.aspx, you might go to a single page for all employees, passing their first and last names:

```
EmployeeHomePage.aspx?FirstName=John&LastName=Kauffman
```

You would specify the FirstName and LastName fields in DataNavigateUrlFields (separated by a comma) and then use the format string to complete the rest of the URL, as in the following example:

```
    <asp:HyperLinkField DataNavigateUrlFields="FirstName,LastName"
DataNavigateUrlFormatString="EmployeeHomePage.aspx?FirstName={0}&LastName={1}"
```

Try It Out #3 — HyperLink Field Columns

We'll start with a simple example that adds a hyperlink column to a list of employees. Then you will activate the hyperlink to go to another page and display how to carry your employee ID to the new page.

1. Create a new page named TIO-3-Hyperlink.aspx. Add a SqlDataSource control and a GridView to show the employee ID and last name of the Northwind employees. Save the page (in the downloads, this page is named version 1) and take a look at it in the browser.

```
<%@ Page Language="VB" %>
<html>
<head>
    <title>Displaying Data in a GridView - HyperLinkField</title>
</head>
<body>
    <form id="form1" runat="server" Runat="server">
      <asp:GridView ID="GridView1"
         DataSourceID="SqlDataSource1"
         AutoGenerateColumns="False" >
        <Columns>
          <asp:BoundField HeaderText="Employee ID" DataField="EmployeeID" />
          <asp:BoundField HeaderText="First Name" DataField="FirstName" />
          <asp:BoundField HeaderText="Last Name" DataField="LastName" />
        </Columns>
      </asp:GridView>

      <asp:SqlDataSource ID="SqlDataSource1" runat="server"
      ConnectionString="<%$ ConnectionStrings:LocalSqlNorthwind %>"
      SelectCommand="SELECT * FROM Employees" />
    </form>
</body>
</html>
```

2. Close the browser and view the page in Design view. Open the smart task panel and choose Edit Columns. Add a hyperlink column with its DataField set to the photo field. Save the page (version 2) and take a look at it in the browser.

```
<Columns>
 <asp:BoundField HeaderText="Employee ID" DataField="EmployeeID" />
 <asp:BoundField HeaderText="First Name" DataField="FirstName" />
```

```
  <asp:BoundField HeaderText="Last Name" DataField="LastName" />
  <asp:HyperLinkField
   HeaderText="View Photo"
   Text="View Photo..."
   DataNavigateUrlFields="PhotoPath" />
</Columns>
```

3. Last, you will create a second page and see how you can transfer data from the hyperlink. Create a page named `TIO-3-HyperlinkTarget.aspx`, as follows:

```
<%@ Page Language="VB" %>
<html>
<head>
  <title>Employee Details Page</title>
</head>
<body>
  <form id="form1" runat="server">
    <h2>
      Details for Employee
      <%= Request.QueryString("ID") %> :
      <%= Request.QueryString("FirstName") %>
      <%= Request.QueryString("LastName") %>
    </h2>
    To learn in later chapter: Look up more employee details here
  </form>
</body>
</html>
```

4. Now modify your page `TIO-3-Hyperlinks.aspx` with a second Hyperlink column as follows, and save as version 4.

```
  <asp:HyperLinkField
         HeaderText="View Details..."
         Text="View Details..."
         DataNavigateUrlFields="EmployeeID,FirstName,LastName"
         DataNavigateUrlFormatString=
"TIO-3-HyperlinkTarget.aspx?ID={0}&FirstName={1}&LastName={2}" />
```

5. Save both files and view the fruits of your labor in the browser. Notice that when you scroll over the new hyperlinks, the target reflects the data for the correct record. When a hyperlink is clicked, the appropriate information is sent to the target page.

How It Works #3 — Hyperlink Field Columns

We began in step 1 with a page that did not contain a hyperlink. Step 2 added a hyperlink field that rendered a hyperlink to a target page specified by the PhotoPath field. In this case, the field contained the complete target URL, so it was not necessary to use a format string. The text for each link was the same: "View Photo..."

Steps 3 and 4 added another hyperlink field that rendered a link to a target page that accepts field values along the querystring. Step 3 created the target page for these hyperlinks. In step 4, you specified a hyperlink field that passed three field values along the querystring, using the `DataNavigateUrlFields` and `DataNavigateUrlFormatString` properties. Note that the placeholders for the fields in the format string use an incremental number (`{0}`, `{1}`, `{2}`, and so on) to indicate the placement of each field in the URL.

Image Field

Similar to HyperLinkField, ASP.NET 2.0 includes an ImageField type that can be used to render images in the grid. Instead of setting properties for the hyperlink's Text and URL, you set properties for the AlternateText and URL to an image file. The physical location of the image can be anywhere as long as it is URL addressable. For example, the URL might be to a physical image file, such as `Banner.jpg`, or to a dynamic Web page that returns an image based on field values passed to the URL, such as `GetImage.aspx?ImageID=1234`. While the latter approach is outside the scope of this book, the former approach is demonstrated in the following example.

Like HyperLinkField, you can set the URL to the image as a static value using the `ImageUrl` property, but this would render the same image for all rows. A more useful approach is to specify the `DataImageUrlField` property to a field of the data source and use the `DataImageUrlFormatString` property to complete the URL with `http://` or other literal characters.

Alternatively, you may have a database field containing the name of an image file outside the database. In this case, you switch the mode to ImageURL. The trick is in the formatting. The image file name is likely to be stored in your database image name field, such as one of the following values:

1. `JaneDoe`
2. `JaneDoe.jpg`
3. `Images\JaneDoe.jpg`

You must do some modifications to get that value in a form usable as a URL. That reformatting is done with the value in the `ImageUrlFormatString`. The syntax is of two parts. The value from the database is represented as `{0}`. Anything you need to add you type as a literal. So, in the case of the preceding first option, and where the image file is stored in the same folder as the ASPX page, you would use the following to add the file extension to the stored value:

```
ImageUrlFormatString = "{0}.jpg"
```

In the case of the second option, the image files are located in a sister folder named `images`; you would use the following:

```
ImageUrlFormatString = "../images/{0}"
```

In the case of the third option, you can just use the field value by itself, with no format string specified.

Command Field

Adding a Command Field allows you to offer the user one of three behaviors: deleting, editing, or selecting. We'll focus on selecting later in the master-details chapter of this book. The general syntax for a select column follows:

```
<asp:GridView ID="GridView1" Runat="server"
        DataSourceID="AccessDataSource1">
        <Columns>
                <asp:CommandField ButtonType="Button"
                        ShowSelectButton="True">
                </asp:CommandField>
        </Columns>
</asp:GridView>
```

Alternatives for the show buttons include the following:

```
ShowEditButton ShowDeleteButton ShowCancelButton ShowInsertButton
```

You can also customize the exact text for each of the buttons that is rendered by the Command Field. Note that when CommandField is rendered in a control in Edit or Insert mode, it renders different buttons than in Read-Only mode. Also note that it is not sufficient to support updating, inserting, or deleting merely by adding a Command Field; there are other steps that need to be taken to fully configure a GridView for these scenarios. Updating, inserting, and deleting data are covered in later chapters.

For now, we simply demonstrate that adding a Command Field to the GridView renders the appropriate button to perform a selection.

Try It Out #4 — Command Field Columns

Consider this exercise a preview of techniques discussed in detail later, namely, modifying data and using data from a selection in an event.

1. Create a new page named `TIO-5-CommandColumns.aspx`. Add a data source control and a GridView to show the `ProductID`, `ProductName`, and `Unit Price` fields from the Products table in Northwind.
2. Now use the smart task panel and Edit Columns to add a Command Field. In the Properties window, set both the `ShowSelectButton` and `ShowEditButton` to `true`. Save and take a look in your browser to see the command buttons. Note that with zero coding they work; you can click Edit for a record and change its values. Note that if you click Update while the GridView is in Edit mode, it will not work yet. Editing data is examined in a later chapter.

```
<%@ Page Language="VB" %>
<html>
<head>
    <title>Displaying Data in a GridView - CommandField</title>
</head>
<body>
    <form id="form1" runat="server">
      <asp:GridView ID="GridView1" Runat="server"
DataSourceID="SqlDataSource1"
AutoGenerateColumns="False" OnSelectedIndexChanged="GridView1_SelectedIndexChanged"
DataKeyNames="ProductName">
        <SelectedRowStyle BackColor="#cccccc" />
        <Columns>
          <asp:CommandField ShowEditButton="true" ShowSelectButton="true"/>
          <asp:BoundField HeaderText="Product ID" DataField="ProductID" />
          <asp:BoundField HeaderText="Product Name" DataField="ProductName" />
          <asp:BoundField HeaderText="Unit Price" DataField="UnitPrice" />
        </Columns>
      </asp:GridView>

      <asp:SqlDataSource ID="SqlDataSource1" runat="server"
      ConnectionString="<%$ ConnectionStrings:LocalSqlNorthwind %>"
      SelectCommand="SELECT * FROM Products" />
    </form>
</body>
</html>
```

3. Close the browser and return to VWD. This time, go to Source view and add the following procedure:

```
<%@ Page Language="VB" %>
<script runat="server">

Sub GridView1_SelectedIndexChanged(ByVal sender As Object, ByVal e As
System.EventArgs)
    Response.Write("You Selected: " & GridView1.SelectedValue)
End Sub
</script>
<html>
 ...
```

Or you can write it in C#, as follows:

```
<%@ Page Language="C#" %>
<script runat="server">
void GridView1_SelectedIndexChanged(object sender, EventArgs e)
{
    Response.Write("You selected: " + GridView1.SelectedValue + "<br/>");
}
</script>
<html>
 ...
```

How It Works #4 — Command Field Columns

The real story here is how little you actually had to do to add tremendous functionality to the GridView. Simply adding a CommandField and setting one property modified our page so that it renders Edit and Select buttons. Note that when the GridView is in Edit mode, the CommandField renders appropriate buttons for that mode: Update and Cancel. We also enabled the selection of rows by setting `DataKeyName` to a field to use as the grid's SelectedValue.

In the final step, we demonstrated the availability of values once a row is selected. The GridView triggers an event named `SelectedIndexChanged` whenever the user clicks on the Select button you enabled. Your single line of code then reads the selected value from the GridView and writes it to the page. Don't worry if you don't understand the relationship between all these properties right now. Future chapters will look at more sophisticated uses of the SelectedValue; for example, Chapter 10 explains how to use a selection in one control to limit the records in another control.

Button Field

Button Fields provide a way for a user to invoke code the programmer writes. Compare that to a Command Field that can invoke one of several built-in operations (edit, select, delete). Confusion arises because a Button Field can be set to invoke a built-in behavior just like a Command Field, but it is predominantly used to invoke user-defined code. Note that button columns have nothing to do with radio buttons (option buttons).

Button columns offer one of three appearances by the `ButtonType` property (note that the Text and Image options both require a JavaScript-capable browser to work).

- **Text** — Enables the `Text` property so that GridView will display its value in an appearance of a clickable string (typically blue with an underline).
- **Button** — Will display a small button icon with your text on the button.
- **Image** — Will display a picture that is clickable.

You set the text for the button by setting the `Text` property, and you set a special command name for the button using the `CommandName` property. The command name can be anything you want, such as "Buy," "Sell," or "Authorize." This name will be passed to the event where your code to handle the command is written. This handler also receives a CommandArgument, which is set to the index of the row that fired the command by default.

The custom code will be held in a procedure named `MyGridView_RowCommand` within the script tags. The procedure will fire when a button is clicked. When there is more than one button field, you can determine which one was clicked using the CommandName passed in the list of arguments to the procedure. The intricacies of handling events are discussed in Chapter 16, but for now a simple Try It Out follows.

Try It Out #5 — Button Field Columns

In this exercise, you create the front end to enable a buy or sell click for each product of Northwind.

1. Create a page named `TIO-5-ButtonColumns.aspx`. Use it to display the `ProductID` and `ProductName` values from all the records of the Products table of Northwind. Test the page and then close your browser.
2. Back in VWD, in Design view, open the common task panel and then click Edit Columns. Add a ButtonField and set its `CommandNameProperty` to "Buy" and the `Text` property to "Buy This Product," and then repeat using "Sell" and "Sell This Product." The button does not do anything yet, but you can check your work in the browser.

```
<%@ Page Language="VB" %>
<html>
<head>
    <title>Displaying Data in a GridView - ButtonField</title>
</head>
<body>
    <form id="form1" runat="server">
      <asp:GridView
        ID="GridView1"
        Runat="server"
        DataSourceID="SqlDataSource1"
        AutoGenerateColumns="False">
        <Columns>
          <asp:BoundField HeaderText="Product ID" DataField="ProductID" />
          <asp:BoundField HeaderText="Product Name" DataField="ProductName" />
          <asp:ButtonField CommandName="Buy" Text="Buy" />
          <asp:ButtonField CommandName="Sell" Text="Sell" />
        </Columns>
      </asp:GridView>

      <asp:SqlDataSource ID="SqlDataSource1"
      ConnectionString="<%$ ConnectionStrings:LocalSqlNorthwind %>"
```

```
        SelectCommand="select * from Products"
        Runat="server" />
    </form>
</body>
</html>
```

3. Now you will create the custom code to run when the buttons are clicked. First, you must modify the GridView to handle the clicks. Add two lines, as follows:

```
<asp:GridView
  ID="GridView1"
  Runat="server"
  DataSourceID="SqlDataSource1"
  AutoGenerateColumns="False"
  OnRowCommand="GridView1_RowCommand"
  DataKeyNames="ProductName">
```

Next, add the following procedure (in VB or C#) to your page. First is the VB.

```
<%@ Page Language="VB" %>
<script runat="server">
  Sub GridView1_RowCommand(ByVal sender As Object, ByVal e As
  System.Web.UI.WebControls.GridViewCommandEventArgs)
    Response.Write("Commmand Name: " & e.CommandName & "<br/>")
    Dim rowIndex As Integer = e.CommandArgument
    If e.CommandName = "Buy" Then
      Response.Write("You Bought: " & GridView1.DataKeys(rowIndex).Value)
    ElseIf e.CommandName = "Sell" Then
      Response.Write("You Sold: " & GridView1.DataKeys(rowIndex).Value)
    End If
  End Sub
</script>
<html>
...
```

Or you can use the C# version, as follows:

```
<%@ Page Language="C#" %>
<script runat="server">
void GridView1_RowCommand(Object sender,
System.Web.UI.WebControls.GridViewCommandEventArgs e) {
    Response.Write("Commmand Name: " + e.CommandName + "<br/>");
    int rowIndex = Int32.Parse((String)e.CommandArgument);
    if (e.CommandName == "Buy")
      Response.Write("You Bought: " + GridView1.DataKeys[rowIndex].Value);
  else if (e.CommandName == "Sell")
      Response.Write("You Sold: " + GridView1.DataKeys[rowIndex].Value);
  }
</script>
<html>
...
```

How It Works #5 — Button Field Columns

The Button Column enables the GridView to fire custom events that you can handle in your own code. You started by adding the button column just as you would for any other column type. You then specified the Text and CommandName properties for the button.

Then you modified the GridView in two ways. First, you added a property to specify that when a RowCommand is clicked, it should trigger the `GridView1-RowCommand` event handler procedure. Second, you established which column should be the DataKey. (DataKeys are further discussed in the modifying chapters, but for now, understand that a DataKey is a set of identifiers for the records, similar to a primary key in a table.)

```
        OnRowCommand="GridView1_RowCommand"
        DataKeyNames="ProductName">
```

Lastly, you wrote the code in the `GridView_RowCommand` procedure. You had to name the procedure to match your specification in the GridView for the `OnRowCommand` event. When the event is triggered, it will receive a set of `GridViewCommandEvent` arguments that are put into a collection named `e`. One of those arguments is CommandName, the string you provided when you created the button. This will identify which button was pressed if there is more than one button column. A second argument of interest is the CommandArgument, which will be the index of the clicked row within the record set. Because you designated ProductName to be the DataKey name, you can use that number to look up the ProductName by using the index from the event and the DataKeys collection of the GridView. The code is wrapped in an If-Then statement that formats your values into either a "You bought" or "You sold" string.

Note that the `RowCommand` event is also raised automatically when clicking a button rendered by a CommandField column, such as "Update" or "Select." This is another reason why it is important to check the CommandName value before processing the event. In the case of built-in commands from CommandField, GridView automatically handles the command, so you don't need to write code to explicitly handle these types of events.

Template Field

ASP.NET 2.0 allows you to create columns with even more elaborate customization than the column types discussed in the preceding text. The sky is the limit when you use Template Columns. A template column gives you a blank space, almost like a form, upon which you can add controls such as a label or image. Once added to a template, a control can have its properties "data-bound" to fields from the data source of the GridView, and this control will be rendered for each row of the GridView with data-bound values appropriate for each row.

> **Templates in ASP.NET 2.0 contain user-defined controls and HTML elements to be rendered for a region of a control's rendering. Instead of using the control's built-in rendering, a template allows you to replace this rendering with your own. Data-bound controls such as GridView support templates for a variety of regions such as the grid header, footer, pager, and individual column cells. When a template is data-bound, controls inside it can be linked to a data field and their values will stay synchronized with the current record of the data-bound control. Templates give the designer support for multiple controls and flexible layout within a section of a data-bound control. Note that templates are not the same as styles. Templates are discussed in more detail in Chapter 10.**

You can add a template column to the GridView's Columns collection the same way as you do other columns. The TemplateField provides you with a blank workspace. Close the Edit Columns dialog and then choose the Edit Templates task on the GridView control. Select the ItemTemplate for the TemplateField column that you added, and the GridView will render a blank workspace upon which you can drag and drop labels, images, or other controls, as well as type literal strings or HTML tags. More options are covered in Chapter 10. When finished, don't forget to end template editing. An exercise using TemplateField columns follows.

Try It Out #6 — Template Field Columns

You will create a new products table with two new goals. First, you want more than one value in a cell (such as product ID and product name). Second, you want some literal text to be in every cell, for example, the words "in stock" next to the stock amount.

1. Start with a new page named `TIO-6-TemplateColumns.aspx`. Add a SqlDataSource control for the Products table. Add a GridView and select its data source to be the only source on the page. Then choose the GridView "Edit Columns" task and set `AutoGenerateColumns` to `false`. Add a TemplateField and set the `HeaderText` property to "Product," and then add a second template column with the header "Price." Click OK to close the Fields dialog and give the page a test. Notice that you have columns but no values assigned to the columns. Your GridView source code will be similar to that shown here:

```
<asp:GridView ID="GridView1" Runat="server"
            DataSourceID="NorthwindProductsSqlDataSource"
            AutoGenerateColumns="False">
            <Columns>
                <asp:TemplateField HeaderText="Product" />
                   <asp:TemplateField HeaderText="Price" />
            </Columns>
</asp:GridView>
```

2. Close your browser and go back to the Design view. Select the GridView, open the common task panel, and click on Edit Templates. Expand the list of templates to display and select `Column (0) - Product, Item Template`. You are now in template editing mode.

3. Drag a label from the toolbar onto the template. Click on the smart task panel for the label and select Edit Data Bindings. Bind the `Text` property to the field Product ID. If you can't see the fields, click on Refresh Schema. Click OK to close the binding dialog and then close the smart task panel. Strike the right arrow to remove the selection from the label and press Enter. Add another label and bind it to ProductName. You now have two labels in the template, one above the other. Open the GridView (not a label) smart task panel and click End Template Editing. Your GridView source code will now appear, as follows. Save and run in the browser.

```
    <asp:GridView ID="GridView1" Runat="server"
    DataSourceID="NorthwindProductsSqlDataSource"
    AutoGenerateColumns="False">

            <Columns>
                <asp:TemplateField
HeaderText="Product"><ItemTemplate>
                    <asp:Label ID="Label1" Runat="server"
                          Text='<%# Eval("ProductID") %>' />
                    <br />
                    <asp:Label ID="Label2" Runat="server"
```

```
                    Text='<%# Eval("ProductName") %>' />
                <br />
            </ItemTemplate>

            </asp:TemplateField>
            <asp:TemplateField HeaderText="Price" />

        </Columns>
    </asp:GridView>
```

4. Perform a similar set of steps for the second column. Go to Edit Templates, and select the Price Column Item Template. Drag a label onto the template, close its smart task panel, strike a right arrow, and press Enter. Add text and a second label so that it will read `(xx on hand)` when rendered. Now go back and open the labels' smart task panels and bind them to the `Price` and `UnitsOnHand` fields. Don't forget to end template editing. Your GridView source code will be similar to the following. Then save and view in your browser.

```
<asp:GridView ID="GridView1" Runat="server"
        DataSourceID="NorthwindProductsSqlDataSource"
        AutoGenerateColumns="False">

            <Columns>
                <asp:TemplateField HeaderText="Product"><ItemTemplate>
                    <asp:Label ID="Label1" Runat="server"
                            Text='<%# Eval("ProductID") %>' />
                    <br />
                    <asp:Label ID="Label2" Runat="server"
                            Text='<%# Eval("ProductName") %>' />
                </ItemTemplate>
                </asp:TemplateField>

                <asp:TemplateField HeaderText="Price"><ItemTemplate>
                    <asp:Label ID="Label3" Runat="server"
                            Text='<%# Eval("UnitPrice") %>' />
                    <br />
                    (
                <asp:Label ID="Label4" Runat="server"
                            Text='<%# Eval("UnitsInStock") %>' />
                 on hand) 
                </ItemTemplate>
                </asp:TemplateField>
            </Columns>
        </asp:GridView>
```

How It Works #6 — Template Field Columns

Template columns offer tremendous versatility. You get a blank slate upon which you can do almost any arrangement of controls, all bound to the values for the current record. Template columns are added in the same way as other columns.

After adding a template column, you use the GridView's smart task panel to begin editing the templates. Drag and drop labels and then select a field to which they bind. Remember to end template editing. More template techniques are discussed in Chapter 10.

AutoGenerateColumns Property of the GridView

Now that you have examined how to specify the desired columns, look at how the GridView offers a flexible syntax to define the columns in your grid. There are three possibilities involving mixtures of the GridView self-generating the columns and your specific definition of columns.

- **`AutoGenerateColumns = True` and no predefined fields** will give you one column in the GridView for each field in the data source. If you have the right combination of fields in your data source control, you do not have to do any work in the GridView. This option is the easiest and least flexible, and it results in the most compact ASPX page. `AutoGenerateColumns` is, by default, true.

```
<asp:GridView... AutoGenerateColumns="true" ... >
```

- **`AutoGenerateColumns = True` and also some predefined fields** will give you one column in the GridView for each field in the data source, plus it will display your predefined fields from the Columns collection. This option allows you to add a command field, such as Select or Edit, to the GridView, but keep the columns that are autogenerated from the data source. Your ASPX page will be larger, as you have tags and attributes to describe the predefined fields. For example, the following autogenerates all of the columns but also adds another column that creates a column to perform selections:

```
<asp:GridView... AutoGenerateColumns="true" ... >
       <columnfields>
              <asp:CommandField ShowSelectButton="True">
              </asp:CommandField>
       </columnfields>
</asp:GridView>
```

- **`AutoGenerateColumns = False` (must have predefined fields)** will give you nothing beyond the fields that you predefine. If you don't predefine fields, you get nothing. This option gives you the most control over exactly which columns will appear and in what order.

```
<asp:GridView... AutoGenerateColumns="False" ... >
       <columns>
              <asp:BoundField datafield="MySourceField1">
              </asp:BoundField>
              <asp:BoundField datafield="MySourceField2">
              </asp:BoundField>
              <asp:BoundField datafield="MySourceField3">
              </asp:BoundField>
       </columns>
</asp:GridView>
```

In the VS or VB IDE, when you go through the Choose Data Source wizard from the GridView smart task panel, the GridView will automatically create BoundFields for each data field in your data source and will set `AutoGenerateColumns` to `false`. If you want the autogenerate feature turned on, you must uncheck the option. Then you will get the `AutoGenerateColumns` attribute set to `true` and no bound fields showing in your ASPX page.

In summary, for `AutoGenerateColumns`, turn it on when you simply want to display all fields in the data source with no extra columns. Feel free to add a few predefined columns if you want. But if you want a particular selection and arrangement of columns, take the time to set them up by adding explicit fields to the GridView's Column collection (as explained in the next chapter).

Handling Null Field Values

The GridView offers an easy solution for handling null data. Users generally want to have more descriptive content for a cell than just emptiness. The `NullDisplayText` will render an alternate string when the value from the data source control is `NULL`. There is another case wherein the data source control does not return any rows at all — this is handled by the `EmptyDataText` property covered in the next chapter.

Try It Out #7 — Handling Null Values

In this simple exercise, you will handle nulls from two fields of the Suppliers table.

Start with a new page named `TIO-7-HandlingNullValues.aspx` that has a SqlDataSource control to return the fields for Company Name, Region, and Fax from the Suppliers table. Create a GridView that shows these three fields as simple bound columns. Save the page (which should look similar to the following) and check it in your browser. Note that there is some missing data.

```
<%@ Page Language="VB" %>
<html>
<head>
  <title>Displaying Data in a GridView - Handling Null Values</title>
</head>
<body>
  <form id="form1" runat="server">
    <asp:GridView ID="GridView1" Runat="server"
    DataSourceID="NorthwindProductsSqlDataSource"
    AutoGenerateColumns="False">
        <Columns>
            <asp:BoundField DataField="CompanyName" />
            <asp:BoundField DataField="Region"/>
            <asp:BoundField DataField="Fax"/>
        </Columns>
    </asp:GridView>

    <asp:SqlDataSource ID="NorthwindProductsSqlDataSource" Runat="server"
      ConnectionString="<%$ ConnectionStrings:LocalSqlNorthwind %>"
          SelectCommand="Select * FROM Suppliers" />

  </form>
</body>
</html>
```

Close your browser and return to the VWD Design view. Select the GridView and open its smart task panel. Select Edit Columns and, in the lower left, select the Regions field. In the Property window, find the `NullDisplayText` property and enter "Region unknown." For the Fax field, enter `NullDisplayText` = "Not on record." Save and view in the browser. The GridView will be modified, as follows:

```
<asp:BoundField DataField="Region" NullDisplayText="Region Unknown" />
<asp:BoundField DataField="Fax" NullDisplayText="Not on record " />
```

How It Works #7 — Handling Null Values

Handling nulls is very easy; merely set the `NullDisplayText` value to the string you want the user to see when a value is missing. Note that the string is set on a per-column basis, not for the entire GridView.

The DetailsView Control

The GridView displays fields from many records as individual rows in a table. An alternate table-based display might present the fields of one record stacked in a vertical column, as follows.

EmployeeID	0001
First Name	Nancy
Last Name	Davolio
City	Seattle
Postal Code	98122
First << Record # 1 of 10 >> Last Add new Record	

ASP.NET 2.0 accommodates this need with the DetailsView control, a sibling control to GridView. The two controls share almost exactly the same object model, and all of the preceding concepts apply equally to this control, including the field (column) types. Additionally, DetailsView supports inserting rows, which the GridView does not support. DetailsView can also be used in conjunction with a GridView control to insert rows that are displayed in the GridView (discussed in Chapter 9).

DetailsView Rendering Elements

The DetailsView rendering is very similar to the FormView in Microsoft Access, rendering its data item as a table of label and value pairs. The DetailsView essentially renders a single data item at a time from its data source, unlike the GridView, which renders all data items at once. It can optionally page over a list of data items.

Header	Single row at the top of DetailsView that contains a header for the DetailsView as a whole (usually the name of the item). It can be specified by HeaderText or HeaderTemplate properties.
Data Fields	Each data row in the DetailsView corresponds to a single data field from the data source, for the current item rendered.
Data Field Headers	The leftmost cell of each data field contains the header for the data field. This is the same value that is normally rendered as a column header in GridView.
Footer	Single row that contains footer information
Pager	Single row that holds page navigation tools
Empty Data Row	A single cell shown as an alternative to the DetailsView if there are no records provided by the data source control

Like the GridView, DetailsView offers an alternate one-cell rendering if there are no records available from the data source control. The layout and values for this case are held in the Empty Data Template.

Connecting the DetailsView to Data

The GridView and DetailsView controls are derived from the same class, so their behavior and syntax are almost identical. The DetailsView is connected by the `DataSourceID` property to a data source control. The DetailsView retrieves data from the data source and automatically generates a table of values for the first record.

```
<%@ Page Language="VB" %>
<html>
<head><title>Displaying Data in a DetailsView</title></head>
<body>
    <form id="form1" runat="server">

      <asp:DetailsView ID="DetailsView1" Runat="server"
        DataSourceID="SqlDataSource1" />

      <asp:SqlDataSource ID="SqlDataSource1" Runat="server"
      ConnectionString="<%$ ConnectionStrings:LocalSqlNorthwind %>"
        SelectCommand="select * from Products"/>
    </form>
</body></html>
```

In this example, the DetailsView control automatically generates the default vertical layout of each field from the first record returned by the data source control. As with the GridView, you can exercise much more control over how the data is displayed by setting additional properties.

The VWD designer facilitates the addition and modification of a DetailsView control. The first option is to go to the smart task panel of the DetailsView control and turn on paging. Another option is Edit Fields, which corresponds to the same dialog that we used to customize the GridView columns. This dialog allows you to add a BoundField, HyperLinkField, CheckBoxField, CommandField, ButtonField, or TemplateField to the DetailsView. Lastly, DetailsView also supports the Edit Templates task for manipulating its templated fields and other top-level template properties, a topic introduced in the preceding text and covered in more detail in Chapter 10.

Like GridView, DetailsView supports editing and deleting data items, but unlike GridView, it also supports inserting new records. This feature is discussed in the chapters on modifying data.

You will note two small but important differences in the syntax of DetailsView from GridView. DetailsView uses the `<Fields>` tag, whereas GridView uses `<Columns>`. DetailsView also has an `AutoGenerateFields` property, whereas GridView has `AutoGenerateColumns`. Both of these differences are logical given that DetailsView does not actually render the fields as columns.

Try It Out #8 — DetailsView Control

In this exercise, you create a DetailsView that shows information about the Northwind products. We'll start with a basic sample and then add paging and templated fields.

1. Create a new page named `TIO-8-DetailsView.aspx`. Add a SqlDataSource control connecting to the Products table of Northwind. Now drag and drop a DetailsView control from the toolbar. On its smart task panel, set the data source to the only available control. Save and run the file to see the default layout. By default, you see every field in the table.

2. Close the browser and use VWD in Design view. Open the DetailsView smart task panel and turn on paging. Then click on Edit Fields to see a dialog very similar to the one for GridView. Select the ProductName bound field and change its `HeaderText` property to just "name." Save and run the page, noting how paging was implemented with a single click and how the `HeaderText` property is rendered to the left of the value.

```
<%@ Page Language="VB" %>
<html>
<head>
  <title>Displaying Data in a GridView - TemplateField</title>
</head>
<body>
  <form id="form1" runat="server">
      <asp:DetailsView ID="DetailsView1" Runat="server"
          DataSourceID="AccessDataSource1"
          DataKeyNames="ProductID"
          AllowPaging="True" AutoGenerateRows="false">
          <Fields>
              <asp:BoundField ReadOnly="True" HeaderText="ProductID"
InsertVisible="False" DataField="ProductID"
                  SortExpression="ProductID" />
              <asp:BoundField HeaderText="Name" DataField="ProductName"
SortExpression="ProductName" />
              <asp:BoundField HeaderText="SupplierID"
DataField="SupplierID" SortExpression="SupplierID" />
              <asp:BoundField HeaderText="CategoryID"
DataField="CategoryID" SortExpression="CategoryID" />
              <asp:BoundField HeaderText="QuantityPerUnit"
DataField="QuantityPerUnit" SortExpression="QuantityPerUnit" />
              <asp:BoundField HeaderText="UnitPrice"
DataField="UnitPrice" SortExpression="UnitPrice" />
              <asp:BoundField HeaderText="UnitsInStock"
DataField="UnitsInStock" SortExpression="UnitsInStock" />
              <asp:BoundField HeaderText="UnitsOnOrder"
DataField="UnitsOnOrder" SortExpression="UnitsOnOrder" />
              <asp:BoundField HeaderText="ReorderLevel"
DataField="ReorderLevel" SortExpression="ReorderLevel" />
              <asp:CheckBoxField HeaderText="Discontinued"
SortExpression="Discontinued" DataField="Discontinued" />
          </Fields>
      </asp:DetailsView>

     <asp:SqlDataSource ID="SqlDataSource1" Runat="server"
       ConnectionString="<%$ ConnectionStrings:LocalSqlNorthwind %>"
         SelectCommand="SELECT * FROM Products" />
  </form>
</body>
</html>
```

How It Works #8 — DetailsView Control

As you can see, the DetailsView control is very similar to the GridView. They have the same properties and source code. But the DetailsView shows just one record at a time. Note that the label to the left of the value is actually called the HeaderText. In the next few chapters, you will return to this control to see how it works in a master-details scenario and how it is used to add new records to a GridView.

Common Mistakes

Following are some common mistakes made in trying to display data in tables:

- Attempting to render a GridView from a data source control that does not return data. If there is no data returned and the `EmptyDataText` or `EmptyDataTemplate` are not defined, the GridView will not render anything at all.
- Forgetting to set `AutoGenerateColumns=false` when explicit columns are defined.
- Attempting to show values from two data sources in one GridView control. The GridView itself is not able to join data from multiple tables. That must be done either in the RDBMS or in the SelectCommand of the data source control.
- Attempting to set the properties of a GridView when it is not selected. If your properties options are ASP.NET, Body, and Misc, you have the page (background) selected, not the GridView. Click once on the middle of the GridView to select it; then you should have the property options Accessibility, Appearance, and so on.
- Malformed tags. It is easy when typing and rearranging many attributes in the Source view of a GridView to end up without a closing angle bracket on the GridView tag. The error message "The server tag is not well formed" stops on the line the tag starts, which misleads your eye from the position of the problem — after the last attribute at the absence of the tag ending bracket (>).
- Attempting to display a field in a data-bound control when that field was not included in the data source control.
- Using the wrong name for a field in a data-bound control. This arises from an error in typing or an error recalling the name of the field. Whenever possible, in an IDE, use a pick list or drag-and-drop.
- Committing a SQL mistake when using the `AS` clause in a SQL statement that also has a `WHERE` or `ORDER BY` clause. Use the alias (new name) in the `WHERE` if the `AS` clause is in the data store's query or view. Use the old name in the `WHERE` clause if the `AS` clause is in the data source control's SELECT statement.

Summary

Recall from earlier chapters that the basic architecture to display data on an ASP.NET 2.0 page utilizes two controls: a data source control and a data-bound control. Data source controls can connect to Access, SQL, Oracle, or other sources. The data-bound controls work, for the most part, with any data source control. This interoperability reduces the learning curve and maintenance costs as databases and displays are modified over the life of a Web site.

With almost no coding, the GridView provides many of the functions that you had to create by hand in earlier versions of ASP. In most cases, the GridView can be created and modified through the VWD Design view tools, eliminating the need to work with tags. The GridView binds to a data source control and then displays the data in tabular form, that is, one or more columns and all of the rows sent from the data source.

The GridView's columns can be created automatically (one for each field) using `AutoGenerateColumns=true` or by specific definitions. Columns can be added, deleted, moved, and modified through the GridView's smart task panel ⇨ Edit Columns. If you use both, you will get one column for each field, plus any columns you defined by hand. Columns that display values from the database have an option to set a string to be displayed if the data source sends a NULL to the GridView.

The basic type of column that shows a value is the Bound Field. The value to display can be formatted into standard presentations for numbers or dates and can include leading or trailing text. These formatting features use the `DataFormatString`.

A CheckBox Field binds to Boolean data and then automatically formats the results as a check box icon. A hyperlink column allows you to redirect the user on a click. Each hyperlink in the GridView will point to an appropriate target for its record. First, you must set the hyperlink text that will appear in the hyperlink column and then the hyperlink's target. You will probably have to add strings using the `DataNavigateFormatString` to get a properly formed URL.

GridView offers ImageField columns that will pick up an image and prepare it properly for the browser. The image comes from a value in the database referencing an external file (`mode=ImageURL`). You may need to modify the value's string to properly point to the image file, for example, by adding the path or extension.

CommandField columns and ButtonField columns both invoke code. The Command Column will run one of several standard operations provided by the GridView, including edit, select, and delete. A Button Column will trigger events wherein you write custom code.

The most flexible column is the Template Field. This option provides a blank space into which you can place controls bound to values, HTML tags, or text. This flexibility allows you to completely customize the rendering for a GridView cell.

The DetailsView is a sibling control to the GridView in appearance, function, and internal design. Whereas the GridView displays a table of many records and a series of vertical columns, the DetailsView displays a single column showing values from just one record. It is easy to add page navigation, and the ability to modify its templates offers great freedom in layout.

This chapter explained how to build the structure of GridView and DetailsView controls. The next chapter looks at techniques to improve their overall appearance using styles.

6

Customizing the Appearance of Tables

The GridView and DetailsView controls offer a wide variety of options for formatting the appearance and style of their major rendering elements. Whereas the last chapter focused on creating the structure of these controls from the fields in the data source, this chapter focuses on their overall appearance, covering six major areas:

- Customizing Appearance
- Customizing Individual Styles
- Using Cascading Style Sheets (CSS)
- Precedence of Styles
- Using AutoFormat in Visual Studio
- Themes and Skins

You'll practice techniques discussed in this chapter with eight Try It Out exercises:

Try It Out	Topic
1	Colors, Gridlines, and Backgrounds
2	Headers, Footers, Alignment, and ToolTips
3	Formatting Row Styles
4	Empty Tables
5	DetailsView Styles
6	Column Styles
7	Formatting by Cascading Style Sheet
8	Precedence of Styles

Customizing Appearance

The properties, events, and methods of a GridView or DetailsView can be roughly categorized into two areas: those that affect appearance and those that affect behavior. Each of these areas has several subcategories. Behavioral properties include the access key, ToolTips, autogeneration of columns, clickable elements, and scripted actions. Formatting features include colors, lines, styles, and the control of formatting by a Cascading Style Sheet (CSS). Furthermore, you can divide the formatting properties into those that affect the GridView as a whole and those that are specific to only some columns, rows, or cells. The appearance of a table can be modified quickly using the design features of Visual Web Developer (VWD) or Visual Studio (VS). The resulting source code is also provided so that you can create the page using another editor.

BackColor and BackImageUrl

You can specify a background color for the entire grid. There are three ways to specify a color. The Visual Studio backcolor property dialog box divides these options across three tabs:

- First is RGB with three hexadecimal values for Red, Green, and Blue in the format RRGGBB. Each value ranges from 00 to FF. A good tool to experiment with the RGB hexadecimal color system is the VWD Custom Color tab in the dialog box for setting a GridView's border color. The custom tab colors are a basic palette offering 48 values in a range of hues and intensities that will insert an RGB value into the tag. RGB colors are a logical selection for desktops but do not always translate well to the Web. The syntax follows for a purple, where Red is a medium value (C0), Green is nothing (00), and Blue is also medium (C0).

  ```
  <asp:gridview ... backcolor="#C000C0" ... >
  ```

- The second option is the palette of approximately 150 specific colors that have been recognized and named by the WWW Consortium. They should be available in every modern Web browser. VWD offers this palette in the Web tab, or typists can find the list in an HTML book.

  ```
  <asp:gridview ... backcolor="DarkMagenta" ... >
  ```

- The third option, System, will display a color that depends on the user's Windows settings. Most Windows users right-click on the desktop and then select Properties ➪ Appearance ➪ Scheme and change from Windows Standard to something like Wheat or Spruce. That scheme then sets a color for each part of a window, including the Button Face, Border of an Active Window, Disabled Menu Options, and Menu Bar Background. By selecting a Windows system color, your GridView background color will be set to match that Window part for each user. For example, you might set your GridView backcolor to "MenuBarBackgound." If visitor A to your Web site is using the Spruce scheme (which has an Active Title color = green), her GridView backcolor will autoset to green. Other visitors will have other backgrounds depending on their personal Windows settings. The net result is that your page looks well integrated with every user's Windows system.

  ```
  <asp:gridview ... backcolor="MenuBar" ... >
  ```

An alternative to a backcolor is a background image. GridView handles GIF, JPG, BMP, and WMF file formats. However, be aware that some older browsers don't support formats such as .png and .bmp (GIF and JPG are safest). Considering that your entire Web site may move to different folders or machines, it is best to use a path to the image file that is relative to the page that contains the GridView, instead of a fully qualified path that depends on the file system of your development machine. In VWD, simply navigate to and select the image; for typists, use the following syntax:

```
<asp:gridview ... backimageurl="MyCompanyLogoInBlackAndWhite" ... >
```

Carefully consider the user experience with background images. Most images interfere with the legibility of the data in the grid. Because a background image will have a variety of color hues, it will be difficult to select any font color that will contrast with all areas of the image. A second problem with background images is that they are not scaled or stretched to fit the GridView. A large image will have only its top left corner visible in a small GridView. A small image will be repeated in a large GridView, with parts of its right and bottom sides cut off. Considering that the dimension of a GridView will change with each request according to the amount of data and the size of the browser display, your chances of obtaining a consistent GridView background image are small.

I know of only two cases where a background image works well. First is a single color image with a very low contrast, such as a faint watermark of a company logo. Another is to have an artist design an "image," which is just a gradation of color from the very faintest to light as you go from left to right. Make this image a little larger than the largest the GridView can render. When a "wash" like this cuts off, it will not be troublesome to the eye.

Using a background image will override a backcolor setting.

Font and ForeColor

You can set the characteristics of the text displayed in the entire table. This operation is no different than modifying the font in standard HTML. Keep in mind that selecting the table control and setting font attributes makes changes to the entire table; changes to specific columns and rows will come in the next section of this chapter. General characteristics of the font can be changed in the font property of the table control (note the plus sign [+] for expansion to the left of the property name in the property window).

```
<asp:gridview ... font-bold="True" font-underline="False" ... >
<asp:gridview ... font-name="Verdana" font-size="10pt" ... >
<asp:gridview ... forecolor="#10E4DD" ... > color according to the RGB Hexadecimal
code
<asp:gridview ... forecolor="PeachPuff" ... > one of the standard WWW colors
<asp:gridview ... forecolor="ActiveCaptionText" ... > color of user's Windows setup
```

Height and Width

The GridView control will automatically size itself to accommodate the values on the screen. However, you have the ability to override this default and specify a custom width and height. Select the table and use the VWD Properties window to specify the height and width. The result will be as follows:

```
<asp:GridView ID="GridView1" Runat="server"
    ...
    Height="5cm"
    Width="200">
```

The available units are in for inches, cm for centimeters, and px for pixels (the default). Although these options are available, you gain flexibility by leaving them out and letting the table size itself to the values. On the other hand, absolute values for a table reduce the amount of time it takes the browser to generate the HTML.

CellSpacing and CellPadding

Cell spacing determines the distance between cells. Effectively, that becomes the width between the gridlines around each cell. Cell padding creates space inside the cell between the values and the cell walls. Increasing padding gives the values more space between each other. Units for both of these properties are always in pixels.

```
<asp:gridview ... cellpadding="2" cellspacing="5" ... >
```

Borders and Gridlines

Borders refer to the single rectangle around the entire GridView or DetailsView control. Gridlines refer to the internal lines that separate the cells; they can be modified two ways. Default settings for the entire table control are done as described here. Specific columns, rows, or cells can then override the default, as described in the later section on styles.

Change the gridlines for the entire table by setting the GridLines property to one of the following four values. The default is both.

```
<asp:GridView...  gridlines="None"...
<asp:GridView...  gridlines="Horizontal"
<asp:GridView...  gridlines="Vertical"
<asp:GridView...  gridlines="Both"
```

The border color is set in the same manner as the table's background color, using either a standard WWW named color or a color that the browser picks up from the user's Windows settings or an RBG hexadecimal value.

The border width can be set in the Properties window when the table is selected. The options for units include in, cm, and px. The border style can be one of ten options, as follows:

```
<asp:GridView... borderstyle="NotSet"...>
or
<asp:GridView... borderstyle=0 ...>

NotSet (0)       None (1)
Dotted (2)       Dashed (3)      Solid (4)              Double (5)
Groove (6)       Ridge (7)       Inset (8)              Outset (9)
```

Note that those on the bottom row will render the four borders in different configurations to create a 3-D effect. The value in parentheses is the integer setting held by the control and the value reported if you look at the contents of the property. The double style must have a width of at least 3 to accommodate the dimensions of two lines; widths less than 3 will appear as a single line. Don't be surprised that when using a setting of `none`, depending on the `GridView.Gridlines` value, there will still be some or all lines around the table. Note that when setting any of these values using the English name in code, you'll need to qualify the value with the BorderStyle enumeration, as follows:

```
GridView1.BorderStyle = BorderStyle.Dashed
```

The preceding properties will change the appearance of the entire GridView. However, two more-effective ways will be discussed shortly. Themes and Style Sheets make it easier to change all of the grids in your site at once. You can also apply several formatting changes at once using the Auto Format feature of Visual Web Developer.

Try It Out #1 — Colors, Gridlines, and Backgrounds

In this exercise, you will create two GridViews, separated by a horizontal line `<hr/>`. Both will show the first and last names of the first three Northwind employees, but with different appearances. Of course, you can use more colorful options, but in this exercise you will use shades of black, white, and gray so that they are obvious in the black-and-white printing of the book.

1. Create a folder named `C:\Websites\BegAspNetDB\ch06` and, within it, a page named `TIO-2-GridViewColorAndBorder.aspx`. Add a single SqlDataSource control named NorthWindEmployees pointing to your Northwind database hosted by MSDE. Select the LastName and FirstName of all employees. Cover up the code solution following step 4 and try creating the page as follows.
2. Create two GridViews with IDs set to "White" and "Black," both linked to the NorthWindEmployees data source.
3. In VWD's Design view, select the GridView and then turn your attention to the Properties window. Format the GridView with ID "White" to have a wide dark-gray border that appears outset. Set the font to be a typeface that is *sans serif* and about a quarter inch tall. There should be no internal lines dividing cells.
4. Format the GridView with ID "Black" to have a black background with white letters in a block font with bold italics. Set the border to be double and display white lines between all cells. Your page will resemble the following, which you can view in your browser:

```
<%@ page language="VB" %>
<script runat="server">
</script>

<html>
<head id="Head1" runat="server">
    <title>Ch06-TIO-1 GridView Colors and Borders</title>
</head>
<body>
    <form id="Form1" runat="server">
        <H4>Chapter 6 Try It Out #1 - GridView Colors and Borders</H4>
        <asp:AccessDataSource ID="NorthwindEmployees" Runat="server"
            DataFile="~/Data/Northwind.mdb"
            SelectCommand="SELECT TOP 3 FirstName,LastName FROM [Employees]" />
        <br/>
        <br />
        <asp:gridview id="White" runat="server"
          datasourceid="NorthWindEmployees"
```

```
            autogeneratecolumns="True"
            font-names="Arial" font-size="Large" gridlines="None"
            borderwidth="7px" borderstyle="Outset" bordercolor="LightGray">
          </asp:gridview>
          <br />
          <hr />
          <br />
          <asp:gridview id="Black" runat="server"
            datasourceid="NorthWindEmployees"
            autogeneratecolumns="True"
            backcolor="Black"
            forecolor="White" font-italic="True" font-bold="True" font-names="Tahoma"
            borderstyle="Double" borderwidth="5px">
          </asp:gridview>
      </form>
  </body>
  </html>
```

How It Works #1 — Colors, Gridlines, and Backgrounds

These concepts are simple; you just have to know the exact name of each property and where to find it in the properties list. When you set the font using VWD, you do not get a sample (as in Word) in a dialog box, so it is best to try different fonts until you find one that you like. You will probably be most comfortable with one of the three color-naming methods, but keep in mind that pages you view from other programmers may use another method. Be prepared to work in all three methods.

HorizontalAlign

The entire table can be located on the page at the left, center, or right as per the HorizontalAlign property. Keep in mind that when this property is used in the GridView or DetailsView control, it applies to the location of the entire table (not the values within the cells). Alignment of values within cells is covered later in this chapter.

ShowHeader and ShowFooter

A GridView, by default, will show a header but not a footer. The header will contain the names of the fields in the data source, as column headers. If you want to show a footer, you must set the ShowFooter property to `True` and specify a value to display in the footer style (covered shortly). A DetailsView control has an optional header that goes at the top of the control. For DetailsView, *Field Headings* refers to the column of labels stacked along the left side, next to the values.

ToolTip

A ToolTip specific to a control appears whenever the mouse is held over the control. For example, in almost any Microsoft toolbar, if you hold the mouse over one icon, you will get a short text identifying the tool. These are easy to implement for a GridView using the ToolTip property to create source code, as follows:

```
<asp:gridview ... tooltip="My tooltip text message goes here" .../>
```

You can have a very long ToolTip, although text over a few hundred characters has been found to be unstable (sometimes flashes). You cannot include any formatting characters such as `vbTab` or `chr(10)` or a `Shift+Return`.

ToolTips are particularly useful to remind users that clicking on the column heading will perform a sort. In some applications, selecting a record will automatically start a process or lead to a new page — that can also be indicated in a ToolTip.

Try It Out #2 — Headers, Footers, Alignment, and ToolTips

In this exercise, you will experiment with the three behaviors of the GridView previously listed.

1. Create a new page named `TIO-2-GridViewBehavior.aspx`. View the Database Explorer, expand your connection to `LocalSqlNorthwind`, and expand the Employees table. Select the employee's ID and both names and drag them to the page.
2. Add a ToolTip for the entire GridView with the text, "Employee list is updated each midnight."
3. Turn on the ShowFooter and turn off the ShowHeaders. Save the page and look at it in your browser. Note that the footers are empty by default.
4. Close the browser and set the entire GridView to be on the right side of the page. Save and observe in the browser. The final page should be similar to the following:

```
<%@ page language="VB" %>
<scrip0t runat="server">
</script>
<html>
<head id="Head1" runat="server"><title>Ch06-TIO-2 BasicBehavior</title></head>
<body>
    <form id="Form1" runat="server">
        <H3>Chapter 6 Try It Out #2 - Headers, Footers, Alignment and Tooltips</H3>

        <asp:gridview id="GridView1" runat="server"
          datasourceid="NorthWindEmployees"
          ToolTip='Employee list is updated each midnight.'
          ShowHeader="false"
          ShowFooter="true"
          HorizontalAlign="Right">
        </asp:gridview>

        <asp:SqlDataSource ID="NorthwindProductsSqlDataSource" Runat="server"
            ConnectionString="<%$ ConnectionStrings:LocalSqlNorthwind %>"
            SelectCommand="SELECT EmployeeID,FirstName,LastName FROM [Employees]"/>
    </form>
</body>
</html>
```

How It Works #2 — Headers, Footers, Alignment, and ToolTips

With this exercise, you see a ToolTip in action and then observe the default and modified behavior of ShowHeader and ShowFooter. Last, you modified the HorizontalAlign property of the GridView. Keep in mind that the Horizontal Align property of the GridView moves the entire table. When I discuss column-level formatting, I will cover how to align data within a cell.

Customizing Individual Styles

We've looked at a number of properties that affect the appearance of the GridView as a whole, from colors and borders to alignment and ToolTips. This next section examines the set of style properties that can be applied to individual elements in the GridView (and DetailsView) renderings. A *style* in ASP.NET is a collection of properties that affect the look and feel of a control rendering. The properties you can set on an ASP.NET style roughly correspond to the same style properties you might apply to an HTML tag directly. In fact, some of the GridView properties we've looked at so far are in fact style properties (inherited by the base ASP.NET Control class). However, this section looks at additional styles that apply at a more granular level to the control rendering. In particular, there are styles that apply to rows in the table, and there are styles that apply to columns and cells.

GridView and DetailsView Styles

The GridView and DetailsView control renderings are made up of table rows, and these controls provide a set of properties you can set for applying style customizations to a row or group of rows in this rendering. The following style properties are supported:

- **RowStyle** — Applies to each row containing data from the data source.
- **AlternatingRowStyle** — Applies to every other row containing data from the data source. The properties set on this style override the same property on RowStyle, if applicable.
- **HeaderStyle** — Formats the header row when `ShowHeader=true`.
- **FooterStyle** — Formats the footer row when `Showfooter=true` (`false` by default).
- **SelectedRowStyle** — Formats a row after it has been selected. This style is used only when the GridView has a CommandField with the `ShowSelect` set to `true`.
- **EditRowStyle** — Formats a row that has been shifted into Edit mode, for example, when a user clicks an Edit button rendered by a CommandField with `ShowEditButton` set to `true`.
- **PagerStyle** — Formats the pager row (usually merged into a single cell) that contains tools for navigations, such as buttons for First, Last, Previous, and Next.
- **EmptyDataRowStyle** — Applies to the row rendered when there is no data. It is a bit misleading in its name. This is not for a phantom record that does not have data. Rather, this is a single row that is substituted for the entire table control (GridView or DetailsView) when the data source control delivers zero records.

With VWD, you can modify the format of a row style by using the properties of the control. You will see a long list of options for each row type (you may have to click the plus sign to expand the options). If you are typing in another editor, styles for a type of row are held in `<style>` tags within the control tag. They can be located before or after the `<Columns>` tag but not within the `<Columns>` tags. For example, the following creates white characters on a black background for the header row:

```
<asp:GridView ID="GridView1" Runat="server">

    <HeaderStyle
            BackColor="black"
            ForeColor="white">
    </HeaderStyle>
```

```
        <Columns>
          <asp:BoundField DataField="MyField1"></asp:BoundField>
          <asp:BoundField DataField="MyField2"></asp:BoundField>
          <asp:BoundField DataField="MyField3"></asp:BoundField>
        </Columns>

    </asp:GridView>
```

There is an alternative syntax supported for setting styles that does not require a separate `<style>` inner tag. Instead, you can type the name of the style property, followed by a dash, followed by the property of the style you wish to set, as an attribute of the GridView tag itself.

```
    <asp:GridView ID="GridView1" HeaderStyle-BackColor="black" HeaderStyle-
ForeColor="white" Runat="server">
```

Note that if the style property has subproperties, these can be nested using additional dashes between the property names. The most common example of this is the `Font` style property.

```
    <asp:GridView ID="GridView1" HeaderStyle-Font-Bold="true" HeaderStyle-Font-
Name="Verdana" Runat="server">
```

Try It Out #3 — Formatting Row Styles

This exercise formats row styles.

1. Create a new file named `TIO-4-FormatRows` and use it to simply display the ProductID, ProductName, and UnitPrice of the first ten items in the Products table. Save the file and check it in your browser to see that, by default, there is no formatting other than the default bold applied to the header row.

```
<%@ page language="VB" %>
<html>
<head runat="server">
    <title>TIO # 4 Format Rows</title>
</head>
<body>
<h2>Ch06 TIO # 4 Format Rows</h2>
    <form runat="server">
        <asp:SqlDataSource ID="NorthwindProductsSqlDataSource" Runat="server"
            ConnectionString="<%$ ConnectionStrings:LocalSqlNorthwind %>"
            SelectCommand="SELECT ProductID, ProductName, UnitPrice
                FROM Products
                WHERE ProductID <= 10">

        <asp:gridview id="NorthwindProductsGridView" runat="server"
            datasourceid="NorthwindProductsSqlDataSource">
        </asp:gridview>
    </form>
</body>
</html>
```

2. Create a HeaderRowStyle with a larger font, as follows. Select the GridView; then go to the Properties window. Expand the HeaderStyle pane and then expand the Font pane. Change the size to large.

3. Now set your basic rows to be italic using similar steps. Note that you don't have to worry about selecting rows. Just select the GridView as a whole and find the appropriate property. This time, you change the `RowStyle/Font/Italic`.

4. Now differentiate every other row by giving it a very faint gray background using `AlternatingRowStyle/Backcolor` set to something like `#E0E0E0`.

5. Turn on paging (GridView/smart task panel) and then set the PagerStyle to a sans serif font such as Arial. Save the file and take a look in the browser.

```
<asp:gridview id="GridView1" runat="server"
  datasourceid="NorthWindEmployeesSqlDataSource"
  AllowPaging="True"
  PageSize="5">
    <PagerStyle
        ForeColor="Black"
        BackColor="White"
        Font-Names="Arial" />
    <HeaderStyle Font-Size="Large" />
    <AlternatingRowStyle BackColor="#E0E0E0" />
    <RowStyle Font-Italic="True" />
</asp:gridview>
```

How It Works #3 — Formatting Row Styles

Formatting rows is easy; however, there are a few syntax tricks. Note that VWD created `<XXXstyles>` within the GridView but outside the `<Column>` tags. When you set a style, it applies to the appropriate row for all of the columns.

Empty Tables

The last chapter discussed how to use the NullDisplayText to display a string when a single value is `NULL`. But what if the data source control returns no records at all? Perhaps there was an error connecting to the database, or perhaps the SelectCommand had a `WHERE` clause (for example, `DOB < 1/1/1800`) that is unfulfilled by any of the records. The result will be that your GridView or DetailsView does not render at all; you get blank space on the page. You can improve the appearance using the properties for EmptyDataRow.

> **The terminology here is confusing. *EmptyDataRow* implies that one row of a GridView is empty, but the term actually means that the set of data is empty of any rows at all. If there is one "empty" row, it will not show up in the GridView. An empty cell will show up blank.**

EmptyDataRowText allows you to substitute a literal text where the table control would have been. Having a value for EmptyRow text actually does two things. First, it creates a table of one row and one column. Second, it renders the text into the single cell of that little table. Once you have a value in EmptyDataRowText, you can set any of the dozen or so formatting properties of that little table (background, width, and so on) by using the EmptyDataRowStyle.

Try It Out #4 — Empty Tables

In this exercise, you will build three versions of a page. The first will display the employee's data in a DetailsView. The second will seek to retrieve employees whose ID = 999, and there will be no result. In the third version, you will handle the lack of results by displaying an alternate message in the EmptyRowsStyle.

1. Create a new file named `Tio-4-EmptyTable-ver1.aspx`. Add a SqlDataSource control that gets the ID and name fields from Employees in Northwind. Add a DetailsView control bound to the DataSource control, save, and check the page, which should be similar to the following:

```
<%@ page language="VB" %>
<script runat="server">
</script>
<html>
<head id="Head1" runat="server"><title>Ch06-TIO-4-EmptyTable</title>
</head>
<body>
    <form id="Form1" runat="server">
        <H3>Chapter 6 Try It Out #4 - Empty Table </H3>
            <asp:DetailsView ID="DetailsView1" Runat="server"
                DataSourceID="NorthwindEmployeesSqlDataSource"
                AllowPaging="True" />

        <asp:SqlDataSource ID="NorthwindEmployeesSqlDataSource"  Runat="server"
            ConnectionString="<%$ ConnectionStrings:LocalSqlNorthwind %>"
            SelectCommand="
                SELECT EmployeeID,FirstName,LastName
                FROM [Employees]" />

    </form>
</body>
</html>
```

2. Run the page and observe that you get a normal list of employees. Save the page as version 2 and change the SelectCommand so that it has a `WHERE` clause that will return no records, for example, `WHERE EmployeeID = 999`. Save as version 2 and note that the GridView does not render at all.

```
SelectCommand="
    SELECT EmployeeID,FirstName,LastName
    FROM [Employees]
    WHERE EmployeeID = 999" />
```

3. Close the browser and save the page as version 3. In Design view, select the GridView, go to the Properties window to find EmptyRowText, and set its value to "No employees match your criteria." Then go to the EmptyDataRowStyle and assign a font of Arial Bold in size Large. Save as version 3 and run in your browser.

```
<asp:DetailsView ID="DetailsView1" Runat="server"
    DataSourceID="NorthwindEmployeesSqlDataSource"
    AllowPaging="True"
    EmptyDataText="No employees match your criteria">
    <EmptyDataRowStyle Font-Names="Arial Black" Font-Size="Large" />
</asp:DetailsView>
```

How It Works #4 — Empty Tables

This exercise starts by displaying a DetailsView without problems. When you change the select command to return no records, the page does not give the user good feedback about the absence of the DetailsView control. There is no error, but the user is left wondering whether there might be an error. You recover by adding an EmptyDataText and formatting the resulting EmptyDataRowStyle.

DetailsView-Specific Styles

Because of its different layout (fields stacked vertically rather than laid out horizontally) and capabilities (able to insert new records), the DetailsView has some special styles.

- **FieldHeaderStyle** — This region is the vertical list of field names to the left of the values. Functionally it is the same as a header row in a GridView, but it is located to the left and rotated in a DetailsView. The header row in DetailsView doesn't contain column names, rather, just the value of HeaderText, if set on the DetailsView control.
- **CommandRowStyle** — When a CommandField, such as Edit, Delete, or Insert, is used in the DetailsView, it creates a new row for the command(s). This row can be styled in the same way as other regions of the DetailsView.
- **InsertRowStyle** — Although the GridView and DetailsView are very similar, they have one major functional difference: DetailsView can add ("insert") new records. The functionality is enabled when a CommandField with `ShowInsertButton="true"` is added to the DetailsView. The DetailsView control then offers a special style for data rows when they are in insertion mode.

Try It Out #5 — DetailsView Styles

In this short exercise, you will modify the three styles mentioned in the preceding bulleted list.

1. Get a quick start by opening your `TIO-4-EmptyTableStyleVer1.aspx` and save it as `TIO-5-SpecialStylesForDetailsView.aspx`. Change the title in the head and the H3 and H4 text in the <body> using the text in the code list below.
2. In VWD Design view, select the DetailsView control and open the smart task panel. Click on Edit Columns and add a column of type Command Field/"New, Insert, Cancel." Close the Edit Columns dialog and the panel. Observe that you now have a command row that holds the button "New."
3. Select the DetailsView control and look in the Properties window to find the CommandRow Style and set the `font/Italics` to `true`.
4. Scroll down in the Properties window to the InsertRowStyle and set its background to light gray.
5. Last, with the DetailsView control still selected, look in the Properties window for the FieldHeaderStyle and change the font to Arial Black. Save the page; the source code should look like the following listing. Observe the results in your browser.

```
<%@ page language="VB" %>
<script runat="server">
</script>
```

```
<html>
<head runat="server"><title>Ch6-TIO-5-SpecialStylesForDetaislView</title>
</head>
<body>
    <form id="Form1" runat="server">
        <H3>Chapter 6 Try It Out #5 - Special Styles for DetailsView control</H3>

            <asp:DetailsView ID="DetailsView1" Runat="server"
                DataSourceID="NorthwindEmployeesSqlDataSource"
                AllowPaging="True">
                <CommandRowStyle Font-Italic="True" />
                <Fields>
                    <asp:CommandField ShowInsertButton="True" />
                </Fields>
                <FieldHeaderStyle Font-Names="Arial Black" />
                <InsertRowStyle BackColor="Silver" />
            </asp:DetailsView>

        <asp:SqlDataSource ID="NorthwindEmployeesSqlDataSource"  Runat="server"
            ConnectionString="<%$ ConnectionStrings:LocalSqlNorthwind %>"
            SelectCommand="
                SELECT EmployeeID,FirstName,LastName
                FROM [Employees]" />
    </form>
</body></html>
```

How It Works #5 — DetailsView Styles

You can use the FieldHeaderStyle to format the left column where the names of fields are listed. When the DetailsView contains a CommandField, the command buttons rendered by that field will be formatted according to the CommandRowStyle. Also, recall that the DetailsView offers the ability to add new records (called inserting), a function not available in the GridView (specifics are discussed starting in Chapter 12). The insertion function is available once there is a CommandField of the type Insert. When the Insert button (New) is clicked, the DetailsView control changes to Insert mode. The CommandRow now offers two different commands: Insert and Cancel. When in Insert mode, the body of the DetailsView changes to the format of InsertRowStyle.

Column Styles and Field Styles

Similar to rows, individual columns (in GridView) or fields (in DetailsView) can also have formatting. However, whereas some rows have styles that span multiple rows (RowStyle and AlternateRowStyle), each column or fields style applies to only that column or field. Recall from Chapter 5 that we used the "Edit Columns" or "Edit Fields" task to add individual fields, such as BoundField or HyperLinkField, to the GridView and DetailsView controls. In addition to setting properties of these fields to determine their behavior, you can also set properties to determine the style of a given field.

The style for a field or column is broken down into four parts. In other words, you do not apply a style to an entire column. You apply four separate styles to the four parts of a field/column: the header, footer, item (data cell), and controls in the item. Note that you must define your columns or fields to apply styles to their cells. You cannot use AutoGenerateColumns or AutoGenerateFields.

The following styles apply to only the cell(s) within one column or field. They can be seen in source code as an `<xxxStyle>` tag within an `<asp:xxxField>` tag. If you want to change the style of all of the cells in a row, use the GridView or DetailsView row styles. In other words, use these styles when you want cells of one column to be different from the cells of the rest of the columns in the GridView.

- **HeaderStyle** — Affects the header of the field or column. In a GridView, that is the cell holding the column name.
- **FooterStyle** — Affects the footer of the field or column. In a GridView, this is an optional cell at the bottom of the column.
- **ItemStyle** — Affects the actual data value cells in the middle of the column or field.
- **ControlStyle** — Affects the appearance of a control in the data value cells of a field. For example, the button or hyperlink cells rendered by a ButtonField or HyperLinkField would have this style applied. In a BoundField column, this style also applies to the editable input control when the GridView row is put into Edit mode by the user clicking the Edit command button.

> **Note that the syntax is RowStyle (and AlternateRowStyle) for the GridView-level style. For the column-level equivalent, the syntax is ItemStyle. There is no AlternateItemStyle within a single column.**

Try It Out #6 — Column Styles

In this exercise, you will set some overall formatting for a GridView. But you want one column to stand out, so giving its cells special formatting is necessary.

1. Create a new file named `TIO-6-ColumnStyles.aspx`. Add a GridView to display the EmployeeID and first and last names from the Employees table of Northwind.
2. Select the GridView and set some basic styles, as follows, using the Properties pane: HeaderStyle = Large font size and RowStyle = light gray background. Save and view in your browser (download file version 1). Observe that the GridView row styles apply to cells in all columns.
3. Close the browser and now, in Design view, select the GridView. Choose Edit Columns, select the FirstName column, and go to the Properties section of the dialog box. Expand the HeaderStyle section and set the background to black, set the forecolor to white, and turn on italics. Do the same for the ItemStyle. Save (equals download version 2) and check in the browser. You may also want to examine the following source code to see the relationships between the controls:

```
<asp:GridView ID="GridView1" Runat="server"
    DataSourceID="NorthwindEmployeesSqlDataSource"
    DataKeyNames="EmployeeID"
    AutoGenerateColumns="False">
    <HeaderStyle Font-Size="Large" />
    <RowStyle BackColor="#E0E0E0" />
    <Columns>
        <asp:BoundField HeaderText="EmployeeID"
            DataField="EmployeeID"
```

```
                    SortExpression="EmployeeID">
                </asp:BoundField>
                <asp:BoundField HeaderText="FirstName"
                    DataField="FirstName"
                    SortExpression="FirstName">
                    <ItemStyle
                        ForeColor="White"
                        Font-Italic="True"
                        BackColor="Black" />
                    <HeaderStyle
                        ForeColor="White"
                        Font-Italic="True"
                        BackColor="Black" />
                </asp:BoundField>
                <asp:BoundField HeaderText="LastName"
                    DataField="LastName"
                    SortExpression="LastName" />
            </Columns>
        </asp:GridView>

        <asp:SqlDataSource ID="NorthwindEmployeesSqlDataSource"  Runat="server"
            ConnectionString="<%$ ConnectionStrings:LocalSqlNorthwind %>"
            SelectCommand="SELECT EmployeeID,FirstName,LastName FROM [Employees]"/>
    </form>
```

How It Works #6 — Column Styles

The key to understanding this exercise is to know what syntax applies to which section of the GridView and where to make the changes in the VWD designer. To apply formatting to the entire GridView, you select the GridView and use the editor's main Properties window.

To change just the cells of one column, select the GridView and then expand the smart task panel and click on Edit Columns. Select the column to change and then modify the style properties such as ItemStyle, HeaderStyle, and FooterStyle in the Properties window that is within the Edit Columns dialog box.

Using Cascading Style Sheets

Cascading Style Sheets (CSS) are a system to create a single set of appearance definitions for an entire Web site and to do so with a minimum of coding and information transfer across the network. The sheet defines styles and then, for each style, provides a format consisting of the font, colors, indentation, and almost any other HTML formatting tag. Then, any control on the site with formatting (including table controls) can use a set of styles by setting a single CssClass property. Three objectives are achieved:

- All pages will look the same because the style comes from one source.
- The description of the style must only be transmitted once across the connection.
- The Webmaster only has to make a change in one place (the style sheet) to affect stylistic changes across every page of the site.

You can build a CSS definition quickly and accurately in Visual Studio by adding a new item to the root of your site of the type "Style Sheet" ending with the extension .css. By default, there will be a body{} definition. You can add a new style by right-clicking after the braces and selecting Build New Style. The dialog box accepts your input and then builds a syntax similar to the following. There are many books on the market that explain more details of style sheets and their many syntactic permutations.

```
body{
}

.MyStyleGridView{
 color: white;
 font-family: Tahoma;
 background-color: black;
 text-align: right;
}
```

Then, in your ASPX page, you must add two items. In the <head> there must be a <link> to the CSS file, as follows (assuming that the CSS is in the root of your site). This establishes the style sheet for the entire page. In VWD, select the page and look in the Properties window. Double-check that the object selected in the top of the Properties window is the document; then set the StyleSheet to your CSS file.

```
<head runat="server">
<link rel="Stylesheet" type="text/css" href="~/MyStyleSheet.css" />
</head>
```

And finally, you set a property that determines which of the style classes in the CSS to apply to the GridView. Although you must have a leading period before your class name in the CSS file, you do not use the leading period in the GridView property:

```
<asp:gridview ... cssclass="MyStyleForGridView" ... >
```

You can even add to your CSS parameters to apply styles to individual HTML elements within the GridView rendering, for instance, styles to apply to hyperlinks. For example, add the following to your style definition:

```
.MyStyleGridView a {
    color: Aqua
}

.MyStyleGridView a:hover {
    color: Yellow
}
```

When you create the CSS file, you have to translate the ASP.NET 2.0 control properties into the syntax allowed for style sheets. The complete list of allowed style sheet format names can be found at www.w3.org/TR/REC-CSS1 or http://msdn.microsoft.com/library/default.asp?url=/workshop/author/css/reference/attributes.asp.

Here are the some of the conversions that trip up new designers:

Description	ASP Control Syntax	CSS Syntax
Text color	`Forecolor`	`Color: Green;` `Color: rgb(120,140,88);`
Background color	`Backcolor`	
Italics	`Font-Italic="true"`	`Font-Style: italic;`
GridView border	`BorderColor`	`Table-border-color-light: Green;` `Table-border-color-dark: Red;`

Try It Out #7 — Formatting by Cascading Style Sheet

In this exercise, you will create a style for a GridView and use it on three GridViews spread across two pages. Then you will change the style and see how it rolls out to all of the GridViews. Last, you will create a second style and apply it to some of the GridViews. Note that the downloads provide more than one CSS to reflect its state after various steps. On your machine, you will create just a single CSS and change it as instructed.

1. Create a style sheet in the root of your site named `StyleSheetCh06-ver01.CSS`. Within it, create a style named GridViewOverall and add formatting as follows: a black background with white letters in a block font with bold italics. Set the border to be double. Double-check that the syntax is correct per the preceding paragraphs on style sheets. The page should look similar to the following (you may have picked a different font name and the attributes may be in a different order):

```
body {
}

.GridViewOverallForTio3{
background-color: black;
font-family: Arial;
color: white;
font-style: italic;
font-weight: bold;
border-style: double;
border-width: 5px;
}
```

2. Now create a page named `TIO-7-GridViewFormatByStyleSheet-1.aspx` in your `ch06` folder. Add two data source controls pointing to Northwind in SSE and two GridViews. The first should show the last names from Employees, the second the names of categories from the Categories table (see earlier TIOs if you forget the steps). Select the document and sets its `StyleSheet` to `StyleSheetCh06.CSS`. Now select each GridView and set its GridView CSS to your GridViewOverall from step 1 with the following highlighted lines:

```
<%@ Page Language="VB" %>
<html xmlns="http://www.w3.org/1999/xhtml" >
<head runat="server">
    <title>Ch06-TIO-7 GridView Formatting with Style Sheets - Page 1</title>
    <link href="~/StyleSheetCh06.css" type="text/css" rel="stylesheet" />
</head>
<body>
```

```
    <h3>Ch06-TIO-3 GridView Formatting with Style Sheets - Page 1</h3>
    <form id="form1" runat="server">

        <asp:GridView ID="NwEmployeesGridView" Runat="server"
                DataSourceID="NorthwindEmployeesSqlDataSource"
                CssClass="GridViewOverall" /> </div>

        <asp:GridView ID="NwCategoriesGridView" Runat="server"
                DataSourceID="NorthWindCategoriesSqlDataSource"
                CssClass="GridViewOverall" />

        <asp:SqlDataSource ID="NorthwindEmployeesSqlDataSource"  Runat="server"
            ConnectionString="<%$ ConnectionStrings:LocalSqlNorthwind %>"
          SelectCommand="Select LastName FROM Employees"/>

        <asp:SqlDataSource ID="NorthWindCategoriesSqlDataSource"  Runat="server"
            ConnectionString="<%$ ConnectionStrings:LocalSqlNorthwind %>"
          SelectCommand="Select CategoryName FROM Categories"/>
    </form>
</body></html>
```

3. Create a second page named `\ch06\TIO-7-GridViewFormatByStyleSheet-2.aspx` upon which you will display the CompanyName field from the Shippers table of Northwind. Again, format from the style sheet, as follows (in part):

```
<title>Ch06-TIO-7 GridView Formatting with Style Sheets - Page 2</title>
   ...
    <asp:GridView ID="NwShippersGridView" Runat="server"
    DataSourceID="NorthWindCategoriesSqlDataSource"
    CssClass="GridViewOverall" />

    <asp:SqlDataSource ID="NorthWindCategoriesSqlDataSource"  Runat="server"
        ConnectionString="<%$ ConnectionStrings:LocalSqlNorthwind %>"
      SelectCommand="Select CompanyName FROM Shippers"/>
```

4. Browse to the two pages and see how one style can be implemented to GridViews on any page in the Web site.

5. Change your style sheet to make GridViewOverall a wide gray border that appears outset, and make the font a typeface that is sans serif and about a quarter inch tall. Save the style sheet with the same name. In your browser, refresh your two ASPX pages to see the changes rolled out to all three grids.

```
body {
}

.GridViewOverallForTio3{
border-width: 10px;
border-color: Gray;
border-style: Outset;
font-family: Sans-Serif;
font-size: larger;
}
```

6. Now create a second style in your style sheet called GridViewBig, which does only one thing—sets the font to large.

```
body {
}

.GridViewOverallForTio3{
border-width: 10px;
border-color: Gray;
border-style: Outset;
font-names: SanSerif;
font-size: larger;
}

.GridViewBig{
font-size: xx-large;
}
```

7. Change the Categories GridView to utilize the GridViewBig style and view in your browser (as in download file version 3).

```
...
        <asp:GridView ID="NwCategoriesGridView" Runat="server"
            DataSourceID="NorthWindCategoriesSqlDataSource"
            CssClass="GridViewBig" />
...
```

How It Works #7—Formatting by Cascading Style Sheet

You start by creating your style sheet. With the VWD dialog for styles sheets, the `Body{}` style is automatically added by VWD. If you are not using VWD, keep in mind that you create additional CSS class definitions with a period at the beginning of the name. Don't forget the braces (`{}`) and use the syntax with a colon and semicolon. Do not use quotes around text values. The keywords for style sheets are different from what you use in attributes or properties. The CSS file is normally saved in the site's root.

You then created two pages with GridViews. You employ the style sheet with two commands. First, in the `<head>` you create a `<link>` to the name of the style sheet file. Note how easy it is to create the link's proper syntax by just clicking through the Properties pane in the designer. The second type of command is a property to set which style to use for each GridView.

When you make a change to the style sheet, the new format is automatically used by all GridViews employing that style. Likewise, it is very easy to switch a GridView to a different style.

Precedence of Styles

This and the preceding chapter have discussed many ways of formatting; in fact, there are six ways to set a format for a cell in a GridView. In the end, what is the order of precedence of these settings? There are two basic rules. First, smaller groups of cells have precedence over larger groups. So a setting for a column overrides a setting for the GridView. Second, formatting properties in the control have precedence over the same setting made in a CSS style sheet. Written out, you could view the hierarchy as follows, with a top-level GridView CSS having the least precedence and a column/field ItemStyle property taking precedence over all others:

GridView CssClass < GridView Style property < RowStyle CssClass < RowStyle property < Column/Field ItemStyle CssClass < Column/Field ItemStyle property

Because a row can be in a variety of states (alternating, selected, editable) at different times, it is possible for a row to have more than one applicable RowStyle at a time. When there are multiple conflicting RowStyles defined, they are applied in the following order of precedence:

RowStyle < AlternatingRowStyle < SelectedRowStyle < EditRowStyle or InsertRowStyle

If the properties of styles at different levels of precedence do not conflict with each other, the styles are merged instead. So, for example, if RowStyle defines `Font-Name="Arial"`, AlternatingRowStyle defines `BackColor="Green"`, and SelectedRowStyle defines `Font-Bold="true"`, the resulting rendered style for a selected alternating row would be Arial Bold with green background color.

Try It Out #8 — Precedence of Styles

In this exercise, you will set GridView cells to a background color in six different places and examine the results. You will use the colors in the following table. Note that the CSS value is always lighter but is the same hue as the value set in the equivalent specific attribute. Also note that the colors of lower frequency (red) are the least powerful in precedence, and the colors of highest frequency (green) are of the highest precedence. In general, the exercises of this book avoid color because they will not appear on the printed page, but in this case, color is a very useful tool for seeing the level of precedence.

Level	Background Color with Official WWW3 Name
GridView CSS	Light red ("pink")
GridView Style Property	Red ("red")
RowStyle CSS	Light yellow ("lemonchiffon")
RowStyle Property	Yellow ("yellow")
Column ItemStyle CSS	Light green ("lightgreen")
Column ItemStyle Property	Green ("green")

1. Start by creating a CSS style sheet named `PrecedenceStyleSheet.css` in the root of your site. Under the body style, create three substyles, as outlined in the following code. Note how all of the colors in the style sheet are the light-colored tints.

```
body {
}
.GridView{background-color: pink; }
.Row{background-color: lemonchiffon; }
.ColumnItem{background-color: lightgreen; }
```

2. Now create a new file named `TIO-8-Precedence.aspx`. Drag the ProductName, UnitPrice, and CategoryID columns from the Products table onto the page and complete the wizards. The page should now resemble the following (version 1 in downloads). Note that there is no color in the GridView.

```
<%@ page language="VB" %>
<script runat="server">
</script>

<html>
<head id="Head1" runat="server">
    <title>TIO-8 Precedence</title>
</head>
<body>
    <form id="Form1" runat="server">
        <H3>Chapter 6 TIO #8 Precedence</H3>

            <asp:GridView ID="GridView1" Runat="server"
            DataSourceID="NorthwindProducts"
            AutoGenerateColumns="False">
                <Columns>
                    <asp:BoundField HeaderText="ProductName"
                        DataField="ProductName"
                        SortExpression="ProductName" />
                    <asp:BoundField HeaderText="UnitPrice"
                        DataField="UnitPrice"
                        SortExpression="UnitPrice" />
                    <asp:BoundField HeaderText="CategoryID"
                        DataField="CategoryID"
                        SortExpression="CategoryID" />
                </Columns>
            </asp:GridView>

        <asp:SqlDataSource ID="NorthwindProducts"  Runat="server"
            ConnectionString="<%$ ConnectionStrings:LocalSqlNorthwind %>"
            SelectCommand="SELECT ProductName,UnitPrice,CategoryID FROM Products"/>

    </form>
</body>
</html>
```

3. Close the browser and, in Design view, select the page (document). In the Properties window, set the `StyleSheet` to `PrecedenceStyleSheet`. Now you can use the CSS styles in your controls.

4. Set the GridView property `CssClass="GridView"`. Save and take a look in the browser (version 2 in download) to observe the application of the pink backcolor.

5. Close the browser and, in VWD Design view, change the GridView backcolor to use a local attribute (not the CSS) set to Red. Now save and take a look in the browser (version 3 in download). Observe that a local setting (red) takes precedence over the `StyleSheet` setting (pink).

6. Let's move to the Row. Close the browser and switch to VWD in Design view. Select the GridView, and in the Properties window, find RowStyle and expand to find CSSClass. Set it to Row, save, and take a look in the browser (version 4 in the downloads). Observe that the data rows are now light yellow.

7. To see the precedence of local settings over CSS values, change the RowStyle to format the background with an attribute set to bright yellow (version 5 in the downloads). Do this in the designer by selecting the GridView and in the Properties window by setting RowStyle/backcolor to bright yellow. Save and take a look in the browser. Observe that a local setting overrides the CSS setting.

8. Last, you will work with the Column Item styles. Close the browser, and in the Designer view, select the GridView. Select Edit Columns and select UnitPrice. In the properties section of the dialog box, set ItemStyle/CssClass to ColumnRow. Save (as in download version 6) and take a look in the browser.

9. As with the other settings, you can override the CSS setting with a specific attribute in the UnitPrice column's ItemStyle to set the background to green (as in download version 7).

```
            <asp:GridView ID="GridView1" Runat="server"
            DataSourceID="NorthwindProducts"
            AutoGenerateColumns="False" CssClass="GridView" BackColor="Red">
                <Columns>
                    <asp:BoundField HeaderText="ProductName"
DataField="ProductName" SortExpression="ProductName" />
                    <asp:BoundField HeaderText="UnitPrice" DataField="UnitPrice"
SortExpression="UnitPrice">
                        <ItemStyle CssClass="ColumnItem" BackColor="Lime" />
                    </asp:BoundField>
                    <asp:BoundField HeaderText="CategoryID" DataField="CategoryID"
SortExpression="CategoryID" />
                </Columns>
                <RowStyle BackColor="Yellow" CssClass="Row" />
            </asp:GridView>
```

How It Works #8 — Precedence of Styles

Although repetitious, this exercise reviews almost all of the formatting you have done to sections of the GridView and emphasizes the priority given to each style setting when rendering the GridView. You can set the entire GridView background by a CSS or local attribute. Then you do the same with rows and column cells (items). Note that local settings take precedence over CSS settings and that smaller units of cells take precedence over larger blocks of cells.

Themes and Skins

One of the principal advantages of CSS style sheets is that they allow the look and feel of your pages to be maintained centrally in a single file, so it is not necessary to update multiple pages in your site just to change a style setting you want to propagate to all pages. Although CSS is a great way to define styles in the W3C standard format that applies to the HTML elements rendered by the control, there are many control properties that affect the look of a control that cannot be represented in a CSS style sheet. For example, consider the GridView GridLines property. It would be nice if you could also define this property in a single place to be used by all GridView controls in the site. Fortunately, ASP.NET 2.0 allows you to do this using a new feature called Themes.

A *theme* in ASP.NET 2.0 is a collection of skin files that are stored under an `App_Themes` subdirectory in the application root directory. A *skin file* is saved with the `.skin` extension and consists of a collection of control definitions with properties set on them. Each control definition will determine the properties to set for that control type across the entire site. For example, you could create a directory under the Web site root for a CustomBlue theme:

```
/ApplicationRoot
    /App_Themes
        /CustomBlue
            CustomBlue.skin
```

Inside the skin file, you can define a GridView control as follows. Note that the ID and DataSourceID properties on this control are intentionally left out, because they are not supported in a theme definition. The `<Columns>` collection is also left out, because each GridView in our site is likely to have a different set of fields. In fact, each control defines the set of properties that are themeable, which varies from control to control. Most often, the appearance properties of a control are themeable, whereas the behavioral properties are not. We set a few appearance and style properties on this control that we want to apply to all GridView controls in our site.

```
    <asp:GridView Font-Italic="true" ForeColor="LightBlue" BackColor="DarkBlue'
runat="server"/>
```

We then reference the theme from a page in our site that contains a GridView control with no style formatting specified on it (but bound to an appropriate data source). This is done using a `Page` directive at the top of the page:

```
<%@Page Theme="CustomBlue" %>
...
<asp:GridView ID="GridView1" DataSourceID="SqlDataSource1" runat="server"/>
```

Although the GridView in the page has no style properties defined on it, when you run the page, the properties defined in the skin file are automatically applied. So a theme is very much like a style sheet in that it can define a set of appearance/style definitions that can be maintained centrally but applied globally. In fact, a theme can also contain a CSS style sheet as well, so you can apply a CssClass property as part of a skin. Note that if you place a CSS style sheet named `CustomBlue.css` in the `CustomBlue` directory, it will automatically be applied to pages that reference this theme, without having to define a `<link>` tag on each page.

A skin file can also define properties that apply to only some (but not all) GridView controls in your site. To do this, add a SkinID property to the control definition in the skin file:

```
    <asp:GridView SkinID="RedGrid" BackColor="Red" runat="server"/>
```

Any GridView control in your site with a matching SkinID property will have this skin applied instead of the default GridView skin that applies to all other GridView controls.

Themes can actually be applied to a page in one of two ways:

- **As a Theme** — When applied as a Theme, the properties on the control are applied first, followed by any properties defined in the skin for the control. This is the setting used in the preceding example. This mode is typically used to customize the look of a site that was previously developed without a theme. In this mode, the theme style settings (properties defined in the skin file) always win over style settings defined by control properties in the target page.

- **As a StyleSheetTheme** — When applied as a StyleSheetTheme, the properties defined in the skin files for the theme will be applied first, followed by the properties defined on the control in the target page. In this mode, the control properties always win over the theme. This mode is useful when you want to use a theme like a style sheet, that is, when you are developing an application to serve as a central place to define the styles for controls in the application.

In the preceding example, if you try to set the ForeColor to Yellow on the GridView, the Theme ForeColor will win and it will be LightBlue anyway. If you want the control properties in the page to be applied *after* the theme properties, set the Theme as a StyleSheetTheme instead:

```
<%@Page StyleSheetTheme="CustomBlue" %>
...
<asp:GridView ID="GridView1" DataSourceID="SqlDataSource1" ForeColor="Yellow"
runat="server"/>
```

I recommend that you use `StyleSheetTheme` to apply your themes when you develop applications. Another big advantage of using `StyleSheetTheme` is that the VWD designer shows a preview of what the control will look like with the theme applied. As you will see in the following section, the AutoFormat dialog also allows you to easily preview and choose from the set of available skins in a StyleSheetTheme for a particular control.

Using Auto Format in Visual Studio

Visual Studio (and VWD) offers a smart task option for automatically formatting a GridView and other controls using a set of predefined style settings. This is a great way to get a nice-looking grid without having to define each and every style setting yourself.

To invoke the Auto Format dialog, first switch to Design view using the tabs at the bottom left. Select your GridView or DetailsView and open the smart task panel. Click Auto Format... and review the dozen or so Auto Format schemes. These designs include row colors, formatting of the header and footer, line settings, forecolor and backcolor, and other features. If you do not like the settings, note that there is a remove option at the top of the list. When you click OK, the Auto Format dialog applies its settings as a single operation. There is no ongoing enforcement of those settings, so you can first apply an AutoFormat and then make changes to individual properties within the control tag.

The Auto Format dialog will also show you the set of skins available in the applied StyleSheetTheme, if applicable. You can preview the look of each skin in the dialog, and when you choose to apply a skin, the dialog sets the SkinID on the control to apply the styles.

Common Mistakes

Following are some common mistakes made while customizing the appearance of tables:

- Using the wrong syntax or wrong keywords in a Cascading Style Sheet. The names of attributes in style sheets are different from those used in `asp:control` properties. You can get the correct set of keywords from `www.W3.org` or from style sheets you can examine by searching your drive for `*.css`. In addition, VS and VB IDEs will give you IntelliSense options for the correct keywords while editing a style sheet.

- Expecting a style setting to be applied but having that style overridden by a style of higher precedence.
- Improper placement of style tags within the GridView or DetailsView tag structure. If you are using VS or VWD, it is best to rely on the designer to automatically generate these tags as you make customizations through the property grid.
- Omitting the handling of empty datasets and `NULL` values.
- Attempting to set the properties of a GridView when the GridView is not selected. If your properties options are ASP.NET, Body, and Misc, you have the page (background) selected, not the GridView. Click once on the middle of the GridView to select it, and then you should have the property options Accessibility, Appearance, and so on.
- Malformed tags. It is easy, when typing and rearranging many attributes in a GridView, to end up without a closing angle bracket on the GridView tag. The error message "The server tag is not well formed" stops on the line the tag starts, which misleads your eye from the position of the problem — after the last attribute at the absence of the tag ending bracket (>).
- Changing the right property in the wrong control. In a large page with many asp:controls, it is easy to change a common tag or attribute in the wrong control and then wonder why your change is not taking effect.
- Forgetting that ControlStyle applies settings to controls in a GridView, such as HyperLinks or TextBox input controls in Edit mode.
- Attempting to use an incorrect `Theme` directory and file structure or attempting to use incorrect skin file contents (for example, setting properties in a skin that are not themeable, such as ID or DataSourceID).
- Trying to override a Skin property for a theme that is not applied as a StyleSheetTheme.

Summary

This chapter explained how to change the appearance of tabular data-bound controls, namely, the GridView and DetailsView. It discussed formatting at the levels of the entire table, rows, and cells within one column. Many formatting options in this chapter require the use of defined fields or columns, so AutoGenerateColumns must be turned off and your columns must be explicitly defined within `<Columns>` tags. The entire GridView is formatted by properties such as backcolor and font. These settings will be the defaults unless overridden by some finer degree of formatting.

You format entire rows using style properties of the GridView control. Each type of row can be specified, with RowStyle being the basic style applied to the records. AlternateRowStyle modifies the RowStyle for every other record. Header and Footer styles will be shown only if those rows are set to be visible in the GridView.

You can specify styles for cells within a single column using column or field ItemStyles. Note that you do not format an entire column. Rather, you set the formatting for one of the four kinds of cells within a column. This level of formatting is used when you want one column or a few columns to stand out from the default formatting of the table. These will get the highest precedence if there is a conflict of values for a given setting.

The lowest priority goes to formatting applied to the GridView as a whole. For each level, a format can be set either in the tag as a specific attribute or by reference to a Cascading Style Sheet. The advantage of the CSS is that it can then be applied to (and easily maintained for) many GridViews in your site.

The most effective way to handle formatting is with a CSS that is set up in a separate file. The ASPX page must have a `<LINK>` to the CSS file. Then, within a table control, row style, or column style, you set the CssClass to a style in the style sheet. A setting in a style sheet is overridden by a setting that is made directly in the control's property.

Another method for defining your site styles in a central location is using a Theme/StyleSheetTheme. A theme allows you to specify control properties and/or CSS style settings that should apply globally for all controls in your site. It is a powerful alternative to using CSS style sheets alone.

If no records are supplied by the Data Source, a single cell is created with the format of the GridView's EmptyDataRowStyle and EmptyDataText. It is easy to add a ToolTip to the GridView so that users have an additional item of explanation for the control.

VWD offers a tool to automatically apply a set of formats with a single click. This is a one-time operation at design time, and each setting can then be modified as desired. It also allows you to set skin definitions found in the applied StyleSheetTheme for your page.

The last chapter explained how to create the structure of GridViews and DetailViews. This chapter explained how to modify their appearance. The next chapter looks at how to change their behavior in two major ways: breaking a large set of records into smaller pages and sorting the set of records.

Exercises

1. Compare and contrast the term *header* as used in the GridView and the DetailsView controls.
2. State the precedence of formatting in different tags and files.
3. Describe the difference between the terms *borders* and *gridlines*.
4. Describe the three systems for defining a color in data-bound controls.
5. Describe the difference between cell spacing and cell padding.
6. Write the proper syntax for a dotted cell border.
7. Write the two syntaxes for setting a property for a style.
8. In what situation will the EmptyRowStyle be applied to a data-bound control?
9. Why does the DetailsView control have an InsertRow style but the GridView lacks that style?

7

Paging and Sorting Data

Paging and sorting in the GridView control represent the archetype of the advances in ASP.NET version 2.0. Microsoft saw features that everyone wants to utilize but that take considerable time and expertise to code in a set of functions. The ASP.NET team wrapped up the hundreds of lines of code that were necessary in ASP.NET 1.0 and exposed them as simple Boolean (true/false) properties in ASP.NET 2.0. With a single click of a check box in the designer, you can now add paging or sorting to a table.

This chapter discusses the basics of sorting and paging and then covers some embellishments that solve common real-world problems. You will do six exercises, as follows:

Try It Out	Topic
1	Sorting Basics
2	Requirements for Sorting
3	Sort Expressions
4	Paging Basics
5	Pager Settings
6	Paging, Sorting, and Selecting Together

Paging is the ability to display only portions of the records at one time in a GridView — for example, just the first ten products. A set of navigational controls then allows the viewer to switch to seeing other sets, or pages, of products. Paging gives the page designer the opportunity to reduce "information overload" for the user, albeit at some loss in comprehensiveness. Note that this "paging" is not concerned with switching between full ASPX pages in a Web site. That is a job for the site navigation features.

Sorting is the ability to change the order in which records are listed in a GridView. With Sorting enabled, a user can find a given record more easily and make associations between similar records (such as all employees from one state). These techniques are very flexible in ASP.NET 2.0, so you will start with some basic scenarios and then study the enhancements and potential conflicts.

Sorting

Sorting is a special modification of the header row in GridView. When turned on, the header text for each column becomes a clickable hyperlink. When clicked, a header's column will resort itself according to the values in the column, toggling between an ascending or a descending sort order each time the link is clicked. The GridView first checks whether the column is currently sorted. If not, it sorts the records in increasing order based on the field values under the clicked header. If the column is already sorted on that field, the GridView reverses the sort order. Note that the DetailsView control does not support sorting because only one record is displayed at a time. However, you can change the order in which records will be displayed by using an `ORDER BY` clause in the SelectCommand.

Try It Out #1 — Sorting Basics

This exercise gives the Northwind employees a way to look at all of the products in a sortable GridView (just the ID, Name, and Price fields).

1. Create a new folder for Chapter 7 and a file named `TIO-1-SortingBasics.aspx`. Add code to create a GridView of the Northwind Products' ID, Name, and Price fields. Recall that since Try It Out #2 of Chapter 2, you have been using a connection string stored in the Web.config. Review that Try It Out if you are unsure of the connection code that follows.
2. Open the GridView's smart task panel and turn on Enable Sorting. Save the page and observe the results in your browser.

```
<%@ Page Language="VB" %>
<html xmlns="http://www.w3.org/1999/xhtml" >
<head runat="server"><title>Ch07-TIO1-SortingBasics</title></head>
<body>
    <h3>Chapter 7 TIO #1 Sorting Basics</h3>
    <form id="form1" runat="server">
    <div>

        <asp:SqlDataSource ID="NorthwindProductsSqlDataSource"  Runat="server"
          ConnectionString="<%$ ConnectionStrings:LocalSqlNorthwind %>"
          SelectCommand="
            SELECT ProductID, ProductName, UnitPrice
            FROM Products"/>

        <asp:GridView ID="GridView1" Runat="server"
            DataSourceID="NorthwindProductsSqlDataSource"
            AllowSorting="True"
            AutoGenerateColumns=true>
        </asp:GridView>
    </div>
    </form>
</body>
</html>
```

How It Works #1 — Sorting Basics

Enabling sorting in Visual Web Developer just means putting a check in the Enable Sorting check box in the GridView smart task panel. In ASP.NET, this corresponds to a Boolean `AllowSorting` property set to `true`. The following source code enables sorting:

```
<asp:GridView
        ID="GridView1"
        Runat="server"
        AutoGenerateColumns=true
        DataSourceID="... "
        AllowSorting=true />
```

Requirements to Enable Sorting

As you saw in the preceding simple case, sorting works with a single click in the designer. However, it will work only if the data source supports sorting. Different data sources support sorting under different conditions, and some data sources do not support sorting at all (for example, XmlDataSource). The SqlDataSource control supports sorting when its `DataSourceMode` = `DataSet`. Similarly, the ObjectDataSource control supports sorting when the `SelectMethod` returns a DataSet, DataTable, or DataView. The reason for this is that the data source directly applies the `SortExpression` from the GridView to the `DataView.Sort` property, which can be obtained from any of the aforementioned types. When the `SqlDataSource.DataSourceMode` = `DataReader`, sorting is not supported.

In addition to data source support, GridView requires four prerequisites for sorting to be allowed. These are often set by the designer by default, but if you begin to customize columns, you will have to ensure that you meet the following requirements. Note that some of these requirements are set at the level of the GridView and some within each field to be sorted. A fifth, optional prerequisite is generally also used.

- **`GridView.ShowHeader`** — Because the sort interface is rendered in the header, the GridView as a whole must have `ShowHeader` set to `true`. `True` is the default, but if you change it to `false`, you eliminate sorting.
- **`HeaderText`** — This property is set on a field object (for example, BoundField) in the GridView's Columns collection. Again, because sorting is exposed to the user through the header, you need some text rendered so that the user can click to invoke sorting. Again, this is the default, so generally this is not a problem.
- **`GridView.AllowSorting`** — This property, when set to `true`, makes the built-in sorting method available.
- **`SortExpression`** — This property is set on a field object (for example, BoundField) in the GridView's Columns collection. Sorting works only if you have designated what values to use in the sort for each column. By default, the `SortExpression` is set to the data field name.
- **`Header Style` (Optional)** — This property is set on a field object (for example, BoundField) in the GridView's Columns collection. Although the default is fine, most designers want to enhance the item that can be clicked to invoke sorting. This formatting can be set for all headers in the `GridView.HeaderStyle` or for only one column in the `Field.HeaderStyle`.

With the preceding settings, all columns will be sortable. But that does not always make sense; for example, it does not make sense to sort BLOB or GUI data types. To turn off sorting for one column, open the GridView's Edit Column dialog, select the column, and set its `SortExpression` to an empty string (nothing).

There is an advanced sorting technique supported by both SqlDataSource and ObjectDataSource that is not discussed in detail in this text. You can set the `SortParameterName` property to the name of a parameter in your SelectCommand (or SelectMethod) that corresponds to the `SortExpression`, and then in the implementation of your stored procedure or method you can apply your own sorting (using `ORDER BY`) by parsing the expression that is passed in. This technique makes it possible to support sorting even in DataReader mode.

Try It Out #2 — Requirements for Sorting

This exercise returns to the Northwind Employees table but with a GridView that adds sortable columns rather than using `AutoGenerateColumns=true`. To review the sorting requirements previously mentioned, you will then create some points of failure. You finish with some formatting at two levels.

1. Create a new file named `TIO-2-SortRequirements.aspx`. Add a GridView that displays BoundFields for EmployeeID and both first and last names of employees from Northwind in the local SSE. Enable sorting with the check box in the Edit Columns dialog or turn on sorting from the GridView's smart task panel. Test the page; the source code will be similar to the following:

```
<%@ Page Language="VB" %>
<html xmlns="http://www.w3.org/1999/xhtml" >
<head runat="server"><title>Ch07-TIO2-SortingRequirements</title></head>
<body>
    <h3>Chapter 7 TIO #2 SortingRequirements</h3>
    <form id="form1" runat="server">
    <div>

        <asp:SqlDataSource ID="NorthwindEmployeesSqlDataSource"  Runat="server"
          ConnectionString="<%$ ConnectionStrings:LocalSqlNorthwind %>"
          SelectCommand="
            SELECT EmployeeID, FirstName, LastName, Photo
            FROM Employees"/>

        <asp:GridView ID="GridView1" Runat="server"
            DataSourceID="NorthwindEmployeesSqlDataSource"
                AutoGenerateColumns="False"
                AllowSorting="True">
            <Columns>
                <asp:BoundField HeaderText="EmployeeID"
                        DataField="EmployeeID"
                        SortExpression="EmployeeID" />
                <asp:BoundField HeaderText="FirstName"
                        DataField="FirstName"
                        SortExpression="FirstName" />
                <asp:BoundField HeaderText="LastName"
                        DataField="LastName"
                        SortExpression="LastName" />
            </Columns>
        </asp:GridView>
        </div>
    </form>
</body>
</html>>
```

2. Now let's see how this page fails when you leave out some of these requirements. Using the GridView Edit Columns dialog, do the following; after each modification, test the page in the browser:

   a. Remove the header text from the FirstName column.

   b. Remove the sort expression from the EmployeeID column.

   c. Set the sort expression for the LastName column to `EmployeeID`.

   d. Save the page as `TIO-2-SortRequirements-2.aspx` and test. The page source code should now be similar to the following:

```
<asp:GridView ID="GridView1" Runat="server"
        DataSourceID="NorthwindEmployeesSqlDataSource"
        AutoGenerateColumns="False"
        AllowSorting="True">
    <Columns>
        <asp:BoundField HeaderText="EmployeeID"
                DataField="EmployeeID" />
        <asp:BoundField
                DataField="FirstName"
                SortExpression="FirstName" />
        <asp:BoundField HeaderText="LastName"
                DataField="LastName"
                SortExpression="LastName" />
        <asp:ImageField HeaderText="Photo"
                DataField="Photo"
                SortExpression="LastName" />
    </Columns>
</asp:GridView>
```

How It Works #2 — Requirements for Sorting

When setting up a GridView to be sortable, you must complete several tasks. First, double-check that your data source (including its modes) supports sorting. Then check that each column that should be sortable has a heading text and a sort expression. Double-check that the sort expression matches the field of the column. Of course, all of this is done automatically and correctly for you when you turn on sorting in the VWD.

Sort Expressions

ASP.NET 2.0 GridView separates the properties for the data to display and the data to use in the sorting. In most cases, these will be the same. But you will look at some cases where you may want to break out of the mold.

First, your initial order of records should be set in the SQL clause of the data source select command. This is not a GridView sort expression issue, but it answers a common question. The SQL `ORDER BY` clause also offers the `DESC` option to reverse the sort order. For example, to display employee records starting with the most recently hired, use the following:

```
SelectCommand="
  SELECT EmployeeID, FirstName, LastName, HireDate
  FROM Employees
  ORDER BY HireDate DESC"
```

Second, you can perform sorting on an alternate field when a column is unsortable. For example, if a user clicks on the heading for an employee photo, the GridView will actually sort by last name.

Sometimes you want to sort on a value that is not in any field, for example, the result of a string function such as `TRIM()`, `LEFT()`, or `MID()`. This cannot be done directly in the sort expression. However, you can add a column to your data source control SelectCommand (SQL `SELECT` statement) and use it as a sort expression rather than display the column in the GridView.

Tie breaking in the sort requires some custom code. The way a sort works is to check if there is an `ASC` or a `DESC` at the end of the SortExpression of the column that was clicked to sort. If there is an `ASC` or a `DESC`, the control deletes it and replaces it with the opposite. If there is no `ASC` or `DESC`, a `DESC` is added (because the default is `ASC`). The problem comes if there is a tie-breaking field, which has the syntax `PrimaryField ASC, Tie-BreakerField ASC`. When ASP.NET 2.0 reverses the direction at the end of the expression, there is no change to the primary sort field. You can solve the problem by ignoring the built-in sort feature and substituting your sort expressions based on a sort order that you track in a variable held in `ViewState`. The specifics follow in an exercise.

> *More information on tiebreaking is available at* `http://msdn.microsoft.com/library/default.asp?url=/library/en-us/cpref/html/frlrfsystemdatadataviewclass sorttopic.asp`.

Try It Out #3 — Sort Expressions

This exercise presents the table of orders from Northwind with several sorting options. First, you build the default. Then, limit the sort to just Employees and use CustomerID for a tiebreaker. You will see some problems, however, and replace the default sorting behavior with custom code.

1. Create a page named `TIO-3-SortExpressionBasic` and build a GridView to show just the OrderID, CustomerID, and EmployeeID from the Orders table of Northwind. Using the GridView's smart task panel, turn on sorting. Save and test the page, which will be similar to the following code. Depending on how you build the page (dragging fields from database explorer versus dragging controls from the toolbar and setting properties), there may be more or less lines in your page, particularly sets of `<parameters>`.

```
<%@ Page Language="VB" %>
<!DOCTYPE html PUBLIC "-//W3C//DTD XHTML 1.1//EN"
"http://www.w3.org/TR/xhtml11/DTD/xhtml11.dtd">
<script runat="server">
</script>
<html xmlns="http://www.w3.org/1999/xhtml" >
<head runat="server">
    <title>Ch07-Tio-03-SortExpressions-ver1</title>
</head>
<body>
    <h2>
        Chapter 7 Tio #03 Sort Expressions version 1
    </h2>
    <form id="form1" runat="server">
    <div>
        <asp:GridView ID="GridView1" Runat="server"
                DataKeyNames="OrderID"
```

```
                DataSourceID="SqlDataSource1"
                EmptyDataText="There are no data records to display."
                AutoGenerateColumns="False"
AllowSorting="True">
            <Columns>
                <asp:BoundField ReadOnly="True" HeaderText="OrderID"
DataField="OrderID" SortExpression="OrderID"></asp:BoundField>
                <asp:BoundField HeaderText="CustomerID" DataField="CustomerID"
SortExpression="CustomerID"></asp:BoundField>
                <asp:BoundField HeaderText="EmployeeID" DataField="EmployeeID"
SortExpression="EmployeeID"></asp:BoundField>
            </Columns>
        </asp:GridView>
        <asp:SqlDataSource ID="SqlDataSource1" Runat="server"
       ProviderName="<%$ ConnectionStrings:LocalSqlNorthwind.ProviderName %>"
      SelectCommand="SELECT [OrderID], [CustomerID], [EmployeeID] FROM [Orders]"
        ConnectionString="<%$ ConnectionStrings:LocalSqlNorthwind %>">
        </asp:SqlDataSource>
    </div></form></body></html>
```

2. For the rest of this exercise, you will work on the objective of being able to sort the table on EmployeeID with CustomerID as a tiebreaker. Regardless of whether the EmployeeID is ascending or descending, the CustomerIDs within one employee should always be ascending. Start with two steps: First, eliminate sorting on columns other than Employees by deleting their sort expressions and then change the sort expression for EmployeeID to have a tiebreaker, as follows. You can make the change in Source view either directly in the code or in the Properties window after selecting the bound field in Source view. Save as version 2, open in the browser, and observe the problem. You can try adding sort directions as in the alternate code following this listing.

```
<asp:GridView
...
   <Columns>
     <asp:BoundField
        ReadOnly="True"
         HeaderText="OrderID"
         DataField="OrderID"></asp:BoundField>
     <asp:BoundField
         HeaderText="CustomerID"
         DataField="CustomerID"></asp:BoundField>
     <asp:BoundField
         HeaderText="EmployeeID"
         DataField="EmployeeID"
         SortExpression="EmployeeID,CustomerID"></asp:BoundField>
   </Columns>
        </asp:GridView>
```

Here is the alternate code to try for the preceding sort expression:

```
SortExpression="EmployeeID ASC,CustomerID ASC"
```

or

```
SortExpression="EmployeeID DESC,CustomerID ASC"
```

3. Before adding the custom script, look more closely at what is happening. Add two labels and then the following code. The code will display the contents of two sort properties in the labels: sort order and sort expression. Save as version 3 and experiment with the preceding alternate sort expressions. The object e in the script represents the GridView. This script is running before the re-sort is performed by the GridView.

```
<%@ Page Language="VB" %>
<!DOCTYPE html PUBLIC "-//W3C//DTD XHTML 1.1//EN"
"http://www.w3.org/TR/xhtml11/DTD/xhtml11.dtd">
<script runat="server">

Sub Page_Load(ByVal sender As Object, ByVal e As System.EventArgs)
        If Not IsPostBack Then
            ViewState("SortAscending") = False
        End If
    End Sub


    Sub GridView1_Sorting(ByVal sender As Object, ByVal e As
System.Web.UI.WebControls.GridViewSortEventArgs)
        Label1.Text = "Sort Expression = " & e.SortExpression
        Label2.Text = "Sort Direction = " & e.SortDirection
    End Sub
</script>
<html xmlns="http://www.w3.org/1999/xhtml" >
...
    <div>
        <asp:Label ID="Label1" Runat="server" Text="Label"></asp:Label><br />
        <asp:Label ID="Label2" Runat="server" Text="Label"></asp:Label><br />
        <asp:GridView
          ...
```

4. Now add the following code to solve the problem (discussed in depth in the How It Works section that follows). Save the page as version 4 and test.

```
...
<script runat="server">
    Sub GridView1_Sorting(ByVal sender As Object, ByVal e As
System.Web.UI.WebControls.GridViewSortEventArgs)
        Label1.Text = "Sort Expression = " & e.SortExpression
        Label2.Text = "Sort Direction = " & e.SortDirection

        If ViewState("MyKey") Then
            e.SortExpression = "EmployeeID DESC,CustomerID ASC"
        Else
            e.SortExpression = "EmployeeID ASC,CustomerID ASC"
        End If
        ViewState("MyKey") = Not ViewState("MyKey")
    End Sub
</script>
...
```

How It Works #3 — Sort Expressions

In version 1, you just set up a page and turn on sorting. If you drag and drop from the database explorer, you will have additional lines such as insert and update commands and parameters. They do not affect the exercise.

Version 2 adds a tiebreaker `SortExpression="EmployeeID,CustomerID"`, but this creates problems. When the GridView sorts, it reads the order from the end of the sort expression, deletes it, and replaces it with the opposite. So, in this case, it is reading the sort order from CustomerID. By default, that is `ASC`, so `ASC` is clipped off and replaced with `DESC`. The next time, `... CustomerID DESC` is changed to `... Customer ASC`. Notice that our primary sort field, EmployeeID, is never touched.

You can get a glimpse of the behavior using a standard troubleshooting technique, displaying control properties on a development page. Version 3 shows you the sort properties. Coding is covered in detail at the end of the book, but for now, notice the new property of the GridView control to run the Sub named `GridView_OnSorting`. This Sub will use `e` to represent the GridView and picks up two of the GridView's properties to display in the labels.

The problem is solved in several steps. First is to create a variable in the ViewState named `SortAscending` that keeps track of the current sort order. This relieves the page of relying on the GridView's `SortOrder` property, which checks only the last field. When the `ViewState("SortAscending")` is set to `TRUE`, the first item on the page is loaded in the Sub named `Page_Load`. Subsequent sorts will cause the `ViewState("SortAscending")` to flip to the opposite value.

Second, you create an exact sort expression for each of the two cases:

- Employees `ASC` with tiebreaker of Customer `ASC`
- EmployeeID `DESC` with tiebreaker of Customer `ASC`

Then an `IF` structure decides which sort expression to use. Each time a sort occurs, there is an inversion of the value for a variable stored in the ViewState named `SortAscending`; it flip-flops between `true` and `false`. The first time the page loads, the GridView will be in the order of the primary key in the table (OrderID). At this point, the custom code has not been executed. The first sort click will run the Sub and check `ViewState("SortAscending")` to find that the variable does not exist, which evaluates to `false`, so the `e.SortExpression` is set to the one with EmployeeID `ASC`. At the end of the Sub, the value in `ViewState("SortAscending")` is flipped to its opposite.

Paging

When paging is added to a GridView or DetailsView, the following happens:

- Only a portion of the total number of records is shown.
- The GridView creates a pager UI used to navigate between records.

DetailsView displays one record of the total records at a time, as opposed to GridView, which displays a few records of the total at a time.

> ***Paging* is a feature to control the display of sets of records within a GridView. Do not confuse paging with *page navigation,* which is a set of features to help the user move between entire pages on the site.**

Enabling Paging

Paging can work only if the data source supports paging directly or returns a list that implements the ICollection interface. The GridView uses this interface to determine the total number of rows in the collection (using the `Count` property) and for random access into the collection at a specified index (so that it can display the correct subset of rows). When `DataSourceMode=DataSet`, paging will work because the DataView retrieved from the DataSet implements ICollection (DataSet is special-cased). GridView paging will not work if `DataSourceMode=DataReader`. For an ObjectDataSource, your SelectMethod must return a DataSet, DataTable, or DataView or a list that implements ICollection in order for paging to work.

To summarize:

1. ICollection is required for GridView to perform paging.
2. This "just works" for DataSet and DataTable, because GridView knows how to extract the ICollection from the corresponding DataView.
3. GridView is requesting all rows from the data source and only rendering a subset.

To do custom paging where only the subset of rows is selected in the first place (a performance optimization), use `ObjectDataSource.EnablePaging` (this technique is outside the scope of this book).

Enabling paging requires only one setting in the GridView control to work: set `AllowPaging=true`. This single setting sets up the entire paging function with defaults, a procedure that would have taken at least several hours of programmer time in the older versions of ASP.NET. A simple ASPX page like the following yields a HTML page as shown. Note the grid-wide pager column at the bottom.

Try It Out #4 — Paging Basics

Create a new page named `TIO-4-PagingBasics.aspx`. Drag onto the page the OrderID, CustomerID, OrderDate, and Freight fields from the Orders table of Northwind. On the GridView's smart task panel, enable paging. Open the page in your browser and enjoy one-click paging.

```
<%@ Page Language="VB" %>
<!DOCTYPE html PUBLIC "-//W3C//DTD XHTML 1.1//EN"
"http://www.w3.org/TR/xhtml11/DTD/xhtml11.dtd">
<html xmlns="http://www.w3.org/1999/xhtml" >
<head runat="server">
    <title>Ch7-TIO-4-PagingBasics</title>
</head>
<body>
<h3>Chapter 7 TIO #4 Paging Basics</h3>
```

```
<form id="form1" runat="server">
<div>
    <asp:SqlDataSource ID="NorthwindOrdersSqlDataSource"  Runat="server"
      ConnectionString="<%$ ConnectionStrings:LocalSqlNorthwind %>"
      SelectCommand="
            SELECT OrderID, CustomerID, OrderDate, Freight
            FROM Orders"/>;

    <asp:GridView ID="GridView1" Runat="server"
        DataSourceID="NorthwindOrdersSqlDataSource"
        AutoGenerateColumns=true
        AllowPaging=true>
    </asp:GridView>
</div>
</form></body></html>
```

How It Works #4 — Paging Basics

In earlier versions of ASP.NET, this task took hours to custom code. Today, it requires a single click of a check box in the designer. Notice in the following code that a single `AllowPaging` property of the GridView turns on paging.

```
<asp:GridView ID="GridView1" Runat="server"
    DataSourceID="NorthwindOrdersSqlDataSource"
    AutoGenerateColumns=true
    AllowPaging=true>
      </asp:GridView>
```

This is almost criminally easy.

Customizing Paging and the Pager

Paging creates a new row in the GridView called the pager row. This is different from sorting, which modifies the header row. You can format the pager row as a whole and format the clickable navigation links within the pager.

The properties to control and format paging are located across three locations on the GridView:

- Some are simple properties directly on the GridView control, such as `PageSize`. These control the basic pager settings.
- Some are subproperties on the GridView `PagerStyle` property, persisted as a `<PagerStyle>` subtag under the `<GridView>` tag. These control the appearance of the pager.
- Some are subproperties on the GridView `PagerSettings` property, persisted as a `<PagerSettings>` subtag under the `<GridView>` tag. These control the behavior of the pager.

A confusing point is that some of these are available in more than one location. When there are multiple options, your best choice is in the `PagerSettings` tag to improve readability and conform to the practice of the VWD designer.

Location	Paging Properties

In the `<GridView>` tag	`AllowPaging`
	`PageSize`
	`PageCount` (read-only)
	`PageIndex`

In the `<PagerStyle>` tag	Font, color CSS class Alignment (other formatting)
In the `<PagerSettings>` tag	`Mode` (what links will be shown in the pager) `ImageURLs` and `Text` for pager links `PageButtonCount` Position

`AllowPaging` within the `<GridView>` tag was already mentioned; the other option is to set the `PageSize` property of the GridView in the designer. The resulting code follows.

```
<asp:GridView ID="GridView1" Runat="server" ...
AllowPaging="True"
PageSize="5"
...>
```

The `PagerStyle` contains the same kinds of formatting that we discussed regarding other row styles. You can set the color, font, and alignment of the text in the pager cell. If working in Source view, recall that any row styles, including `PagerStyle`, must be wholly located between the `<asp:GridView>` and `</asp:GridView>` tags, as follows:

```
<asp:GridView ...>
          <Columns>
                    ...
          </Columns>

        <PagerStyle ... >
         </PagerStyle>

        <PagerSettings ... >
         </PagerSettings>

</asp:GridView>
```

`PagerSettings` contains the most interesting and individualized properties for paging. `Mode` defines what kinds of clickable links to display in the pager cell.

```
<PagerSettings
     Mode=NextPreviousFirstLast
</PagerSettings>
```

The most constrained mode option is `Next Previous`, which does not allow the user to jump out of the page sequence. An alternative is `Numeric`, which gives the user the ability to jump to any page. Both of these options can be combined with `First Last` and `Next Previous`.

`PagerSettings` also supports flexibility in how a clickable link is rendered. The properties that end in "text" (`FirstPageText`, `LastPageText`, and so on) accept a literal value such as "Click here for last page." The properties that end in "URL" (`LastPageURL`, `NextPageURL`, and so on) typically accept the name of an image file. If you specify both a text and an image, ASP.NET will use the `ImageURL`.

```
<PagerSettings
    Mode=NextPreviousFirstLast
    FirstPageText="Jump to first page"
    NextPageImageUrl="PageDown.gif"
    PreviousPageImageUrl="PageUp.gif"
    LastPageText="Jump to last page">
</PagerSettings>
```

The final setting in `<PagerSettings>` is for the `PageButtonCount`, which determines, if the mode is set to `Numeric`, how many numbers are shown. If more pages are available than shown, an ellipsis appears.

Simple design changes can improve the appearance of your GridViews with paging enabled. If your data values are of different widths, your resulting GridView will become wider or narrower as the user pages because the browser will render each column only wide enough to accommodate the longest values in that set of records. Setting your column widths as follows gives a consistent appearance.

Try It Out #5 — Pager Settings

The Products table has about 80 items, but only about 25 rows fit in the vertical height of a screen. Let's enable paging and present some GIF images to allow the user to click through the pages.

1. Download from the Wrox site and save in your `ch07` folder two GIF images named `PageUp` and `PageDown`. Alternatively, search your hard drive for `*.gif` and pick two that look appropriate.
2. Create a page named `TIO-5-PagerSettings-1.aspx` and drag from the DataExplorer the ProductID, Name, and UnitPrice fields from the Products table of the `(local)\SqlExpress` connection onto the page. To start, do not do any modification of the GridView beyond the defaults. The source code should be similar to the following. Note that the lines in gray may or may not be added by VWD, depending on whether you do a drag-and-drop from DataExplorer or whether you drag controls from the toolbar. There may also be some variation in the final beta release. In any case, the gray lines do not affect our discussion of paging. Save and check in your browser.

```
<%@ Page Language="VB" %>
<!DOCTYPE html PUBLIC "-//W3C//DTD XHTML 1.1//EN"
"http://www.w3.org/TR/xhtml11/DTD/xhtml11.dtd">
<script runat="server">
</script>
<html xmlns="http://www.w3.org/1999/xhtml" >
<head runat="server">
    <title>ch07-TIO-05-PagingFormat-1</title>
</head>
<body>
```

```
    <h3>Chapter 07 TIO #05 Paging Formats version 1</h3>
    <form id="form1" runat="server">
    <div>
        <asp:GridView ID="GridView1" Runat="server"
            DataKeyNames="ProductID"
            DataSourceID="SqlDataSource1"
            EmptyDataText="There are no data records to display."
            AutoGenerateColumns="False"
            >
            <Columns>
                <asp:BoundField ReadOnly="True" HeaderText="ProductID"
DataField="ProductID" SortExpression="ProductID"></asp:BoundField>
                <asp:BoundField HeaderText="ProductName" DataField="ProductName"
SortExpression="ProductName"></asp:BoundField>
                <asp:BoundField HeaderText="UnitPrice" DataField="UnitPrice"
SortExpression="UnitPrice"></asp:BoundField>
            </Columns>
        </asp:GridView>
        <asp:SqlDataSource ID="SqlDataSource1" Runat="server"
            ProviderName="<%$ ConnectionStrings:LocalSqlNorthwind.ProviderName %>"
            SelectCommand="SELECT [ProductID], [ProductName], [UnitPrice] FROM
[Products]"
            ConnectionString="<%$ ConnectionStrings:LocalSqlNorthwind %>">
            <DeleteParameters>
                <asp:Parameter Type="Int32" Name="ProductID"></asp:Parameter>
            </DeleteParameters>
            <InsertParameters>
                <asp:Parameter Type="String" Name="ProductName"></asp:Parameter>
                <asp:Parameter Type="Decimal" Name="UnitPrice"></asp:Parameter>
            </InsertParameters>
            <UpdateParameters>
                <asp:Parameter Type="String" Name="ProductName"></asp:Parameter>
                <asp:Parameter Type="Decimal" Name="UnitPrice"></asp:Parameter>
                <asp:Parameter Type="Int32" Name="ProductID"></asp:Parameter>
            </UpdateParameters>
        </asp:SqlDataSource>
    </div>
    </form>
</body>
</html>
```

3. Select the GridView, and in the Properties window, enable paging of seven records per page; in the pager settings, set the mode to display page links for next, previous, first, and last. Save `TIO-5-PagerSettings-2.aspx` and have a look in your browser.

```
        <asp:GridView ID="GridView1" Runat="server"
            DataSourceID="SqlDataSource1"
            DataKeyNames="ProductID"
            EmptyDataText="There are no data records to display."
            AutoGenerateColumns="False"
            AllowPaging="True"
            PageSize="7">
            <PagerSettings Mode="NextPreviousFirstLast"></PagerSettings>
            <Columns> ... </Columns>
        </asp:GridView>
```

4. Again, select the GridView in Design view, and in the Properties window ➪ Paging ➪ Pager Settings, set the first- and last-page links to display text, as follows. You may want to include some spaces as shown. Save as version 3 and examine in your browser, jumping to the first and last page to see all options of the pager text.

```
<PagerSettings
    Mode=NextPreviousFirstLast
    FirstPageText="Jump to first page    "
    LastPageText="    Jump to last page">
</PagerSettings>
```

5. Improve the pager by giving it a gray background and using the icons to represent moving to the next and previous pages. These properties are in the Properties window ➪ Styles ➪ Pager Style. Save as version 4 and inspect in your browser.

```
<asp:GridView ID="GridView1" Runat="server"
DataSourceID="adsNW"
AutoGenerateColumns=false
AllowPaging="true"
PageSize=7>

         <PagerStyle
             Backcolor=#f0f0f0>
         </PagerStyle>

         <PagerSettings
             Mode=NextPreviousFirstLast
             FirstPageText="Jump to first page"
             NextPageImageUrl="PageDown.gif"
             PreviousPageImageUrl="PageUp.gif"
             LastPageText="Jump to last page">
         </PagerSettings>
...
</asp:GridView>
```

6. Save as version 5 and switch the mode to `NumericFirstLast`. Note that when you use `Numeric` there is no opportunity for setting text or images.

```
<PagerSettings
    Mode=NumericFirstLast
     FirstPageText="Jump to first page"
    NextPageImageUrl="PageDown.gif"
    PreviousPageImageUrl="PageUp.gif"
    LastPageText="Jump to last page">
</PagerSettings>
```

How It Works #5 — Pager Settings

You turned on paging with a single property in the GridView control: `AllowPaging`. You then began to override defaults, starting with setting the page size (also in the GridView). In step 5, you changed the `PagerStyle` in the same way that you changed the `HeaderStyle` in a previous chapter.

You can make modifications to the appearance of the pager links themselves. You observed both creating your own text and using an image instead of the default >> and << symbols. Last, you observed how the `Numeric` option gives useful feedback but is not modifiable.

Note that there is another option for customizing the pager that is not discussed here, which is using the `PagerTemplate` property to fully customize the UI for paging. Templates are discussed in more detail in Chapter 10.

Paging Theory and Alternatives

Paging is performed at the level of the data-bound control. The data source control retrieves all of the records from the database, as defined in the SELECT command, and puts them into a data set. The data-bound control gets all of the records from the data source control, displays the current set, and destroys the rest. This model works well for one-click enablement, as you have observed in this chapter. However, records can be retrieved from the database and stored in the data sets that are never used.

An alternative is to have data source–level paging that would work with the database to retrieve only one set of records at a time, thus reducing the database read and reducing the size of the data set held in server memory. This option can be implemented in the beta release using an `ObjectDataSource` control. Look to future releases (or third-party controls) for implementation with Microsoft SQL Server.

Relationship of Sorting, Paging, and Selecting

A number of questions arise when paging and sorting are used together. Fortunately, they are resolved in a logical way by the internal GridView code. But it is important for you as a designer to understand what will happen when these features intersect.

- When you perform a sort, it is for all of the records in the GridView, not only those that are in the set of the current page.
- When you perform a sort, your page is automatically reset back to page 1 of the new sort order.
- If a row is selected and a new sort is performed, the selected style stays on the physical row. The style does not move with the record.

By design, selection corresponds to the UI, not the underlying data row. You can set `SelectedIndex = -1` in the sorting and paging events to unselect the row when one of these operations is performed. The more difficult task is retaining the selection on the specific data row after data is paged and sorted or rows are inserted/deleted/updated. To do this, you would retain the `SelectedDataKey` for the user-selected row and then enumerate each visible row in the GridView looking for this key to programmatically set the selection after a sort, a page, or an insert event.

Try It Out #6 — Paging, Sorting, and Selecting Together

In this exercise, you will create a GridView that has paging, sorting, and selecting all enabled. Then you will observe its behavior.

1. Create an ASPX file named `TIO-6-PageAndSortAndSelect` that displays the ID, Name, and Price fields of the Products table, with the ability to page five records at a time, sort, and select a record. Make the selected record appear with a light gray background. Save and compare with the following solution:

```
<%@ Page Language="VB" %>
<html xmlns="http://www.w3.org/1999/xhtml" >
<head runat="server">
    <title>Ch07-Tio6-PagingAndSortingAndSelecting</title>
</head>
<body>
    <h3>Chapter 7 TIO # 6 Paging and Sorting and Selecting Together</h3>
    <form id="form1" runat="server">
    <div>
        <asp:SqlDataSource ID="NorthwindProductsSqlDataSource" Runat="server"
          ConnectionString="<%$ ConnectionStrings:LocalSqlNorthwind %>"
          SelectCommand="
            SELECT ProductID, ProductName, UnitPrice
            FROM Products"/>

        <asp:GridView ID="GridView1" Runat="server"
            DataSourceID="NorthwindProductsSqlDataSource"
            AllowSorting="True"
            PageSize="5"
            AllowPaging="True">
            <Columns>
                <asp:CommandField ShowSelectButton="True" />
            </Columns>
            <SelectedRowStyle BackColor="Silver" />
        </asp:GridView>
      </div>
    </form>
</body>
</html>
```

2. View the page in your browser. When first opened, the page will be sorted by Product ID because that is the sort order of the primary key back in the database's table. Observe that if you sort on Price, it sorts all of the records, not just the five shown in this page.
3. Without changing the sort based on price, go to page 6 to see items in the $15 range. Now re-sort on ID. Note that your page goes back to page 1.
4. Observe selection issues with sorting; select Item #5, the gumbo mix. Its background should pick up the `SelectedRowStyle` of gray. Now jump to page 10 and observe that the selection remains on the bottom row, thus applying to a different product.

How It Works #6 — Paging, Sorting, and Selecting Together

This selection does not require intricate coding; you are looking at a basic page to understand how sorting and paging work together. When you perform a sort, the paging is reset back to the first page of the new sort order. Note that when you have a selection and then page or sort, the wrong record could be selected.

Common Mistakes

Following are some mistakes commonly made while attempting to page and sort data:

- Attempting to set the initial sort order in the GridView. It should be set in the data source control's SELECT command.

- Attempting to sort a column that does not have a sort expression.
- Attempting to sort a column that does not have header text.
- Attempting to enable sorting or paging when the data source does not support sorting, for example when `SqlDataSource.DataSourceMode=DataReader`. Only `DataSet` mode supports sorting and paging. Paging is also only supported on `ObjectDataSource` (discussed later in the book) when the `SelectMethod` returns a `DataSet, DataView, DataTable` or a collection that implements the `ICollection` interface.

Summary

This chapter covered two tools that are high on the priority list for many clients: the abilities to sort and page within a table. Although powerful, the code is prewritten in the GridView, and your task as a designer is very simple.

To sort, you must turn on sorting and show headers in the GridView object. Within each tag, you need header text and a sort expression. Optionally, you can set the appearance for all the headers (using the header row style of the GridView) or you can set the appearance of just one header (using the column's header style property).

To add paging to a GridView, your minimum act is to set `AllowPaging` to `true` within the GridView. This simple setting enables the paging behavior and creates a pager cell at the bottom of the GridView. You can apply a style to the pager using the `PagerStyle` like any other row style. You can use the pager mode to determine which items of page navigation are available, including numeric, next, previous, first, and last. These options can be presented to the user as ASCII arrows (default), literal text, or images.

This chapter concludes the discussion of tabular data-bound controls (GridView and DetailsView). Next you look at a different group of data-bound controls, the list controls.

Exercises

1. What is necessary to enable paging in a GridView control?
2. What two event arguments are useful when creating custom sort expressions?
3. Describe the syntax of the `SortExpression` property.
4. Name the interfaces that enable the user to navigate through pages in a GridView or DetailsView control.
5. Where in the Properties window do you set the kind of paging links shown (First/Last, Numeric, and so on)?
6. Describe how a user might be misled about which record is currently selected.

8

Displaying Data in Lists

The last three chapters discussed tables, both the GridView and the DetailsView. This chapter studies lists. Whereas tables present data in a two-dimensional format (rows and columns), lists present data in a single dimension, such as a bulleted list, a list box, a drop-down list, radio buttons, or sets of check boxes. Some types of links support selection and hyperlinks, making them a tool for user input. In the simplest case, you can provide the items in the list from literal statements in your code. Populating a list from a data source is also explained.

The chapter covers the following four topics, in addition to the usual list of common mistakes and a summary.

- Concepts Common to List Controls
- Data-Binding List Controls
- Drop-Down List Control
- Handling Selection in a List

> **Although the DataList control has *list* in its name, it is completely templated and so is discussed in Chapter 10 with other templated controls.**

You will find that the Try It Out exercises, which help you practice the concepts of data lists, do not complete the kinds of objectives needed for most sites. The next few chapters will build on these listing techniques to allow user interaction with lists to set properties of other controls. For example, a selection from a list of customers can change a GridView to show only orders from the selected customer.

Try It Out	Topic
1	Populating Static List Items
2	Data-Binding a BulletedList Control
3	Data-Binding a DropDownList Control
4	Data-Binding Other List Controls
5	Handling Selection with the Submit Button
6	Handling Selection with Automatic Postback

Introduction

GridView and DetailsView provide information in two dimensions. Lists present information in a single dimension. But beyond the presentation of data, lists are the most useful and common form of user input. Rather than allowing users to type in their region, for example, lists offer them a set of acceptable choices in a list. Site designs that offer only acceptable choices fail less frequently.

Transition from GridView to Other Formats

Before starting with lists, let's review the way data-bound controls are categorized.

- **Tabular controls** present data in a two-dimensional table. GridView offers many rows and fields, whereas DetailsView is specialized to offer two columns, the left for labels and the right for data, describing a single record.
- **List controls** present data in one dimension and include the BulletedList, ListBox, DropDownList, CheckBoxList, and RadioButtonList, as discussed in this chapter.
- **Templated controls** provide an empty space into which controls can be placed. Once placed into the template, the controls become data-wise and show the appropriate value for the current record. Templates include the DataList, FormView, and templated portions of other controls (see Chapter 10).
- **Hierarchical controls** display nested relationships like trees. The ones covered in this book are the TreeView, Menu, and Site Navigation controls (see Chapter 14).

DataList is a crossover of these categories. It is a list in the sense of repeated display on page and is a list in name; however, the DataList is more like a templated control in that the DataList renders in a side-by-side format, whereas FormView renders just one record at a time, the top one of a stack of all the records. Therefore, the DataList is covered in Chapter 10 on templates.

Types of List Controls

ASP.NET 2.0 (beta 2 version) provides five types of list controls, as follows:

- `<asp:BulletedList>` provides a list with an image or icon next to each item. Items in a bulleted list can lead to hyperlinks, but a bulleted list does imply to users a sense of selectability that can be identified to the rest of the page.
- `<asp:ListBox>` provides a list of items in a standard format, indicating to the user that a selection is expected.
- `<asp:DropDownList>` provides a format similar to the list box but using less space when not in use.
- `<asp:CheckBoxList>` provides a list of items from which the user can select any number of items from zero to all.
- `<asp:RadioButtonList>` provides a list of items in a group from which the user can select only one.

Concepts Common to List Controls

Lists have a set of values that are presented in a consistent and repeating format. These data are called *items*, a term used extensively throughout the chapter. The source of items can be from a list hard-coded into the page (static) or from a data source control (dynamic). When using a data source control, the list of items can be filtered, renamed, or ordered using the appropriate SQL statement.

The user can select the items in a list. The selection can be used later in the page life, or the selection can invoke an immediate hyperlink or page refresh and update. You will work with both possibilities in this chapter and the next. Note that the bullet list provides flexibility on this point. It can merely present information, or it can present items that are indicated to the user as selectable.

List controls have a standard hierarchy of organization. Lists consist of a collection of list items, represented by `<asp:ListItem>` objects in ASP.NET. You can assign `<asp:ListItem>` objects to the list control's Item collection property, as in the following example:

```
<asp:BulletedList>
<Items>
  <asp:ListItem Text="Item One"/>
  <asp:ListItem Text="Item Two"/>
  <asp:ListItem Text="Item Three"/>
</Items>
</asp:BulletedList>
```

Of course, Visual Web Developer and Visual Studio handle the creation of lists of items through a simple dialog box.

Text versus Value in List Items

A list item has two important properties, `Text` and `Value`. The `Text` property represents the text to display in the rendering of the list item; it is what the end user will see in the page rendering. The `Value` property is held in the background and will not be rendered. This dual property design proves useful when you want to show the user a text such as "CanadaPost" but want to use a value of the shipper's ID code to process a selection in the list such as in a `WHERE` clause. The source code is organized as follows, with the `Text` and `Value` properties both explicitly stated within the item tag.

```
<asp:ListBox>
 <Items>
   <asp:ListItem Text="Canada Post" Value="111"/>
   <asp:ListItem Text="Royal Mail" Value="222"/>
   <asp:ListItem Text="US Postal Service" Value="333"/>
 </Items>
</asp:ListBox>
```

An alternative is to locate the text between opening and closing tags without the `Text` property identifier or the equals sign or quotation marks, as follows:

```
<asp:ListBox>
<Items>
   <asp:ListItem Value="111"/>Canada Post</asp:ListItem>
   <asp:ListItem Value="222"/>Royal Mail</asp:ListItem>
   <asp:ListItem Value="333"/>US Postal Service</asp:ListItem>
 </Items>
</asp:ListBox>
```

If you want to use a single value for each list item, to both display and serve as the underlying value, you may set either the `Text` or `Value` property and leave the other property unset. In this case, the property that is set will assume the role of the one that is not set. Note that the `Value` property of `ListItem` is generally useful only if the control allows user selection. It makes little sense for `asp:BulletedList`, which only renders the items (no selection).

The following exercise is a simple example that creates a list of items that are hard-coded into the page.

Try It Out #1 — Populating Static List Items

1. Create a new folder named `C:\Websites\BegAspNet2DB\ch08` and then a new page named `TIO-01-BulletedList-HardCode.aspx`.

2. Drag a bulleted list from the toolbar onto the page. In the smart task panel, click Edit Items and then click the Add button. In the right panel, set the `Text` property to one of your favorite authors. Add several more authors and click OK to close. Save and take a look at the resulting source code. Observe the page in your browser.

```
<%@ Page Language="VB" %>
<html>
<head>
    <title>Ch08-TIO-1-DisplayingDataInABulletedList-HardCode</title>
</head>
<body>
```

```
Chapter 8 TIO #1 Displaying Static Data In A BulletedList
  <form id="form1" runat="server">
    <div>
         <asp:BulletedList ID="BulletedList1" Runat="server">
            <asp:ListItem>Allen</asp:ListItem>
            <asp:ListItem>Beckett</asp:ListItem>
            <asp:ListItem>Cavellari</asp:ListItem>
        </asp:BulletedList>
    </div>
  </form>
</body>
</html>
```

How It Works #1 — Populating Static List Items

In this exercise, you had two simple objectives: first, to practice using the designer interface in VWD that allows you to easily add items to lists; second, to observe the resulting code. Note the `<Items>` collection within the list tag and then the tags for each item in the collection. VWD creates code with the text between tags rather than setting the text string as a property within a tag.

Data-Binding List Controls

Setting list items statically (as in the preceding exercise) provides good performance if items do not change (for example, a few types of membership categories). But if the list varies and the items are represented in your database, it behooves you to create the items collection dynamically. With ASP.NET 2.0, this is very easy. The list controls are data-bound controls that behave at design time and runtime almost the same as other data-bound controls. The list's `DataSourceID` property can be set to any data source control. You then have to set the `Text` and `Value` properties of the list control to fields that are available from the data source control's SelectCommand.

DataTextField and DataValueField

Recall from the introduction to list controls the need for separate `Text` and `Value` properties; `Text` is shown to the user, whereas `Value` is the datum available to other controls or processes after a selection. `Text` might be "Canada Post," but the `Value` represents that shipper's code of "101." When list controls are data-bound, you can specify separate fields to bind to the `Text` property and the `Value` property. Generally, you would bind the DataTextField to the more understandable field, like ShipperName, and the DataValueField to the primary key like ShipperID field.

Many developers forget to set the DataTextField or DataValueField or get them reversed. Using VWD's tools reduces errors. "Choose Data Source" link opens a dialog for choosing the data source and then reflects against the data source schema to allow (and remind) the user to choose field associations for DataTextField and DataValueField.

```
<asp:BulletedList ID="BulletedList1" Runat="server"
  DataSourceID="SqlDataSource1"
  DataTextField="Field1"/>

<asp:SqlDataSource ID="SqlDataSource1" Runat="server"
```

```
        SelectCommand="SELECT Field1 FROM MyTable"
        ConnectionString=" ... "/>
```

Note that you do not need to create an items collection; that will be done automatically by ASP.NET 2.0. However, you must be sure that the DataTextField is one of the fields in the data source control's SelectCommand. Before going further, let's create a bulleted list that is dynamic.

Try It Out #2 — Data-Binding a BulletedList Control

In the last exercise, you created a bulleted list using items (favorite authors) that were hard-coded (static) in the page. This time, you will generate the list from the authors in the Pubs database.

1. If you did not create a connection string for Pubs in Chapter 3, you should do so now. Add to your Web.config file:

```
<?xml version="1.0"?>
<configuration>
<connectionStrings>
    <add name="LocalSqlNorthwind"
       connectionString="Server=(local)\SQLExpress;
       Integrated Security=True;
       Database=Northwind;
       Persist Security Info=True"
       providerName="System.Data.SqlClient" />
    <add name="LocalSqlPubs"
       connectionString="Server=(local)\SQLExpress;
       Integrated Security=True;
       Database=Pubs;
       Persist Security Info=True"
       providerName="System.Data.SqlClient" />
</connectionStrings>
 <system.web>
        <compilation debug="true"/></system.web></configuration>
```

2. Create a new page named `TIO-2-BulletedList-Dynamic.aspx`. Drag a SqlDataSource onto it and set it to Pubs using a SELECT command to retrieve just the authors' last names.

3. Drag a bulleted list object onto the page and, in the smart task panel, select Choose Data Source. Click Refresh Schema. Select the SqlDataSource control and, for the data field, select the only field, `au_lname`. You do not have to worry about the field for the value. Click OK, save the page, and view it in your browser.

```
<%@ Page Language="VB" %>
</script>
<html>
<head><title>Ch08-TIO-2-DisplayingDataInAListBulletedList-Dynamic</title></head>
<body>
  <h3>Chapter 8 TIO #2 Displaying Data In A BulletedList With a Dynamic
Source</title>
  <form id="form1" runat="server">
    <div>
      <asp:BulletedList ID="BulletedList1" Runat="server"
        DataSourceID="SqlDataSource1"
        DataTextField="au_lname" OnClick="BulletedList1_Click" />
```

```
        <asp:SqlDataSource ID="SqlDataSource1" Runat="server"
          SelectCommand="SELECT [au_lname] FROM [authors]"
          ConnectionString="<%$ ConnectionStrings:LocalSqlPubs %>"
/>
      </div>
    </form></body></html>
```

How It Works #2 — Data-Binding a BulletedList Control

Now you employ a list that displays information from a database, thus creating a dynamic list. The technique was simplicity itself in VWD where you just dragged and dropped. Now your bulleted list will automatically be current with the database.

DropDownList Control

A bullet list presents items, and those items can have hyperlinks. But a bullet list does not signal to the user that a selection is expected. For that job, you move to list boxes. Drop-down lists and list boxes are covered here at three levels: simple presentation, allowing selection with processing after a button is clicked, and allowing selection with automatic processing (AutoPostBack).

For simply presenting items, you can use the same technique as the bulleted lists. The only change is the name of the control. You still bind to a data source control and, in the list control, identify one field as the source of items in the list.

```
<asp:DropDownList ID="DropDownList1" Runat="server"
  DataTextField="Field1"
  DataSourceID="SqlDataSource1" />

<asp:SqlDataSource ID="SqlDataSource1" Runat="server"
  SelectCommand="SELECT Field1 FROM MyTable"
  ConnectionString=" ... "/>
```

Try It Out #3 — Data-Binding a DropDownList Control

In this example, you provide a list of authors in a drop-down list control.

1. You can start from scratch and create `TIO-3-DropDownList.aspx` or you can open the file from the `TIO-2` and save as `TIO-3`.
2. Add a SqlDataSource control and set it the same as in `TIO-2` (just author last name from authors table in the Pubs database).
3. If revising `TIO-2`, merely change the `<asp.bulletedlist...>` to `<asp:dropdownlist...>`. Change the closing tags, as well.
4. If working from scratch, drag a drop-down list onto your page. In the smart task panel, do not enable AutoPostBack. Set the data source to your SqlDataSource. Refresh the schema and then set the data field to display the only option — `au_lname`. Save and view in your browser. (At this point, there will be no action when you select a name.)

```
<%@ Page Language="VB" %>
<html>
<head>
```

```
    <title>Ch08-TIO--Displaying Data In A List - DropDownList</title>
  </head>
  <body>
    <form id="form1" runat="server">
      <div>
        <asp:DropDownList ID="DropDownList1" Runat="server"
          DataValueField="au_id"
          DataTextField="au_lname"
          DataSourceID="SqlDataSource1" />
      </div>
      <div>
        <asp:SqlDataSource ID="SqlDataSource1" Runat="server"
          SelectCommand="SELECT [au_id], [au_lname] FROM [authors]"
          ConnectionString="<%$ ConnectionStrings:LocalSqlPubs %>"/>
      </div>
    </form>
  </body>
  </html>
```

How It Works #3 — Data-Binding a DropDownList Control

Displaying a dynamic list of items in a drop-down list box is as easy as for the bulleted list. You merely create a data source control and then set the list's DataSourceID to the data source control.

Other list controls are just as easy to create. In the following exercise, you review the drop-down list box and then demonstrate the very similar syntax for list boxes, radio button lists, and check box lists.

Try It Out #4 — Data-Binding Other List Controls

In this page, you will create a single data source control and then display four lists from the one control.

1. Create a new page named `TIO-4-OtherListControls.aspx`. Add a SqlDataSource control to read the author last names from the authors table of the Pubs database.
2. Drag a DropDownList control onto the page and set its DataSource to the SqlDataSource control. Set the Data Field to Display to `au_lname`.
3. Repeat for ListBox, CheckBoxList, and RadioButton controls. Save and observe the file in your browser.

```
<%@ Page Language="VB" %>
<html>
<head>
  <title>Ch08-TIO-4-DisplayingDataInAList-OtherListControls</title>
</head>
<body>
<h3>Chapter 8 TIO #4 Displaying Data In A List - Other List Controls</h3>
  <form id="form1" runat="server">

    <asp:SqlDataSource ID="SqlDataSource1" Runat="server"
        SelectCommand="SELECT [au_id], [au_lname] FROM [authors]"
        ConnectionString="<%$ ConnectionStrings:LocalSqlPubs %>"/>
    <br /><br />

    <h2>DropDownList</h2>
    <asp:DropDownList ID="DropDownList1" Runat="server"
```

```
        DataValueField="au_id"
        DataTextField="au_lname"
        DataSourceID="SqlDataSource1" />
    <br /><br />

    <h2>ListBox<h2 />
    <asp:ListBox ID="ListBox1" Runat="server"
        DataSourceID="SqlDataSource1"
        DataTextField="au_lname"
        DataValueField="au_id" />
    </h2>
      <h2>
          CheckBoxList</h2>
    <asp:CheckBoxList ID="CheckBoxList1" Runat="server"
        DataSourceID="SqlDataSource1"
        DataTextField="au_lname"
        DataValueField="au_id" />
    <br /><br />

    <h2>RadioButtonList</h2>
    <asp:RadioButtonList ID="RadioButtonList1" Runat="server"
        DataSourceID="SqlDataSource1"
        DataTextField="au_lname"
        DataValueField="au_id" />
  </form>
</body>
</html>
```

How It Works #4 — Data-Binding Other List Controls

VWD offers a consistent pattern to create list controls. You drag the control to the page and set its data source control. Then you specify a field to provide the text property. The resulting code generated by VWD is also very consistent — only the names of the controls change.

Handling Selection in a List

It's time to move on to a more interactive level, where you permit the user to select one item in the list and you react to that selection. Note that you can use the selected item at two points in time. If you enable AutoPostBack, the act of selecting causes the page to refresh, probably using the selected value. If you do not use autopostback, the page waits for the user to click on a button (typically "submit") before you use the selected item. For example, if a user is entering information as a new member, you may want to wait until selections are made from many lists before you process the page. In this case, AutoPostBack should be off. Both techniques are demonstrated shortly.

SelectedIndex and SelectedValue

When the user selects an item in a list control, three of the control's properties will receive values:

- The SelectedItem.Text, which holds the string that was shown in the list control
- The SelectedValue, which is the datum in the `Value` property for the selected item
- The SelectItemIndex, which is the number (starting with zero) of the item in the list

The index is useful if a list is generated from an array and you want to go back and look up data in the array (perhaps an additional dimension). However, if the list's item collection is being generated dynamically, the index can vary from page to page and is thus less useful. Most of the examples in this book will be using the selected item's value to use in a lookup back in the database.

If you work on more advanced scenarios of custom code, it is useful to know that SelectedIndex may be set declaratively in code at runtime. SelectedValue can only be read at runtime.

Try It Out #5 — Handling Selection with the Submit Button

In this exercise, you will present a drop-down list box of authors. The user can select one and then click a submit button. You report back on the page on which author was selected. For the benefit of the student programmer, also report the selection's value and index.

1. Create a new page named `TIO-5-DropDownList-Select.aspx`. Add a SQL data source control as you did earlier, but this time read two fields: author ID and author last name.
2. Add a drop-down list with a connection to your data source control. But this time set the `Text` (display) field to the `au_lname` and the `Value` property to the `au_id field`.
3. Drag an `asp:` button control onto the page. With the button selected, in the Properties window set the name to `button1` and the `OnClick` to `Button1_Click`.
4. Staying in VWD, go to the Source view and create the procedure in the `<script>`, as shown here for Visual Basic:

```
<%@ Page Language="VB" %>
<script runat="server">
  Sub Button1_Click(ByVal sender As Object, ByVal e As System.EventArgs)
        Response.Write("You Selected: " & DropDownList1.SelectedItem.Text)
        Response.Write("<br />(value: " & DropDownList1.SelectedValue & ")")
        Response.Write("<br />(index: " & DropDownList1.SelectedIndex & ")")
    End Sub
</script>
<html>
<head><title>Ch08-TIO-5-DisplayingDataInAList-DropDownList</title></head>
<body>
<h3>Chapter 8 TIO #5 Displaying Data In A List - DropDownList<h3/>
  <form id="form1" runat="server">
    <asp:DropDownList ID="DropDownList1" Runat="server"
        DataValueField="au_id"
        DataTextField="au_lname"
        DataSourceID="SqlDataSource1"/>

    <asp:Button ID="Button1" Runat="server"
        Text="Submit"
        OnClick="Button1_Click" />

    <asp:SqlDataSource ID="SqlDataSource1" Runat="server"
        SelectCommand="SELECT [au_id], [au_lname] FROM [authors]"
        ConnectionString="<%$ ConnectionStrings:LocalSqlPubs %>"/>
  </form></body></html>
```

If you prefer C#, the following procedure can be used:

```
<%@ Page Language="CS" %>
<script runat="server">

  void Button1_Click(Object sender, EventArgs e)
        {
        Response.Write("You Selected: " + DropDownList1.SelectedItem.Text);
        Response.Write("<br />(value: " + DropDownList1.SelectedValue + ")");
        Response.Write("<br />(index: " + DropDownList1.SelectedIndex + ")");
        }

</script>
```

5. Save and test in your browser.

How It Works #5 — Handling Selection with the Submit Button

This exercise differs from earlier exercises in several ways. First, you are going to handle selections and you don't want to use the string that was presented in the list. So, you specify a second property for the items and value, and you set it to the `au_ID`. As you will see in the next chapter, having that ID in hand makes it easy to create a `WHERE` clause that would look up only books from the selected author.

Second, you added a button to the page that, when clicked, triggers a procedure named `button1_click`. Third, you wrote the procedure (more details on handling events are presented in Chapter 16). The button-click event will send to the procedure `EventArgs` (arguments). These include, in the case of a click on a list, three arguments of use to us: the list's selected item's text, value, and index number.

Automatic Postback

For some pages, you will want to react as soon as the user makes a selection in your list. Rather than having a button that requires a second user action, you can enable an automatic submit, that is, AutoPostBack. You can specify a procedure to perform when the automatic postback is invoked. That procedure can utilize the selected item's text, value, and index. However, turning on AutoPostBack is not for every case, and the application developer needs to make a decision on which is the best choice. For example, if the DropDownList is being used to alter the value of a record during editing, chances are good that you don't want the postback to happen until after the client has filled out all other input fields. In this case, a button submit (Update) makes more sense than AutoPostBack.

Try It Out #6 — Handling Selection with Automatic Postback

This exercise builds on the last by adding a drop-down list that automatically posts back.

1. Open your `TIO-5` and save as `TIO-6-DropDOwnList-AutoPostback.aspx`.
2. Add a second DropDownList that is the same as the first with three exceptions. First, name it `DropDownList2`. Second, set `AutoPostBack=true`. Third, set its `OnSelectedIndexChanged` property to the procedure named `"DropDownList2_SelectedIndexChanged"`.

3. Add a second procedure named "`DropDownList2_SelectedIndexChanged,`" as shown in the following code. Save and observe in your browser.

```
<%@ Page Language="VB" %>
<script runat="server">

  Sub Button1_Click(ByVal sender As Object, ByVal e As System.EventArgs)
        Response.Write("You Selected: " & DropDownList1.SelectedItem.Text)
        Response.Write("<br />(value: " & DropDownList1.SelectedValue & ")")
        Response.Write("<br />(index: " & DropDownList1.SelectedIndex & ")")
    End Sub

  Sub DropDownList2_SelectedIndexChanged(ByVal sender As Object, ByVal e As
System.EventArgs)
        Response.Write("You Selected: " & DropDownList2.SelectedItem.Text)
        Response.Write("<br />(value: " & DropDownList2.SelectedValue & ")")
        Response.Write("<br />(index: " & DropDownList2.SelectedIndex & ")")
    End Sub
</script>
<html>
<head><title>Ch08-TIO-6-DisplayingDataInaList-DropDownList</title></head>
<body>
<h3>Chapter 8 TIO #6 Displaying Data In A List - DropDownList</h3>
  <form id="form1" runat="server">
    <h2>Button Postback</h2>
    <asp:DropDownList ID="DropDownList1" Runat="server"
        DataValueField="au_id"
        DataTextField="au_lname"
        DataSourceID="SqlDataSource1" />

    <asp:Button ID="Button1" Runat="server"
        Text="Submit"
        OnClick="Button1_Click" />
    <br /><br />

    <h2>Automatic Postback</h2>
    <asp:DropDownList ID="DropDownList2" Runat="server"
        DataValueField="au_id"
        DataTextField="au_lname"
        DataSourceID="SqlDataSource1"
        AutoPostBack="True"
        OnSelectedIndexChanged="DropDownList2_SelectedIndexChanged" />
    <br /><br />

    <asp:SqlDataSource ID="SqlDataSource1" Runat="server"
        SelectCommand="SELECT [au_id], [au_lname] FROM [authors]"
        ConnectionString="<%$ ConnectionStrings:LocalSqlPubs %>"/>
  </form></body></html>
```

You can also write the code in C# as follows:

```
<%@ Page Language="CS" %>
<script runat="server">

void Button1_Click(Object sender, EventArgs e)
        {
```

```
        Response.Write("You Selected: " + DropDownList1.SelectedItem.Text);
        Response.Write("<br />(value: " + DropDownList1.SelectedValue + ")");
        Response.Write("<br />(index: " + DropDownList1.SelectedIndex + ")");
        }

void DropDownList2_SelectedIndexChanged(Object sender, EventArgs e)
        {
        Response.Write("You Selected: " + DropDownList2.SelectedItem.Text);
        Response.Write("<br />(value: " + DropDownList2.SelectedValue + ")");
        Response.Write("<br />(index: " + DropDownList2.SelectedIndex + ")");
        }

</script>
```

How It Works #6—Handling Selection with Automatic Postback

When you added the second button, you introduced two new properties. The `AutoPostBack=True` means that a selection in the list will also automatically perform the equivalent of a click on a submit button. Second, you set a procedure to be run when that submission occurs.

```
<asp:DropDownList ID="DropDownList2" Runat="server"
    DataValueField="au_id"
    DataTextField="au_lname"
    DataSourceID="SqlDataSource1"
    AutoPostBack="True"
    OnSelectedIndexChanged="DropDownList2_SelectedIndexChanged" />
```

The actual procedure is the same as in the previous example, except that you now write the data from the selected item of the second drop-down list.

Common Mistakes

The following are mistakes commonly made while trying to display data in lists:

- Forgetting to set `AutoPostBack=true` when you want an automatic postback (nothing happens when you select from the list).
- Forgetting to set DataTextField or DataValueField (nothing renders in the list, or it renders the same thing for all items, such as `System.Data.DataRowView` when bound to a DataSet).
- Using `Text` when you want to use `Value`, and vice versa. These can be used interchangeably only when they point to the same field or value.
- Setting a list's `Text` or `Value` property to a field that is not included in the data source control's SelectCommand statement.
- Expecting the `List.SelectedItem.Index` to be the same from page to page when the list is generated dynamically.
- Setting a list's `Text` or `Value` property to the original name of a field but the field's name has been changed with an alias in the select command.

Summary

The last few chapters presented data in tables consisting of grids of rows and columns. When you have only one dimension of data, you can use one of the list controls, including the BulletedList, DropDownList, ListBox, CheckBoxList, or RadioButtonList.

They all work in very similar ways. A list contains a collection of items that will be displayed. Items have a `Text` property that is shown to the user. They also have a `Value` property that holds a datum that is hidden from the user but may be more useful when set for your code. Last, there is an `Index` property for each item.

The items can come from one of two sources. Static loads the list from lines of code that contain literal strings. Or you can load the list from the data output by a data source control. Using this dynamic method, you get lists that are responsive to the current situation of the site and its business.

Lists go beyond just displaying data; they can also accept a user's click and react. At the time of reaction, three important bits of data will be available regarding the item that was selected: the aforementioned `Text`, `Value`, and `Index` properties. In this chapter, we reacted with a simple procedure that wrote the data to the page.

There are two options for when to react. First, a submit button can be on the page. After performing multiple tasks on a page, the user can click the submit button. Alternatively, you can have the page automatically and immediately perform a postback when the select is performed.

The exercises in this chapter were trivial; they did not solve real-world problems. But future chapters use the techniques of lists as building blocks for more complex solutions. For example, in the next chapter, you will react to a selection by rerendering a GridView to show only the books of the selected author.

9

Filtering and Master-Child Data

The last few chapters discussed several data-bound controls, each with its own advantages. This chapter discusses how they can work together. You will work with multiple controls, using the specialized strengths of each. For example, you will select one record from a GridView and display further details about that record in a DetailsView control. These concepts start our discussion of how to bring together multiple controls to create an efficient user interface.

This chapter tackles six major ideas:

- Filtering GridView records from a querystring
- Filtering GridView records from user input in a TextBox
- The theory of selection and ControlParameters
- Filtering GridView records from user selection in a list control
- Showing a record in DetailsView based on a user selection in a GridView
- Cascading lists

You will practice these concepts with the following Try It Out exercises:

Try It Out	Topic
1	Filtering GridView Records Using a QueryString
2	Limiting GridView Records Using a TextBox
3	Using the SQL LIKE and IN Clauses
4	Filtering GridView Records Using a DropDownList
5	Filtering GridView Records Using a Bound DropDownList
6	Displaying Details Using a GridView and DetailsView with All Items
7	Displaying Details Using a GridView and DetailsView on the Same Page
8	Displaying Details Using a GridView and DetailsView on Different Pages
9	Displaying Related Records Using a GridView and a GridView
10	Using Cascading DropDownLists

This chapter addresses how to give the user the capacity to change the scope of records or fields displayed in a data-bound control. It has two major objectives:

- **Showing only a subset of all the records in a control.** For example, you may want to see the orders for only one customer.
- **Showing more fields for just one of the records.** For example, after picking an employee from a GridView, you may want to see additional details about that employee.

Both of these cases are solved in the same way: use one data-bound control to change the scope (number of records or number of fields) of a second data-bound control.

> *The term filtering is often used in this chapter. Filtering in this chapter is the limiting of records to display by setting a* `WHERE` *clause in a data source control. This includes the case of displaying just one record when filtering determines which record. Note that this chapter does not discuss the* `FilterExpression/FilterParameters` *properties of SqlDataSource. That property is typically used in special cases of caching, which are covered in Chapter 15.*

Because you are using one data-bound control to filter another data-bound control, accurate wording must denote the two controls. The master control will be the one that accepts the user's input. The details (or child) control is the one that reacts with a filtered display. Note that the details (reacting) control does not have to be a DetailsView control. Almost all controls can interact as master or child controls in a filtering scenario. For example, a GridView can be either the child control (another control determines which record GridView shows) or a master control (GridView determines which record is displayed in a DetailsView). Also keep in mind that you may have two data source controls on a page, one to supply the master data-bound control and a second to supply the child data-bound control.

The basic theory for filtering involves three steps. In most cases in this chapter, that will mean the following:

1. You obtain a criterion from a master control.
2. You apply the criteria to the `WHERE` clause of the data source for the child control.
3. (Automatic) The child control will display a modified scope of records or fields.

The second step is the focus of much of our discussion. ASP.NET 2.0 passes the user's selection by first putting the value(s) into a parameter. The parameter is then read into the criteria of the `WHERE` clause.

Filtering GridView Records Using a QueryString

We'll start with a focus on how the child control scope can be modified. This first example is so simple that it does not even use a master control; the criteria are provided in a querystring. Recall that a querystring is merely names and values added to the end of a URL. For example, a querystring indicating a membership number could be sent to a site as follows:

```
www.YachtClub.org?MemberNumber=123
```

The value `123` can be used in the page by asking the server for the querystring value named `MemberNumber`. Querystrings are intrinsic to all HTML pages; they are not special to ASP.NET.

The flow of information starts with the request for the page containing a querystring. In this simple example, you will type the querystring. Then, on your page, the data source control will pick up the value from the querystring and put it into a parameter. The `WHERE` clause of the SelectCommand of the data source will pick up the value from the parameter and use it as its criteria to scope (limit) records. The data-bound control will then show the scoped set of records and fields. Note that the `WHERE` clause gets a new substitution of query-string value for every page request; thus the page is dynamic. The VWD IDE walks you through this setup, so you do not actually have to write code.

Try It Out #1 — Filtering GridView Records Using a QueryString

You want a page that accepts a request with a querystring that indicates a state. The resulting GridView of authors will show writers from only the specified state. In this exercise, your input is not from a control but rather from the querystring, and your scoping is to filter the records shown in a GridView.

1. Create a new folder named `C:\Websites\BegAspNet2Db\ch09` and a new page named `TIO-01-QueryString.asp`. If you did not install the Pubs database to your SSE (or SQL Server or SSE) as per Chapter 1, do so now.
2. Add a SqlDataSource control to the page. Use the smart task panel and select Configure Data Source to connect to Pubs. You can keep the connection string in the application configuration file or not (we keep it on the page for clarity in this book). Then select from the authors table the ID, names, city, and state. Click on `WHERE` and set `Column = state`, `Operator` to `equals`, and `Source` to `querystring`. Note that a Parameters Properties panel specific for querystrings opens. Set `Field = State` and a default of `CA`.

3. Click on Add and note how the `WHERE` clause box now displays that the state will be set to the `Request.QueryString` value for `State`. Test the query, accepting the default.

4. Staying in the wizard's test page, try testing again using a different value; overtype `CA` with `IN` to see a different set. Click Finish.

5. Add a GridView to display records from the data source you just created. Your results should be similar to the following:

```
<%@ Page Language="VB" %>
<html>
<head>
  <title>Ch09-TIO-01-QueryString</title>
</head>
<body><h3>Chapter 9 TIO #01 QueryString </h3>
There are authors in CA, OR, KS, IN and others.
  <form id="form1" runat="server">
    <asp:GridView ID="GridView1" Runat="server"
         DataSourceID="SqlDataSource1"
         AutoGenerateColumns="False"
         AllowPaging="True"
         AllowSorting="True">
      <Columns>
        <asp:BoundField HeaderText="au_id"
                DataField="au_id" SortExpression="au_id" />
        <asp:BoundField HeaderText="au_lname"
                DataField="au_lname" SortExpression="au_lname" />
        <asp:BoundField HeaderText="au_fname"
                DataField="au_fname" SortExpression="au_fname" />
        <asp:BoundField HeaderText="city"
                DataField="city" SortExpression="city" />
        <asp:BoundField HeaderText="state"
                DataField="state" SortExpression="state" />
      </Columns>
    </asp:GridView>
    <asp:SqlDataSource ID="SqlDataSource1" Runat="server"
        ConnectionString="<%$ ConnectionStrings:LocalSqlPubs %>"
        SelectCommand="SELECT * FROM [authors] WHERE state = @state" >

      <SelectParameters>
        <asp:QueryStringParameter Name="state"
            DefaultValue="CA"
            QueryStringField="state" />
      </SelectParameters>
    </asp:SqlDataSource>
  </form>
</body>
</html>
```

6. Test the page by first just opening it. Notice that the GridView is filtered by the `WHERE` clause applying the default querystring value of `CA`. Now go to the address line of your browser and type the URL with a querystring such as the following:

```
http://localhost/BegAspNet2Db/ch09/TIO-01-QueryString.aspx?state=IN
```

How It Works #1 — Filtering GridView Records Using a QueryString

First, keep in mind that this is a preliminary example. Instead of using a master control, you are using a value typed into the querystring. Within the data source control, note that the `WHERE` clause is not hard-coded. Rather, the value for state shall come from a parameter named `state`. The `@` symbol indicates that the following term is a parameter.

```
SelectCommand="SELECT * FROM [authors] WHERE state = @state"
```

Now turn your attention to a new structure called the parameters collection. This example uses a `QueryStringParameter`. Give the parameter the same name as that used in the `WHERE` clause, in this case, `state`. Two properties are assigned to the parameter. The first is that the value shall come from the querystring field named `state`. If there is no `state` value, you will use a default of `CA`.

```
<SelectParameters>
  <asp:QueryStringParameter Name="state"
      DefaultValue="CA"
      QueryStringField="state" />
</SelectParameters>
```

The overall flow of information was as follows. The user typed into the URL address bar a page name and value and then pressed Enter to request the page. At the server, that value was automatically put into the querystring collection. Your page then read the value from the querystring collection into your select parameters collection. When the data source control executed its SelectCommand, the `WHERE` clause read the value from the parameters collection. Thus, the data source control created a set of records scoped down to just certain records. That smaller set of records was sent to the data-bound control for display.

Filtering GridView Records Using a TextBox

A value appended to a querystring works fine if it is generated by another ASPX page. But querystrings are awkward for direct input from a user. A better alternative is to give the user a TextBox and use that as the source for the parameter. This means that you are actually using one control to scope another. As with the last exercise, it is easy to create the page by clicking through the VWD designer.

The architecture of ASP.NET 2.0 provides programmers a very consistent syntax for parameters. Switching from a querystring to a TextBox requires only changing your `SelectParameter` type from `QueryStringParameter` to `ControlParameter` and adding a property to specify the control.

Try It Out #2 — Limiting GridView Records Using a TextBox

This time you want the user to be able to type a state into a TextBox on the page rather than into the URL.

Create a new page named `TIO-02-TextBox.aspx`. Start with adding a TextBox named `TextBox1` and a button control named `Button1`. Then add a SqlDataSource control to the page and configure to connect to Pubs with the same data as the previous exercise (from the authors table, the ID, names, city, and state). As in the last exercise, click on `WHERE` and set `Column = state` and `Operator` to `equals`. But now you want the source set to a control. In the parameters properties, set the `ControlID = TextBox1` and a default of `CA`. Add a GridView to display the records; your results should be similar to the following:

```
<%@ Page Language="VB" %>
<html>
<head>
  <title>Ch09-TIO-02-Filtering a GridView Using TextBox</title>
</head>
<body>
  <form id="form1" runat="server">
    Enter a state:  
    <asp:TextBox ID="TextBox1" Runat="server" />

         <asp:Button ID="Button1" Runat="server" Text="Button" />
    <br /><br />

   <asp:GridView> ... </asp:GridView>

   <asp:SqlDataSource ID="SqlDataSource1" Runat="server"
        ConnectionString="<%$ ConnectionStrings:LocalSqlPubs %>"
      SelectCommand="SELECT * FROM [authors] WHERE state = @state">
      <SelectParameters>
        <asp:ControlParameter Name="state"
                PropertyName="Text"
                DefaultValue="CA"
                ControlID="TextBox1"
                />
      </SelectParameters>
    </asp:SqlDataSource>
  </form>
</body>
</html>
```

How It Works #2—Limiting GridView Records Using a TextBox

Your improvement here allows the user to type a state into a TextBox rather than into the browser's address tool. The primary change was in your `SelectParameters` collection. Instead of an `<asp:QueryStringParameter>`, you used an `<asp:ControlParameter>`. Without regard to the parameter type, the data source control just looks through the list of parameters until it finds one with a name to match its `@` in the `WHERE` clause.

Using ASP.NET 2.0 data parameters like ControlParameter and QueryString parameter helps improve the overall security of your site. An insecure approach to designing this page would be to concatenate the text into the `WHERE` clause. Such an approach would open your database to a SQL injection attack where a nefarious user could enter a string that aborts the encoded SQL statement and instead adds its own statement, such as `DELETE FROM Authors`. The code presented in the preceding Try It Out takes the text entry and SQL encodes the string into a parameter that is more difficult to hack. As an additional measure towards security, it is also recommended that you perform validation on parameter inputs to ensure they conform to the values you expect. You can use the ASP.NET 2.0 validation controls or write your own code using the techniques of Chapter 16 on handling events.

Using the SQL LIKE Operator

Although they are not a feature of ASP.NET 2.0, you can accommodate some of that variability in your SELECT command using SQL clauses. `LIKE` allows you to specify only part of the string to match. If you use the clause `...WHERE Name LIKE Per%`, you will get records matching Person, Personn, Persone, and Persom. Although they are not covered in this book, you may want to check a SQL text to understand the power of additional operators, including `BETWEEN`, `IN`, and nested SQL statements. Also, take a look at other wildcards in the SQL syntax.

Try It Out #3 — Using the SQL LIKE and IN Clauses

This exercise allows the user to enter text in a TextBox and do a search for similar (not just exact) last name matches.

Create a new page named `TIO-03-TextBoxSearch.aspx`. As with the last page, add a TextBox and button. Make the data source control show the authors' ID, names, city, and state. When you go through the Configure Data Source wizard, select `WHERE` and set the column to `au_lname`. But for `Operator`, select `LIKE`. The source will be the control named `TextBox1`. Don't forget to click Add. In the text screen, look at the SQL statement. The `WHERE` clause criteria have been given the `LIKE` keyword and the percent symbols have been added, meaning "substitute any number of any characters here." Add a GridView and run; your source code should be similar to the following:

```
<%@ Page Language="VB" %>
<html>
<head>
  <title>Ch09-TIO-03-FilteringGridViewUsingTextBoxSearch</title>
</head>
<body><h3>Chapter 9 TIO # 3 Filtering a GridView Using a TextBox Search</h3>
  <form id="form1" runat="server">
    Enter a character(s) in the author's last name:
    <br/><br />
    <asp:TextBox ID="TextBox1" Runat="server" />
    <asp:Button ID="Button1" Runat="server" Text="Button" />
    <br /><br />

    <asp:GridView> ... </asp:GridView>

    <asp:SqlDataSource ID="SqlDataSource1" Runat="server"
        ConnectionString="<%$ ConnectionStrings:LocalSqlPubs %>"
        SelectCommand="
            SELECT * FROM [authors]
            WHERE ([au_lname] LIKE '%' + @au_lname + '%')" >
      <SelectParameters>
        <asp:ControlParameter
            Name="au_lname"
            Type="String"
            ControlID="TextBox1"
            PropertyName="Text" />
      </SelectParameters>
    </asp:SqlDataSource>
  </form>
</body>
</html>
```

How It Works #3 — Using the SQL LIKE and IN Clauses

When you pass a SELECT command, as follows, to SQL Server:

```
...WHERE au_lname LIKE %smith%
```

it will match any values that have "smith" in them, including Smith, Goldsmith, and Smithers. The only trick is in making up the preceding string. You have to concatenate the percent symbols as a literal within quotes.

Note that you use the term `au_lname` twice in the `WHERE` clause. The first time refers to the field in the table. The second time, with the `@`, refers to the parameter value, which comes from the TextBox.

The Theory of Selection and ControlParameters

The overall pattern of the theory behind selection in ASP.NET 2.0 data-bound controls follows, where you have two data-bound controls named "master" and "child."

1. The user makes a selection in a selectable master control.
2. The page automatically posts back and puts the selected value into any `ControlParameters` on the page that specify the master control as their source.
3. One of those control parameters is in the data source control of the child control. The child's data source control uses the value of the control parameter as a criterion in a `WHERE` clause.
4. The child control shows the set of data limited by the child's data source control.

Tracing the process backward, you see that in the end you have the child control showing a limited set of records. That set is limited because the child's data source control used a `WHERE` clause. The criteria of the `WHERE` clause came from a control parameter in the child's data source control. The control parameter was filled at postback by a value in the master control. The postback occurred because the user clicked on a selectable master control.

The following controls support selection and are discussed in this book (other controls, such as Calendar, support selection but are not covered in this text):

- GridView (with a select command column)
- DetailsView and FormView (current data item)
- ListBox and DropDownList
- CheckBoxList and RadioButtonList
- TreeView and Menu

TextBox can be bound to a `ControlParameter`, so it can behave like a selection although, strictly speaking, it is not selectable.

In the VWD designer, when you use the `WHERE` dialog box to configure the select command of a data source control you see only the data-bound controls in the preceding list. Each selectable control has one or more properties with values useful for control parameters as well as properties of no use to control parameters (for example, backcolor, font). When a control parameter is created, it only needs to specify which control to get a value from. There is no need to specify the property because ASP.NET 2.0 recognizes a default property for each selectable control. Defaults are listed in the following table. Note that you always have the option to bind to a property other than the default by specifying it in the standard `Object.Property` syntax.

Data-Bound Control	Default Property for Binding to a Control Parameter
TextBox, Label	`Text`
CheckBox, RadioButton	`Checked`
ListBox, DropDownList, CheckBoxList, RadioButtonList	`SelectedValue`
GridView, DetailsView, FormView	`SelectedValue` (first field in the list of data key names)
TreeView, Menu	`SelectedValue`
Calendar	`SelectedDate`

In the case of a ListBox and related controls, be aware that there is both a text and a value property for each item in the box. The *text* for all items is shown to the user; the *value* is picked up by the control parameter for the one item that the user selected. For example, in Northwind you might show a list of employees' names in the text property but store their employee ID in the values. The user would interact with the name, but under the covers, you would use the ID value as the selected value to put into the control parameter.

The case of the GridView as a master control is more complex (several examples appear at the end of this chapter). There may not be a single field in a GridView that uniquely identifies one record. So, when a GridView is created, you can specify a `DataKeyNames` property consisting of one or more field names. By default, this will be the table's primary key, which can consist of one or more fields (usually one). When a row is selected in a GridView, the automatic postback occurs, and control parameters that use the GridView will be filled with the value from the GridView's `SelectedValue` property, which will be the value of the first field specified in `DataKeyNames`. In most cases, the data key name field will be the table's primary key and the control parameter will end up holding the primary key value of the selected record. That is precisely what you want for criteria in the `WHERE` clause of the child's data source control.

On rare occasions, you will need to fill a control parameter with a value from a property other than the default. In these cases, you can override the default by using the `PropertyName` property of the control parameter.

To summarize selection in data-bound controls, ASP.NET 2.0 takes care of coordinating all of the values behind the scenes when you use the VWD designer. If you look at the resulting source code, you will see that the master control does an automatic postback after the user makes a selection. The appropriate value of the user's choice is put into a control parameter of the child's data source control. That value is used by the `WHERE` clause so that only a limited set of data is fed to the child data-bound control.

Filtering GridView Records Using a List Control

Whenever you use a TextBox, you open the possibility of getting errant data from the user. The standard Windows interface for selecting from a finite number of choices is a list box. Switching from a querystring or TextBox to a list box is easy because the ASP.NET 2.0 architecture uses a consistent parameters collection. There is no difference in theory between using a drop-down list box and a simple list box. Populating the list box is discussed in three ways:

- Populate the list box from hard-coded values
- Populate the list box from data source
- Populate the list box using the SQL keyword `DISTINCT`

When using the TextBox, you had to include a button because the TextBox doesn't have a built-in sense of when the user is done typing, so you must solicit user action (the button) to begin the filtering of the GridView. Alternatively, you can set the Enter key to be an automatic postback in a TextBox. But in a list box, when `AutoPostBack` is set to `true`, a click sends to the page which item was selected and that also means the selection process is finished so the page can begin processing the selection. Therefore, you can build a page with master-child data-bound controls with no other controls. The ASPX page takes care of triggering events and reacting appropriately.

Master Control by DropDownList with Hard-Coded Items

If the items in the DropDownList do not change frequently, you can add them to the Item collection in the page code. The VWD designer walks you through the process and then builds the set of `ListItem` tags.

Try It Out #4 — Filtering GridView Records Using a DropDownList

You will offer the user a list of three states that you will hard-code. Upon selection, the GridView will display only authors from the selected state.

1. Create a page named `TIO-04-DropDownList` and drag a drop-down list from the toolbar onto it.
2. In the smart task panel, select Edit Items. Click Add and set `text = CA` and `value = CA`. Click Add again and repeat for `UT` and `IN`, and then press OK to save.
3. Keeping the list box selected, check its properties and be sure that `AutoPostBack` is set to `true`.
4. Add a SQL data source control to display author information as in the previous exercises, but this time in the `WHERE` clause set your source to `Control = DropDownList1` and the `value = SelectedValue`. Save and test in your browser.

```
<%@ Page Language="VB" %>
<html>
<head>
  <title>Ch09-TIO-04-FilteringGridViewUsingDropDownList</title>
</head>
```

```
<body><h3>Chapter 9 TIO #4 Filtering a GridView Using A DropDownList</h3>
  <form id="form1" runat="server">
    Choose a state:
    <asp:DropDownList ID="DropDownList1"
        AutoPostBack="true"
        Runat="server">
        <Items>
         <asp:ListItem Value="CA" />
         <asp:ListItem Value="UT" />
         <asp:ListItem Value="IN" />
       </Items>
    </asp:DropDownList>
    <br /><br />

    <asp:GridView> ... </asp:GridView>

    <asp:SqlDataSource ID="SqlDataSource1" Runat="server"
        ConnectionString="<%$ ConnectionStrings:LocalSqlPubs %>"
        SelectCommand="SELECT * FROM [authors] WHERE state = @state" >
      <SelectParameters>
        <asp:ControlParameter
            Name="state"
            ControlID="DropDownList1"
            PropertyName="SelectedValue" />
      </SelectParameters>
    </asp:SqlDataSource>
  </form>
</body>
</html>
```

How It Works #4—Filtering GridView Records Using a DropDownList

This example sticks with using a control for the source of a value in the parameter used in the `WHERE` clause. However, the control you use is a DropDownList. You set up the DropDownList using the VWD designer and double-check that you add a string to both the text and value properties.

This example does not have a button because the page performs an automatic postback after a selection in the DropDownList. This behavior is automatic only if the master control (the DropDownList) has its `AutoPostBack` property set to `true`.

Master Control by List Boxes with Data-Bound Items

Creating a list box with items added in the code works, but it would be a nightmare to maintain if the choices changed on a regular basis. Fortunately, the list box is a data-bound control (as discussed in Chapter 8). You can have a page with two data source controls. The first supports the GridView, as before, and takes its `WHERE` clause criteria from your list box. But now your list box also has a data source control #2, which provides just the list of values held in the `State` field of the authors table. Note that SQL's keyword `DISTINCT` is used so that you do not get duplicates, such as `CA` listed eight times for the eight records of Californian authors. It would also be possible to load the list box from a new table named States, and in fact this would be faster if there were hundreds of authors.

Try It Out #5 — Filtering GridView Records Using a Bound DropDownList

In this exercise, you want to re-create your list of authors, but with the master control DropDownList dynamically created.

1. Create a page named `TIO-05-DropDownList_Bound.aspx`. Drag a SQL data source control onto it and name it `SqlDataSourceStates`. Set its select command to `SELECT DISTINCT State FROM Authors`. You can turn on the check in the SqlDataSource wizard that says "Return only unique rows," or you can directly add the word `DISTINCT` after `SELECT` in the SelectCommand in the Source view.

2. Now drag to the page a DropDownList and set its source to the `SqlDataSourceStates` control. Both the text and value should be set to the state field. Check that the list has its `AutoPostBack` set to `true`. Save and test the DropDownList.

3. Now you will add the child control. Add a SQL data source control named `SqlDataSource1` with its `WHERE` clause criteria obtained from the `SelectedValue` of the DropDownList. Finish with a GridView that shows the records from `SqlDataSource1`. The page should be similar to the following; save and test.

```
<%@ Page Language="VB" %>
<html>
<head>
  <title>Ch09-TIO-05-FilteringGridViewUsingDataBoundDropDownList</title>
</head>
<body><h3>Chapter 9 TIO #5 Filtering a GridView Using A Data-bound DropDownList
</h3>
  <form id="form1" runat="server">
    Choose a state:
    <asp:DropDownList ID="DropDownList1"
         AutoPostBack="True"
         Runat="server"
         DataSourceID="SqlDataSourceStates"
         DataTextField="state"
         DataValueField="state"/>

    <asp:SqlDataSource ID="SqlDataSourceStates" Runat="server"
        SelectCommand="SELECT DISTINCT [state] FROM [authors]"
        ConnectionString="<%$ ConnectionStrings:LocalSqlPubs %>" />

    <br /><br />

    <asp:GridView> ... </asp:GridView>

    <asp:SqlDataSource ID="SqlDataSource1" Runat="server"
        ConnectionString="<%$ ConnectionStrings:LocalSqlPubs %>"
      SelectCommand="SELECT * FROM [authors] WHERE state = @state" >
      <SelectParameters>
        <asp:ControlParameter Name="state"
            ControlID="DropDownList1"
            PropertyName="SelectedValue" />
      </SelectParameters>
    </asp:SqlDataSource>
  </form>
</body>
</html>
```

How It Works #5 — Filtering GridView Records Using a Bound DropDownList

In this exercise, you did not make changes to your GridView or its source control (`SqlDataSource1`). But you did add a new data source control for the DropDownList to reap the list of state values from the authors table. The `DISTINCT` keyword in SQL filters out duplicate values in the list generated by `SqlDataSourceStates`. You also checked to be sure that the DropDownList as a master control had its `AutoPostBack` property set to `true`.

Note how the two data source controls operate completely independently. Also note that because the queries to retrieve the data for the GridView and DropDownList are different, we need to create two separate SqlDataSources. Although there may be data source controls in the future that can be configured for multiple queries simultaneously, the SqlDataSource control included in ASP.NET 2.0 only supports a single SelectCommand query at a time.

Master Control by List Boxes with a Default Setting That Initially Hides the GridView

The last exercise limited the GridView records based on a user's selection in a DropDownList, but when the page first opened, it displayed one state by default in the DropDownList and only that state's records in the GridView. For example, the last exercise started off with `CA` by default in the DropDownList and just the authors from California visible in the GridView. A better interface would render a DropDownList without a selection and no GridView until the user makes a selection.

The ASP.NET 2.0 team has built in the means to achieve the better scenario. There are a few logical twists and turns in the scenario, so don't worry if you find the next few paragraphs overwhelming. You can just emulate the highlighted code after each paragraph or follow the steps of the Try It Out.

1. In the DropDownList control, add an item with a value of an empty string and a short message to the user in the `Text` property, as follows:

```
<asp:DropDownList ID="DropDownList1"
  ... >
   <Items>
     <asp:ListItem Text="(Choose a state)" Value="" />
   </Items>
</asp:DropDownList>
```

2. Set to `true` a property called `AppendDataBoundItems`. When the page first loads, the DropDownList control will put the hard-coded item at the top of its list. Then, because of the `AppendDataBoundItems` property, the DropDownList continues to populate the rest (bottom) of the list with the records returned by its `DataSourceID`.

```
<asp:DropDownList ID="DropDownList1"
AppendDataBoundItems="true"
...
DataSourceID="SqlDataSource2"
DataTextField="state"
DataValueField="state">
```

3. Next, understand that in ASP.NET 2.0 when an empty string value is passed to a `ControlParameter` (in this case, in the GridView's SqlDataSource), the empty string is converted to `NULL` by default. Also by default, when the page is first loaded, the first item in the DropDownList will be selected. In this case, that will be the message "Choose a state" with the value of an empty string, which will be sent to the `ControlParameter` of the SqlDataSource for the GridView and converted to `NULL`.

4. Normally, the SqlDataSource does not execute the SelectCommand command when it sees a `NULL` for any parameter used in the SelectCommand. Because the select operation should execute in this case, even when the parameter is `NULL`, set `CancelSelectOnNullParameter=false` (in other words, go ahead with the selection even though a `NULL` is present) on the SqlDataSource used by the GridView, as follows:

```
<asp:SqlDataSource ID="SqlDataSourceForGridView"  Runat="server"
    ConnectionString='<%$ ConnectionStrings:LocalSqlPubs %>'
    CancelSelectOnNullParameter=false
...
</asp:SqlDataSource>
```

Consequently, the SelectCommand is actually executed even though it sees a `NULL` value in a parameter it needs to use. It may seem counterintuitive to execute the `SELECT` because our objective is to get no rendering of the GridView on first view, but we will solve that in the next step.

5. You learned a little about parameters earlier in this chapter with master-detail pages. They will be discussed more in Chapters 11 and 12. For now, note that a control parameter holds a value that is supplied by another control on the page. In the following case, the parameter named `state` (and referred to by `@state`) holds the `SelectedValue` from the `DropDownList1` control.

```
<asp:SqlDataSource ID="SqlDataSourceForGridView"  Runat="server"
    ...
  <SelectParameters>
    <asp:ControlParameter Name="state"
        ControlID="DropDownList1"
        PropertyName="SelectedValue" />
  </SelectParameters>
</asp:SqlDataSource>
```

6. With the preceding control parameter established, the value in `DropDownList1.SelectedValue` can be used in a `WHERE` clause of a SelectCommand by using `@state`.

Analyze the results in the case of the page first loading where the DropDownList supplies an empty string as its value, which is then converted to `NULL` by the `ControlParameter`. In the `WHERE` clause, `State=@state` would resolve to `State = NULL`. To the right of the `AND`, `State = Isnull (@state,state)` resolves to `state = state`, so it will be true for all records. But the left term, `State = NULL`, will not match records and, thus, none are returned.

Try It Out #6 — Displaying Details Using a GridView and DetailsView with All Items

In this exercise, the objective is to render the page on first view with all of the records on display in the GridView. Start with the page built in the last Try It Out and walk through the exercise, adding in the code to achieve the goal.

1. Open your page from the last exercise, `TIO-05-DropDownList_Bound.aspx`, and save it as `TIO-06-DropDownListBetter`. Change the title and `<H2>` text to reflect this new exercise. To make your changes more clear, use the Menu ➪ Edit ➪ Find/Replace to change all references to `SqlDataSource1` to `SqlDataSourceForGridView`.

2. Start by looking at it with the DropDownList control. If it is in the single-tag format (as follows), change to the two-tag format.

```
<asp:DropDownList ID="DropDownList1"
      ...  />
```

Two-tag format:

```
<asp:DropDownList ID="DropDownList1"
      ... >
</asp:DropDownList>
```

3. Add an `Item` tag to the DropDownList, as follows (available as version 1 in the downloads):

```
<asp:DropDownList ID="DropDownList1"
    AutoPostBack="True"
    Runat="server"
    DataSourceID="SqlDataSourceStates"
    DataTextField="state"
    DataValueField="state">
      <Items>
        <asp:ListItem Text="(Choose a state)" Value="" />
      </Items>
</asp:DropDownList>
```

4. Save and run the page. Notice that although you have added an item by hand, the DropDownList overwrites your item when it loads data from its data source control. Change that behavior by setting the `AppendDataBoundItems=True`. Save and test the page (version 2 in the downloads).

```
<asp:DropDownList ID="DropDownList1"
    ...
    AppendDataBoundItems=true >
    ...
</asp:DropDownList>
```

5. Ensure that in the SqlDataSource for the GridView, the SelectCommand will still be executed even if there is a `NULL` in a control parameter (version 3 in the downloads).

```
<asp:SqlDataSource ID="SqlDataSourceForGridView"
    ...
    CancelSelectOnNullParameter="false"
    ...
</asp:SqlDataSource>
```

6. Last, you can change your WHERE clause so that it handles both the case of NULL and the case of a value from the DropDownList (version 4 in the downloads).

```
<asp:SqlDataSource ID="SqlDataSourceForGridView"
    ...
  SelectCommand="SELECT * FROM [authors]
    WHERE state=@state AND state = IsNull(@state,state) " >
    ...
</asp:SqlDataSource>
```

How It Works #6—Displaying Details Using a GridView and DetailsView with All Items

In Try It Out #5, the page displayed, on first rendering, a default value in the DropDownList (CA) and a GridView that displayed only authors from California. This exercise provides a more intuitive first rendering of the page that shows all of the GridView records until the user makes a selection from the DropDownList. The improvement required four changes.

First, after checking that the DropDownList was in two-tag form, an item in hard code was added that displayed a message to the user and held a value of an empty string. Because the behavior of a DropDownList is to use the first item in the list as a default, this will be the default when the page is first opened. Recall that an empty string will be converted to a NULL when it is received into a ControlParameter used in a SqlDataSource control.

Second, to still add the states to the DropDownList, a property was turned on that kept the hard-coded item and then appended the items received from the data binding.

Third, this page requires overcoming a default behavior in the SqlDataSource control for the GridView. Normally, if a NULL value is present in a control parameter, the SqlDataSource control will just not execute its SelectCommand. That is fine in most cases because the NULL will cause no records to return, so there is no reason to execute the SelectCommand. But this employs a clever WHERE that handles NULLs, so the SelectCommand should execute even when a NULL is in the ControlParameters. This requires the following double negative. By setting CancelSelectOnNullParameter to false, the SelectCommand is executed.

```
<asp:SqlDataSource ID="SqlDataSourceForGridView"
     v...
    CancelSelectOnNullParameter=false
     ...
</asp:SqlDataSource>
```

Fourth, the WHERE clause of the GridView's data source control is modified to handle two cases. On first load, the ControlParameter will get a NULL. On subsequent loads, the ControlParameter will get the value of a state. To understand the solution, you must be comfortable with the two-argument behavior of ISNULL(argument1,argument2). If the first argument is not NULL, it is returned. If the first argument is NULL, the second argument is returned. As written in the code, the WHERE clause follows.

```
WHERE state=@state AND state = IsNull(@state,state) " >
```

When the page first renders, a NULL will be in the @state parameter. The left side of the AND will require records to have a state value of NULL, which should return no records. The right side of the AND will determine that `@state` is `NULL` and thus return `state`. To visualize the clause that SQL Server executes, substitute these results into the `WHERE` to get the following pseudo code, which will return no records.

```
WHERE state=NULL AND state = state" >
```

After the user selects a state in the DropDownList, a value will be in the `@state` parameter. The left side of the `AND` will require records to have a state equal to the value. The right side of the `AND` will determine that `@state` is not `NULL` and thus return the value in `@state`. As before, you can visualize the substitution of values into the `WHERE` to get the following pseudo code:

```
WHERE state=value AND state = value" >
```

The result is a redundant check to select only records where `state=value`. Good data servers eliminate that double request in their optimization schemas.

Displaying Details Using a GridView and DetailsView on the Same Page

The GridView optimizes the display of a few fields of many records. If you want to see many fields for just one record, you use DetailsView control, as discussed earlier. This inverts earlier examples in this chapter because GridView is now the master instead of the child control. When the GridView is the master, you use a CommandField column with the `ShowSelectButton` set to `true` to render a button for selecting a row in the grid. As with the list box as a master control, all handling of events and postback can be automated by ASP.NET 2.0.

Before starting the next exercise, let's look at pseudo code that explains what is required. These four blocks present the most basic properties (and ignore `ID` and `runat` properties). You will work with two data source controls and two data-bound controls. The first pair supports the display of a selectable GridView showing all authors. When a SELECT is performed, the other two controls come into play to show additional fields for the selected row. So start with the data source control for the GridView, as follows. Note that you are picking up only a few fields from the table.

```
<asp:SqlDataSource ID="MasterSource" ...
     SelectCommand="SELECT PKField, Field1, Field2 FROM MyTable />
```

Use that data source to support a GridView that must include a select column. The GridView must also designate a `DataKeyName`, which is, essentially, a primary key to uniquely identify the records in the GridView. `DataKeyNames` are discussed in more detail in Chapters 11 and 12 on modifying data.

```
<asp:GridView ...
     DataSourceID="MasterSource"
     DataKeyName="PKField">
      <Columns>
         <asp:BoundFields ... />
         <asp:CommandField
                ShowSelectButton="True"
                SelectText="View Details..." />
         </Columns>
</asp:GridView>
```

The second data source control, shown in the following pseudo code, supports the DetailsView. When the user clicks on the preceding GridView's select button, the value from the data key name field for that record is passed into a select parameter named, in this case, `ForeignKey` in the following data source control. That value is then read into the `WHERE` clause and only the single matching record is requested from the database. The `@` symbol means that the following text is a parameter name.

```
<asp:SqlDataSource  ID="DetailsSource"
        SelectCommand="SELECT * FROM MyTable WHERE (ForiegnPrimaryKey =
@ForeignKey)">
      <SelectParameters>
        <asp:ControlParameter
         Name="ForeignKey"
         Type="String"
         ControlID="GridView1"/>
      </SelectParameters>
</asp:SqlDataSource>
```

Last, the child control (in this case, a DetailsView control) displays the limited set of records and fields that were summoned by its data source control.

```
<asp:DetailsView
 DataSourceID="DetailsSource"
      <Fields>
         <asp:BoundFields .../>
      </Fields>
    </asp:DetailsView>
```

Now put the theory into practice with the following Try It Out.

Try It Out #7 — Displaying Details Using a GridView and DetailsView on the Same Page

In this exercise, you will create a GridView that displays just the author names and state fields plus a select button for each row. When the user clicks the select button, all of the fields for the selected employee will display. Even though you are not displaying the author ID, you will use it as the data key name, which becomes the `SelectedValue` for the GridView when a row is selected.

Note that the four controls (`GridViewAuthorNames`, `SqlDataSourceGV`, `DetailsView`, and `SqlDataSourceDetails`) can be in any order down the page. In this case, set the two data-bound controls side by side using an HTML table so they can be rendered side by side.

1. Create a new page, named `TIO-7-MasterDetails_SamePage.aspx`. In Design view, create a table using Menu: Layout(insert table with one row, two columns, and no border. Drag a GridView into the left cell, Choose Data Source as New and name it SqlDataSourceGV that reads the au_id and two name field from the Authors table of Pubs. Do not use a `WHERE` clause, because you want to see all of the authors. Enable Selection in the GridView by clicking the checkbox in its smart tasks panel. Save and test the page (the selection commands will not do anything yet). Close the browser.

2. Back in VWD Design view, drag into the right cell of the table a DetailsView control and configure its data source to a new control named `SqlDataSourceDetails`. Configure it to read all of the fields from the authors table and then click the WHERE button. Set the column for `au_id` equal to a control, then set the `ControlID` to `GridViewAuthorNames`. Leave the default value blank. Save the page and test in the browser.

```
<%@ Page Language="VB" %>
<html>
<head>
  <title>Ch09-TIO-7-MasterDetailsSamePage</title>
</head>
<body><h3>Chapter 9 TIO #7 Master-Details In The Same Page </h3>
  <form id="form1" runat="server">

    <table>
      <tr>
        <td valign="top">

          <asp:GridView ID="GridViewAuthorNames" Runat="server"
                AllowSorting="True"
                DataSourceID="SqlDataSourceGV"
                AutoGenerateColumns="False"
                AllowPaging="True"
                DataKeyNames="au_id">
            <SelectedRowStyle BackColor="#cccccc" />
            <Columns>
              <asp:BoundField HeaderText="au_lname"
                DataField="au_lname" SortExpression="au_lname" />
              <asp:BoundField HeaderText="au_fname"
                DataField="au_fname" SortExpression="au_fname" />
              <asp:CommandField ShowSelectButton="True"
                SelectText="View Details..." />
            </Columns>
          </asp:GridView>

        </td>
        <td valign="top">

          <asp:DetailsView ID="DetailsView1" Runat="server"
            DataSourceID="SqlDataSourceDetail"
            AutoGenerateRows="False"
            DataKeyNames="au_id">
            <Fields>
              <asp:BoundField ReadOnly="True" HeaderText="au_id"
                DataField="au_id" SortExpression="au_id" />
              <asp:BoundField HeaderText="au_lname"
                DataField="au_lname" SortExpression="au_lname" />
              <asp:BoundField HeaderText="au_fname"
                DataField="au_fname" SortExpression="au_fname" />
              <asp:BoundField HeaderText="phone"
                DataField="phone" SortExpression="phone" />
              <asp:BoundField HeaderText="address"
                DataField="address" SortExpression="address" />
              <asp:BoundField HeaderText="city"
```

```
                DataField="city" SortExpression="city" />
              <asp:BoundField HeaderText="state"
                DataField="state" SortExpression="state" />
              <asp:BoundField HeaderText="zip"
                DataField="zip" SortExpression="zip" />
              <asp:CheckBoxField HeaderText="contract"
                DataField="contract" SortExpression="contract" />
            </Fields>
          </asp:DetailsView>

        </td>
      </tr>
    </table>

    <asp:SqlDataSource ID="SqlDataSourceGV"
        ConnectionString="<%$ ConnectionStrings:LocalSqlPubs %>"
        SelectCommand="SELECT * FROM [authors]"
        Runat="server">
    </asp:SqlDataSource>

    <asp:SqlDataSource ID="SqlDataSourceDetail"
      Runat="server"
         ConnectionString="<%$ ConnectionStrings:LocalSqlPubs %>"
      SelectCommand="SELECT * FROM [authors] WHERE ([au_id] = @au_id)">
      <SelectParameters>
        <asp:ControlParameter
          Name="au_id"
          Type="String"
          ControlID="GridViewAuthorNames"/>
      </SelectParameters>
    </asp:SqlDataSource>
  </form>
</body>
</html>
```

How It Works #7 — Displaying Details Using a GridView and DetailsView on the Same Page

This page contains four controls: a GridView and its supporting data source control and a DetailsView with its supporting data source control. The GridView is the master because it accepts the user's click, and the DetailsView is the child. Let's analyze each of the four controls from the standpoint of its source code.

The `SqlDataSourceGV` presents nothing special other than a limited set of fields. Note that the `au_ID` field is included even though you do not intend to display it because you need it as the primary key for the data key names that are used in the selection process.

The `GridViewAuthorNames` displays the names fields plus the column created holding the Select buttons. Note in the source code that Visual Web Developer has checked the table's primary key and used that field for the `DataKeyNames` property.

The SqlDataSourceDetails does the actual filtering so that the DetailsView control will display data for the single selected author. There are two sections of interest. First is the collection of SelectParameters, within which is one member of the type ControlParameter. The designer, following your clicks in the dialog box, gave the parameter a name of au_id and set it to pick up the default property from the GridViewAuthorNames. Second, the SelectCommand is written to pick up your parameter named au_id for the criteria of the WHERE clause.

```
<asp:SqlDataSource ID="SqlDataSourceDetail"
  Runat="server"
     ConnectionString="<%$ ConnectionStrings:LocalSqlPubs %>"
  SelectCommand="SELECT * FROM [authors] WHERE ([au_id] = @au_id)">
  <SelectParameters>
    <asp:ControlParameter
      Name="au_id"
      Type="String"
      ControlID="GridViewAuthorNames"/>
  </SelectParameters>
</asp:SqlDataSource>
```

Last, the DetailsView simply displays all of the fields from the one record returned by the SqlDataSourceDetails control.

What happens when the user clicks on the GridView? An automatic postback is triggered that fills the au_id value of the selected record into the ControlParameter of the SqlDataSourceDetails control. That control then gets all the field values for that single matching record, and those field values are displayed in the DetailsView control.

Displaying Details Using a GridView and DetailsView on Different Pages

Frequently a client wants details for a record shown on a separate page. This allows more fields to be shown and involves fewer layout constraints (and perhaps a new advertisement). The technique combines ideas from Try It Out #7 and Try It Out #1 (transfer of values by QueryString).

There are two changes from the last exercise, one on the master control page and one on the child control page. Recall that in the last exercise (same page for DetailsView), you used in the master control (GridView) a SelectCommand column. To display in a different page, you must use a HyperLinkField column instead. Within that hyperlink are two critical settings:

- DataNavigateUrlField normally holds a URL, but in this case, it will hold the primary key value of the selected field. You set it to the field holding the ID (primary key) for the records.
- DataNavigateUrlFormatString. You will use this to specify the details page's URL and to append the ID value from the preceding property.

The resulting code for the master control follows.

```
<asp:GridView ID="GridView1" Runat="server"
    DataSourceID="MyDataSource"
    DataKeyNames="MyPrimaryKeyField">
  <Columns>
     <asp:BoundField ... />
    <asp:HyperLinkField
            HeaderText="ViewDetails..."
            Text="View Details..."
            DataNavigateUrlFields="MyPrimaryKeyField"
            DataNavigateUrlFormatString="MyDetailsPage.aspx?ID={0}"/>
  </Columns>
</asp:GridView>
```

When the user clicks on a hyperlink button of the GridView, the record's primary key value is put into the variable `{0}` and that is used as the querystring on the end of the literal URL `MyDetailsPage.asp?ID=` of the `DataNavigateUrlFormatString`.

On the details page, you now pick up the value from the querystring, the same as in the first example of this chapter. The data source control would be as follows:

```
<asp:SqlDataSource ID="SqlDataSource1" Runat="server"
  ConnectionString="<%$ ConnectionStrings:LocalSqlPubs %>"
  SelectCommand="
          SELECT * FROM MyTable
          WHERE (MyPrimaryKeyField = @ID)">
  <SelectParameters>
    <asp:QueryStringParameter Name="ID"
      DefaultValue="123"
      QueryStringField="ID"
      Type="String" />
  </SelectParameters>
</asp:SqlDataSource>
```

When the details page opens, it reads the querystring and puts the values into the `QueryStringParameter`. When the data source control builds its `WHERE` clause, it will pull in the value of the record ID from the querystring parameter.

Of course, the VWD designer can generate all of this code automatically, as demonstrated in the following exercise.

Try It Out #8 — Displaying Details Using a GridView and DetailsView on Different Pages

This exercise is very similar in objective to the last exercise, but now you want the DetailsView control to appear on a second page named `TIO-08-Details.aspx`. You can start with the previous exercise, rename it, and make changes in the source, or you can take the following steps to build from nothing.

1. Create a page named `TIO-08-MasterDetails_DifferentPage.aspx`. Add a SqlDataSource control to pick up the `au_id` and names fields from the authors table of Pubs. Don't use a `WHERE`

clause, because you want to see all of the authors' names. Add a GridView and click on Edit Columns to add bound fields for the three author fields plus a hyperlink field. Staying in the Edit Columns dialog box, set four properties for the hyperlink field.

HeaderText=	ViewDetails...
Text=	View Details...
DataNavigateUrlFields=	au_id
DataNavigateUrlFormatString=	TIO-08-Details.aspx?ID={0}/>

2. The field should be similar to the following listing. Save the file and test it (the hyperlinks are not enabled yet).

```
<%@ Page Language="VB" %>
<html>
<head>
  <title>Ch09-TIO-08-MasterDetailsToDifferentPageSameRecord</title>
</head>
<body><h3>Chapter 9 TIO #8 Master-Details To A Different Page - Same Record </h3>
  <form id="form1" runat="server">

    <asp:GridView ID="GridView1"
        AllowSorting="True"
        Runat="server"
        DataSourceID="SqlDataSource1"
        DataKeyNames="au_id"
        AutoGenerateColumns="False"
        AllowPaging="True">
      <Columns>
        <asp:BoundField HeaderText="au_lname"
                DataField="au_lname" SortExpression="au_lname" />
        <asp:BoundField HeaderText="au_fname"
                DataField="au_fname" SortExpression="au_fname" />
        <asp:HyperLinkField HeaderText="ViewDetails..."
                Text="View Details..."
                DataNavigateUrlFields="au_id"
               DataNavigateUrlFormatString="TIO-08-Details.aspx?ID={0}"/>
      </Columns>
    </asp:GridView>

    <asp:SqlDataSource ID="SqlDataSource1"
        ConnectionString="<%$ ConnectionStrings:LocalSqlPubs %>"
        SelectCommand="SELECT au_id, au_fname, au_lname FROM [authors]"
        Runat="server">
    </asp:SqlDataSource>
  </form>
</body>
</html>
```

3. Now create `TIO-08-Details.aspx` and give it a SqlDataSource control that picks up all of the fields from the authors table. Set its `WHERE` clause to make the column `au_id` equal to a querystring field named `au_id`. Give it a default value of `213-46-8915`.

4. Now add a DetailsView control that connects to the data source. The Autogenerate Fields option is fine here, so turn it on in the Edit Columns dialog box. Finish the page by adding a simple hyperlink back to `TIO-08-MasterDetails_DifferentPage.aspx` and save.

```
<%@ Page Language="VB" %>
<html>
  <head runat="server">
    <title>Ch09-TIO##-View Author Details</title>
  </head>
  <body><h3>Chapter 9 TIO # </h3>
    <form id="form1" runat="server">
      <asp:DetailsView ID="DetailsView1" Runat="server"
        DataSourceID="SqlDataSource1"
        AutoGenerateRows="True"
        HeaderText="Author Details"
        EmptyDataText="There are no records to display"
        DataKeyNames="au_id">
      </asp:DetailsView>

      <asp:SqlDataSource ID="SqlDataSource1" Runat="server"
        ConnectionString="<%$ ConnectionStrings:LocalSqlPubs %>"
        SelectCommand="SELECT * FROM [authors] WHERE ([au_id] = @au_id)">
        <SelectParameters>
          <asp:QueryStringParameter Name="au_id"
            DefaultValue="213-46-8915"
            QueryStringField="ID"
            Type="String" />
        </SelectParameters>
      </asp:SqlDataSource>
       
      <br />
      <a href="TIO-08-MasterDetails_DifferentPage.aspx">Back To Grid</a>
    </form>
  </body>
</html>
```

5. Open the first page (`TIO-08-MasterDetails_DifferentPage.aspx`). Select an author, and more data about that person will be shown in the details page.

How It Works #8 — Displaying Details Using a GridView and DetailsView on Different Pages

When the user clicks a select command in the master page GridView, an automatic postback is invoked. Back on the server, ASP.NET 2.0 picks up the `au_id` from the selected row and copies the value into the details page's `QueryStringParameter`. When the details page data source control builds its select command, it will substitute the actual ID value for the `@au-id`. When that SQL statement executes, you get back only the one matching record. The fields of that record are then displayed in the DetailsView.

The same technique works if you want to display data from related tables. For example, page 1 may show a list of customers with selectability. Upon clicking, the user is directed to page 2, which shows all of the orders for the clicked customer. The only difference is in how you use the identification value received in the second page. For related records, you use it in a SQL statement that includes a `JOIN`. This is not an ASP.NET 2.0 topic, but it is worth an exercise so that you can see all of the code.

Try It Out #9 — Displaying Related Records Using a GridView and a GridView

This exercise uses the same GridView of authors as the master control, but on selecting an author, you jump to a page with all of the books by the selected author. Note that Marjorie Greene and Charlene Locksley have written more than one book.

1. Open your page from the last exercise (`TIO-08`) and save as `TIO-09-MasterDetails_AllRelatedRecords.aspx`. Change the target of the hyperlink to a new page by setting the `GridView.HyperlinkField.DataNavigationUrlFormatString` to the following:

```
        <asp:HyperLinkField HeaderText="ViewDetails..."
            Text="View Details..."
            DataNavigateUrlFields="au_id"
            DataNavigateUrlFormatString="TIO-09-DetailsAllRecords.aspx?ID={0}" />
    </Columns>
</asp:GridView>
```

2. Open your details page from the last exercise (`TIO-8-Details.aspx`) and save as `TIO-09-DetailsAllRecords.aspx`. Then change the SQL statement for the data source control, title, and hyperlink, as follows:

```
<title>Ch09-TIO 09-View Book Details</title>


<asp:SqlDataSource ID="SqlDataSource1" Runat="server"
        SelectCommand="
            SELECT authors.au_id, titles.title_id,
                titles.title, titles.type,
                titles.price, titles.notes
            FROM authors
                INNER JOIN titleauthor ON authors.au_id = titleauthor.au_id
                INNER JOIN titles ON titleauthor.title_id = titles.title_id
            WHERE (authors.au_id = @au_id)"


<a href="TIO-09-MasterDetails_AllRelatedRecords.aspx">Back To Grid</a>
```

3. Save and test the page.

How It Works #9 — Displaying Related Records Using a GridView and a GridView

The main change here is the SQL statement for the data source control of the details page. You select fields about titles (books) that come from tabular joins between `Authors` and `TitleAuthor` and then between `TitleAuthor` and `Titles`. This allows you to use the `au_id` value to select only those titles that match with a given author. More detail on the syntax of `JOINs` is available from a SQL text or the appendix at the back of this book.

Cascading DropDownLists

One of the most intuitive user interfaces is a cascade of lists. The user selects from the first list, for example, Countries, and then a second list is populated with appropriate choices, for example, Regions. The Regions choices would be only those regions within the selected country. The second list, when selected, can govern the population of a third list, such as Cities. In this architecture, the first list is a master. The second becomes both a child to the first and a master to the third. You need a data source control for each list. The child data source control will have a `ControlParameter` that points to the master data source control and uses the parameter value in its `WHERE` clause.

Try It Out #10 — Using Cascading DropDownLists

In this exercise, you will create a list to show the categories in Northwind. When a category is selected, you will see all of the products in that category.

1. Create a new page named `TIO-10-CascadingDropDownLists.aspx`. Add a DropDownList control, then expand the Choose Data Source drop-down in the smart tag panel (in VWD) and choose "<New Data Source...>". The new data source control should be named `SqlDataSourceCategories` and read the category ID and name from the Categories table of Northwind. When configuring the drop-down list, set the text to `CategoryName` and value to `CategoryID`. Save and test the page.

```
<%@ Page Language="VB" %>
<html>
<head><title>Ch09-TIO10-CascadingDropDownLists</title></head>
<body><h3>Chapter 9 TIO #10 Cascading DropDownLists </h3>
  <form id="form1" runat="server">

    <asp:DropDownList ID="DropDownListCategories" Runat="server"
        DataSourceID="SqlDataSourceCategories"
        DataTextField="CategoryName"
        DataValueField="CategoryID"
        AutoPostBack="True" />

    <asp:SqlDataSource ID="SqlDataSourceCategories" Runat="server"
        SelectCommand="
            SELECT [CategoryID], [CategoryName] FROM [Categories]"
        ConnectionString="<%$ ConnectionStrings:LocalSqlNorthWind %>" />

</form></body></html>>
```

2. Now add a second drop-down list, expand the Choose Data Source drop-down in the smart tag panel (in VWD), and choose "<New Data Source...>." Name it `SqlDataSourceProducts`. This time read the product ID and product name from the Products table. Click the WHERE button and set the CategoryID field equal to the `DropDownListCategories` control. If you check the source code, you should have two new controls, as follows. Save and test the page.

```
<asp:DropDownList ID="DropDownListProducts" Runat="server"
    DataSourceID="SqlDataSourceProducts"
    DataTextField="ProductName"
    DataValueField="ProductID"
    AutoPostBack="True" />
```

```
<asp:SqlDataSource ID="SqlDataSourceProducts" Runat="server"
    SelectCommand="
        SELECT [ProductID], [ProductName] FROM [Products]
        WHERE ([CategoryID] = @CategoryIDParam)"
    ConnectionString="<%$ ConnectionStrings:LocalSqlNorthwind %>">
  <SelectParameters>
    <asp:ControlParameter Name="CategoryIDParam"
        ControlID="DropDownListCategories"
        PropertyName="SelectedValue" />
  </SelectParameters>
</asp:SqlDataSource>
```

How It Works #10 — Using Cascading DropDownLists

The first drop-down list, Categories, presents nothing new. The second list is supported by the `SqlDataSourceControlProducts`. That has a `ControlParameter` to read the selected value from the Categories drop-down list. The value selected is passed into the ControlParameter and then used as the criterion in the `WHERE` clause of the data source column for list 2.

Common Mistakes

Following are mistakes commonly made in filtering and working with master-child data:

- Forgetting to click Add after setting up a parameter in the `WHERE` clause dialog box of the data source control.
- Attempting to use the value property from a list box after only setting the text property for the list box's items. You need to set `DataValueField` in addition to `DataTextField`.
- Expecting a list box selection to automatically update a child control, but the `AutoPostBack` property of the list box is set to `false`. It must be `true` or else you must have a button to submit.
- Utilizing the wrong data source control for a data-bound control when the page contains multiple data sources. Use descriptive names for your data source controls to reduce errors.
- Improperly formatting a URL with a querystring in a hyperlink column. Check the syntax in the examples of this chapter.
- Forgetting to set `DataKeyNames` on GridView when using it as a master control for selection or navigation to a separate page. The field set to `DataKeyNames` is used as a `SelectedValue` for the grid.
- Using a single data source for both the master and details controls. It will often be necessary to use separate data sources for each control because the data they display will be different.

Summary

This chapter demonstrates how one control can establish settings to change the scope of another control. You have implemented multiple scenarios of master-details controls without doing any VB or C# coding or even thinking about events. The chapter walked through dialog boxes and wizards, and then the

VWD designer built all necessary code (with the exception of the complex SQL `JOIN` example). In particular, you used the Parameters dialog box made visible by clicking the WHERE button when configuring the data source control for the child data-bound control.

The basic theory is that the user will select an item on a master control. That will trigger a postback, and the value of the selected item will be placed into any `ControlParameters` on the page. You typically have such a parameter in the data source control for the child control. That data source control will then use the value in the parameter as the criterion for its `WHERE` clause. The resulting data (usually filtered to just one record) is displayed in the child data-bound control.

The first case demonstrated how to pass the value to the page in the querystring. Although the technique is too crude for deployment, you saw how the child control picked up the parameter and used it to filter. Note that when a value comes from the querystring, you must store it in a `QueryStringParameter`. The explanation then moved to the use of TextBox controls to store value in a `ControlParameter`. Although you can use the SQL keyword `LIKE` to overcome some problems, it is poor practice to rely on the user to type accurate input. When you use a list, you know that the user will not type invalid values.

You explored how to use the GridView as a child by adding a parameter to its data source control and using that parameter as the criterion in a `WHERE` clause.

You also explored how to use the GridView as a master by adding a CommandField of the Select type. When the user clicks on the select button of a record, a postback occurs. The selected record's ID (the value in the first field of the `DataKeyNames` property) is deposited in any control parameters on the page that specify the GridView as their source.

If you want the details to appear on a separate page, you use a hyperlink instead of a Select field in the GridView. The hyperlink uses the `DataNavigateUrlField` to hold the value from the ID column. You use the `DataNavigateUrlFormatString` to add the literal name of the details page. That details page then gets the ID value from the querystring, deposits it in a `QueryStringParameter`, and uses the parameter as the criterion in the data source control's `WHERE` clause.

The chapter finished with cascading DropDownList controls. Each list gets its own data source control. The first list has no special modifications. But the second data source control establishes a control parameter with the selected value of the first drop-down list. As per the pattern of this chapter, that parameter is used as the criterion in the `WHERE` clause of the second list's data source control.

The final topic to cover on displaying data involves templates, which are discussed in detail in the next chapter.

Exercises

1. In a data source control SelectCommand `WHERE` clause, what is the difference between `Xxx` and `@Xxx`?
2. Write the syntax to include the value `567` in the MemberID field in a URL that calls a page named `MemberProfile.aspx` at the `MyYachtClub.org` site.

3. Continuing from Question 2, on the page `MemberProfile.aspx`, write the code for a SqlDataSource control to show information for only the member ID passed from the URL.
4. What is the default property for binding to a `ControlParameter` for a DropDownList and a GridView?
5. When populating a DropDownList from a SQL statement, how can you avoid multiple listings of the same value, for example multiple `PA`s when four authors are from Pennsylvania?
6. How can you display in a DropDownList a combination of items from hard coding and from a data source control?
7. How does an ASP.NET 2.0 data source `ControlParameter` handle values that are an empty string?
8. How does a data source control react to a `ControlParameter` containing a `NULL` value?
9. The GridView control was designed to display values for many records. What controls are designed to show values for only one record at a time?
10. Describe the difference between a GridView's `DataNavigateUrlField` and `DataNavigateUrlFormatString` properties.
11. How is the value from the `DataNavigateUrlField` put into the `DataNavigateUrlFormatString`?
12. How are the `DataNavigateUrlField` and `DataNavigateUrlFormatString` properties set when a GridView is calling for details of one record on another page?

10

Displaying Data in Templated Controls

A GridView bound column has one value per cell, and a list box presents its choices in a standard format — these are rigid in their rendering. ASP.NET 2.0 offers a set of controls that support a feature called templates that are more flexible in their rendering. These include the Repeater, the DataList, the FormView, and the templated column/field of the GridView and DetailsView. Within these templated controls, you can add custom markup and one or more simple controls, such as labels or images, to define the rendering of the template. Because the templated control is bound to a data source, controls inside the template can be bound to fields of the data source, and then each of the controls within a template will display the value for the current record as the template is created. When the current record changes, the values of data-bound controls in the template change. The arrangement of the controls in the template is very flexible, as are options for laying the template on the page.

Template behavior is the only option for some controls — the template must be defined in order for the control to provide a rendering. For others, templating is optional and only replaces a region within the built-in control rendering.

This chapter discusses the following topics:

- **Template field in a control (GridView)** — Changing a bound field to a template field; use of `Eval()`
- **DataList and FormView** — Properties to arrange on page
- **Arranging by DataList** — Add a table into the template to arrange internal data-bound controls
- **DataList conversion** — Convert to FormView and enable paging
- **DetailsView** — Review

You will explore template behavior with the following Try It Out exercises:

Try It Out	Topic
1	Convert Column from Bound to Template in a GridView
2	DataList Control Page Layout Properties
3	DataList Control Internal Layout
4	DetailsView and FormView

The last few chapters discussed techniques to display data in tables. These controls offer quick results, but they have a prescribed layout for their format. To provide more flexibility, ASP.NET 2.0 offers several controls within which a designer can easily build a custom set of data-bound controls. These workspaces are called templates.

The templated control as a whole is bound to a data source control, and the templates themselves can hold controls such as labels, hyperlinks, and images. Properties of these controls within a template can then be bound to a field of the templated control's data source using a data binding expression (discussed later in this chapter). The control will show the value from its data-bound field for the template's current record. As you read this chapter, keep in mind these two levels of binding: the templated control bound to a data source control and the internal control inside the template bound to a field of the data source.

Note that not all templated controls are data-bound, but for the sake of the discussion in this book we only look at templated data-bound controls (with an associated data source). For more information on non-data-bound template customization, refer to a more general ASP.NET reference.

Templates can represent a set of multiple data records in one of two ways: repeated iterations of the template on the page for each data item in the data source, or a single iteration of the template for the current data item, with paging enabled to move between data items. The DataList, Repeater, and GridView template column controls provide a repeated format, whereas the DetailsView and FormView provide a single record presentation (optionally with paging enabled to move between records). You can see the repeated layout at the top of the page (solid border) shown in Figure 10-1 and the single record layout in the lower part of the page (dotted border). You can download the file for this page, named `Demo-1-TemplateLayout.aspx`, from Chapter 10.

Templated controls can actually have more than one templated area. For example, the GridView and DetailsView TemplateField allows you to define a template for the header and footer of the column (the HeaderTemplate and FooterTemplate properties of TemplateField, respectively) in addition to the individual cells in the column (called the ItemTemplate on TemplateField). Note that unlike the item template, which can contain data-bound controls to data source fields, the header and footer templates are not data-bound and can only contain static controls and markup (HTML). The GridView and DetailsView also provide top-level templates for the pager (PagerTemplate) and empty data row (EmptyDataTemplate). Other controls, such as DataList and Repeater, provide a different set of templates, but the concept is still the same.

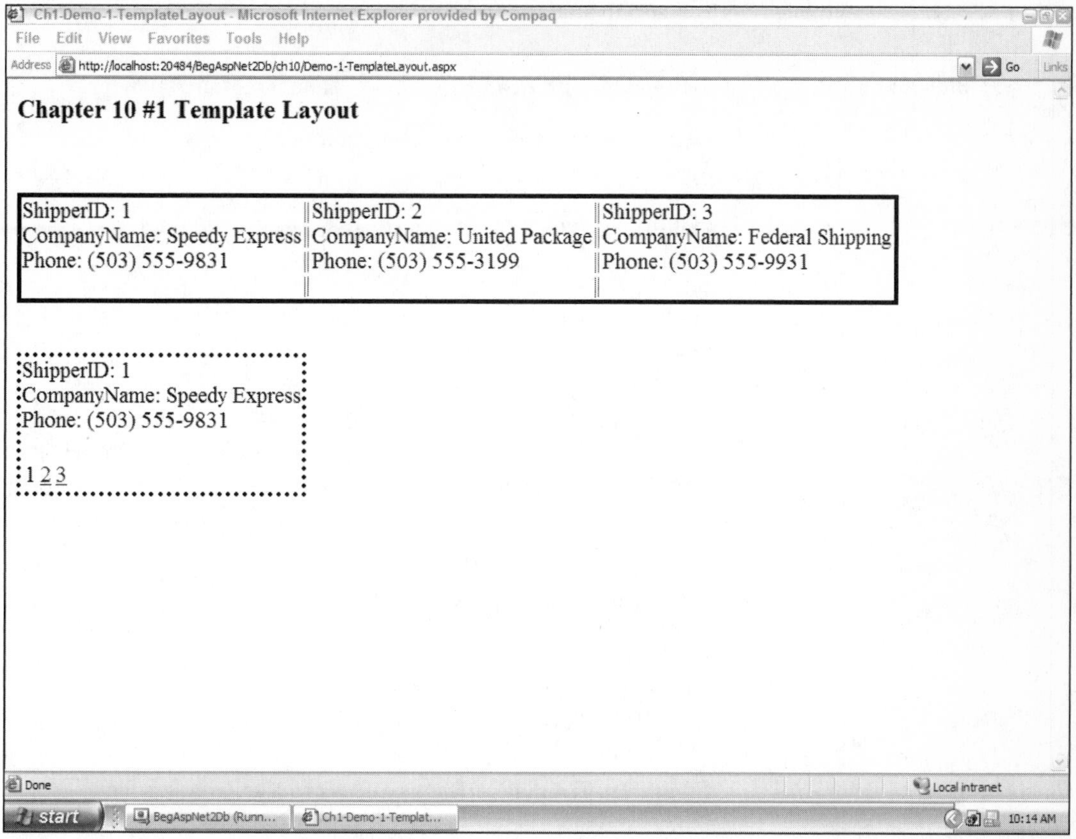

Figure 10-1

You have encountered templated controls twice before: GridView templated columns in Chapters 5 and 6 and the DetailsView in Chapter 9. In each case, you followed the pattern just described. A template space held other controls that were bound to a data source field. In the previous chapter's example of Master-Details using GridView and DetailsView, the record selected in the master GridView determined the record of choice for the child DetailsView control. In the case of the templated field within the GridView, each cell was an iteration of the ItemTemplate and showed the appropriate data for its row.

The ASP.NET 2.0 templated controls and their associated template properties are defined as follows:

Templated Control	Template Properties	ItemTemplate Behavior
GridView	EmptyDataTemplate PagerTemplate **TemplateField** AlternatingItemTemplate * EditItemTemplate * FooterTemplate HeaderTemplate ItemTemplate *	GridView repeats Template Field.ItemTemplate once per row for each record in the data source.
DetailsView	EmptyDataTemplate PagerTemplate HeaderTemplate FooterTemplate **TemplateField** AlternatingItemTemplate * EditItemTemplate * FooterTemplate HeaderTemplate InsertItemTemplate * ItemTemplate *	DetailsView renders Template Field.ItemTemplate for field's data cell the current record in the data source.
FormView	EmptyDataTemplate PagerTemplate HeaderTemplate FooterTemplate ItemTemplate * EditItemTemplate * InsertItemTemplate *	FormView renders the ItemTemplate for the current record in the data source.
DataList	HeaderTemplate FooterTemplate AlternatingItemTemplate * ItemTemplate * EditItemTemplate * SelectedItemTemplate * SeparatorTemplate	DataList repeats the ItemTemplate once for each record in the data source.
Repeater	HeaderTemplate FooterTemplate AlternatingItemTemplate * ItemTemplate * SeparatorTemplate	DataList repeats the ItemTemplate once for each record in the data source.

Note that this chapter will discuss using tables at several levels. On the grandest scale, you may add a table to a page to arrange controls such as two GridViews. Then, a control may generate an overall table such as one GridView, with each record getting an entire cell. At the finest level, you may add a table to a template to organize the internal data-aware controls.

Using Templated Controls

Templated controls are added to the page in seven steps using the VWD designer (we will look at the source code in a minute):

1. Add the templated control to the page.
2. Bind the templated control to a data source control (existing or created at the moment).
3. If using GridView or DetailsView, add a TemplateColumn to the Columns or Fields collection.
4. Switch to Edit Template mode and select Edit the ItemTemplate.
5. Add controls from the toolbox to the template region, using the "Edit Databindings..." task to bind them to fields of the data source.
6. (Optional) Edit other templates such as header, footer, and pager.
7. Click on end Template Editing.
8. (Optional) Set other properties on the templated control as needed.

In step 1, you drag and drop the template from the toolbar to the page. A smart task panel opens to help with step 2, where you select an existing data source control or create a new one.

Once the entire template is bound, you can look on the smart task panel for the Edit Templates item. When you click it, you get a drop-down list of templates. Select the Item template and you are in Edit Template mode. There are up to seven choices of templates to edit, including header, footer, and pager. In the Item template, a control can be added and bound to a field of the data source. Note that some templated controls, such as DataList and FormView, automatically created default content for their templates based on the available fields in the data source. You can alter this default template content to your liking, or delete it entirely and start from scratch.

In Edit Template mode (step 4 in the preceding list), you can add controls such as labels, images, and hyperlinks from the toolbox to the template. After adding the control, click on its smart task panel option to Edit Data Bindings. You can select a bindable property (such as the `Text` property of a TextBox or Label), and then on the right, select Field Binding and select a field from the drop-down list. Click OK and the control within a template is bound.

After editing the templates as desired, select the templated control as a whole (click on its title bar) and reopen the template's smart task panel. Click End Template Editing to perform step 6 in the preceding list. You can then finish with setting properties of the templated control such as its layout pattern.

Data Binding in Templates

Data-binding expressions are created from the designer when using Visual Web Developer (VWD) or Visual Studio (VS). But it is worth understanding the source code for binding so that you can troubleshoot and maintain the page. Recall that you data-bind at two levels of controls: the *templated control* itself is bound to a data source control and the *controls within a template* that you add onto the template's workspace, such as labels and images, are bound to fields of the data source.

The templated control itself is bound to a data source control. That binding enables two features. First, it makes the fields of values from the data source control available to the controls within a template. Second, the templated control can set the current record and determine which record's values to display in the control within a template. The source code for a typical bound control within a template follows.

```
<asp:DataList ID="DataList1" Runat="server"
  DataSourceID="NorthwindShippersSqlDataSource"
  <ItemTemplate>
         <asp:Label />
         <asp:Image />
  </ItemTemplate>
</asp:DataList>
```

The controls within a template are bound to fields of the data source. They must be bound to fields that are made available by the templated control's data source control. They can be bound as read-only or read-write (although write is not available for all templated controls). When you bind a control within a template to be read-only, you use the `Eval()` function. To add write capability, you use the `Bind()` function. In the VWD, you can set writability by checking the "Two Way Binding" box when binding the control within a template. Note that `Bind()` is available on only the controls that were released with ASP.NET version 2.0: GridView, DetailsView, and FormView. DataList and Repeater do not support `Bind()`. The writing of data from ASPX pages to a database is discussed in detail in Chapters 11 and 12. The source code for a typical read-only bound control within a template follows.

```
<asp:DataList ID="DataList1" Runat="server"
         DataSourceID="MySqlDataSource">
                <ItemTemplate>
                        <asp:Label Text='<%# Eval("MyField") %>'  runat="server"/>
                </ItemTemplate>
</asp:DataList>
```

Content Suitable for Addition to a Template

As previously mentioned, templates can contain either markup (HTML), server controls, or a mixture of both. For example, it is often desirable to add an HTML table to a template simply for providing an overall layout structure to the template to contain data-bound server controls. You can drag and drop a table from the toolbar, or if you position the cursor within the template and click through the menu (Layout ➪ Insert Table), you will get a handy dialog box to build the table with a GUI.

Any server control can be added to a template, although some controls make more sense in certain templates than others. In the ItemTemplate, which is rendered for the read-only view of a data-bound control, you will most often place server controls that are simply for rendering the data, such as a Label control or Image control.

```
<ItemTemplate>
    <asp:Label Text='<%# Eval("CustomerName") %>'  runat="server"/>
    <asp:Image ImageUrl='<%# Eval("FileName", "~/Images/{0}") %>' runat="server"/>
</ItemTemplate>
```

In templates meant for editing, you will most likely place server controls that support input of data, such as a TextBox or CheckBox control.

```
<EditItemTemplate>
    <asp:TextBox Text='<%# Bind("CustomerName") %>'  runat="server"/>
    <asp:CheckBox ImageUrl='<%# Bind("IsActive") %>' runat="server"/>
</EditItemTemplate>
```

An edit template may also contain list controls, such as a DropDownList. As demonstrated in Chapter 8, the items in the list can be created statically or by binding the list to its own data source control.

```
<EditItemTemplate>
    <asp:DropDownList SelectedValue='<%# Bind("CustomerName") %>'
DataSourceID="CustomersDataSource" DataTextField="CustomerName"  runat="server"/>
</EditItemTemplate>
```

Editing will be discussed in detail in the following chapters, so it is not treated in depth here.

GridView and DetailsView Template Fields

We've already seen that you can add various field objects to the GridView Columns collection and DetailsView Fields collection. The TemplateField is one of these fields that allows you to define the contents of the column or field as a template region. The GridView's template column renders with multiple iterations on the page, so it is like the other repeated templates in that all of the records are visible at once. DetailsView renders the field once for the current data records, and you can page between records if paging is enabled on the control.

The template column offers layout flexibility not provided by other field objects like BoundField. You can use spaces and CR/LF (Carriage Return/Line Feed) to arrange the internal controls in the template as well as tables for more complex layouts. When adding a table in VWD, go to Menu ➪ Layout ➪ Insert Table to take advantage of the design tool. The VWD allows easy conversion of a bound field to a templated field so that you can enhance a template without having to re-drag and bind its first data-aware control.

Try It Out #1 — Convert Column from Bound to Template in a GridView

In this first exercise, you will create a page (named version 1) displaying a GridView with four bound columns from the Northwind Employees table. You will then (in version 2) convert one of those columns from a bound column to a template column and arrange within that template column three fields.

1. Create a new folder for this chapter named `C:\Websites\BegAspNet2Db\ch10`. Create a new page named `TIO-1-ConvertBoundToTemplate-1.aspx`. Add a data source control and GridView to display the IDs, names, and hire dates for employees of Northwind. Format the hire date to short date using `{0:d}`. The code should be similar to the following. Save the page and observe in your browser. Recall that in this book, connection strings are stored in the Web.config file as per Try It Out #2 in Chapter 3.

```
<%@ Page Language="VB" %>
<!DOCTYPE html PUBLIC "-//W3C//DTD XHTML 1.1//EN"
"http://www.w3.org/TR/xhtml11/DTD/xhtml11.dtd">
```

```
<html xmlns="http://www.w3.org/1999/xhtml" >
<head runat="server"><title>Ch10-TIO-1-ConvertBoundToTemplate-Ver1</title></head>
<body>
<h3>Chapter 10 TIO #1 <BR />
GridView - Convert Bound Column to Template Column<br />
Bound column version</h3>
    <form id="form1" runat="server">
    <div>
        <asp:SqlDataSource ID="NorthwindEmployeesSqlDataSource"  Runat="server"
            ConnectionString="<%$ ConnectionStrings: LocalSqlNorthwind %>"
          SelectCommand="Select EmployeeID,FirstName,LastName, HireDate
                FROM Employees"/>

        <asp:GridView ID="GridView1" Runat="server"
            DataSourceID="NorthwindEmployeesSqlDataSource"
            AutoGenerateColumns="False">
            <Columns>
                <asp:BoundField DataField="EmployeeID" HeaderText="ID"/>
                <asp:BoundField DataField="FirstName" HeaderText="First Name"/>
                <asp:BoundField DataField="LastName" HeaderText="Last Name"/>
                <asp:BoundField DataField="HireDate"
                    DataFormatString="{0:d}" HeaderText="Date of Hire"/>
            </Columns>
        </asp:GridView>
    </div>
    </form>
</body>
</html>
```

2. Save the page as `TIO-1-ConvertBoundToTemplate-2.aspx`. Now perform the following steps in the VWD Design view. Select the GridView, open the smart task panel, and click on Edit Columns. In the Selected Fields box, delete the two name fields.

3. Click on the EmployeeID field. In the lower right of the Fields dialog, click on "Convert this field to a Template Field." Click OK to close the Fields dialog.

4. With the smart task panel still open, click on the leftmost column of the GridView to select it. Click on Edit Templates. You have a `Label1` on your template that was created by the conversion. Click just to the right of the `Label1` and strike Enter to go to a new line. From the toolbox, drag and drop a label to the beginning of the second line and select Edit Data Bindings to set the `Text` to `LastName` (if the Field Binding list box is not populated, click the Refresh Schema button). Continuing in the template, add a comma and space. Now drag and drop another label and bind it to the first name. You now have in your template the employee ID and names in a free-form layout within the cell. The source code will be similar to the following. Save and observe in your browser.

```
<asp:GridView ID="GridView1" Runat="server"
    DataSourceID="NorthwindEmployeesSqlDataSource"
    AutoGenerateColumns="False">
    <Columns>
        <asp:TemplateField>
                <EditItemTemplate>
                        <asp:TextBox Runat="server"
                        Text='<%# Bind("EmployeeID") %>' ID="TextBox1" />
```

```
                    </EditItemTemplate>
                <ItemTemplate>
                        ...
                </ItemTemplate>
            </asp:TemplateField>
            <asp:BoundField DataField="HireDate" DataFormatString="{0:d}" />
        </Columns>
    </asp:GridView>
```

How It Works #1 — Convert Column from Bound to Template in a GridView

This exercise walked through the conversion of a GridView bound column to a template column, followed by modifications to that template column. In the following analysis, you will see how the VWD designer produces slightly different code for the two kinds of labels.

First, in version 2 of the page, note that the template field now has a different control than the bound field.

```
    <asp:GridView ID="GridView1" Runat="server"
        DataSourceID="NorthwindEmployeesSqlDataSource"
        AutoGenerateColumns="False">
        <Columns>
            <asp:TemplateField>
```

Second, skip your attention to the following lines. Recall from the introductory section of this chapter that there are two bindings: `Eval()` is read-only, whereas `Bind()` is read/write (more on writing data in Chapters 11 and 12).

```
Please remove shading on the words Bind and Eval from following dozen lines up to
my stop note.              <ItemTemplate>
                        <asp:Label ID="Label1" Runat="server"
                               Text='<%# Bind("EmployeeID") %>' />
    <br />
                        <asp:Label ID="Label2" Runat="server"
                               Text='<%# Eval("LastName") %>' />
    ,  
                        <asp:Label ID="Label3" Runat="server"
                               Text='<%# Eval("FirstName") %>' />
                </ItemTemplate>
            </asp:TemplateField>
```

Also observe in the following code how the VWD designer added layout code and text for a return `<br/>`, comma, and space as per your keystrokes. You will see later in the chapter that even more complex layout (such as tables) can be added to a template.

```
            <ItemTemplate>
                        <asp:Label ID="Label1" Runat="server"
                               Text='<%# Bind("EmployeeID") %>' />
    <br />
                        <asp:Label ID="Label2" Runat="server"
                               Text='<%# Eval("LastName") %>' />
```

```
            ,  
                              <asp:Label ID="Label3" Runat="server"
                                    Text='<%# Eval("FirstName") %>' />
                          </ItemTemplate>
```

Now return your attention to the GridView as a whole. Any time there is an editable field, the GridView will have an additional tag for `EditItemTemplate` (discussed in more detail in Chapters 11 and 12).

```
<asp:GridView ... runat="server"
 <Columns>
        <asp:TemplateField>

              <EditItemTemplate>
              ...
              </EditItemTemplate>

               <ItemTemplate>
                     <asp:Label ... Text='<%# Bind("MyField") %> />
               </ItemTemplate>
        </asp:TemplateField>
 </Columns>
</asp:GridView>
```

DataList Control

Like the GridView, the DataList control offers a technique to display all of the records on the page at once, with each record getting a cell within an overall HTML table. DataList is the first example of a control we've encountered that actually requires you to define templates (at least, the ItemTemplate) in order for the control to render. Unlike GridView and DetailsView, DataList does not provide a built-in rendering for data records other than the outer table used to lay out the content defined in its templates.

The DataList can be formatted at two levels. At the larger level, the arrangement of the overall HTML table can be controlled, including the number of columns and horizontal or vertical ordering of records. Then, within each cell, you have a templated space to lay out the fields for one record. That layout can include small tables to arrange the internal controls within the DataList's templates within the overall table.

The arrangement of records is established by the DataList Page Layout Properties. Note that the formatting properties for the overall table are actually divided into two panels of the Properties window in the categorized view: Appearance and Layout. Within Layout, Direction determines whether the records will be ordered across the page (horizontal) or down the columns (vertical). `RepeatColumns` determines the number of columns. Note that if you change the `RepeatLayout` to `flow` (default is `table`), you will lose the overall HTML table that holds the records.

Within the Appearance panel of the DataList properties window, you can set the borders. The properties that begin with "Border..." affect the single rectangle around the entire DataList (all columns and rows). The `2border` settings within the `ItemStyle` (and `Alternating ItemStyle`) determine the appearance of dividing lines between the records. Like any HTML table, you have properties for cell padding (space between the inside of the cell wall and the contents) and cell spacing (width of the space between cells).

Try It Out #2 — DataList Control Page Layout Properties

In this exercise, you will lay out a DataList of employees and experiment with the appearance of the overall table.

1. Create a new page named `TIO-2-DataListPageArrangements-ver1.aspx`. Add a data source that reads the IDs, names, and hire dates from the Northwind Employees table. Add a DataList to the page and bind it to the data source control. Use the smart task panel to enter Edit Template mode for the Item template. Drag and drop labels for the text fields. If you want, add text or returns to change the layout of the group of fields. End template editing and save the page, which should look similar to the following. View in your browser. By default, the DataList will show the records in a table one column wide, so they will run straight down the page.

```
<%@ Page Language="VB" %>
<!DOCTYPE html PUBLIC "-//W3C//DTD XHTML 1.1//EN"
"http://www.w3.org/TR/xhtml11/DTD/xhtml11.dtd">
<html xmlns="http://www.w3.org/1999/xhtml" >
<head runat="server"><title>Ch10-TIO-2-DataList-PageArrangement-Ver1</title></head>
<body><h3>Chapter 10 TIO #2 DataList - arrangement on the page</h3>
    <form id="form1" runat="server">
    <div>
        <asp:SqlDataSource ID="NorthwindEmployeesSqlDataSource"  Runat="server"
        ConnectionString="
<%$ ConnectionStrings:LocalSqlNorthwind %>"
        SelectCommand="SELECT EmployeeID,FirstName,LastName,HireDate
            FROM Employees"/>
    </div>
    </form>
    <asp:DataList ID="DataList1" Runat="server"
         DataSourceID="NorthwindEmployeesSqlDataSource">
        <ItemTemplate>
            <asp:Label ID="Label1" Runat="server"
                Text='<%# Eval("EmployeeID") %>' />
            <asp:Label ID="Label4" Runat="server"
                Text='<%# Eval("HireDate", "{0:D}") %>' />
         <br />
            <asp:Label ID="Label2" Runat="server"
                Text='<%# Eval("FirstName") %>' />
          
            <asp:Label ID="Label3" Runat="server"
/>
        </ItemTemplate>
    </asp:DataList>
</body>
</html>
```

2. Close the browser and, in VWD Design view, save as `TIO-2-DataListPageArrangements-ver2.aspx`. Select the DataList control and, on its smart task panel, click on the Property Builder. Select two columns and the direction of horizontal. Save (source code similar to the following) and view in the browser. You now display the records in two columns with the records (sorted by EmployeeID) from left to right horizontally.

```
<asp:DataList ID="DataList1" Runat="server"
 DataSourceID="NorthwindEmployeesSqlDataSource"
 RepeatColumns="2"
 RepeatDirection="Horizontal">
       <ItemTemplate>
       ...
       </ItemTemplate>
</asp:DataList>
```

3. Close the browser. Save as version 3 and change the layout to vertical and the column count to 3 (as in the following code). Notice in the browser how the increasing employee numbers go vertically downward and then wrap up to the top of the next column.

```
<asp:DataList
     ...
     RepeatColumns="3">
</asp:DataList>
```

or

```
<asp:DataList
     ...
     RepeatColumns="3">
     RepeatDirection="Vertical">
</asp:DataList>
```

4. Finish by saving as version 4. Reopen the property builder for the DataList. This time, click the Borders tab on the left side. Add both gridlines of a gray color and a width of 3 points. Set the cell spacing to 2.

```
<asp:DataList ID="DataList1" Runat="server"
     DataSourceID="NorthwindEmployeesSqlDataSource"
     RepeatColumns="3"
     CellSpacing="2"
     BorderColor="LightGray"
     BorderWidth="3pt"
     GridLines="Both">
</asp:DataList>
```

How It Works #2 — DataList Control Page Layout Properties

In this exercise, you experimented with the overall layout of the DataList. You can see that the number of columns and the flow of information (repeat direction) are similar to those of any other HTML table. Note that the default repeat direction is vertical, as shown in the first sample code of step 3.

Recall that the DataList can be formatted at two levels. The last section focused on the overall HTML table where each cell holds one record of information. Now we turn our attention to the templated space within each cell. VWD offers an intuitive tool to add a table to a template. Select the templated control and then edit the Item template. Click through the menu: Menu ➪ Layout ➪ Insert Table. You will see some predefined options at the top of the dialog box under Templates. Below that are tools to design a custom table, including the appearance of borders. Click the Cell properties to set defaults for all cells in the table. Even if you do not intend to display a border in the final version, you may want to turn on a border of width 1 to help in navigation while adding controls to the table. In the end, a typical table in a template might appear as follows:

```
<asp:DataList ID="DataList1" Runat="server"
    DataSourceID="NorthwindEmployeesSqlDataSource"
    RepeatColumns="3"
    GridLines="Both">
    <ItemTemplate>
            <table>
               <tr>
                   <td>
                       <asp:Label ID="Label1" Runat="server"
                           Text='<%# Eval("Field1") %>' />
                   </td>
                   <td>
                       <asp:Label ID="Label2" Runat="server"
                           Text='<%# Eval("Field2") %>' />
                   </td>
                </tr>
                <tr>
                   <td>
                       <asp:Label ID="Label3" Runat="server"
                           Text='<%# Eval("Field3") %>' />
                   </td>
                   <td>
                       <asp:Label ID="Label4" Runat="server"
                           Text='<%# Eval("Field4") %>' />
                   </td>
                </tr>
           </table>
    </ItemTemplate>
</asp:DataList>
```

Try It Out #3 — DataList Control Internal Layout

In this exercise, you will present the employees' information in a more pleasing layout within each record. You will start with a page from the last exercise, add a table, and relocate the fields into the table.

1. Start with your file `TIO-2-DataListPageArrangements-ver3.aspx` from the last exercise and save as `TIO-3-DataListWithInternalTable.aspx`. In the data source control, add the field for Notes.

```
<asp:SqlDataSource
 ...
SelectCommand="SELECT EmployeeID,FirstName,LastName,HireDate,Notes
    FROM Employees"/>
```

2. In the VWD Design view, switch to the DataList's Edit Template mode. Click anywhere in the template; to create some working space at the top of the template, strike Ctrl+Home to locate the insertion bar at the top of the Item template, strike a few returns, and then strike Ctrl+Home again.

3. Click through Menu ➪ Layout ➪ Insert Table and add a table of three columns and three rows. Click OK. Now select the three cells in the bottom row. Click through Menu ➪ Layout ➪ Merge Cells.

4. Move or add controls so that the template's internal table will display as follows. Note each cell's horizontal alignment, which is set by clicking in the cell and striking Ctrl+L, Ctrl+R, or Ctrl+E.

	LastName, FirstName	**HireDate (in short format)**
Employee ID		
Notes		

5. End template editing and go to the property builder of the DataList. Select the Borders category and add both gridlines. Save the file (source code follows) and view in the browser.

```
<%@ Page Language="VB" %>
<!DOCTYPE html PUBLIC "-//W3C//DTD XHTML 1.1//EN"
"http://www.w3.org/TR/xhtml11/DTD/xhtml11.dtd">
<html xmlns="http://www.w3.org/1999/xhtml" >
<head runat="server"><title>Ch10-TIO-3-DataList-InternalTable</title></head>
<body>
<h3>Chapter 10 TIO #3 DataList - Internal Table</h3>
    <form id="form1" runat="server">
    <div>
        <asp:SqlDataSource ID="NorthwindEmployeesSqlDataSource"  Runat="server"
        ConnectionString="
<%$ ConnectionStrings:LocalSqlNorthwind %>"
        SelectCommand="SELECT EmployeeID,FirstName,LastName,HireDate, Notes
            FROM Employees"/>
    </div>
    </form>
    <asp:DataList ID="DataList1" Runat="server"
         DataSourceID="NorthwindEmployeesSqlDataSource"
         RepeatColumns="3"
         GridLines="Both">
        <ItemTemplate>
            <table><tr>
                <td style="width: 100px; height: 21px"> </td>
                <td style="width: 100px; height: 21px">
                        <asp:Label ID="Label3" Runat="server"
                                Text='<%# Eval("LastName") %>' />,
                        <asp:Label ID="Label2" Runat="server"
                                Text='<%# Eval("FirstName") %>' />
                </td>
                <td style="width: 100px; height: 21px">
                        <asp:Label ID="Label4" Runat="server"
                                Text='<%# Eval("HireDate", "{0:d}") %>' />
                </td>
         </tr><tr>
```

```
                    <td style="width: 100px">
                        <asp:Label ID="Label1" Runat="server"
                            Text='<%# Eval("EmployeeID") %>' />
                    </td>
                    <td style="width: 100px">
                    </td>
                    <td style="width: 100px">
                    </td>
                </tr>
                <tr>
                    <td colspan="3">
                        <asp:Label ID="Label5" Runat="server"
                            Text='<%# Eval("Notes") %>' />
                    </td>
                </tr>
            </table>
          </ItemTemplate>
      </asp:DataList>
  </body>
  </html>
```

How It Works #3 — DataList Control Internal Layout

Here you see how you can achieve a spectrum of HTML table format options within each iteration of a template. Adding the table from the Layout menu gives you the dialog box for easy design (in the beta version of VWD, that dialog box is not available if you add a table by dragging and dropping from the toolbar). Within the table, you were able to merge cells and set horizontal alignment. In the final source code, you can also see the normal table elements such as `<td>`.

Repeater Control

The Repeater is similar to the DataList in that it iterates one template to the page for each record. The difference is that the Repeater does not wrap the iterations in an overall HTML table. Because there is no overall table, there are no properties for repeat direction, number of columns, or table elements such as border and cell padding. Otherwise, DataList and Repeater are the same, including support for tables within a template.

Note that in templated controls, data and literal text must be within a template tag, most frequently, the `<ItemTemplate>`. It is easy to be in Source view and begin adding labels and images without first creating an `ItemTemplate`. The result is an error message that the Repeater does not have a property named "label." It is the `ItemTemplate` that actually exposes as a public property) the `<asp:label>` control. (See a demonstration of the failure in the download file `Demo-3-RepeaterWithNoItemTemplate.aspx`.)

```
  <asp:Repeater ID="Repeater1" runat="server"
      DataSourceID="NorthwindEmployeesSqlDataSource">
      <ItemTemplate>
           Id #
          <asp:Label ID="Label1" runat="server" Text='<%# Eval("EmployeeID") %>' />
           =
```

```
        <asp:Label ID="Label2" runat="server" Text='<%# Eval("LastName") %>' />
        .<br />
    </ItemTemplate>
</asp:Repeater>
```

Because the Repeater does not automatically generate an overall table, the designer has greater control over the rendering. The DataList provides less flexibility but much greater convenience. Of these two iterated (tiled) controls, DataList will cover most of your needs.

DetailsView Control

The DataList, Repeater, and GridView template columns all repeat their ItemTemplate for each record in the data source; that is, they showed all of the records on the page at once. We now switch gears to the controls that render the ItemTemplate once for the currently displayed record: DetailsView and FormView. Although similar in appearance, they differ in the automatically generated structure of the Item template. DetailsView creates an internal table of all fields and their names, while FormView is a blank slate, within which you define the overall structure of controls in the template. That makes DetailsView faster to set up, but FormView is more flexible.

You've already encountered DetailsView to support a drill-down of data from a selection in a GridView. You will encounter it again in the next two chapters as the control to add a new record when working with a GridView. Like the GridView template column, the DetailsView Edit Fields dialog allows you to switch a bound field to a templated field.

DetailsView's smart task panel offers options to edit fields, just as GridView had an option to edit columns. You can also click to edit the template, select the Item template, and rearrange the fields to your heart's content.

Navigation in Templated Controls

Templated controls that display only one record at a time (DetailsView and FormView) offer navigation tools for the user to move from record to record. The tools are hyperlinks generated by ASP.NET 2.0 in response to property settings. These tools are generally held in a special cell that reaches across the bottom of the control called the pager (and under the control of the `PagerStyle`). We've already looked at paging in Chapter 7, so this is just a review of those concepts as they apply to rendering templated content.

> **The terms *page* and *paging* are used for two similar meanings. When paging in a GridView, you are dividing the total set of records into groups on the page. This type of paging has implications for the number and timing of records that the data source control will fetch from the database. In DetailsView and FormView, you use the term *paging* to describe navigation through the current records in order to display the template for each data record.**

The navigation tools can be divided into the following types:

- **Page Numbering** provides a series of numbers across the bottom of the control that represent hyperlinks to each record.
- Move to **Previous** or **Next** Page displays hyperlinks to move to adjacent pages.
- Jump to **First** or **Last** Page offers the user a hyperlink to the first record or the last record.
- Various combinations of the preceding tools.

These properties can be set in VWD in three steps:

1. Turn on paging using the check box in the control's smart task panel.
2. Go to the control's properties and expand the Paging section and then the `PagerSettings` to select a mode (one of the preceding choices).
3. The third step formats the display of the page navigation hyperlinks. For each hyperlink displayed on the pager, you get two options: format text or replace the text with a graphic. For the text, the default is the display of greater-than and less-than signs designated in the Properties window as `<` and `>` (two signs can be concatenated with no connecting symbol). But these can be easily replaced with words such as *Jump To Most Recent Order* without the need for quotes. When using numbers, the `PageButtonCount` determines how many numbers will be displayed across the pager.

FormView Control

The FormView is very similar to the DetailsView. They both show only one record at a time and support paging over records. They also both support reading, writing, and creating new records. The difference is that the DetailsView automatically creates an internal HTML table structure that holds the names and values of the fields. The FormView offers just a blank area (actually a single cell of a one-row table) in which to add controls. Unlike the DetailsView, which has a built-in rendering (using AutoGenerateField, or explicit fields defined in the Fields collection), the FormView actually requires you to define its ItemTemplate in order to provide the rendering for the control. It is more similar to DataList and Repeater in this regard, as it is an entirely templated control. As with other controls, you can add an HTML table by hand to organize your controls.

Try It Out #4 — DetailsView and FormView

Northwind occasionally has a need to look at employees from the perspective of when they were hired. You want to create a page that displays information on one employee at a time with the order from longest serving to most recently hired. Suppose your client has asked for easily understood aids for navigating through the list of employees.

1. Create a new page named `TIO-4-DetailsViewAndFormView-ver1.aspx`. Add a SqlDataSource for the IDs, names, and hire dates of the employees of Northwind ordered by hire date (use ascending order).

2. Add a DetailsView and bind to the data source. Click on the Allow Paging option in the smart task panel. Save and run the page, noting how an internal table was automatically generated and populated with the names and values of fields.

```
<%@ Page Language="VB" %>
<!DOCTYPE html PUBLIC "-//W3C//DTD XHTML 1.1//EN"
"http://www.w3.org/TR/xhtml11/DTD/xhtml11.dtd">
<html xmlns="http://www.w3.org/1999/xhtml" >
<head runat="server">
    <title>Ch10-TIO-4-DetailsViewAndFormView-Ver1</title>
</head>
<body>
<h3>Chapter 10 TIO #4 DetailsView And FormView version 1</h3>
    <form id="form1" runat="server">
    <div>
        <asp:SqlDataSource ID="NorthwindEmployeesSqlDataSource"  Runat="server"
        ConnectionString="
<%$ ConnectionStrings:LocalSqlNorthwind %>"
        SelectCommand="Select EmployeeID,FirstName,LastName,HireDate
            FROM Employees
            ORDER BY HireDate ASC"/>

        <asp:DetailsView ID="DetailsView1" Runat="server"
            DataSourceID="NorthwindEmployeesSqlDataSource"
            AllowPaging="True" />
    </div>
    </form>
</body>
</html>
```

3. Save as version 2 and go to the properties of the DetailsView control. Select the DetailsView control and, in the Properties window, expand the paging option and then the `PagerSettings` option. Change the mode to `NextPreviousFirstLast`. Revise the `LastPageText` property to be `"     Last hired     "` and the `FirstPageText` to `"     First hired     "`. Add five or so spaces on either side of the text.

4. Change the `NextPageText` to `"     Later hired     "` and the `PreviousPageText` to `"     Earlier hired     "`. Save the page and view in the browser.

```
        <asp:DetailsView ID="DetailsView1" Runat="server"
            DataSourceID="NorthwindEmployeesSqlDataSource"
            AllowPaging="True">
            <PagerSettings
                Mode="NextPreviousFirstLast"
                LastPageText="  Last hired  "
                NextPageText="  Later hired  "
                FirstPageText="  First hired  "
                PreviousPageText="  Earlier hired  " />
        </asp:DetailsView> 
```

5. Save as version 3 and drag and drop a FormView to the page. Bind the FormView to the data source control. In the smart task panel, set Enable Paging to `true`. Save and view in the browser. The FormView renders nothing in the item template by default. However, the control does render the pager cell if paging is turned on.

```
        <asp:SqlDataSource .../>

        <asp:DetailsView ... >...</asp:DetailsView>

        <asp:FormView ID="FormView1" Runat="server"
                DataSourceID="NorthwindEmployeesSqlDataSource"
                AllowPaging="True"  />
    </div>
    </form></body></html>
```

6. Close the browser and, back in the VWD designer, save as version 4. Open the FormView's smart task panel and click on Edit Templates ➪ Item Template. Add a label for the employee's last name and check that the two-way binding option remains off. Save and close. View in your browser and note that although they have the same data source control, the two templated controls navigate independently.

```
<asp:FormView ID="FormView1" Runat="server"
         AllowPaging="True"
         DataSourceID="NorthwindEmployeesSqlDataSource">
            <ItemTemplate>
                <asp:Label ID="Label1" Runat="server"
                        Text='<%# Eval("LastName") %>' />
            </ItemTemplate>
        </asp:FormView>
```

How It Works #4 — DetailsView and FormView

When you add a DetailsView control and bind to a data source control VWD automatically gives you a default layout within the Item template. You can also turn on paging (page navigation) and specify custom text for the navigation hyperlinks. In contrast, the FormView does not render anything automatically — you must define an ItemTemplate in order to provide the rendering elements. You can add a pager with a single property, but the ItemTemplate remains unrendered until you add a data-bound control. When you have more than one data-bound templated control, they can share the same data source. However, they will navigate through the records independently.

Comparing and Selecting the Templated Controls

ASP.NET 2.0 supports five templated data-bound controls. The following information will help you decide which templated control to use. Historically speaking, the DataList and Repeater were available in ASP.NET version 1.x, while GridView, DetailsView, and FormView came out only with version 2.0.

First, we have already considered controls that render their templates once per data record (DetailsView and FormView) versus those that repeat their templates (GridView Template Control, DataList, and Repeater).

Now think of the templated controls in a range from most rigid to most flexible:

[Most flexible] GV template field, DetailsView, FormView, DataList, Repeater [Just a frame]

Although there may be variations, here is a list of considerations when deciding which control best suits your scenario. Although we haven't discussed updating, deleting, and inserting data in detail (those topics are reserved for the next three chapters), we list below which controls support which operations to help you decide the right control to use.

Choosing a control based on Display, Update, Delete, and Insert capability:

1. If you want to insert new records, your only choices are DetailsView and FormView (Group 3, described shortly).
2. If you want to update or delete data (but not necessarily insert new records), choose between GridView, DetailsView or FormView. Although DataList is capable of providing UI for editing, it does not take advantage of the data source's ability to do this automatically like GridView and you'll need to write custom code to make it work. Refer to an ASP.NET v1 reference for more information (the topic is outside the scope of this book).
3. If you only want to display read-only values, you can use any of the templated controls we've discussed within this chapter.

Choosing a control based on formatting and layout of the data records:

1. If you want to display multiple data records at the same time, choose between GridView, DataList, and Repeater:

    a. GridView — Displays each data record as a row in a table. Fields of the data record are displayed in the table cells (one field per cell, or using a template, as many fields per cells as you need). The contents of each cell are defined by the TemplateField.ItemTemplate property.

    b. DetailsView — Displays each data record as a table of two columns, where each row typically contains a single field (the left cell is the header and the right cell the value). Using TemplateField, you can define the contents of each value cell using the `TemplateField.ItemTemplate` property.

    c. FormView — Displays each data record as a single cell in a table with one row. The contents of the table cell are defined by the FormView's `ItemTemplate` property.

    d. DataList — Displays each data record as a cell in a table. The number of data records per row in the table is determined by the DataList's `RepeatColumns` property. The `ItemTemplate` property allows you to define the template rendering of each data record within the table cell.

    e. Repeater — Displays each data record as a user-defined item, defined by the Repeater's `ItemTemplate` property. There is no built-in table for layout, so the items simply flow from one to the next (within a `<span>` tag, so styles are applied).

To finish the comparison, study the following table.

	GridView	DataList	Repeater	DetailsView	FormView
From version 1.x?	No	Yes	Yes	No	No
Number of records shown at once	Multiple	Multiple	Multiple	Single	Single
Can update records?	Yes	No*	No	Yes	Yes
Can delete records?	Yes	No*	No	Yes	Yes
Can insert records?	No	No	No	Yes	Yes
Can select records?	Yes	No*	No	Yes**	Yes**
Supports paging?	Yes	No	No	Yes	Yes
Renders data record as...	Row in multi-column table	Cell in multi-row/column table	Item in a <span> (no table)	Single table of two columns	Single cell in a one-row table
Templates are optional?	Yes	No	No	Yes	No
Supports header/footer	Yes	Yes	Yes	Yes	Yes

Although the DataList provides the ability to render Edit and Delete UI (through custom command buttons in the ItemTemplate and EditItemTemplate), it does not automatically perform these operations through data source controls like GridView, DetailsView, and FormView. For more information about using DataList to update and delete data, consult a reference for ASP.NET version 1.x.

Unlike GridView, selection in FormView and DetailsView is not performed through a Select command button, but rather through paging between data records. The `SelectValue` property reflects the DataKey of the currently rendered data item.

Common Mistakes

Following are some mistakes commonly made in trying to display data in templates:

- Forgetting to end Edit Template mode and then not finding desired options on the smart task panel.
- Attempting to bind controls in a template when the outer templated control as a whole has not been bound to a data source.
- Attempting to use Eval in an edit template, where Bind is required.
- Not seeing the fields available for binding to controls in a template. Click on Refresh Schema in the dialog box, and the drop-down list of fields will be repopulated.
- Building contents of a Repeater control in Source view without including a set of `<ItemTemplate>` tags.

Summary

This chapter presented data-bound controls that have templated regions that offer a canvas upon which you can add and arrange data-bound controls (such as labels, hyperlinks, and images), literal values (such as dashes or commas), and HTML tags (such as `<br>` or `<table>`). The data-bound controls will display values for the current record of the templated control. Keep in mind that data binding occurs at two levels. The templated control as a whole is bound to a data source control. Then, within the template, each control that displays values is bound to a field.

Templated controls display the multiple records in one of two ways: either in a repeated fashion or singly. DataList, Repeater, and the template column of the GridView display values from all of the records at once in some type of repeated arrangement. The DetailsView and FormView display just one record at a time, as if you were seeing the top record of a stack.

Templates are built by selecting the control, opening the smart task panel, and entering Edit Template mode. Controls can be dragged from the toolbar; then a smart task panel for that control offers to expedite data binding. The Data Binding dialog box has a drop-down section to select a display format for the value. Don't forget to reopen the smart task panel and select End Template Editing to restore the normal options in the smart task panel.

HTML tables are used in two ways with templated controls. In some templated controls, all of the records will be rendered onto a cell within an *overall* HTML table. The second use of tables is *inside* a template to organize various fields in the display of one record. Be careful to keep the two uses of tables differentiated in your mind when selecting which templated control to use and when maintaining code in Source view.

In the DetailsView and FormView, ASP.NET 2.0 offers tools to navigate through the stack (from record to record). These navigation controls are generally in a pager cell with a `PagerStyle`. They provide navigation by listing the record numbers or displaying Next/Previous or jumps to First and Last pages.

Selecting the control to use can be confusing. Keep these points in mind to differentiate data-bound controls by read and write capability.

- If you want to insert new records, your only choices are DetailsView and FormView.
- If you want to update or delete data (but not necessarily insert new records), choose between GridView, DetailsView, or FormView.
- If you only want to display read-only values, you can use any of the templated controls we've discussed within this chapter.
- Select a control based on layout as follows: If you want to display multiple data records at the same time, choose between GridView, DataList, and Repeater; To display one record at a time, select between FormView (an empty template space) and DetailsView (with a default internal table).

You are about to move on to the fourth section of this book: how to use an ASPX page as a user interface to modify data stored in a database.

Exercises

1. Describe the differences between a bound field and a templated field.
2. Which controls can contain a templated field?
3. Which controls can and cannot create new records?
4. What is the fundamental difference between DetailsView and FormView?
5. Which two data-bound controls covered in this chapter are holdovers from earlier versions of ASP.NET and thus are not written in fully managed code?
6. Does ASP.NET 2.0 support HTML tables within a template? Explain.
7. Once a column is added to a GridView as a bound type, can it be converted to a template?
8. What is the main difference between the DataList and Repeater controls?

11

Updating and Deleting Data

This chapter and the next cover the modifying of data. This chapter discusses how to change values in existing records (updating) and how to remove a record (deleting).

As with almost every task in ASP.NET 2.0, the Visual Web Designer (VWD) makes the creation of a data-modifying page very easy. This chapter walks you through the drag-and-drop and then explains the source code. Beneath the surface lies some theory that is trickier than what has been discussed to date; this chapter explains those ideas. I finish with some special examples and the techniques to delete a record.

You will practice with the following Try It Out exercises:

Try It Out	Topic
1	Command Field
2	Update Simple
3	DataKeyNames
4	Update Using the DetailsView
5	Handling NULLs
6	Delete

In several exercises, you will modify or delete data. To help you return to the original state after having made some edits, here is the information for the first author:

ID = 172-32-1176 First name = Johnson Last name = White City = Menlo Park

There are some constraints on the ID field. When changing the ID on the author Johnson, you can use a new value of 172-32-1177 or 172-32-1178.

Overview of Modifying

First, for readers who have not worked with SQL, there are three terms used for modifying data:

- **Update** — To change values for records that already exist
- **Delete** — To remove an entire record
- **Insert** — To create a new record (usually with a set of values, but it could be empty)

These SQL terms carry over into the terminology of ASP.NET 2.0 and this book. Similar terms are used by ASP.NET 2.0 for similar operations.

- **New** — Used to invoke an Insert (create new record)
- **Edit** — To update values within an existing record. Used to invoke an Update (change in an existing record.

> **There is a technical difference between the operation of the SQL terms and the ASP.NET 2.0 terms. The SQL keywords cause an operation to be performed on the data. The ASP.NET 2.0 New and Edit terms are not true substitutes for Insert and Update. They are command button keywords used to cause data-bound controls to transition UI states (*e.g.*, from Read-Only mode to Edit mode). In some cases, for example when in Edit mode and clicking on Update, that change in UI state triggers the execution of the appropriate SQL statement.**

Although these are good descriptive terms to display to the site user, they can cause some confusion when the designer has to translate that into the proper SQL terminology. Sometimes there is confusion about the term *delete*. If you want to remove just one value from a record, you use update and replace the existing value with a `NULL`. The term *delete* is used only when removing an entire record.

ASP.NET 2.0, particularly with VWD or Visual Studio (VS), makes it easy to create pages that allow a user to modify values in a database. The ease derives from the capabilities that are built into the data source and data-bound controls. There are four basic concepts to understand, two regarding the data source controls and two regarding the data-bound controls.

- **Data source controls have a built-in capability to modify data.** You've already read about some built-in capabilities, such as sending a SELECT command to the database. ASP.NET 2.0 data source controls also have three capabilities to modify data: update, insert, and delete.
- **Data source controls have properties to enable the capability to modify data.** The modification capabilities can be turned on or off.
- **Data-bound controls can automatically use capabilities that have been turned on in the data source control.** Smart data-bound controls "know" which capabilities are turned on for their data source control. However, this sensing is only for smart controls, including GridView, DetailsView, and FormView.

- **Data-bound controls have properties that enable use of their source control capability.** The developer can set properties of the smart data-bound control to enable the control to invoke operations such as showing Edit/Cancel or Delete buttons. When the user clicks on the data-bound control buttons, the data-bound control sends the appropriate information to its data source control.

To summarize, data source controls have the ability to modify data, and that ability can be turned on by setting properties of the control. Similarly, data-bound controls have the ability to send modification commands to their data-bound control, and that ability can be turned on by also setting properties of the control. These concepts are covered here in reverse order, starting with the basics of displaying commands and moving back through the preceding list.

Keep in mind that the techniques for this chapter are for the ASP.NET 2.0 smart data-bound controls (GridView, DetailsView, and FormView). Legacy controls from version 1.x, such as DataGrid, are supported in version 2.0, but they do not have the "smarts" to perform the techniques of this chapter. Also note that these techniques are not available for list controls such as the DataList or the Repeater. If you want to modify data using version 1.x controls, you must use the version 1.x techniques of instantiating and using ADO.NET objects directly.

Command Fields

Recall that for a smart control you can open the smart task panel and edit the columns or fields. One of your choices is to add a column of the Command type. Your choices are fourfold:

- Edit/Update/Cancel is for updating values in an existing record.
- Delete is for removing an entire record.
- New/Insert/Cancel is for adding an entire new record.
- Select (not directly part of modifying data).

GridView does not have the New/Insert/Cancel command because the control does not support the insertion of a new record. To insert a new record from a GridView, use a SelectCommand in the GridView to switch to a DetailsView or FormView that does support an insert.

Try It Out #1 — Command Field

As a review, you will simply add nonfunctional commands to several smart data-bound controls.

1. Create a new folder named `ch11` and, within it, create a page named `TIO-1-CommandFields.aspx`. Add a SqlDataSource control named `AuthorsSqlSource` pointing to the Pubs database on your server. Recall that in this book, connection strings are stored in the Web.config file as per Try It Out #2 in Chapter 3.
2. Add a GridView to the page, edit columns, and turn off autogenerate fields. Refresh the schema. Add four bound fields for authors' ID, names, and city. Open the list of command fields and add an Edit, Update, Cancel command — note that GridView does not offer a New command to insert a new record. Test the page and note that ASP.NET 2.0 has rendered the Edit column in the GridView.

3. Add a DetailsView to the page and set its source to the same `AuthorsSqlSource`. Edit fields and note that, by default, with DetailsView you get all of the fields in the control. Delete all but the basic four fields for ID, names, and city. Take a look at the command field options and note that you now have a New/Insert/Cancel option. Add that to the DetailsView, save, and try in your browser.

4. With the page open in the browser, try clicking on one of the Edit buttons in the GridView and change a phone number. Click Update and the page fails. Go back and scroll down to the DetailsView. Click New, enter some information, and click Insert. Again, a failure. This is because we have not yet configured the data source for editing or inserting.

5. Save the page (similar to the following listing).

```
<%@ Page Language="VB" %>
<!DOCTYPE html PUBLIC "-//W3C//DTD XHTML 1.1//EN"
"http://www.w3.org/TR/xhtml11/DTD/xhtml11.dtd">
<html xmlns="http://www.w3.org/1999/xhtml" >
<head runat="server">
    <title>Ch11-TIO-1-CommandFields</title>
</head>
<body>
    <h3>Chapter 11 TIO#1 Command Fields</h3>
    <form id="form1" runat="server">
    <div>

    <asp:SqlDataSource ID="AuthorsSqlSource" Runat=server
        ConnectionString="
<%$ ConnectionStrings:LocalSqlPubs %>"
        SelectCommand="SELECT au_id,au_lname,au_fname,city FROM [authors]"/>
</div><div>
    <asp:GridView ID="GridView1" Runat="server"
            DataSourceID="AuthorsSqlSource"
            AutoGenerateColumns="False">
                <Columns>
                    <asp:BoundField DataField="au_id"/>
                    <asp:BoundField DataField="au_fname" />
                    <asp:BoundField DataField="au_lname" />
                    <asp:BoundField DataField="city" />
                    <asp:CommandField ShowEditButton="True" />
                </Columns>
            </asp:GridView>
</div><div>
        <asp:DetailsView ID="DetailsView1" Runat="server"
            DataSourceID="AuthorsSqlSource"
            AutoGenerateRows="False"
            DataKeyNames="au_id">
                <Fields>
                    <asp:BoundField HeaderText="ID" DataField="au_id" />
                    <asp:BoundField HeaderText="au_lname" DataField="au_lname" />
                    <asp:BoundField HeaderText="au_fname" DataField="au_fname" />
                    <asp:BoundField HeaderText="city" DataField="city" />
                    <asp:CommandField ShowInsertButton="True" />
                </Fields>
            </asp:DetailsView>
</div></form></body></html>
```

How It Works #1 — Command Field

In this exercise, you reviewed the design tools of VWD to add a command to a smart control. You saw that the data-bound control has the capability to turn on features for modifying data. This turning-on process is accomplished by simply adding appropriate fields to the control. And you see the big difference between GridView and DetailsView for modifying — GridView does not support inserts.

When you attempted to try the modification techniques in the browser, they failed. The reason is that you have not yet performed the necessary steps to enable modification by the data source control.

Simple Update

Recall the four concepts for data modification in ASP.NET 2.0:

- Data source controls have a built-in capability to modify data.
- Data source controls have properties to enable the capability to modify data.
- Data-bound controls can automatically use capabilities that have been turned on in the data source control.
- Data-bound controls have properties that enable use of their source control capability.

You tested the last concept in the preceding exercise. The second to last is automatic. Now you want to enable the properties of the data source control so that you can modify data. The property to enable updating on the SqlDataSource control is the UpdateCommand (`UpdateQuery in the property grid of Visual Web Developer`), and its argument is the SQL statement to perform the update. This is very similar to the data source control's read capability that is enabled by having a SQL `SELECT` statement in the `SelectCommand` property.

As a note for readers not familiar with SQL, the `UPDATE` statement has three clauses: an `UPDATE MyTable clause`, then a `SET clause`, which names the new values, and, finally, a `WHERE` clause that identifies which record to change. A typical statement follows.

```
UPDATE MyTable
SET
 Phone = 5551234,
 Name = 'My New Name'
WHERE Field_PrimaryKey = 'MyID'
```

Now the trick is how to pass the new values entered by the user into this sort of syntax. ASP.NET uses parameters, which are a collection of values. The collection is automatically created and filled with the values the user types into the textboxes. The SQL `UPDATE` statement then reads those values from the parameters collection. You can see in the following statement how you refer to values in the parameter collection with an `@` preceding their field name.

```
UPDATE MyTable
SET
 Field1 = @Phone,
 Field2 = @Name
WHERE Field_PrimaryKey = @ID
```

Try It Out #2 — Update Simple

In this exercise, you will enable the data source control to support editing changes in your GridView. We will not enable updating of the au_id field that is the primary key.

1. In the `ch11` folder, open the `TIO-1` and save as `TIO-2-UpdateSimple.aspx`.
2. In Source view, add the following SQL statement to the `UpdateCommand` property of the `AuthorsSqlSource`. (Double-check that you are adding to the SQL source control, not the GridView.)

```
<asp:SqlDataSource
 ID="SqlDataSource1"
 ConnectionString= " ... "
 SelectCommand="SELECT * FROM [authors]"
 UpdateCommand="UPDATE [authors]
  SET

    [au_lname] = @au_lname,
    [au_fname] = @au_fname,
    [city] = @city
  WHERE [au_id] = @original_au_id"
 Runat="server" />
```

3. Looking at the source code for the GridView, set AutogenerateColumns=False and then add a ReadOnly=True for the ID field which is the primary key.

```
<asp:GridView ID="GridView1" DataSourceID="SqlDataSource1"
AutoGenerateColumn="false" Runat="server"
...
             DataKeyNames="au_id">
                 <Columns>
<asp:CommandField ShowEditButton="true"/>
<asp:BoundField ReadOnly="true" DataField="au_id"/>
...
                 </Columns>
</asp:GridView>
```

4. Save the page (as shown) and view it in your browser. Test the page by changing the name, city, and phone number. The author ID field is read-only, so it cannot be changed. The entire source code appears listed below.

```
<%@ Page Language="VB" %>
<!DOCTYPE html PUBLIC "-//W3C//DTD XHTML 1.1//EN"
"http://www.w3.org/TR/xhtml11/DTD/xhtml11.dtd">
<script runat="server">
</script>
<html xmlns="http://www.w3.org/1999/xhtml" >
<head runat="server">
    <title>Ch11-TIO-2-UpdateSImple</title>
</head>
<body>
    <h3>Chapter 11 TIO#2 Update Simple</h3>
```

```
    <form id="form1" runat="server">
    <div>

    <asp:SqlDataSource ID="AuthorsSqlSource" Runat=server
        ConnectionString='<%$ ConnectionStrings:LocalSqlPubs %>'
        SelectCommand="SELECT * FROM [authors]"
        UpdateCommand="
            UPDATE [authors]
            SET
                [au_id] = @au_id,
                [au_lname] = @au_lname,
                [au_fname] = @au_fname,
                [city] = @city
            WHERE [au_id] = @original_au_id" />
        </div>
        <div>
        <asp:GridView ID="GridView1" Runat="server"
            DataSourceID="AuthorsSqlSource"
            AutoGenerateColumns="False"
            DataKeyNames="au_id">
                <Columns>
                    <asp:BoundField ReadOnly="true" DataField="au_id"
HeaderText="ID"/>
                    <asp:BoundField DataField="au_fname" HeaderText="First Name" />
                    <asp:BoundField DataField="au_lname" HeaderText="Last Name" />
                    <asp:BoundField DataField="city" HeaderText="City" />
                    <asp:CommandField ShowEditButton="True" />
                </Columns>
            </asp:GridView>
        </div>
    </form>
</body>
</html>
```

How It Works #2 — Update Simple

In this exercise, you enabled updating in the data source control. Turning on that capability is simply a matter of adding an `UpdateCommand`. The SQL `UPDATE` statement, in its simplest form, specifies what value from the parameters collection to send to the database. The parameters collection is created automatically by the SqlDataSource control using the values given to it by the GridView.

Note that in order for the parameter values passed by the GridView to match up with the names of the parameters in the UPDATE statement, a naming convention is used. For parameters that correspond to values typed in by the user into the GridView edit mode TextBoxes, the parameter names in the UPDATE statement match the names of the fields in the SELECT command. The parameter name f or the primary key matched in the `WHERE` clause is an exception to this rule. In this case, the parameter is given an "original_" prefix. The reason is because the GridView passes fields defined in DataKeyNames as a separate "keys" dictionary to the data source control, and the SqlDataSource automatically renames these special values with the "original_" prefix (defined by the SqlDataSource `OldValuesParameterFormatString` property, which is set to "original_{0}" by default, although you can edit this property to change the prefix used). As we will see in the next Try It Out example, this prefix is required in order to differentiate the original key value to match in the `WHERE` clause from the new value of the key field when you want to support updating the primary key.

DataKeyNames and Updates

DataKeyNames solve a specific set of problems that can occur behind the scenes when a page supports updates. In an update, you must use a WHERE clause that equals the primary key in the table. In the preceding cases, you used the au_id field as the primary key. Frequently, the primary key is set by the database; for example, an exclusive serial number is created for each author. The database schema would not permit external values to be set for the field, in which case you'll make the key field read-only, as you saw in the previous example. But if the primary key is updateable, you face a potential problem. A user could change the primary key value in an update in a data-bound control. If you used the same parameter name for both the new value and the value to match in the WHERE clause, then when the UpdateCommand is executed, the WHERE could no longer match the original value of the primary key in the table. It would try to match the original value in the SQL statement's WHERE clause with the new value changed by the user in the GridView's TextBox for the updateable primary key.

Data-bound and data source controls handle this problem by using a naming convention to differentiate between the new values and old (original) values for parameters. When the data-bound control (in this case, GridView) applies the update operation of its associated data source, it takes the original value of the primary key specified by DataKeyNames and stores it in a separate "keys" dictionary from the "values" dictionary that contains values edited by the user in the GridView input TextBoxes. When the update operation of the data source is invoked, GridView passes both of these dictionaries to the data source. The data source then prepends each parameter name in the keys dictionary with a special prefix used to differentiate these original values from the new values. The prefix is defined by a property of the SqlDataSource called OldValuesParameterFormatString, set to "original_{0}" by default. Like other format strings we've examined in this text, the {0} placeholder is substituted with the field name at runtime. For example, if the field name is au_id, the parameter name is formatted to become original_au_id. The SqlDataSource then applies the newly formatted parameters to the UpdateCommand before executing the statement. So now, even if the primary key has been changed, the update is still able to create a WHERE clause that can find the correct record to apply the update to in the table.

Sometimes, the primary key (and thus the WHERE clause) uses more than one field (a multikey primary key). If you are matching all of these fields in the WHERE clause, they should all be included in the DataKeyNames property (comma-separated).

Before you try using DataKeyNames, here are two advanced ideas to keep in mind:

- There is a complication when using Access as a database. The OLEDB provider for Access uses parameters by the *order* in which they were entered into the parameters collection, not as requested by parameter *name*. This makes the storing of parameters trickier because you have to be sure that the new value of a primary key is read from the parameters collection into the SET clause before the old value is read out in the WHERE clause. ASP.NET 2.0 arranges the parameter values so that new values are applied before key (original) values, so that parameters are applied in the order they most likely appear in the UPDATE statement.
- I haven't discussed optimistic concurrency yet, but essentially this means you are matching all the original values of the row, not just the primary key values. Data sources support this option by allowing you to include all original values as parameters of the WHERE clause, where each parameter is formatted using the "original_" prefix, just as is done for keys. If you are using optimistic concurrency, you are attempting to ensure that no one else will be changing a value in the same record at the same time. You can check whether that was the case by getting an argument back from the database for the number of rows that were actually affected. Hopefully the value is 1; if it is 0 (zero), your update was not applied. You can hand that value to an event handler (see Chapter 16) that checks for rows =0 and responds with a failure notice to the user (or retries the update).

Try It Out #3 — DataKeyNames

In this exercise, you will modify the previous example to support modifying the primary key, while also matching the original value in the `WHERE` clause.

1. Open the `TIO-2` page you created in the last exercise, and save it as `TIO-3-DataKeyNames`. Remove the ReadOnly attribute on the ID field (Primary Key) so it can be modified in edit mode. Ensure that au_id is also specified in DataKeyNames (same as previous example) so the original value is round tripped to the data source.

```
<asp:GridView ID="GridView1" Runat="server"
            DataSourceID="AuthorsSqlSource"
            AutoGenerateColumns="False"
            DataKeyNames="au_id">
                <Columns>
                    <asp:BoundField DataField="au_id"/>
                    <asp:BoundField DataField="au_fname" />
                    <asp:BoundField DataField="au_lname" />
                    <asp:BoundField DataField="city" />
                    <asp:CommandField ShowEditButton="True" />
                </Columns>
</asp:GridView>
```

Also add a "SET au_id = @au_id" clause to the `UPDATE` statement:

```
<asp:SqlDataSource
 ...
 UpdateCommand="UPDATE [authors]
  SET
    [au_id] = @au_id,
    [au_lname] = @au_lname,
    [au_fname] = @au_fname,
    [city] = @city
  WHERE [au_id] = @original_au_id"
 Runat="server" />
```

Viewing the page in your browser, jot down on a sheet of paper an author's ID and last name (for example, Johnson White is 172-32-1176). Click Edit for that author and change only his or her last name. Click Update and see that there is no problem. You changed a field that was not a primary key.

How It Works #3 — DataKeyNames

This exercise solves the problem of changing the value in the primary key of a table. The dilemma arises from the SQL statement needing two different values for the primary key field. The *original* value must be used in the `WHERE` clause to find the correct record to change. The *new* value must be used in the `SET` clause.

The internal behavior of ASP.NET 2.0 DataKeyNames differentiates and saves the old and new values, in this case for au_id. The multiple values are held in a dictionary with an entry for each field listed in DataKeyNames. The original value has been stored for us with the "original_" prefix, while the new value is without a prefix.

When the `SQL UPDATE` statement is written, we use the un-prefixed field name parameter (@au_id). Without a prefix, the DataKeyNames dictionary will provide the new value that the user typed into the text box in edit mode. In the `WHERE` clause, we want the old value provided by the DataKeyNames because we request it with the `original_` prefix.

```
UpdateCommand="
    UPDATE [authors]
    SET
        [au_id] = @au_id,
        [au_lname] = @au_lname,
        [au_fname] = @au_fname,
        [city] = @city
    WHERE [au_id] = @original_au_id"
```

The preceding statement will actually be filled with values from the parameters collection behind the scenes by ASP.NET 2.0, as follows (assuming you also changed Johnson's au_id to 999-88-7777):

```
UpdateCommand="
    UPDATE [authors]
    SET
        [au_id] = 999-88-7777
    WHERE [au_id] = 172-32-1176"
```

Update in a DetailsView

The theory and practice remain the same when you switch from the GridView to the DetailsView or FormView. In the DetailsView, the command will be called a field instead of a column.

Try It Out #4—Update Using the DetailsView

In this exercise, you add editing (with ability to change the ID field) to a DetailsView control.

1. Reopen `TIO-3-DataKeyNames.aspx` and save as `TIO-4-UpdateDetailsView.aspx`. Delete the GridView control and add a DetailsView control with its data source = AuthorsSqlSource.

2. Select the DetailsView control. If you haven't done so yet, turn on paging. Edit the fields and remove the New/Insert/Cancel field (left over from Try It Out #1). Add a command field for Edit/Update/Cancel. In the Properties window, find `DataKeyNames` and drop down the list of values. Select `au_id`. Save the page (partially shown as follows) and view in the browser. You should have no problems changing names or ID numbers. To preserve the integrity of the database, change the ID numbers back to the original values.

```
<h3>Chapter 11 TIO #4 Update in DetailsView</h3>
    <form id="form1" runat="server">
    <div>

    <asp:SqlDataSource ID="AuthorsSqlSource" Runat=server
        ConnectionString="
<%$ ConnectionStrings:LocalSqlPubs %>"
        SelectCommand="SELECT * FROM [authors]"
        UpdateCommand="
```

```
        UPDATE [authors]
        SET
            [au_id] = @au_id,
            [au_lname] = @au_lname,
            [au_fname] = @au_fname,
            [city] = @city
        WHERE [au_id] = @original_au_id" />

    <asp:DetailsView ID="DetailsView1" Runat="server"
            DataSourceID="AuthorsSqlSource"
            AutoGenerateRows="False"
            DataKeyNames="au_id"
            AllowPaging="True">
            <Fields>
                <asp:BoundField HeaderText="au_id" DataField="au_id"/>
                <asp:BoundField HeaderText="au_lname" DataField="au_lname" />
                <asp:BoundField HeaderText="au_fname" DataField="au_fname" />
                <asp:BoundField HeaderText="city" DataField="city" />
                <asp:CommandField ShowEditButton="True" />
            </Fields>
        </asp:DetailsView>
    </div></form></body></html>
```

How It Works #4 — Update Using the DetailsView

Enabling the update capability in a data-bound control that displays one record at a time (DetailsView or FormView) is very similar to the process for the controls that show many records (e.g., GridView). You render an interface on the data-bound control by adding a command field. That field then activates the capability of the data-bound control to re-render for Edit mode and to send the appropriate values to the data source control. The data source control was already enabled for modifying because in an earlier Try It Out, you added an `UpdateCommand`.

Parameters Collections

The parameters collection has been mentioned several times in this chapter. You may have been wondering why ASP.NET 2.0 creates an entire structure just to pass values from one control to another. The reason is to allow you, the designer, more control over how those values are passed. Three major areas are available for manipulation, although the exact capabilities will depend on the provider.

- Parameters can be typecast. This means that although incoming data may appear of one type (perhaps the string `111`), they can be forced into another type (for example, the integer 111). When you use VWD's parameter builder, this is done automatically.
- Parameters can be set to be read-only or write-only. The `Direction` property offers choices for `Input` (write-only), `Output` (read-only), or `InputOutput` (read and write). If you attempt to update a field whose parameter is set to `Output`, the result will be a `NULL` in the field because the new value was not accepted to be saved.
- Parameters can be given a default value. This chapter focuses on updating, and the default value is generally left blank so that the old value stands. But in the next chapter, when inserting new records is discussed, it will be useful to have a default value.

The VWD automatically creates the hierarchy of parameter objects and their properties when you drag fields from the Data Explorer onto the page. A collection is created for each of the data source control's commands. If you drag a DataSource control to the page, you can walk through the Configure Wizard. After selecting the data connection, you have the opportunity to specify the columns. Click on Advanced Options and turn on Generate Insert, Update, and Delete Statements. When you finish off this wizard, VWD will not only build the commands but also create collections of parameters to feed the appropriate values into the `SelectCommand`.

If you are working in a non-VWD editor or need to make changes in Source view, you will work directly with the hierarchy. Note that not all collections must be present and that the parameters collections are nested within the data source control (not the data-bound control). Note also that the properties (typing, direction, and default) are described within each parameter.

```
<body><form id="form1" runat="server">
...
<asp:SqlDataSource ...
 SelectCommand="SELECT * FROM [authors]"
 DeleteCommand="DELETE ... "
 UpdateCommand="UPDATE ... "
 <SelectParameters>
          <asp:Parameter Type="String" Name="Field_ID" />
 </SelectParameters>
 <DeleteParameters>
          <asp:Parameter Type="String" Name="Field_ID" />
 </DeleteParameters>
 <UpdateParameters>
          <asp:Parameter Type="String" Name="Field_ID" />
          <asp:Parameter Name="Field1"
               Type="Int32"
               DefaultValue=999
               Direction="Output"/>
          <asp:Parameter Name="Field2"
               Type="DateTime"
               DefaultValue="1/1/2005"
               Direction="InputOutput"/>
 </UpdateParameters>
</asp:SqlDataSource>
</div></form>
...
```

Handling NULLs in Updates

When users enter Edit mode, they are expected to enter or revise a value for each editable field. What happens if they leave a field blank? Conversely, the database may have a `NULL` and the data-bound control shows a hole in the textbox for editing. You work with `NULL`s in several ways when modifying data.

- A database may not have a value for a given field of a given record. You can display a literal text as an alternative to an empty space. This property is set for the bound field as the `NullDisplayText`. When the user modifies data, if the `NullDisplayText` is left as-is, ASP.NET will convert it back to a `NULL` value when the update is performed.

- When the user updates a record but leaves a textbox empty, you can substitute a default value. This property is set in the default value of the parameter object in the parameters collection. This property has no effect on reading, but if a user does not enter a value in a textbox when updating, ASP.NET will automatically substitute the default value.
- Confusion arises when a user enters an empty string into a textbox. Databases don't always record an empty string as a proper `NULL`. Within each parameter object, there is a property to change empty strings to true `NULL`s for storage in the database.

Try It Out #5 — Handling NULLs

In this exercise, you will modify a page to handle the absence of data in two scenarios.

1. In the `ch11` folder, open `TIO-4` and save as `TIO-5-NullHandling.aspx`.
2. First create a `NULL` in the database by deleting the city for the first author, Johnson White. Edit his record, delete the city, and update the changes. Note that his `city` field is empty. Close the browser and go back to VWD Design view. Select the GridView, open the smart task panel, and edit the columns. Select the `city` bound field and, in the Properties window (within the dialog box), change the `NullDisplayText` to "not known." Save and view the page in the browser to see that the city is now not known.
3. Now you will update the record with no city and observe the use of the default. Close the browser and use the Source view in VWD. Select the `<AuthorsSqlSource><Update Parameters><Parameter Name="city">`. In the Properties window, set the default value to "Anytown." Save the page and view in the browser. Edit the author and delete the old value for city. Click on Update. Note that ASP.NET 2.0 uses "Anytown" when no value is provided.

```
<%@ Page Language="VB" %>
...
<head runat="server"><title>Ch11-TIO-6-NullHandling</title></head>
...

    <asp:SqlDataSource ID="AuthorsSqlSource" Runat=server
        ConnectionString="
<%$ ConnectionStrings:LocalSqlPubs %>"
        SelectCommand="SELECT * FROM [authors]"
        UpdateCommand="
            UPDATE [authors]
            SET
                [au_id] = @au_id,
                [au_lname] = @au_lname,
                [au_fname] = @au_fname,
                [city] = @city
            WHERE [au_id] = @original_au_id" >
        <UpdateParameters>
          <asp:Parameter Type="String" Name="au_id" />
          <asp:Parameter Type="String" Name="au_lname" />
          <asp:Parameter Type="String" Name="au_fname" />
          <asp:Parameter Type="String" Name="city"
                DefaultValue="Anytown" />
        </UpdateParameters>
    </asp:SqlDataSource>
        </div>
        <div>
```

```
            <asp:GridView ID="GridView1" Runat="server"
                DataSourceID="AuthorsSqlSource"
                AutoGenerateColumns="False"
                DataKeyNames="au_id">
                    <Columns>
                        <asp:BoundField DataField="au_id"/>
                        <asp:BoundField DataField="au_fname" />
                        <asp:BoundField DataField="au_lname" />
                        <asp:BoundField DataField="city"
                            NullDisplayText="not known" />
                        <asp:CommandField ShowEditButton="True" />
                    </Columns>
                </asp:GridView>
    ...
    </form></body></html>
```

How It Works #5 — Handling NULLs

This exercise demonstrates that you can display an alternate text instead of a blank space when the database offers up a `NULL` value as established in the following:

```
<asp:GridView ... ><Columns>
                    <asp:BoundField DataField="city"
                        NullDisplayText="not known" />
```

The second step created a default value for when the user did not enter any value in the textbox while in Edit mode.

```
<asp:SqlDataSource ...>
 <UpdateParameters>
        <asp:Parameter Type="String" Name="city"
               DefaultValue="Anytown" />
```

Note the difference in location in the source code of these two properties. The `NullDisplayText` is located in the GridView control, while the default is a property of the data source control.

Delete to Remove Entire Records

Deleting an entire record is similar in practice to updating. The main difference is that there are issues that must be considered in terms of how the delete affects the rest of the database.

Recall from the introduction to this chapter that in SQL, *delete* means to remove an entire record. If you want to delete just one value from a record (but keep the remainder of the record), use Update (Edit) to change the one field to a `NULL`.

To perform deletion using the data-bound control, you must first change the rendering of the data-bound control and then enable the capabilities of the data source control. You enable deletions in the data source control by specifying a `DeleteCommand`, which is a proper SQL `DELETE` statement. The command will have to identify which record to delete, so there will be a `WHERE` clause. The `WHERE` clause typically sets the record to be deleted based on its primary key (generally an ID field). If you set the

DataKeyNames property of the data-bound control to the primary key, ASP.NET 2.0 automatically feeds the original value when the parameters are requested in the WHERE clause. Switching attention to the data-bound control, the smart control merely needs a new command column (or field) of the delete type.

The biggest problem with a delete is the potential for conflicts in the database. For example, the Pubs database has an authors-titles table that determines the author for each book (title). If you delete an author, you are left with an orphaned book. To prevent these problems, a database will normally have constraints on deletions. If you attempt to delete a constrained record, the database will raise an error and pass it back up to ASP.NET 2.0. At this point, you will see the error in a form for designers to use in programming. Chapter 16 will discuss how to handle this error with grace.

Try It Out #6 — Delete

In this exercise, you add the capability to delete an author, but then you see that the operation is blocked by the database.

1. In the ch11 folder, go back to TIO-3 (DataKeyNames). Open it and save as TIO-6-Delete-author.aspx.
2. Modify the data source control to enable deleting by adding a DeleteCommand, as follows:

```
<asp:SqlDataSource
    ...
    SelectCommand=" ... "
    UpdateCommand="... "
    DeleteCommand="DELETE FROM [authors] WHERE [au_id] = @Original_au_id"
  />
```

3. Modify the data-bound control (the GridView) to enable deletions as follows. Select the GridView, open the smart task panel, and edit the columns. Add a command column for Delete. Save the page and test. When you attempt to delete, the page works fine, but a message materializes from the database that a constraint has been violated.

```
<asp:GridView ID="GridView1" Runat="server"
    DataSourceID="AuthorsSqlSource"
    AutoGenerateColumns="False"
    DataKeyNames="au_id">
        <Columns>
            <asp:BoundField DataField="au_id"/>
            <asp:BoundField DataField="au_fname" />
            <asp:BoundField DataField="au_lname" />
            <asp:BoundField DataField="city" />
            <asp:CommandField ShowEditButton="True" />
            <asp:CommandField ShowDeleteButton="True" />
        </Columns>
    </asp:GridView>
```

How It Works #6 — Delete

This exercise walks you through the two steps to enable deleting of entire records. In the data source control you enable deletions by adding a DeleteCommand, as follows. Note that because you have a DataKeyName set to the primary key (au_id), ASP.NET 2.0 will automatically handle the populating of the parameter. You just have to specify in the WHERE clause that you want to use the original value for au_id.

```
<asp:SqlDataSource
    ...
    SelectCommand=" ... "
    UpdateCommand="... "
    DeleteCommand="DELETE FROM [authors] WHERE [au_id] = @Original_au_id"
  />
```

Then in the data-bound control (the GridView), you have two steps. First, you set the `DataKeyName` (actually already done in prior a prior Try It Out). Second, you enable the feature in the rendering by adding a Delete command column.

```
<asp:GridView ID="GridView1" Runat="server"
    DataSourceID="AuthorsSqlSource"
    AutoGenerateColumns="False"
    DataKeyNames="au_id">
        <Columns>
            <asp:BoundField DataField="au_id"/>
                ...
            <asp:CommandField ShowEditButton="True" />
            <asp:CommandField ShowDeleteButton="True" />
        </Columns>
    </asp:GridView>
```

Common Mistakes

Following are mistakes commonly made in attempting to update or delete data:

> **Whenever possible, use VWD tools (dialogs, wizards, IntelliSense and properties window) to add properties or set options, since VWD will use the correct placement and syntax.**

- Forgetting to use the `DataKeyNames` property and then not being able to update changes to the database.
- Forgetting to use the "original_" prefix for parameter names in the `WHERE` clause.
- Having a different number of (or incorrect names for) parameters in the `UPDATE` or `DELETE` statements from parameters that are passed by the data-bound control. Make sure you only have as many parameters as editable fields plus fields specified by DataKeyNames.
- Allowing the user to update fields that should be locked (direction is output only).
- Not handling the error of a delete that was not performed by the database (generally because of relational dependencies).
- Failure to typecast, causing an error when a wrong data type is rejected by the database.
- Accidentally changing the wrong set (Select, Update, Insert) of parameters when working in Source view.

- Placing the parameters collections in the data-bound control when coding without the VWD.
- Confusing the location of similar properties. `NullDisplayText` is in the `BoundField` object of the Columns or Fields collection. `DefaultText` is in the parameter object of one of the parameters collections.

Summary

This chapter explained two modification techniques: updating values in an existing record and deleting an entire record.

Data source controls have the capability of modifying data. They will automatically create and manage the appropriate ADO.NET objects to complete the modification. You enable these capabilities by adding an `UpdateCommand` or a `DeleteCommand` property. The argument for these commands is a suitable SQL statement.

The SQL statement generally needs to use values that were entered by the user. In the case of an update, these will be the new values; in the case of a delete, it will be the ID of the record to be deleted. Values are held in collections of parameters. There is one collection for each command object (`DeleteParameters`, `UpdateParameters`, and so on). In many cases, you can accept the default parameters collections made by ASP.NET 2.0, which will have a value for each field name. If you want to change the data type, set defaults, or limit the direction of information flow, you have to explicitly state the parameters and their properties.

Using the data-bound control requires you to go through the following steps. First, turn on the modification capability by adding a command field or command column. This enables a whole set of behaviors including re-rendering the screen when the user switches into Edit mode. When the user clicks Delete or Update, the data-bound control will automatically write the user's input values into the parameters collection and instruct the data source control to perform the modification.

A special case arises when the primary key (usually an ID field) can be edited. The new value will inhibit the lookup of the record in the table containing the old values. The problem is solved by assigning the name of the primary key field(s) to the data-bound control's `DataKeyNames` property and using the `original_{0}` prefix for parameters in the `WHERE` clause.

The next chapter discusses the third modification option: creating new records with the `INSERT` command.

Exercises

1. What is the difference between the SQL terms `UPDATE` and `INSERT`?
2. What is the difference between the commands New and Edit?
3. How do you configure a GridView to create a new record?
4. How does a command field know which command to execute?

5. What is the purpose of a `DataKeyNames` property in a data-bound control?
6. What is the difference between a command field and a command column?
7. Values that a user types into a textbox will always be of the data type string. How can a typed value be changed to a number for a numeric field?
8. What property adds the capacity to delete records to a DetailsView control?

12

Inserting New Records

The last chapter discussed how to change values in existing records and how to delete an entire record. This chapter covers the third leg of modifying data — creating a new record. It starts with a section on theory and a comparison of the insert capabilities of ASP.NET 2.0 controls. It then examines enabling inserts in the data source controls and the data-bound controls in more detail. Next is a quick example of inserts with templates and then a more careful study of specific controls on a template. And the final section discusses issues specific to the FormView.

This chapter walks you through the following Try It Out exercises:

Try It Out	Topic
1	Simple Insert by DetailsView
2	Setting Up a Data Source Control to Support Inserts
3	Insert Using DetailsView, Starting from GridView
4	Insert Using Template Fields in DetailsView
5	Insert with a List Box and Radio Buttons
6	FormView for Inserting New Records

Several times in this chapter, you will add a new author to the authors table in the Pubs database. Note the following constraints on data for an author:

- For ID, use *nnn-nn-nnnn*, where *n* is a number.
- Phone numbers should be of the form *nnn-nnnn.*
- For the state, use CA.
- For the zip code, use 12345.
- For the other fields, use any values, but do not leave any blank.
- If you add more than one record, you must use different ID numbers.

Inserting, on a theoretical level, requires five operations. These are handled almost automatically in ASP.NET 2.0.

1. Provide a way to begin the insertion, typically a button.
2. Change to the insert interface, a display to accept values for the new record.
3. Provide a button to end the input and create the record (or cancel).
4. Send the command to the database.
5. Check for success and handle errors.

Although all of these operations were possible in version 1.x, many designers stumbled on the syntax and location of operations in the correct events. ASP.NET 2.0 handles all of those tricky parts and exposes a highly simplified (abstracted) interface for the designer to add insert capability.

ASP.NET 2.0 insertion uses a particular set of vocabulary to describe the operations in an insertion:

- **New** — This button performs the change from Display to Insert mode.
- **Insert** — This button actually executes the insertion using the values entered by the user and returns to Display mode.
- **Cancel** — This button aborts the insertion and returns to Display mode.

> **Remember that Insert creates an entire new record in the table. To add or change a value in an existing record, use the Update command with an UPDATE SQL statement as discussed in Chapter 11.**

Support for Insert

Not all of the data-bound controls support ASP.NET 2.0 inserts. DetailsView and FormView do; GridView does not (you must shift to DetailsView or FormView to perform the insert). Although cumbersome, you can perform inserts on almost any control using ASP.NET 1.x techniques.

How do you choose between DetailsView and FormView? They both present one record at a time and both support inserting new records. DetailsView provides a very simple layout with a simple enablement of inserts, but you may not find the automatic layout to your liking. FormView requires you to build the insert capability in several steps but gives you complete freedom in layout.

Unlike FormView, DetailsView does not, even after enabling inserts, offer top-level templates for Item and InsertItem. However, you can add a template field to the DetailsView, and that template field will have its own template for Item and InsertItem for a specific row in the DetailsView table.

What Happens under the Hood?

ASP.NET controls automatically carry out many tasks in reaction to user clicks. You can use Visual Web Designer (VWD) to design pages that insert new records, and you never have to worry about the underlying operations. But it helps in troubleshooting to have some knowledge of what happens. The theory can be broken into three parts: the setup, the rendering modes, and the action after clicks.

Setup for Insert

The SqlDataSource control can be enabled to perform inserts by setting an `InsertCommand` property. The argument will be a standard SQL INSERT INTO statement. Also in the data source control, within the parameters collection, there must be an InsertParameters collection that defines the parameters in the `INSERT` statement. This collection will be used to transfer values from the data-bound control's input controls to the data source control's InsertCommand.

Insertion Mode

The DetailsView control supports three different rendering modes: ReadOnly, Edit, and Insert. We have already seen the ReadOnly and Edit modes in the previous chapters. Recall that DetailsView changes from ReadOnly to Edit mode when an "Edit" command button is clicked in the control. In Edit mode, the DetailsView renders input controls for modifying the data of the current record. Similarly, DetailsView supports an Insert mode for rendering input UI to define a new record. DetailsView will change into this mode from ReadOnly mode when a button with CommandName="New" is clicked inside the control. There are three ways to include this button in the DetailsView rendering: 1) you can set AutoGenerateInsertButton="true" on DetailsView, 2) you can set ShowInsertButton="true" on a CommandField object in the DetailsView.Fields collection, or 3) you can add a Button control with CommandName="New" to a TemplateField in the Field collection.

During Insert mode, the display of values changes from labels to input controls (textboxes, lists, radio buttons, and so on) to allow the user to type values for the new record. Once in Insert mode, the DetailsView will submit the newly entered record in response to an "Insert" button command. Like Edit mode, Insert mode can be cancelled (without performing the record insert) by clicking a Cancel button command. In both cases, the DetailsView reverts to ReadOnly mode (or to the mode set by DetailsView.DefaultMode, if set).

Action Performed by ASP.NET 2.0 on Insert

When the Insert button is pressed in Insert mode, the form is posted back to the server along with the values entered by the user in the DetailsView input UI. The DetailsView collects the input values from these inner controls and creates a dictionary to pass to the data source Insert operation. When the data source receives these values, it appends them to the InsertCommand, using the types specified by parameters in the InsertParameters collection. The data source then executes the command to insert the new record. The data source control automatically creates the appropriate ADO.NET objects and calls the methods on those objects to perform the insert into the database. The database returns any error messages that can be handled.

Database Considerations When Inserting

There are several basic database rules that require your attention when adding new records. Tables will have a primary key (a field or fields together that have values that are unique for each row). Primary key values can be entered by hand or auto-generated. If the value is auto-generated, you must prevent the ASP.NET page from trying to add the value when it performs the insertion, by omitting the field from Insert mode altogether. You can do this by setting InsertVisible=false on the corresponding field object, or remove from the `InsertItemTemplate`, as we will discuss below. If you decide to make the primary key field editable and allow the user to enter a value by hand, the entered value cannot match a value that has already been taken by another record. Therefore, you will have to check whether the user's entered value for the primary key was accepted or rejected by the database.

Some tables are designed so that a given field's value must match a value in the primary key of another table. For example, in an Orders table, the value in the Customer ID field must match a value in the Customer ID field of the Customers table. The best solution is to use an input control that accepts only valid values, such as a list or radio button.

Basic Insert Using DetailsView

DetailsView has a simple designer interface to turn on inserting using a checkbox on the DetailsView smart task panel. However, the capability to insert must first be enabled in the data source control before this checkbox will appear.

You can achieve this in two steps. When you create the data source control, you step through the configuration wizard. On the page for configuring the select statement, click on Advanced Options and then click on Generate Insert, Update, and Delete Statements. This performs both steps of enabling insertions by the data source control (creating an InsertCommand and creating the InsertParameters collection). Then, in the DetailsView control's smart task panel, you can simply click on Allow Insert to enable the two requirements in the data-bound control: Allow Inserts and add the New button.

Try It Out #1—Simple Insert by DetailsView

In this exercise, you will create a page that uses the DetailsView control with insert capability to add a new author and then view some errors.

1. Create a folder named `C:\BegAspNetDb\ch12` and, within it, a page named `TIO-1-InsertSimple.aspx`. Drag and drop a DetailsView control onto the page and configure it to use a new data source.
2. Select the Database type and give it an ID of AuthorsSqlSource. Choose a New data connection and enter your server name. Use Windows Integrated Security and the Pubs database. Save the connection string as LocalSqlPubs in the Web.config file. Configure the Select statement to use the authors table and check the asterisk for all fields.
3. To enable inserting, click on the Advanced Options and turn on Generate Insert, Update, and Delete Statements. Test if you want and finish.
4. Select the DetailsView control and enable paging and inserting.
5. To check your tests, add a GridView to the bottom of the page that displays authors (you can use the same data source control). Save the page, as follows:

```
<%@ Page Language="VB" %>
<html>
<head><title>Ch-12-TIO-InsertSimple-</title></head>
<body>
<h3>Chapter 12 TIO #1 Insert Simple with DetailsView  </h3>
  <form id="form1" runat="server">

      <asp:DetailsView ID="DetailsView1" Runat="server"
        DataSourceID="AuthorsSqlSource"
        AutoGenerateRows="False"
        DataKeyNames="au_id"
        AllowPaging="True">
          <Fields>
```

```
                <asp:BoundField ReadOnly="True" HeaderText="au_id" DataField="au_id"/>
                   ...
                 <asp:BoundField HeaderText="zip" DataField="zip" />
                 <asp:CheckBoxField HeaderText="contract" DataField="contract" />
                 <asp:CommandField ShowInsertButton="True"></asp:CommandField>
            </Fields>
        </asp:DetailsView>

        <asp:SqlDataSource ID="AuthorsSqlSource" Runat="server"
           ConnectionString="<%$ ConnectionStrings:LocalSqlPubs
%>"SelectCommand="SELECT * FROM [authors]"
            InsertCommand="INSERT INTO [authors]
                  ([au_id], [au_lname], [au_fname], [phone],
                          [address], [city], [state], [zip], [contract])
                   VALUES (@au_id, @au_lname, @au_fname, @phone,
                          @address, @city, @state, @zip, @contract)"
            DeleteCommand=" ... "
            UpdateCommand=" ... ">

            <DeleteParameters> ... </DeleteParameters>
            <UpdateParameters> ... </UpdateParameters>

            <InsertParameters>
                <asp:Parameter Type="String" Name="au_id"></asp:Parameter>
                <asp:Parameter Type="String" Name="au_lname"></asp:Parameter>
                <asp:Parameter Type="String" Name="au_fname"></asp:Parameter>
                <asp:Parameter Type="String" Name="phone"></asp:Parameter>
                <asp:Parameter Type="String" Name="address"></asp:Parameter>
                <asp:Parameter Type="String" Name="city"></asp:Parameter>
                <asp:Parameter Type="String" Name="state"></asp:Parameter>
                <asp:Parameter Type="String" Name="zip"></asp:Parameter>
                <asp:Parameter Type="Boolean" Name="contract"></asp:Parameter>
            </InsertParameters>
        </asp:SqlDataSource>

        <asp:GridView ID="GridView1" Runat="server"
          DataSourceID="AuthorsSqlSource"
          DataKeyNames="au_id"
          AutoGenerateColumns="true">
        </asp:GridView>
    </form>
</body>
</html>
```

6. View in your browser. Add a new author following the constraints outlined in the beginning of the chapter. Click on Insert, observe your new record in the GridView, and page to it in the DetailsView.

7. Try violating a table constraint by adding another author with no phone number. Notice that the Insert fails.

How It Works #1 — Simple Insert by DetailsView

Insert works when the data source control and the data-bound control are both enabled for inserting. The data source control was enabled by having the VWD generate an InsertCommand in step 3. At the same time, VWD automatically generated an InsertCommand and a set of InsertParameters. For our purposes, the command and parameters for Update and Delete can be excised from the page.

The data-bound control (DetailsView) was insert-enabled with a simple check box in the VWD designer. That check added a CommandField that renders a button that will switch from New to Insert and Cancel. Although you cannot access it at design time, at runtime the control will be rendered with textboxes instead of labels.

When the user opens the page, the DetailsView will be in ReadOnly mode. When you click on New, the rendering will change in two ways. First, the buttons change from New to Insert and Cancel. Second, the fields change from showing values in labels for the current record to showing empty textboxes. When the user clicks on Insert, the DetailsView control takes the values and puts them into the data source control's InsertParameters collection. The data-bound control then instructs the data source control to perform the insert. The data source control instantiates and uses ADO.NET objects, as needed. They, in turn, instruct the database to perform the insertion. If there is a problem, an error message will bubble back up through ADO.NET and cause a page error.

Enabling Insert in a Data Source Control

The first step for inserting is to enable the function in the data source control. To do this, you add an InsertCommand and an InsertParameters collection. There is no additional property to set such as `"EnableInsert=true"`; the existence of the `InsertCommand` and `InsertParameters` is all that is needed to enable inserting.

The `InsertCommand` is a standard SQL INSERT INTO statement. It will list values for each of the fields, and those values come from the InsertParameters collection (wholly held within the parameters collection of the data source control). Each parameter derives from its own tag with a type and name. A default value can also be specified. Note that the InsertCommand will read parameters from only the InsertParameters collection, even if there are same-named parameters in other collections (such as EditParameters). Values from parameters are referred to with an @ before their name.

Try It Out #2—Setting Up a Data Source Control to Support Inserts

In this exercise, you start with three steps that create a read-only page showing the authors. You then make the necessary changes to enable the data source control to support inserting. That capability will migrate up to the data-bound control (DetailsView) where you can enable inserting.

1. Create a page named `Tio-2-EnableDataSource.aspx`. Add a DetailsView control with a new data source control. Follow the steps of the previous Try It Out, but do not use Advanced Options in the Select Command dialog box.
2. In the DetailsView smart task panel, enable paging, but note that there is no option to enable inserts.
3. Save and test the read-only page.
4. Now you will convert your data source control to enable inserting. Close the browser and return to the Design view. Select the data source control and, in its smart task panel, click on Configure Data Source. Leave the data connection set to "(Custom)" and click Next twice to get to the Configure Select Statement dialog box. Click Advanced Options and generate the Insert, Update, and Delete statements.

5. Now reopen the DetailsView smart task panel and note how there is an option to enable inserting. Click it to enable inserting.

6. Change to Source view and find the `asp:SqlDataSource`. Scroll down to the InsertParameters collection and click anywhere in the `asp:parameter` tag named "address." In the Properties window, set the default value to "Suite 2.0, Asp Street."

7. Save as version 2 (see following code sample) and open in your browser. Add a new author (see samples of acceptable data in the previous Try It Out or in the GridView) but do not include a value for the address. Insert and observe that your default value was used for your new author.

```
<%@ Page Language="VB" %>
<html>
<head><title>Ch-12-TIO-2-EnablingADataSourceControlForInserts</title></head>
<body>
<h3>Chapter 12 TIO #2 Enabling a Data Source Control For Inserts</h3>
    <p>version 2 - Insert enabled</p>
  <form id="form1" runat="server">
      <asp:DetailsView ID="DetailsView1" Runat="server"
        DataSourceID="AuthorsSqlSource"
        AutoGenerateRows="False"
        DataKeyNames="au_id"
        AllowPaging="True">
          <Fields>
             <asp:BoundField HeaderText="au_id" DataField="au_id" ReadOnly="True"/>
...
              <asp:CheckBoxField HeaderText="contract" DataField="contract" />
          </Fields>
      </asp:DetailsView>
      <asp:SqlDataSource ID="AuthorsSqlSource" Runat="server"
            ProviderName="System.Data.SqlClient"
          ConnectionString="
            Server=HPSERV;
            Integrated Security=True;
            Database=pubs;
            Persist Security Info=True"
          SelectCommand="SELECT * FROM [authors]"
          DeleteCommand="DELETE FROM [authors] WHERE [au_id] = @original_au_id"

          InsertCommand="INSERT INTO [authors] ([au_id], [au_lname], [au_fname],
[phone], [address], [city], [state], [zip], [contract]) VALUES (@au_id, @au_lname,
@au_fname, @phone, @address, @city, @state, @zip, @contract)"

          UpdateCommand=" ... ">

          <DeleteParameters> ... </DeleteParameters>
          <UpdateParameters> ... </UpdateParameters>

          <InsertParameters>
              <asp:Parameter Type="String" Name="au_id"></asp:Parameter>
              <asp:Parameter Type="String" Name="au_lname"></asp:Parameter>
              <asp:Parameter Type="String" Name="au_fname"></asp:Parameter>
              <asp:Parameter Type="String" Name="phone"></asp:Parameter>
              <asp:Parameter Type="String" Name="address"
                    DefaultValue="Suite 2.0 Asp Street"></asp:Parameter>
              <asp:Parameter Type="String" Name="city"></asp:Parameter>
              <asp:Parameter Type="String" Name="state"></asp:Parameter>
```

```
            <asp:Parameter Type="String" Name="zip"></asp:Parameter>
            <asp:Parameter Type="Boolean" Name="contract"></asp:Parameter>
        </InsertParameters>
    </asp:SqlDataSource>
  </form>
</body>
</html>
```

How It Works #2—Setting Up a Data Source Control to Support Inserts

Data source controls can be converted from read-only to enabling insertions. In this exercise, you used three steps to create a read-only page and then modified to enable insertions. To enable inserting in the VWD designer, you merely opened the data source control's smart task panel and walked through the configuration steps for the data source. In the dialog to create the Select statement, you clicked Advanced Options and instructed VWD to create the statements for Insert, Update, and Delete. Note that you do not have a choice here; this designer generates all or none. Although there is no explicit check box, the VWD also generates the InsertParameters collection.

You then observed how the DetailsView is aware of and reacts to changes in its data source control. After enabling the data source, you saw the Enable Insert option in the data-bound control. You finished by modifying an insert parameter. VWD automatically creates name and type attributes; you added a default attribute for the address.

DetailsView INSERT Starting from GridView

As previously mentioned, you can't perform an insert using the GridView control. Instead, you must switch to a DetailsView or FormView control. Starting from a GridView, you have two layout options: locate the DetailsView/FormView on the same page as GridView or on a different page from the GridView. Both of these scenarios are covered in this section.

GridView and DetailsView for Insert on Same Page

A layout of a GridView and DetailsView on the same page works well. Both can use the same data source control, provided the data source control is enabled to perform inserts (has an InsertCommand and a set of InsertParameters). The DetailsView has a `DefaultMode` property that can be set to insert. Its appearance with blank fields and a New button will signify to users its purpose.

GridView on One Page with DetailsView on a Second Page

An alternative is to add a button to a page that jumps to a new page for creating new records. The button can be in the GridView's header or footer or located outside the GridView. The button is nothing more than a hyperlink to the page set up for inserts. The DetailsView on the inserts page should have its DefaultMode set to Insert. Don't forget to add a button to go back to the GridView page (or create an automatic redirection in an event handler, as described in Chapter 16).

Try It Out #3—Insert Using DetailsView, Starting from GridView

In this exercise, you will offer insertions to the authors table in two ways. The first has a GridView and DetailsView on the same page. The second technique is to have a separate page for the insert function.

1. Create a new page named `TIO-3-Both.aspx`. This page will sport three controls: one data source control with insert enabled, a GridView that is read-only, and a DetailsView that is for inserting.
2. Add a GridView and choose a new data source named AuthorsSqlSource to show all of the authors table's fields. Because you will soon be using this control to support insertions in the DetailsView control, in the step for Configure Select Statement, click on Advanced Options. Turn on Generate Insert, Update, and Delete statements. Save and test the page.
3. Now add a DetailsView control, set the data source to the existing AuthorsSqlSource, and enable paging and inserting. Last, go to the Properties window and set DefaultMode (in the Behavior group) to Insert. Save and test the page (keep in mind the constraints on data listed at the beginning of the chapter).
4. Now you will build a two-page solution. Create a new page named `TIO-3-DetailsOnly.aspx` with a DetailsView that displays all the fields from the authors table. Set the default mode to Insert. Add a link button to return to the GridView page with the properties of `ID=ReturnToGridView; text = Return to GridView page; PostBackUrl=Tio-3-GridOnly.aspx`.
5. Create a new page named `Tio-3-GridView.aspx` and repeat step 1 (add a GridView and configure a new SqlDataSource control). Now add a button to the page with the following properties: ID = HyperNewStore; Text = Add a New Author; PostBackUrl="~/ch12/TIO-3-DetailsOnly.aspx". Save and test.

How It Works #3 — Insert Using DetailsView, Starting from GridView

GridView does not support inserting new records, so you use a DetailsView (FormView also works for inserts). The DetailsView enabled for inserting can be on the same page as the GridView or on an alternate page. If it is on the same page, the two data-bound controls can share a single data source control if the data source control is enabled for inserts (has an InsertCommand and has a set of InsertParameters). In your second set of pages, the GridView page sports a button that jumps to the DetailsView page. In both cases, the DetailsView should have its DefaultMode set to Insert so that it is ready for the user to begin entering values for the new record. When a new record is inserted, it automatically shows up in the related GridView control because they are bound to the same data source.

Insert Using Template Fields

DetailsView renders in one of several modes, including ReadOnly mode, Insert mode, and Edit mode. By default, ReadOnly mode shows values in labels and Insert mode displays a textbox for each BoundField. However, in many cases you want your Insert mode to offer a different input control. Instead of a TextBox, you may want a ListBox, Calendar, or set of RadioButtons. You can change the input control type by adding a TemplateField in place of the BoundField and modifying the `InsertItemTemplate` of that field. A template, as discussed in Chapter 10, is a holder for other controls. The DetailsView will render different templates depending on its mode. By editing the `InsertItemTemplate`, you can change the type of input controls rendered to the user during Insert mode.

In Design view of VWD, it is easy to change the input controls. Assuming that the data-bound control is insert-enabled, you can edit the field of the DetailsView to add a TemplateField, and then select the Edit Templates option in the DetailsView smart task panel. Select the `InsertItemTemplate`, delete the TextBox, and substitute another control.

Using the Bind Syntax in InsertItemTemplate

Controls inside the `InsertItemTemplate` must be data-bound to a field of the DetailsView data source. However, instead of using the Eval syntax to data-bind, we use the Bind syntax in order to create a two-way association to the field. This allows the DetailsView control to automatically extract the value from the data-bound control in order to pass to the data source Insert operation. We did not need to specify data-bindings in the previous examples using BoundFields, because the DetailsView itself creates the TextBox input UI and therefore automatically can extract the values from these controls. In a template, the DetailsView doesn't necessarily know from which control property to extract the value unless you specify an explicit data-binding. In the next exercise, you will try this with a calendar control.

Try It Out #4 — Insert Using Template Fields

In this exercise, you will create a DetailsView to add new employees. Instead of a textbox for hire date, you will use the ASP.NET 2.0 calendar control.

1. Create a new page named `TIO-4-TemplateEditing.aspx`. Add a DetailsView control and configure its data source to a new data source named EmployeesSqlSource listing all the fields from the Employees table. Use Advanced Options to generate statements for Insert, Update, and Delete. In the DetailsView, enable paging and inserting. Click Edit Templates and note that you have a very limited set of choices: Footer, Header, EmptyData, and Pager. Save and test the page to see all the fields in Insert mode as the default textboxes.
2. To change the Hire Date field to a calendar control, close the browser and return to the page in VWD Design view. Select the DetailsView control, open the smart tasks panel, and select Edit Fields. In the lower left panel, select HireDate and click on "Convert to Template"; then close the Fields dialog box.
3. With the DetailsView control still selected, click on Edit Templates and select the HireDate-InsertTemplate. Select and delete the default textbox. Drag and drop a calendar control onto the template. The calendar's smart task panel will open; click on Edit Data bindings, select the `SelectedDate` property, and bind it to HireDate. Notice that the two-way data-binding check-box is checked, to indicate that the Bind syntax will be used to create a two-way binding association. Save, end template editing, close, and test.

How It Works #4 — Insert Using Template Fields

When you created the page in step 1, you took a peek at the templates. As the DetailsView is created by the VWD designer, there are just four templates: Footer, Header, EmptyData, and Pager. By default, there is no ItemTemplate or InsertTemplate. Although the DetailsView is very easy to use, it takes some work to modify its basic presentation.

To change from the default textboxes in Insert mode, you have to convert a textbox field to a template field. Now when you open the edit templates, there are many more options because you can edit the template field in each of its modes. Note that instead of an Item and InsertItem template for the entire DetailsView you have an Item and InsertItem template for each templated control. Any BoundFields that are not templated will get the default rendering of label and textbox.

When you add the calendar, ASP.NET 2.0 will do all the work of rendering the calendar and accepting user input such as changing months and selecting a date. You have to set only one property, the binding of the selected date to a field in your table.

Data Entry with RadioButtonLists and DropDownLists

RadioButtonLists provide the best input method when there is a short list of options. DropDownlists and ListBoxes support a greater quantity of choices. These input controls can be populated either from the same data source control used by the DetailsView as a whole or from another data source. A data source control can support only one Select statement, so if the RadioButtonList or DropDownList control is to have a Select that is to use values any different from the DetailsView, the input control must have its own data source control. It is also possible to statically populate the items of the list instead of binding to a data source, but this may not be maintainable if the items change frequently. For the sake of the examples below, we will bind the lists to a data source.

If the list of values includes duplicates, you will probably not want the duplicates in your radio buttons or list box. The SQL keyword DISTINCT will eliminate the redundancy. However, a Select statement that uses DISTINCT will probably no longer be useful for the DetailsView as a whole. You will see this in the next exercise.

The overall technique is a modification of the general template discussion. There are five steps.

1. Create a data source to supply values to the input control.
2. Convert the field to a template field using the DetailsView smart task panel and Edit Fields.
3. Select Edit Templates and, in the InsertItem template, delete the default textbox and replace it with a RadioButtonList or DropDownList.
4. Choose a data source from the input control's smart task panel and set the DataTextField and DataValueField. (Text will be shown to the user while Value will actually be placed into the table.)
5. From the input control's smart task panel, edit the data bindings to set the field in the DetailsView that will receive the selected value.

Although none of these steps is difficult, it is important to perform all of them in the order listed here to ensure success.

Try It Out #5 — Insert with a List Box and Radio Buttons

In this exercise, you will create a DetailsView to add a new sale. Because publishers only sell to a few stores, you will let the user select from a radio button list of stores. But when the user must select from more than fifty titles, a DropDownList is more appropriate. Because the three data-bound controls (DetailsView as a whole, RadioButtonList, and DropDownList) need fundamentally different sets of values, you will have to use three data source controls.

1. Create a new page named `TIO-5-InsertWithListBoxAndRadio.aspx`. Drag and drop a DetailsView control. Name the data source SalesSqlSource and configure to display all fields of the Sales table of Pubs ordered by descending Date (most recent order will be on page 1). Enable inserting when creating the data source control. (These are the same techniques used in previous Try It Outs in this chapter.)

2. Now you will create the data source controls needed for the input controls. Start with the stores radio buttons by dragging an SqlDataSource to the bottom of the page and naming it StoresSqlSource. Display only the Store ID, name, and city, ordered by Store name. Repeat for another data source control named TitlesSqlSource that selects Title_ID and Title ordered by title.

3. Change two of the fields from simple BoundFields to TemplateFields. Select the DetailsView and enable paging and inserting. Select Edit Fields, and in the bottom left, select Store_id and convert to a template field. Repeat for Title_ID. Click OK to close field editing.

4. Replace the Store TextBox with a RadioButtonList control, as follows. Continuing in the DetailsView smart task panel, click Edit Templates. Drop down the list of templates and select Store-ID/InsertItem template. In the control's template workspace, delete the TextBox. From the toolbar, drag and drop a RradioButtonList control onto the template. Configure its data source to StoresSqlSource and click Refresh Schema. Set the display field to Store_name and the field for the value to Store_id. Going back to the radio button's smart task panel, edit data bindings and set the `SelectedValue` property to bind to the Store-ID field. Two-way binding should be turned on.

5. Now change the title input to a DropDownList, as follows. Open the smart task panel for the entire DetailsView control and, if not in template-editing mode, click Edit Templates. Select the Title_ID and InsertItem template. Delete the textbox and drag a DropDownList from the toolbar. Choose the TitlesSqlSource as its data source and refresh the schema. Set the display field to Title and the data field to Title_ID. In the DropDownList's smart task panel, edit data bindings and set the `SelectedValue` property to bind to the Title-ID field. Two-way binding should be turned on.

6. Save and run the page, as follows (large sections of code that were automatically generated for update and delete are replaced with ellipsis). Try adding a new sale and note the ease of selecting a store and a title. For the text fields, use 111 for the order number, 1/1/01 for the date, 1 for the quantity, and Net 60 for the terms.

```
<%@ Page Language="VB" %>
<!DOCTYPE html PUBLIC "-//W3C//DTD XHTML 1.1//EN"
"http://www.w3.org/TR/xhtml11/DTD/xhtml11.dtd">
<html xmlns="http://www.w3.org/1999/xhtml" >
<head><title>Ch-12-TIO-5-InsertWithListAndRadio</title></head>
<body>
<h3>Chapter 12 TIO #5 Insert With ListBox and Radio Buttons</h3>
    <form id="form1" runat="server">
    <div>
        <asp:DetailsView ID="DetailsView1" Runat="server"
            DataSourceID="SalesSqlSource"
            AutoGenerateRows="False"
            DataKeyNames="stor_id,ord_num,title_id"
            AllowPaging="True">
            <Fields>
                <asp:TemplateField SortExpression="stor_id"
HeaderText="stor_id"><ItemTemplate>
                    <asp:Label Runat="server" Text='<%# Bind("stor_id") %>'
ID="Label1"></asp:Label>
                </ItemTemplate>
                    <InsertItemTemplate>
                        <asp:RadioButtonList ID="RadioButtonList1" Runat="server"
                            DataSourceID="StoresSqlSource"
                            SelectedValue='<%# Bind("stor_id") %>'
```

```
                            DataTextField="stor_name"
                            DataValueField="stor_id">
                        </asp:RadioButtonList>
                    </InsertItemTemplate>
                </asp:TemplateField>
                <asp:BoundField ReadOnly="True" HeaderText="ord_num"
DataField="ord_num" SortExpression="ord_num"></asp:BoundField>
                <asp:BoundField HeaderText="ord_date" DataField="ord_date"
SortExpression="ord_date"></asp:BoundField>
                <asp:BoundField HeaderText="qty" DataField="qty"
SortExpression="qty"></asp:BoundField>
                <asp:BoundField HeaderText="payterms" DataField="payterms"
SortExpression="payterms"></asp:BoundField>
                <asp:TemplateField SortExpression="title_id"
HeaderText="title_id"><ItemTemplate>
                    <asp:Label ID="Label2" Runat="server"
                        Text='<%# Bind("title_id") %>'></asp:Label>
                </ItemTemplate>
                    <InsertItemTemplate>
                        <asp:DropDownList ID="DropDownList1" Runat="server"
                            DataSourceID="TitlesSqlSource"
                            SelectedValue='<%# Bind("title_id") %>'
                            DataTextField="title"
                            DataValueField="title_id">
                        </asp:DropDownList>
                    </InsertItemTemplate>
                </asp:TemplateField>
                <asp:CommandField ShowInsertButton="True"></asp:CommandField>
            </Fields>
        </asp:DetailsView>

        <asp:SqlDataSource ID="SalesSqlSource" Runat="server"
            ConnectionString=";
<%$ ConnectionStrings:LocalSqlPubs %>"
            DeleteCommand=" ... "
            InsertCommand="INSERT INTO [sales] ([stor_id], [ord_num], [ord_date],
[qty], [payterms], [title_id]) VALUES (@stor_id, @ord_num, @ord_date, @qty,
@payterms, @title_id)"
            SelectCommand="SELECT * FROM [sales] ORDER BY ord_date DESC"
            UpdateCommand=" ... ">
            <DeleteParameters> ... </DeleteParameters>
            <UpdateParameters> ... </UpdateParameters>
            <InsertParameters>
                <asp:Parameter Type="String" Name="stor_id"></asp:Parameter>
                <asp:Parameter Type="String" Name="ord_num"></asp:Parameter>
                <asp:Parameter Type="DateTime" Name="ord_date"></asp:Parameter>
                <asp:Parameter Type="Int16" Name="qty"></asp:Parameter>
                <asp:Parameter Type="String" Name="payterms"></asp:Parameter>
                <asp:Parameter Type="String" Name="title_id"></asp:Parameter>
            </InsertParameters>
        </asp:SqlDataSource> 

        <asp:SqlDataSource ID="StoresSqlSource" Runat="server"
            ProviderName="System.Data.SqlClient"
            ConnectionString="Server=(local)\SQLExpress;
                Integrated Security=True;
```

```
                Database=pubs;
                Persist Security Info=True"
            SelectCommand="SELECT [stor_id], [stor_name], [city] FROM [stores]">
        </asp:SqlDataSource>

        <asp:SqlDataSource ID="TitlesSqlSource" Runat="server"
            ConnectionString="<%$ ConnectionStrings:LocalSqlPubs %>"
            SelectCommand="SELECT [title_id], [title] FROM [titles] ORDER BY
[title]">
        </asp:SqlDataSource>
    </div></form></body></html>
```

How It Works #5 — Insert with a List Box and Radio Buttons

This type of page can be built in two minutes with drag-and-drop in VWD but generates a lot of source code. You worked with data-bound controls at two levels: the DetailsView as a whole and at a lower level of your two data-bound input controls (RadioButtonList and DropDownList) within that DetailsView.

Your main data-bound control is the DetailsView that is based on a data source enabled for inserts. The DetailsView can sense that enablement and, thus, you can turn on inserts for the user. The DetailsView self-generates an interface of labels in Read-Only mode and textboxes in Insert mode. There is no overall template for the control's Read-Only and Insert modes, but you can convert individual fields to templates that offer you editable templates for ItemTemplate (ReadOnly mode) and `InsertItemTemplate` (Insert mode).

Before you can add specialized data-bound controls within the DetailsView, you need data sources to supply them. Because the set of data to support the internal controls is different from the data source for the entire DetailsView, you must create separate data source controls. You created two, selecting values from the Stores table and the Titles table.

You then carried out several remaining tasks on your two input controls. Within the DataView, you converted the Store and Title fields to templated fields so that you could modify their rendering. Second, within their InsertTemplates, you deleted the textboxes and replaced them with a RadioButtonList and a DropDownList. Then you took two steps from the input control's smart task panel. You configured the data source. In that dialog box, you set a display to a field that would be useful to the human eye, namely store_name and title.

Data Entry with Check Boxes

Check boxes are an odd case. They are automatically generated in DetailsView for fields that the data source control detects as Boolean. So, in most cases, there is no need to convert these fields from bound to templated to use the check box.

However, if you choose to (or are using the FormView), you can add check boxes by hand in two ways. You can add the field as a CheckBoxField in the Edit Fields dialog box, which puts in an `<asp:CheckBoxField>` control into the fields collection that can function without a template. Alternatively, you can create a template field and insert a check box in the same way as previously described for radio buttons. Note that CheckBox is not a data-bound list control, so there is no need to specify a data source; simply two-way data-bind its `Checked` property to a field using "Edit Databindings..."

Inserting with FormView

FormView is similar to DetailsView in that they both display one record at a time and they both support inserting new records (provided, of course, that their underlying data source controls support Insert), but there are a couple of significant differences.

The layout generated by the control differs. DetailsView is created with more automatic layout than FormView. You saw that DetailsView automatically creates a table layout containing headers and values for each field of the data source. DetailsView also uses BoundFields to render a label for the field value in ReadOnly mode, and a TextBox for the value in Edit or Insert mode. Of course, you saw how this can be customized using TemplateField to create custom UI for these modes.

FormView is different from DetailsView in that it does not offer a default table layout or use BoundField or TemplateField objects. Instead, FormView offers only a top-level template for each of its modes. For ReadOnly mode, FormView offers an `ItemTemplate` property. For Edit mode, it offers the `EditItemTemplate`. For Insert mode, it offers the `InsertItemTemplate` property. You can customize these templates to define the UI that FormView should render for each mode, specifying your own custom layout of controls in the template. Unlike TempalteField, which typically contains a single data-bound input control bound to a single field of the data source, the FormView templates will contain multiple data-bound controls.

When FormView is bound to a data source in VWD, it reflects against the schema (fields) of the data source in order to create default templates. If the data source supports Updates or Inserts, it will automatically create the `EditItemTemplate` and `InsertItemTemplate` properties to contain appropriate input controls that are two-way data-bound to the data source fields. You can modify this template content to your liking.

Similar to the way DetailsView works, FormView will switch between its ReadOnly, Edit, and Insert modes in response to command button clicks. The same command names apply: "Edit" to transition from ReadOnly to Edit mode, "New" to transition from ReadOnly to Insert mode, and "Update/Cancel" or "Insert/Cancel" to transition back (aborting the operation if "Cancel" is pressed). Unlike DetailsView however, FormView does not use a CommandField to generate these buttons. The buttons themselves must be defined in the `ItemTemplate`, `EditItemTemplate`, or `InsertItemTemplate` with appropriate command names set for each mode. Fortunately, the FormView will automatically create these buttons as part of the templates generated when it is bound to a data source. If you do not want to support a particular operation, you can delete the buttons that do not apply for your scenario.

Try It Out #6 — FormView for Inserting New Records

In this exercise, you will create a FormView for inserting new records into the Titles table.

1. Create a new page named `TIO-6-FormView.aspx`. Add a FormView that shows all of the fields from the Pubs database Titles table. Enable the data source control for inserts. Turn on paging in the FormView.
2. Select the FormView and, on the smart task panel, click on Edit Templates. Drag a button to the template and set its text to "New Title" and its CommandField to "New." Now go to the `InsertItemTemplate` and drag two buttons named "Create Title" with a CommandName of "Insert" and "Cancel Creation" with a CommandName of "Cancel."
3. Now you need some input controls on the InsertItem template. You could add them for each field by hand from the toolbar. But, instead, save some work by modifying the

EditItemTemplate automatically created by VWD. Switch to Source view and find the EditTemplate set of input controls that VWD automatically created. Select them and copy them into the `InsertItemTemplate`. The control for Title ID needs to be modified. Change its data binding from Eval() to Bind() so that it is two-way. Then change its control type from label to TextBox in both the opening and closing tags.

4. Save (similar to the following) and view the page in the browser. Add a new title with a Publisher ID = 9999. The other fields can be values of your choice.

5. Let's improve that Publisher ID field. Close the browser, and go back to VWD DesignView. Add an SqlDataSource named PublisherSqlSource to read (only) the pub_name and pub-id of the Publishers table. Now select the FormView and edit the InsertItem template. Delete the textbox for Pub_id and drag on a drop-down list box. Configure the data source to PublisherSqlSource and set the DataTextField and DataValueField properties to publisher name and publisher id, respectively. Edit Data Bindings so that SelectedValue is bound to pub_id. Two-way binding must be on. Save again and view in the browser to see an improved data-entry scheme.

```
<%@ Page Language="VB" %>
<html xmlns="http://www.w3.org/1999/xhtml" >
<head runat="server">
    <title>Untitled Page</title>
</head>
<body>
    <form id="form1" runat="server">
    <div>
        <asp:FormView ID="FormView1" Runat="server" DataSourceID="TitlesSqlSource"
DataKeyNames="title_id">
            <InsertItemTemplate>
                title_id:
                <asp:TextBox Text='<%# Bind("title_id") %>' Runat="server"
ID="title_idLabel1">
                </asp:TextBox><br />
                title:
                <asp:TextBox Text='<%# Bind("title") %>' Runat="server"
ID="titleTextBox"></asp:TextBox><br />
                type:
                <asp:TextBox Text='<%# Bind("type") %>' Runat="server"
ID="typeTextBox"></asp:TextBox><br />
                pub_id:
                <asp:DropDownList ID="DropDownList1" Runat="server"
DataSourceID="PublisherSqlSource"
                    SelectedValue='<%# Bind("pub_id") %>' DataTextField="Pub_name"
DataValueField="Pub_ID">
                </asp:DropDownList>
                <br />
                price:
                <asp:TextBox Text='<%# Bind("price") %>' Runat="server"
ID="priceTextBox"></asp:TextBox><br />
                advance:
                <asp:TextBox Text='<%# Bind("advance") %>' Runat="server"
ID="advanceTextBox"></asp:TextBox><br />
                royalty:
                <asp:TextBox Text='<%# Bind("royalty") %>' Runat="server"
ID="royaltyTextBox"></asp:TextBox><br />
                ytd_sales:
```

```
                <asp:TextBox Text='<%# Bind("ytd_sales") %>' Runat="server"
ID="ytd_salesTextBox"></asp:TextBox><br />
                notes:
                <asp:TextBox Text='<%# Bind("notes") %>' Runat="server"
ID="notesTextBox"></asp:TextBox><br />
                pubdate:
                <asp:TextBox Text='<%# Bind("pubdate") %>' Runat="server"
ID="pubdateTextBox"></asp:TextBox><br />           <asp:Button ID="Button1"
Runat="server" Text="insert" CommandName="insert" />
                <asp:Button ID="Button2" Runat="server" Text="cancel"
CommandName="cancel" />
            </InsertItemTemplate>
            <ItemTemplate>
                title_id:
                <asp:Label Text='<%# Bind("title_id") %>' Runat="server"
ID="title_idLabel">
                </asp:Label><br />
                title:
                <asp:Label Text='<%# Bind("title") %>' Runat="server"
ID="titleLabel">
                </asp:Label><br />
                type:
                <asp:Label Text='<%# Bind("type") %>' Runat="server"
ID="typeLabel">
                </asp:Label><br />
                pub_id:
                <asp:Label Text='<%# Bind("pub_id") %>' Runat="server"
ID="pub_idLabel">
                </asp:Label><br />
                price:
                <asp:Label Text='<%# Bind("price") %>' Runat="server"
ID="priceLabel">
                </asp:Label><br />
                advance:
                <asp:Label Text='<%# Bind("advance") %>' Runat="server"
ID="advanceLabel">
                </asp:Label><br />
                royalty:
                <asp:Label Text='<%# Bind("royalty") %>' Runat="server"
ID="royaltyLabel">
                </asp:Label><br />
                ytd_sales:
                <asp:Label Text='<%# Bind("ytd_sales") %>' Runat="server"
ID="ytd_salesLabel">
                </asp:Label><br />
                notes:
                <asp:Label Text='<%# Bind("notes") %>' Runat="server"
ID="notesLabel">
                </asp:Label><br />
                pubdate:
                <asp:Label Text='<%# Bind("pubdate") %>' Runat="server"
ID="pubdateLabel">
                </asp:Label><br />
                <br />
                <asp:Button ID="Button3" Runat="server" Text="New"
CommandName="New" />
```

```
            </ItemTemplate>
        </asp:FormView>

        <asp:SqlDataSource ID="TitlesSqlSource" Runat="server"
            ConnectionString="<%$ ConnectionStrings:LocalSqlPubs %>"
            InsertCommand="INSERT INTO [titles] ([title_id], [title], [type],
[pub_id], [price], [advance], [royalty], [ytd_sales], [notes], [pubdate]) VALUES
(@title_id, @title, @type, @pub_id, @price, @advance, @royalty, @ytd_sales, @notes,
@pubdate)"
            SelectCommand="SELECT * FROM [titles]" >
            <InsertParameters>
                <asp:Parameter Type="String" Name="title_id"></asp:Parameter>
                <asp:Parameter Type="String" Name="title"></asp:Parameter>
                <asp:Parameter Type="String" Name="type"></asp:Parameter>
                <asp:Parameter Type="String" Name="pub_id"></asp:Parameter>
                <asp:Parameter Type="Decimal" Name="price"></asp:Parameter>
                <asp:Parameter Type="Decimal" Name="advance"></asp:Parameter>
                <asp:Parameter Type="Int32" Name="royalty"></asp:Parameter>
                <asp:Parameter Type="Int32" Name="ytd_sales"></asp:Parameter>
                <asp:Parameter Type="String" Name="notes"></asp:Parameter>
                <asp:Parameter Type="DateTime" Name="pubdate"></asp:Parameter>
            </InsertParameters>
        </asp:SqlDataSource>

        <asp:SqlDataSource ID="PublisherSqlSource" Runat="server"
            ProviderName="System.Data.SqlClient"
            ConnectionString="Server=(local)\SQLExpress;
                Integrated Security=True;
                Database=pubs;
                Persist Security Info=True"
            SelectCommand="SELECT Pub_ID, Pub_name FROM [Publishers]" >
        </asp:SqlDataSource>
    </div>
    </form>
</body>
</html>
```

How It Works #6 — FormView for Inserting New Records

In this exercise, you created a FormView that could insert new titles. You started by enabling the inserting capability in the data source control. FormView supports whole-control templates (recall that DetailsView offers field-by-field templates).

You switched to the InsertItem template and added two buttons and got the set of input controls. Of course, such a trick is not without problems. The field for Title-ID was set to read-only in EditTemplate and you need to change it to read-write in `InsertItemTemplate`. You first change the binding code from the Eval() function to the Bind() function. Then you change the control type from Label to TextBox.

In the final step, you converted a textbox to a drop-down list in the same way that you did for DetailsView.

Common Mistakes

- Looking for an insert technique in the GridView. You need to use DetailsView or FormView in combination with GridView for this scenario.
- Changing values in a parameter of the wrong collection. When changing an InsertParameter, double-check that you are not in the list of Update parameters.
- Accidentally editing the Item template instead of the InsertItem template. The former is to display in Read-Only mode, the latter will appear in Insert mode.
- Attempting to insert a value for a primary key field that is auto-generated by the database. In this case, you should remove this field from Insert mode by setting InsertVisible=false on the field or removing the input control for this field from the ItemTemplate.
- Attempting to insert a data for a record that does not conform to the constraints of the underlying database.
- Looking for an Item and InsertItem template in DetailsView. They do not exist; the fields are automatically changed from labels to textboxes. However, if you add a TemplateField to the DetailsView, you can work with an Item and InsertItem template for that field.
- Trying to find a function in the wrong smart task panel of a control. Because controls can be nested (for example, radio buttons within a DetailsView), it is easy to open the smart task panel for the wrong level of control.
- Trying to find a function on a smart task panel when the panel is in template edit mode. End template editing and then you will see the original list of options.
- Setting up a list box or radio button without following each of the five steps listed in this chapter.

Summary

This chapter walked you through increasingly more complex variations in inserting new records. Only the DetailsView and FormViewsupport inserting (not the GridView). Using Insert employs ASP.NET 2.0's ability to change the rendering of the DetailsView from Read-Only to Insert mode. You started with a simple case of drag-and-drop and checked on enabling insertions in the data source control and data-bound control.

Next, you took a closer look at enabling insertions in the data source control. There is no `EnableInsert=true` property; rather, the existence of an InsertCommand and an InsertParameters collection enables inserting. Both of these objects are generated by the data source designer in the dialog box for Select Statement/Advanced Options. Don't be surprised if you look at the source code and see that the designer also generates Update and Delete statements and parameters collections — in this version of VWD you generate all three or none. You can delete the Update and Delete fields to condense code if you don't need them.

The data-bound control can sense the insert enablement in the data source control. By default, DetailsView will provide a label for each field in Read-Only mode and a textbox for each in InsertItem mode. If you want to change that rendering, you can change a field to be a template and then substitute a more robust input control such as radio buttons or a list box. That input control can be populated from a separate data source control, such as a list of states that come from a States table.

Using a templated input control in a DetailsView control is a five-step process:

1. Create a data source control to support the new input control.
2. Change the field in the DetailsView from bound to template.
3. Edit the templates and replace the default textbox with your better input control.
4. Set the input control to read from your data source control of step 1.
5. From the input control's smart task panel, data-bind display and value properties to fields in the input's data source control.

FormView is a less structured control. In contrast with DetailsView, it has Item and InsertItem templates for the control as a whole. By default, VWD seeds the Read-Only template.

You have now completed the first three parts of the book: an introduction, how to read data, and how to modify data. In the last part, you will work with some special data source and address some performance issues.

13

Business Objects as a Source of Data

Developers must realize that there is more to programming than simple code. Application architecture is a very important issue that is often overlooked. For reasons of clean separation and easier maintenance, you should create most Web applications using N-Tier principles. When you work with an N-Tier application, it is most likely that your middle-layer objects will return complex objects that you have to process in your ASP.NET presentation. Keeping this in mind, Microsoft has created a set of new data source controls that will allow you to seamlessly integrate the data returned from the middle-layer objects with the ASP.NET presentation layer. This chapter explains the different variations of the N-Tier application design principle and how they can provide flexible and easily maintainable application architectures. It also demonstrates how the new data source controls provided by ASP.NET 2.0 will aid you in creating true N-Tier applications.

You will find the following Try It Out exercises in this chapter:

Try It Out	Topic
1	Creating a Data Access Logic Component Using Data Component Wizard and Consuming It from within a Web Form
2	Accessing the Data Access Logic Component from a Web Form and Displaying Information in a GridView Control
3	Filtering and Master Details
4	Binding to a Custom Object
5	Implementing Sorting in a Custom Object

Introduction

When you are creating a distributed ASP.NET application, you will most likely split your application into multiple layers, such as presentation, business, and data access. This approach results in an extensible application that can be easily maintained and enhanced over a period of time. ASP.NET complements this type of application design by providing a new ObjectDataSource control that can be used to directly bind an object's methods to data-bound controls such as GridView, DataList, DropDownList, and so on. This approach provides for clean separation and encapsulation of code, eliminating the need to write data access code in the presentation layer. Now that you understand the theory behind the ObjectDataSource control, let's explore N-Tier application design and the different layers that are part of a typical N-Tier application.

Layers of an N-Tier Application

In a typical N-Tier environment, the client implements the presentation logic (thin client). The business logic and data access logic are implemented on an application server(s) and the data reside on a database server(s). N-Tier architecture is typically defined by the following three component layers:

- **Presentation Layer** — A front-end component that is responsible for providing portable presentation logic
- **Business Logic Layer** — Allows users to share and control business logic by isolating it from the other layers of the application
- **Data Access Logic Layer** — Provides access to the database by executing a set of SQL statements or stored procedures

Presentation Layer

The presentation logic layer consists of standard ASP.NET Web forms, ASP pages, documents, Windows forms, and so on. This is the layer that provides an interface for the end user into your application. That is, it works with the results/output of the business logic layer to handle the transformation into something usable and readable by the end user.

Business Logic Layer

This is basically where the brains of your application reside; it contains things like the business rules, data manipulation, and so on. For example, if you're creating a search engine and you want to rate/weight each matching item based on some custom criteria (say a quality rating and number of times a keyword was found in the result), place this logic at this layer. This layer does not know anything about HTML, nor does it output HTML. It does not care about ADO.NET or SQL, and it shouldn't have any code to access the database or the like. Those tasks are assigned to each corresponding layer above or below it.

Data Access Layer

This layer is where you will write some generic methods to interface with your data. For example, write a method for creating and opening an SqlConnection object, create an SqlCommand object for executing the stored procedure, and so on. It will also have some specific methods, such as UpdateProduct, so that when the Product object calls it with the appropriate data, it can persist it to the database. This data access logic layer contains no data business rules or data manipulation/transformation logic. It is merely a reusable interface to the database.

Advantages of N-Tier Architectures

Here are some of the advantages of N-Tier architectures:

- Changes to the user interface or to the application logic are largely independent of one another, allowing the application to evolve easily to meet new requirements.
- Network bottlenecks are minimized because the application layer does not transmit extra data to the client, only what is needed to handle a task.
- When business logic changes are required, only the server has to be updated. In two-tier architectures, each client must be modified when logic changes.
- The client is insulated from database and network operations. The client can access data easily and quickly without having to know where data is or how many servers are on the system.
- Database connections can be "pooled" and shared by several users, which greatly reduces the cost associated with per-user licensing.
- The organization has database independence because the data layer is written using standard SQL, which is platform independent. The enterprise is not tied to vendor-specific stored procedures.
- The application layer can be written in standard third- or fourth-generation languages, such as Java, C, or COBOL, with which the organization's in-house programmers are experienced.
- It is also possible to add total dependence between layers by allowing multiple clients to consume the services of the same business logic layer. For example, both a Windows forms application and a Web application could use the same underlying business tier. This way you can provide a richer experience to folks on the local LAN, but still be able to provide an interface to the application for customers over the Web.

Building a Data Access Logic Layer Using VS DataSets

How does ASP.NET 2.0 facilitate N-Tier application design by providing the ObjectDataSource control that is specifically suited for consuming middle-tier objects? For reasons of clean separation and easier maintenance, most Web applications are constructed using N-Tier principles. When you work with an N-Tier application, your middle-layer objects may return complex objects that you have to process in your ASP.NET presentation. Keeping this in mind, Microsoft has created an easy way to create a data access layer using the Visual Studio designer to generate a DataSet. Once you've created a VS DataSet, you may use the new ObjectDataSource control to seamlessly integrate the data returned from the middle-layer DataSet objects with the ASP.NET presentation layer.

Creating a Data Access Logic Layer Using the VS DataSet Designer

In ASP.NET 2.0, creating a component or class is a very simple process. All you need to do is to create a folder named "App_Code" and place all your components within that folder. Once the components are inside the App_Code folder, they will be automatically referenced and made available to all the pages in the Web application. The examples in this chapter will use the App_Code folder to store all reusable objects. With ASP.NET 2.0, Microsoft has introduced a new DataSet designer that makes creating a data access logic layer class easy. Using the DataSet designer, you can create a data access logic layer component without having to write a single line of code. This increases the productivity of the developers to a great extent. Once you create those objects, you can consume them exactly the same way you consume built-in objects.

Try It Out #1—Creating a Data Access Logic Component Using Data Component Wizard and Consuming It from within a Web Form

In this exercise, you will use the new DataSet project template to easily create a data access logic layer component. This exercise also demonstrates how IntelliSense works with the data access layer components generated as part of this DataSet.

1. Start your page editor and navigate to `C:\Websites\BegAspNet2Db\ch13\`.
2. Create a new DataSet by right-clicking on the Web site and selecting Add New Item... from the context menu. In the Add New Item... dialog box, select DataSet from the list of templates. Leave the name of the file as DataSet.xsd and click Add.
3. When you click Add in the previous step, you will be presented with a dialog box prompting you to choose whether you want to place the DataSet inside a directory called App_Code. Click OK. App_Code directory is a special directory introduced with ASP.NET 2.0. Any reusable component that you want to reference from within your ASP.NET application can be placed in the App_Code directory and referenced directly. Any component placed in this directory will be automatically compiled at runtime into a single assembly. This assembly is automatically referenced and will be available to all the pages in the site. Note that you should only put components and class files in the App_Code subdirectory.
4. When you click OK in the prompt, it will bring up the Table Adapter Configuration Wizard. Click Next in the first step.
5. In the Choose Your Data Connection dialog box that opens, click the New Connection command button and type in the name of your server as (localhost)\SQLExpress. In the Enter Information to Log On to the Server option box, ensure that Use Windows NT Integrated Security is checked. Then select the Pubs database from the Select or Enter a Database Name drop-down list. Click Test Connection to ensure that the connection works properly. Then click OK.
6. You will be prompted to choose whether you want to save the connection string to the application configuration file. Check the check box that says Yes, Save Connection As and give it an appropriate name. Click Next.
7. The wizard will ask you to choose the command type. Select Use SQL Statements from the list of options and click OK.
8. Clicking OK brings up the Generate SQL Statements dialog box wherein you need to either type in the SQL statement or build the SQL using the QueryBuilder. For the purposes of this exercise, just type in `SELECT * FROM Authors` in the SQL Statement textbox and click Next.
9. The Choose Methods to Generate dialog box opens, wherein you can specify the list of methods that you want to add to the Data Component. Change the Method Name from GetData to GetAuthors in the Return a DataTable option and leave all other values. Click Next.

10. In the View Wizard Results dialog box, click Finish. This results in a class named authorsTableAdapter being created.

11. Now that you have created a TableAdapter class in the DataSet, you can access it from a Web form. To this end, add a page named `TO1_BuildingADataComponent.aspx` from the template Web Form. Change to DesignView using the bottom tabs.

12. At the top of the page, add Import directives to import the DataSetTableAdapters and DataSet namespaces. When you created the TableAdapter using the TableAdapter Configuration Wizard, this class and related classes, such as authorsDataTable and authorsRow, were created in these namespaces.

13. Now add the `Page_Load` event to the Web form to create an instance of the authorsTableAdapter class and invoke its GetAuthors method. After modification, your page should appear as follows:

```
<%@ Page Language="VB" %>
<%@ Import Namespace="DataSetTableAdapters" %>
<%@ Import Namespace="DataSet" %>
<script runat="server">
  Sub Page_Load(ByVal sender As Object, ByVal e As System.EventArgs)
     Dim authorsAdapter As New authorsTableAdapter
     Dim authorsTable As authorsDataTable
     authorsTable = authorsAdapter.GetAuthors()
     Response.Write(authorsTable.Item(0).au_id)
  End Sub
</script>
<html>
<head>
  <title>TIO ch13 Building a Data Component</title>
</head>
<body>
 <h3>TIO 1 Demonstration of building a data set and accessing it from a page
 </h3>
<form id="form1" runat="server">
  This shows accessing the data component classes from code in a page
</form>
</body>
</html>
```

14. Open your browser and view `C:\Websites\BegAspNet2Db\ch13\TO1_BuildingADataComponent.aspx`. You will see the page display the author ID for the first author in the table (172-32-1176).

How It Works #1—Creating a Data Access Logic Component Using Data Component Wizard and Consuming It from within a Web Form

In this example, the class named authorsTableAdapter plays an important role and provides the core foundation required for connecting to the database and retrieving the author details from the database. Once you create the DataSet and place it in the Code directory, this class is automatically made available to the Web application. From within your Web form, you use the `Page_Load` event to create an instance of the authorsTableAdapter class and then invoke its GetAuthors method. The GetAuthors method returns an instance of the authorsDataTable. Once you get the authorsDataTable, you can navigate to the data contained in it. In this example, you retrieve the first row in the DataTable using the `Item` property and then display the value contained in the au_id column. As you can see, the au_id column is one of the properties of the authorsRow object. This allows you to access the data contained in the authorsDataTable in a strongly typed manner resulting in less error-prone code. Because of this strongly typed object, you can also take advantage of the IntelliSense to identify the list of data elements of the authors table.

Data-Binding to a DataSet

The previous example looked at how to create an instance of the classes created using the Table Adapter Wizard, part of the Visual Studio DataSet designer. In this exercise, you will understand how to consume those directly by data-binding them to a GridView control using ObjectDataSource.

Try It Out #2 — Accessing the Data Access Logic Component from a Web Form and Displaying Information in a GridView Control

In this exercise, you will utilize the authorsTableAdapter that you created in the previous exercise and bind it to a GridView control.

1. Start your page editor and navigate to `C:\Websites\BegAspNet2Db\ch13\`.
2. Add a page named `TO2_BindingToDataComponent.aspx` from the template Web Form. Change to Design view using the bottom tabs.
3. Display the toolbox (Menu: View/toolbox or Ctrl+Alt+X) and expand the toolbox's Data panel.
4. Drag and drop an ObjectDataSource control onto your page. Modify its declaration to look like the following:

```
<asp:ObjectDataSource ID="ObjectDataSource1" Runat="server"
TypeName="DataSetTableAdapters.authorsTableAdapter" DeleteMethod="Delete"
InsertMethod="Insert"
SelectMethod="GetAuthors" UpdateMethod="Update"/>
```

5. Now drag and drop a GridView control onto the page. Select the GridView control and select Properties Window from the View menu. In the Properties window, set the AutoGenerateColumns, DataKeyNames, and DataSourceID properties to False, au_id, and ObjectDataSource1, respectively.
6. Add the required columns to the GridView control. After adding all the columns, your page should now appear as follows:

```
<%@ Page Language="VB" %>
<html>
<head>
  <title>TIO ch13 Binding to a Data Component</title>
</head>
<body>
  <h3>TIO 2 Demonstration of binding a data component to a GridView control
  </h3>
  <form id="form1" runat="server">
   <asp:GridView ID="GridView1" Runat="server" DataSourceID="ObjectDataSource1"
     AutoGenerateColumns="False" DataKeyNames="au_id">
     <Columns>
```

```
            <asp:CommandField ShowEditButton="True" />
            <asp:BoundField HeaderText="au_id" DataField="au_id" SortExpression="au_id"/>
            <asp:BoundField HeaderText="au_lname" DataField="au_lname"
              SortExpression="au_lname" />
            <asp:BoundField HeaderText="au_fname" DataField="au_fname"
              SortExpression="au_fname" />
            <asp:BoundField HeaderText="phone" DataField="phone"
              SortExpression="phone" />
            <asp:BoundField HeaderText="address" DataField="address"
              SortExpression="address" />
            <asp:BoundField HeaderText="city" DataField="city" SortExpression="city" />
            <asp:BoundField HeaderText="state" DataField="state"
              SortExpression="state" />
            <asp:BoundField HeaderText="zip" DataField="zip" SortExpression="zip" />
            <asp:CheckBoxField HeaderText="contract" SortExpression="contract"
              DataField="contract" />
          </Columns>
        </asp:GridView>
        <asp:ObjectDataSource ID="ObjectDataSource1" Runat="server"
          TypeName="DataSetTableAdapters.authorsTableAdapter" DeleteMethod="Delete"
InsertMethod="Insert"
          SelectMethod="GetAuthors" UpdateMethod="Update"/>
      </form>
</body>
</html>
```

7. Open your browser and view `C:\Websites\BegAspNet2Db\ch13\TO2_BindingToDataComponent.aspx`. Although the GridView looks the same as in previous chapters, we are now actually harvesting data from our data object, not directly from the database. Furthermore, we have saved time by re-using the same data object from the last exercise.

How It Works #2 — Accessing the Data Access Logic Component from a Web Form and Displaying Information in a GridView Control

In this example, the class named authorsTableAdapter plays an important role and provides the core foundation required for connecting to the database and retrieving the author details from the database. Once you create the DataSet and place it in the Code directory, it is automatically made available to the Web application. Instead of creating an instance of this class in `Page_Load` as done in the previous example, this example uses the ObjectDataSource control to make the data from the GetAuthors method available to a GridView on the page. The ObjectDataSource control `TypeName` property was set to the name of the authorsTableAdapter type (qualified by namespace), and the `SelectMethod` property was set to the GetAuthors method. Once the ObjectDataSource is configured, the GridView is associated to this data source through its DataSourceID property. At runtime, the ObjectDataSource instantiates the authorsTableAdapter type and calls the GetAuthors method to return the data to the GridView control.

Implementing Master Details Capability

So far, you have used the DataSet and data controls to display information from the authors table directly. In this example, you will understand how to implement master details capability using multiple TableAdapter classes in a DataSet along with controls such as ObjectDataSource, GridView, and DropDownList.

Try It Out #3 — Filtering and Master Details

In this exercise, you will implement master-detail display capabilities by using the DataSet in conjunction with the declarative attributes of the ObjectDataSource, GridView, and DropDownList controls. You will display the list of states in a DropDownList control and the authors present in that state in a GridView control. When the user selects a different state from the DropDownList, we will refresh the GridView control to display those authors present in that newly selected state.

1. Start your page editor and navigate to `C:\Websites\BegAspNet2Db\ch13\`.
2. Create a new DataSet by right-clicking on the Web site and selecting Add New Item... from the context menu. In the Add New Item... dialog box, select DataSet from the list of templates. Leave the name of the file as DataSet2.xsd and click Add.
3. Next Click OK for the prompt that asks if you want to place your component inside the Code directory.
4. When you click OK in the prompt, it will bring up the Table Adapter Configuration Wizard. Click Next in the first step.
5. The Choose Your Data Connection dialog box opens. In this dialog box, specify the same connection string as you did in your first example.
6. You will be asked whether you want to save the connection string to the application configuration file. Check the check box that says Yes, Save Connection As. Click Next.
7. The wizard will ask you to choose the command type. Select Use SQL Statements from the list of options and click OK.
8. The Generate SQL Statements dialog box opens, wherein you need to either type in the SQL statement or build the SQL using the QueryBuilder. In this case, just type in `SELECT DISTINCT State FROM Authors` in the SQL Statement textbox and click OK.
9. In the resulting Choose Methods to Generate dialog box, you can specify the list of methods that you want to add to the TableAdapter class. Just change the Method Name from GetData to GetStates in the Return a DataTable option and leave all other values. Click Next.
10. You will be presented with the View Wizard Results dialog box. Click Finish in this dialog box. Doing so results in a class named authorsTableAdapter being created. After the Data Component is created, right-click on the Data Component and rename it to statesTableAdapter.
11. Create another TableAdapter by right-clicking on the DataSet2's Design view and selecting Add ➪ TableAdapter... from the context menu.
12. In all the prompts, specify the same information as in the previous example. However, in the Generate SQL Statements dialog box, specify `SELECT * FROM Authors WHERE State = @state` in the SQL Statement textbox and click OK.
13. This results in a Choose Methods to Generate dialog box, wherein you can specify the list of methods that you want to add to the TableAdapter class. In this dialog box, just change the Method Name from GetData to GetAuthorsByState in the Return a DataTable option and leave all other values. Click Next.
14. The View Wizard Results dialog box opens. Click Finish in this dialog box. This results in a Data Component named authorsTableAdapter being created. Right-click on the Data Component and rename it to authors2TableAdapter.

15. Create one more Data Component by right-clicking on the DataSet2's Design view and selecting Add ➪ TableAdapter... from the context menu.

16. In all the prompts, specify the same information as in the first example in this exercise. However, in the Generate SQL Statements dialog box, specify

```
SELECT A.au_id, T.title_id, Title, Type, Price, Notes
              FROM Authors A
              INNER JOIN titleauthor TA ON A.au_id = TA.au_id
              INNER JOIN titles T ON TA.title_id = T.title_id
              WHERE au_id = @au_id
```

in the SQL Statement textbox and click OK

17. This results in the Choose Methods to Generate dialog box, wherein you can specify the list of methods that you want to add to the TableAdapter class. In this dialog box, just change the Method Name from GetData to GetTitles in the Return a DataTable option and leave all other values. Click Next.

18. Now you will be presented with the View Wizard Results dialog box. Click Finish in this dialog box and rename the resulting TableAdapter to titlesTableAdapter.

19. Now that you have created all the TableAdapters in the DataSet, access them from a Web form. To this end, add a page named `TO3_FilteringMasterDetails.aspx` from the template Web Form. Change to Design view using the bottom tabs.

20. Now add two ObjectDataSource controls, a DropDownList, and a GridView control to the page. Modify the controls to use the previously created Data Components as their data source. After modification, your page should appear as follows:

```
<%@ Page Language="VB" %>
<html>
<head>
  <title> ch13 TIO #3 Filtering Master Details Using Data Component</title>
</head>
<body>
  <h3> Ch13 TIO #3 Demonstration of filtering master details using a GridView
control
  </h3>
  <form id="form1" runat="server">
    <asp:DropDownList ID="DropDownList1" Runat="server"
      DataSourceID="ObjectDataSource1"
      DataTextField="state" DataValueField="state" AutoPostBack="True" />
    <asp:ObjectDataSource ID="ObjectDataSource1" Runat="server"
      TypeName="DataSet2TableAdapters.statesTableAdapter"
SelectMethod="GetStates" />
    <br/><br/>
    <asp:GridView ID="GridView1" Runat="server" DataSourceID="ObjectDataSource2"
      AutoGenerateColumns="False">
      <Columns>
        <asp:BoundField HeaderText="au_id" DataField="au_id"
          SortExpression="au_id"/>
        <asp:BoundField HeaderText="au_lname" DataField="au_lname"
          SortExpression="au_lname" />
        <asp:BoundField HeaderText="au_fname" DataField="au_fname"
          SortExpression="au_fname" />
        <asp:BoundField HeaderText="phone" DataField="phone"
          SortExpression="phone" />
```

```
        <asp:BoundField HeaderText="address" DataField="address"
          SortExpression="address" />
        <asp:BoundField HeaderText="city" DataField="city" SortExpression="city" />
        <asp:BoundField HeaderText="state" DataField="state"
          SortExpression="state" />
        <asp:BoundField HeaderText="zip" DataField="zip" SortExpression="zip" />
        <asp:CheckBoxField HeaderText="contract" SortExpression="contract"
          DataField="contract" />
        <asp:HyperLinkField HeaderText="View Details..." Text="View Details..."
          DataNavigateUrlFields="au_id"
          DataNavigateUrlFormatString="Details.aspx?ID={0}" />
      </Columns>
    </asp:GridView>
    <asp:ObjectDataSource ID="ObjectDataSource2" Runat="server"
       TypeName=" DataSet2TableAdapters.authors2TableAdapter"
       SelectMethod="GetAuthorsByState" DeleteMethod="Delete" InsertMethod="Insert"
       UpdateMethod="Update">
      <SelectParameters>
        <asp:ControlParameter Name="state" ControlID="DropDownList1"
           PropertyName="SelectedValue" />
      </SelectParameters>
    </asp:ObjectDataSource>
  </form>
</body>
</html>
```

21. As you can see from the GridView declaration code, you also display an external link to a page named Details.aspx using the asp:HyperLinkField element. To this page, you also pass in the au_id through the querystring.

22. Add a new page named Details.aspx to the Web site. Once the page is created, modify the code in the page, as follows:

```
<%@ Page Language="VB" %>
<html>
<head>
   <title>View Details</title>
</head>
<body>
  <form id="form1" runat="server">
    <asp:DetailsView ID="DetailsView1" Runat="server"
      DataSourceID="ObjectDataSource1" AutoGenerateRows="False" HeaderText="Books
      for Author" AllowPaging="False">
      <Fields>
        <asp:BoundField HeaderText="au_id" DataField="au_id"
          SortExpression="au_id" />
        <asp:BoundField HeaderText="title_id" DataField="title_id"
         SortExpression="title_id" />
        <asp:BoundField HeaderText="title" DataField="title"
          SortExpression="title" />
        <asp:BoundField HeaderText="type" DataField="type" SortExpression="type" />
        <asp:BoundField HeaderText="price" DataField="price"
          SortExpression="price" />
         <asp:BoundField HeaderText="notes" DataField="notes"
          SortExpression="notes" />
```

```
        </Fields>
      </asp:DetailsView>
    <asp:ObjectDataSource ID="ObjectDataSource1" Runat="server"
      TypeName=" DataSet2TableAdapters.titlesTableAdapter"
      SelectMethod="GetTitles">
      <SelectParameters>
        <asp:QueryStringParameter Name="au_id" DefaultValue="213-46-8915"
          QueryStringField="ID" />
        </SelectParameters>
    </asp:ObjectDataSource>
  </form>
</body>
</html>
```

23. Open your browser and view `C:\Websites\BegAspNet2Db\ch13\T03_FilteringMasterDetails.aspx`.

How It Works #3 — Filtering and Master Details

In this example, you used three different TableAdapters in a DataSet to connect to the database and retrieve data from the database. The titlesTableAdapter is used by the Details.aspx, and the remaining two TableAdapters are used in the `T03_FilteringMasterDetails.aspx` page. Let's look at the code of the `T03_FilteringMasterDetails.aspx` page.

In the `T03_FilteringMasterDetails.aspx` page, you declare two ObjectDataSource controls. The first control uses the statesTableAdapter and has its SelectMethod attribute set to GetStates. This ObjectDataSource control also acts as the data source control for the DropDownList that displays the list of states. The second ObjectDataSource control uses the authors2TableAdapter as its TypeName and has its SelectMethod, InsertMethod, UpdateMethod, and DeleteMethod attributes set to GetAuthorsByState, Insert, Update, and Delete, respectively. This control also acts as the data source for the GridView control. In the GridView control, you specify the various elements to be displayed using the `asp:BoundField` and `asp:CheckBoxField` elements. Along with this declaration, you also specify a HyperLink element using the `asp:HyperLinkField` element. You set the HyperLinkField's NavigateUrl to the `Details.aspx` page and also pass in the au_id to the `Details.aspx` page through the querystring.

The `Details.aspx` page is very similar to the previous example except for the following two differences. First, it uses the DetailsView control to display the titles written by a specific author. Second, it uses the querystring value passed from the `T03_FilteringMasterDetails.aspx` page directly in the ObjectDataSource control declaration. Basically, it takes in the supplied querystring au_id value and utilizes it directly in the `asp:querystringparameter` element declaration. The value of the au_id is supplied as an argument while invoking the GetTitles method of the titlesTableAdapter class. The result of the GetTitles method invocation is directly bound to the DetailsView control.

Implementing and Data-Binding to Custom Objects

So far, we have used the TableAdapter Wizard to create our data access logic layer components. Here, you will explore creating a data access logic layer component using ADO.NET and then invoke its methods from a business logic layer component. Finally, you data-bind the results returned by the business logic layer directly to an ObjectDataSource control. Once the information is available in a data source control, you can display it using a variety of data-bound controls, such as GridView, DropDownList, and so on. In this instance, you will also use generic collection objects as the return data type from the business logic layer.

Generics is a new concept introduced with .NET Framework. Generics can be referred to as a class, where you don't force it to be related to any specific type, but you can still perform work with it in a type-safe manner. A perfect example of where you would need Generics is in dealing with collections of items (integers, strings, orders, and so on). You can create a generic collection than can handle any type in a generic and type-safe manner. For example, you can have a single array class that you can use to store a list of users or even a list of products, and when you actually use it, you will be able to access the items in the collection directly as a list of users or products, and not as objects (with boxing/unboxing, casting). Languages such as C# and VB.NET now support this new feature. There are a number of advantages to using Generics, including the following:

- **Type safety** — Generic types enforce type compliance at compile time, and not at runtime (as in the case of using Object). This reduces the chances of data-type conflict during runtime.
- **Performance** — The data types to be used in a generic class are determined at compile time, so there is no need to perform type casting during runtime, which is a computationally costly process.
- **Code reuse** — Because you need to write the class only once and customize it to use with the various data types, there is a substantial amount of code reuse.

The following Try It Out uses Generics in a custom object implementation.

Try It Out #4 — Binding to a Custom Object

In this exercise, you will create a custom object (including data access layer and business logic layer objects) and then bind the business logic layer object to an ObjectDataSource control.

1. Start your page editor and navigate to `C:\Websites\BegAspNet2Db\ch13\`.
2. Add a page named `TO4_BindingToCustomObject.aspx` from the template Web Form. Change to Design view using the bottom tabs.
3. Create a new Class by right-clicking on the Web site and selecting Add New Item from the context menu. In the Add New Item dialog box, select Class from the list of templates. Name the file as AuthorsDB.vb and click Add. As the name suggests, the AuthorsDB.vb file will contain methods to execute Select, Update, or Delete statements against the authors table.
4. A dialog box appears, prompting you to decide whether you want to place your component inside a directory called App_Code. Click OK.
5. Once the file is created, modify the code in the AuthorsDB.vb file to look like the following:

```
Imports System
Public Class AuthorsDB
    Public Sub New()
    End Sub
    Shared Function GetAuthorsByState(ByVal state As String) As System.Data.DataSet
         Dim connectionString As String =
         ConfigurationSettings.ConnectionStrings("Pubs").ConnectionString
         Dim dbConnection As System.Data.IDbConnection = New
```

```
        System.Data.SqlClient.SqlConnection(connectionString)
        Dim queryString As String = "SELECT [authors].[au_id],
        [authors].[au_fname], [authors].[au_lname], [authors].[" & _
        "state] FROM [authors] WHERE ([authors].[state] = @state)"
        Dim dbCommand As System.Data.IDbCommand = New
        System.Data.SqlClient.SqlCommand
        dbCommand.CommandText = queryString
        dbCommand.Connection = dbConnection
        Dim dbParam_state As System.Data.IDataParameter = New
        System.Data.SqlClient.SqlParameter
        dbParam_state.ParameterName = "@state"
        dbParam_state.Value = state
        dbParam_state.DbType = System.Data.DbType.StringFixedLength
        dbCommand.Parameters.Add(dbParam_state)
        Dim dataAdapter As System.Data.IDbDataAdapter = New
        System.Data.SqlClient.SqlDataAdapter
        dataAdapter.SelectCommand = dbCommand
        Dim dataSet As System.Data.DataSet = New System.Data.DataSet
        dataAdapter.Fill(dataSet)
    Return dataSet
End Function

Shared Function GetStates() As System.Data.DataSet
    Dim connectionString As String =
    ConfigurationSettings.ConnectionStrings("Pubs").ConnectionString
    Dim dbConnection As System.Data.IDbConnection = New
    System.Data.SqlClient.SqlConnection(connectionString)
    Dim queryString As String = "SELECT DISTINCT [authors].[state] FROM
    [authors]"
    Dim dbCommand As System.Data.IDbCommand = New
    System.Data.SqlClient.SqlCommand
    dbCommand.CommandText = queryString
    dbCommand.Connection = dbConnection
   Dim dataAdapter As System.Data.IDbDataAdapter = New
    System.Data.SqlClient.SqlDataAdapter
    dataAdapter.SelectCommand = dbCommand
    Dim dataSet As System.Data.DataSet = New System.Data.DataSet
    dataAdapter.Fill(dataSet)
    Return dataSet
End Function

Shared Function UpdateAuthor(ByVal au_id As String, ByVal au_lname As String,
     ByVal au_fname As String, ByVal state As String) As Integer
     Dim connectionString As String =
     ConfigurationSettings.ConnectionStrings("Pubs").ConnectionString
     Dim dbConnection As System.Data.IDbConnection = New
     System.Data.SqlClient.SqlConnection(connectionString)
     Dim queryString As String = "UPDATE [authors] SET [au_lname]=@au_lname,
     [au_fname]=@au_fname, [state]=@state W" & _
     "HERE ([authors].[au_id] = @au_id)"
     Dim dbCommand As System.Data.IDbCommand = New
     System.Data.SqlClient.SqlCommand
     dbCommand.CommandText = queryString
     dbCommand.Connection = dbConnection
     Dim dbParam_au_id As System.Data.IDataParameter = New
     System.Data.SqlClient.SqlParameter
     dbParam_au_id.ParameterName = "@au_id"
```

```
        dbParam_au_id.Value = au_id
        dbParam_au_id.DbType = System.Data.DbType.[String]
        dbCommand.Parameters.Add(dbParam_au_id)
        Dim dbParam_au_lname As System.Data.IDataParameter = New
        System.Data.SqlClient.SqlParameter
        dbParam_au_lname.ParameterName = "@au_lname"
        dbParam_au_lname.Value = au_lname
        dbParam_au_lname.DbType = System.Data.DbType.[String]
        dbCommand.Parameters.Add(dbParam_au_lname)
        Dim dbParam_au_fname As System.Data.IDataParameter = New
        System.Data.SqlClient.SqlParameter
        dbParam_au_fname.ParameterName = "@au_fname"
        dbParam_au_fname.Value = au_fname
        dbParam_au_fname.DbType = System.Data.DbType.[String]
        dbCommand.Parameters.Add(dbParam_au_fname)
        Dim dbParam_state As System.Data.IDataParameter = New
        System.Data.SqlClient.SqlParameter
        dbParam_state.ParameterName = "@state"
        dbParam_state.Value = state
        dbParam_state.DbType = System.Data.DbType.StringFixedLength
        dbCommand.Parameters.Add(dbParam_state)
        Dim rowsAffected As Integer = 0
        dbConnection.Open()
        Try
            rowsAffected = dbCommand.ExecuteNonQuery
        Finally
            dbConnection.Close()
        End Try
       Return rowsAffected
    End Function
End Class
```

6. As you can see from the preceding code, you are retrieving the connection string from the Web.config file. So open up the Web.config file and add the following configuration settings under the configuration element:

```
   <connectionStrings>
    <add name="Pubs"

connectionString="server=(local)\SQLExpress;database=Pubs;trusted_connection=true"/
>
    <add name="Northwind"

connectionString="server=(local)\SQLExpress;database=Northwind;trusted_connection=t
rue"/>
   </connectionStrings>
```

7. Now that you have added the data access logic layer class, create the business logic layer class methods. To this end, create a new class named AuthorsComponent.vb under the Code folder. Like any other business logic layer class, this class will invoke the methods of the AuthorsDB data access layer class for retrieving the necessary data. Now add methods in the AuthorsComponent class to invoke the methods of the AuthorsDB class. After modification, your source code should look like the following:

```
Imports System
Imports System.Data
```

```
Imports System.Collections.Generic
Public Class AuthorsComponent
    Public Sub New()
    End Sub

    Public Function GetAuthorsByState(ByVal state As String) As List(Of Author)
        Dim authors As New List(Of Author)
        Dim ds As DataSet = AuthorsDB.GetAuthorsByState(state)
        Dim row As DataRow
        For Each row In ds.Tables(0).Rows
            authors.Add(New Author(row("au_id"), row("au_fname"), row("au_lname"),
            row("state")))
        Next
        Return authors
    End Function

    Public Function UpdateAuthor(ByVal Original_ID As String, ByVal LastName As
        String, ByVal Name As String, ByVal State As String) As Integer
        Return AuthorsDB.UpdateAuthor(Original_ID, LastName, Name, State)
    End Function

    Public Function GetStates() As List(Of String)
        Dim states As New List(Of String)
        Dim ds As DataSet = AuthorsDB.GetStates()
        Dim row As DataRow
        For Each row In ds.Tables(0).Rows
            states.Add(row("state"))
        Next
        Return states
    End Function
End Class
```

8. Once you have created the business logic layer methods, you can add code to the Web form to invoke the methods of the business logic layer class. Open up the previously created Web form.

9. Now drag and drop an ObjectDataSource control onto your Web form's Design view. Modify its declaration to look like the following:

```
<asp:ObjectDataSource ID="ObjectDataSource1" Runat="server"
TypeName="AuthorsComponent" SelectMethod="GetStates" />
```

10. Drag and drop a DropDownList onto the page. The control's smart task panel should appear automatically, but if not, select the new DropDownList control and then click the top right small arrow to open the smart task panel. Click on the Configure Data Source drop-down list and select ObjectDataSource1 from the list.

11. Drag and drop one more ObjectDataSource control onto your Web form's Design view and then modify its declaration to look like the following:

```
<asp:ObjectDataSource ID="ObjectDataSource2" Runat="server"
   TypeName="AuthorsComponent"  SelectMethod="GetAuthorsByState"
   UpdateMethod="UpdateAuthor">
   <SelectParameters>
      <asp:ControlParameter Name="state" Type="String"
       ControlID="DropDownList1" PropertyName="SelectedValue" />
   </SelectParameters>
</asp:ObjectDataSource>
```

12. Drag and drop a GridView control onto the Web form's Design view and modify its declaration to look like the following:

```
<asp:GridView ID="GridView1" Runat="server" DataSourceID="ObjectDataSource2"
AutoGenerateColumns="False" AllowPaging="True" AllowSorting="True"
DataKeyNames="ID">
<Columns>
  <asp:CommandField ShowEditButton="True" />
  <asp:BoundField ReadOnly="True" HeaderText="ID" DataField="ID"
      SortExpression="ID" />
  <asp:BoundField HeaderText="Name" DataField="Name" SortExpression="Name" />
  <asp:BoundField HeaderText="LastName" DataField="LastName"
      SortExpression="LastName" />
  <asp:BoundField HeaderText="State" DataField="State"
      SortExpression="State" />
</Columns>
</asp:GridView>
```

13. After making all the changes, your Web form should appear as follows:

```
<%@ Page Language="VB" %>
<html>
<head>
   <title>TIO ch13 Binding to a Custom Object</title>
</head>
<body>
<h3>TIO Ch13 Binding a Custom Object to an ObjectDataSource Control</h3>  <form
id="form1" runat="server">
  <asp:DropDownList ID="DropDownList1" Runat="server"
     DataSourceID="ObjectDataSource1" AutoPostBack="True" />
  <asp:ObjectDataSource ID="ObjectDataSource1" Runat="server"
     TypeName="AuthorsComponent" SelectMethod="GetStates" />
  <br/><br />
  <asp:GridView ID="GridView1" Runat="server" DataSourceID="ObjectDataSource2"
     AutoGenerateColumns="False" AllowPaging="True" AllowSorting="True"
     DataKeyNames="ID">
     <Columns>
       <asp:CommandField ShowEditButton="True" />
       <asp:BoundField ReadOnly="True" HeaderText="ID" DataField="ID"
          SortExpression="ID" />
       <asp:BoundField HeaderText="Name" DataField="Name"
          SortExpression="Name" />
       <asp:BoundField HeaderText="LastName" DataField="LastName"
          SortExpression="LastName" />
       <asp:BoundField HeaderText="State" DataField="State"
          SortExpression="State" />
     </Columns>
</asp:GridView>
<asp:ObjectDataSource ID="ObjectDataSource2" Runat="server"
   TypeName="AuthorsComponent" SelectMethod="GetAuthorsByState"
   UpdateMethod="UpdateAuthor">
   <SelectParameters>
     <asp:ControlParameter Name="state" Type="String"
       ControlID="DropDownList1" PropertyName="SelectedValue" />
   </SelectParameters>
```

```
</asp:ObjectDataSource>
</form>
</body>
</html>
```

14. Open your browser and view `C:\Websites\BegAspNet2Db\ch13\T04_BindingToCustomObject.aspx`.

How It Works #4 — Binding to a Custom Object

Here, you use the data access layer class AuthorsDB to execute SQL statements against the Pubs database. The AuthorsDB class contains three methods named GetAuthorsByState, GetStates, and UpdateAuthor. As the name suggests, the GetAuthorsByState method takes in state name as an argument and returns the list of authors in that state in the form of a DataSet object. It does that by executing a Select SQL statement using the SqlCommand, SqlDataAdapter, and DataSet objects. To start with, it creates an SqlCommand object and then sets various properties of the SqlCommand object. Then it creates an instance of the SqlDataAdapter object and sets its SelectCommand property to the previously created SqlCommand object. Finally, it creates an instance of the DataSet object and invokes its Fill method to populate the DataSet object with the results of the SQL query execution. The GetStates and UpdateAuthor methods are similar to the GetAuthorsByState method except that they execute a different SQL statement against the database.

Now let's talk about the implementation of the AuthorsComponent business logic layer class. As previously mentioned, this class utilizes the methods of the AuthorsDB class for performing operations against the authors table. In the GetAuthorsByState method, you start by creating an instance of the generic class named Authors. To the constructor of the generic class, you pass an object named Author. (You can download the code for the Author class along with the support material for this book.) The implementation of the Author class is very simple and provides public properties for setting and getting attributes such as ID, Name, LastName, and State. After creating an instance of the generic class, the method invokes the GetAuthorsByState method of the AuthorsDB class. Then it loops through the resultant DataTable object, loads the values into the Author object, and then moves on to the generic class. Finally, it returns the generic collection object using the return statement. The implementation of the GetStates method is very similar except that it returns a generic object of type string to the caller. The UpdateAuthor method simply invokes the AuthorsDB class's UpdateAuthor method and returns the result of the invocation to the caller.

The Web form contains two ObjectDataSource controls with both of them using the AuthorsComponent class as the object source. The first ObjectDataSource control, named ObjectDataSource1, utilizes the GetStates method of the AuthorsComponent class as its source method by setting its SelectMethod attribute to GetStates. The ObjectDataSource1 control also acts as the data source for a DropDownList control named DropDownList1. The second ObjectDataSource control, named ObjectDataSource2, utilizes the GetAuthorsByState and UpdateAuthor methods by setting its SelectMethod and UpdateMethod attributes to GetAuthorsByState and UpdateAuthor, respectively. While declaring the ObjectDataSource2 control, you also specify the parameter for the GetAuthorsByState method using t he asp:controlparameter element. The value for this parameter comes from the previously declared DropDownList control that displays all the state values from the authors table. You specify this by setting the asp:controlparameter element's ControlID and the PropertyName attributes. The ObjectDataSource2 control also acts as the data source for a GridView control named GridView1. In the GridView control declaration, apart from specifying the fields you want to display in the Web form, you also set the DataKeyNames property to the ID property of the Author object.

If you run the page, you should see CA as the selected state by default in the drop-down list, and the GridView control should display the list of authors present in the CA state. If you change the state in the drop-down list, the GridView will display the corresponding authors data.

Implementing Sorting in a Custom Object

Sorting is nothing but ordering the list of items in a particular way. To sort any object, the underlying system must be able to compare various elements of the list so that they can be rearranged based on the result of comparison. The System.Collections namespace contains an interface called IComparer that can be used to provide such a custom comparison mechanism for your classes. The IComparer interface provides a method named Compare that compares two objects and returns a value indicating whether one is less than, equal to, or greater than the other. The next Try It Out explores how to implement custom sorting behavior and how you can leverage that from within your Web form.

Try It Out #5 — Implementing Sorting in a Custom Object

In this exercise, you will implement sorting in the Author object you used in the previous exercise and then see how it enables sorting in the output of the Web form. You will also utilize the data access layer class AuthorsDB that you created in the previous example.

1. Start your page editor and navigate to `C:\Websites\BegAspNet2Db\ch13\`.
2. Add a page named `TO5_SortingInCustomObject.aspx` from the template Web Form. Change to Design view using the bottom tabs.
3. Create a new class by right-clicking on the Web site and selecting Add New Item from the context menu. In the Add New Item dialog box, select Class from the list of templates. Name the file as AuthorsComponent2.vb and click Add.
4. You are presented with a dialog box prompting you whether you want to place your component inside a directory called Code. Click OK.
5. Once the file is created, modify the code in the AuthorsComponent2.vb file to look like the following:

```
Imports System
Imports System.Data
Imports System.Collections.Generic

Public Class AuthorsComponent2
    Public Sub New()
    End Sub

    Public Function GetAuthorsByState(ByVal state As String, ByVal sortExpression
        As String) As List(Of Author)
        Dim authors As New List(Of Author)
        Dim ds As DataSet = AuthorsDB.GetAuthorsByState(state)
        Dim row As DataRow
        For Each row In ds.Tables(0).Rows
            authors.Add(New Author(row("au_id"), row("au_fname"), row("au_lname"),
                row("state")))
        Next
        authors.Sort(New AuthorComparer(sortExpression))
```

```
        Return authors
    End Function

    Public Function UpdateAuthor(ByVal Original_ID As String, ByVal LastName As
        String, ByVal Name As String, ByVal State As String) As Integer
        Return AuthorsDB.UpdateAuthor(Original_ID, LastName, Name, State)
    End Function

    Public Function GetStates() As List(Of String)
        Dim states As New List(Of String)
        Dim ds As DataSet = AuthorsDB.GetStates()
        Dim row As DataRow
        For Each row In ds.Tables(0).Rows
            states.Add(row("state"))
        Next
        Return states
    End Function
End Class

Public Class AuthorComparer : Implements IComparer(Of Author)
    Private _sortColumn As String
    Private _reverse As Boolean

    Public Sub New(ByVal sortExpression As String)
        _reverse = sortExpression.ToLowerInvariant().EndsWith(" desc")
        If (_reverse) Then
            _sortColumn = sortExpression.Substring(0, sortExpression.Length - 5)
        Else
            _sortColumn = sortExpression
        End If
    End Sub

    Public Function IComparer_Compare(ByVal a As Author, ByVal b As Author) As
        Integer Implements IComparer(Of Author).Compare
        Dim retVal As Integer = 0
        Select Case _sortColumn
            Case "ID"
                retVal = String.Compare(a.ID, b.ID,
                   StringComparison.InvariantCultureIgnoreCase)
            Case "Name"
                retVal = String.Compare(a.Name, b.Name,
                   StringComparison.InvariantCultureIgnoreCase)
            Case "LastName"
                retVal = String.Compare(a.LastName, b.LastName,
                   StringComparison.InvariantCultureIgnoreCase)
            Case "State"
                retVal = String.Compare(a.State, b.State,
                   StringComparison.InvariantCultureIgnoreCase)
        End Select
        Dim _reverseInt As Integer = -1
        If (_reverse) Then
            _reverseInt = 1
        End If
        Return (retVal * _reverseInt)
    End Function
```

```
    Public Function IComparer_Equals(ByVal a As Author, ByVal b As Author) As
         Boolean Implements IComparer(Of Author).Equals
        ' TODO: Implement this, but it's not necessary for sorting
        Return False
    End Function

    Public Function IComparer_GetHashCode(ByVal obj As Author) As Integer
         Implements IComparer(Of Author).GetHashCode
        ' TODO: Implement this, but it's not necessary for sorting
        Return 0
    End Function
End Class
```

6. Once you have created the business logic layer methods, you can add code to the Web form to invoke the methods of the business logic layer class. Open up the previously created Web form and modify the code in the Web form to look like the following:

```
<%@ Page Language="VB" %>
<html>
  <head>
    <title>TIO ch13 Sorting a Custom Object</title>
  </head>
<body>
  <h3>TIO Ch13 Demonstration of Sorting in Custom Object</h3>
  <form id="form1" runat="server">
    <asp:DropDownList ID="DropDownList1" Runat="server"
       DataSourceID="ObjectDataSource1" AutoPostBack="True" />
    <asp:ObjectDataSource ID="ObjectDataSource1" Runat="server"
       TypeName="AuthorsComponent2" SelectMethod="GetStates" />
    <br/><br/>
    <asp:GridView ID="GridView1" Runat="server"
      DataSourceID="ObjectDataSource2" AutoGenerateColumns="False"
      AllowPaging="True" AllowSorting="True" DataKeyNames="ID">
      <Columns>
        <asp:CommandField ShowEditButton="True" />
        <asp:BoundField ReadOnly="True" HeaderText="ID" DataField="ID"
           SortExpression="ID" />
        <asp:BoundField HeaderText="Name" DataField="Name"
           SortExpression="Name" />
        <asp:BoundField HeaderText="LastName" DataField="LastName"
           SortExpression="LastName" />
         <asp:BoundField HeaderText="State" DataField="State"
           SortExpression="State" />
      </Columns>
    </asp:GridView>
    <asp:ObjectDataSource ID="ObjectDataSource2" Runat="server"
      TypeName="AuthorsComponent2" SelectMethod="GetAuthorsByState"
      SortParameterName="SortExpression" UpdateMethod="UpdateAuthor">
      <SelectParameters>
         <asp:ControlParameter Name="state" Type="String"
           ControlID="DropDownList1" PropertyName="SelectedValue" />
      </SelectParameters>
    </asp:ObjectDataSource>
```

```
</form>
</body>
</html>
```

7. Open your browser and view `C:\Websites\BegAspNet2Db\ch13\TO5_SortingInCustomObject.aspx`.

How It Works #5 — Implementing Sorting in a Custom Object

As previously mentioned, you take advantage of the methods of the AuthorsDB class to perform operations against the database. Let us look at the implementation of the GetAuthorsByState method in the AuthorsComponent2 class and the AuthorComparer class. Because the remaining methods in the AuthorsComponent2 are similar to the AuthorsComponent's methods, we will not look at them in detail.

The GetAuthorsByState method starts by creating an instance of the generic collection class that is capable of holding the Author objects. After that, it invokes the GetAuthorsByState method of the AuthorsDB class and gets the results in the form of a DataSet object. Then it loops through the DataTable contained in the DataSet and adds them to the previously created collection object. After that, it invokes the Sort method of the collection class, passing to it an instance of the AuthorComparer object. The AuthorComparer class provides a custom sorting implementation for sorting Author objects by implementing the IComparer interface.

The IComparer interface provides comparison mechanisms with which you can encapsulate the sorting behaviors in custom classes. For example, you can provide sorting of your class on several fields or on several properties. You can also provide a sort in ascending order or in descending order, or both, on the same field. The Compare method of the AuthorComparer is a very important method that determines the actual sorting behavior. In this method, you use the Select Case construct to determine the property of the Author object to be used for sorting. Note that the property of the Author object to use for sorting is determined in the constructor of the AuthorComparer class. Finally, the Compare method returns two objects and returns a value indicating whether one is less than, equal to, or greater than the other.

Now that you have implemented the custom sorting class, let's look at how you use this sorting capability from the Web form. Because the code in the Web form is very similar to previous examples, we will not take a detailed look at the code. However, a discussion of how to specify the sorting expression to the AuthorsComponent2 is warranted. As part of the ObjectDataSource2 declaration, you specify an attribute named SortParameterName and set its value to SortExpression. Once you set the SortParameter to SortExpression, you can use the `SortExpression` property from the GridView control to supply the sorting expression to the AuthorsComponent2 through the ObjectDataSource2 control. As part of the `asp:boundfield` element declarations (that are present inside the Columns element of the GridView control), you set the `SortExpression` property to appropriate values. That's all there is to implementing custom sorting classes and leveraging them from the Web form.

If you run the page, you should see CA as the selected state by default in the drop-down list, and the GridView control should display the list of authors present in the CA state. If you change the state in the drop-down list, the GridView will display the corresponding authors' data. Now you can also sort the authors on ID, LastName, Name, and State columns. If you click on any one of those column names in the column header, you will see that the result set is being sorted based on that selected column.

Common Mistakes

This is a good place to start if you are having problems.

- Using an incorrect connection string. Recheck the connection string specified during the data component creation process. To avoid errors in the connection string, remember to click the Test the Connection command button to check the connection string.
- Inputting an incorrect username or password. Make sure that the connection string contains the correct username and password.
- Trying to use a data-bound control when there is no data source control. A data-bound control must have a source of data, that is, a data source control, specified by its `DataSourceID` property.
- Trying to use a component without creating it in the App_Code directory. Any time you are creating a reusable component, you should create it in the special App_Code directory. Only then will the component be compiled and available for use within the Web application.
- Errors in table or column names. This mistake usually arises when typing; it is less problematic when using the designer wizards or drag-and-drop in Visual Studio and VWD.
- Attempting to sort data using a custom object that does not implement a sorting interface. Remember to set the SortParameterName on the ObjectDataSource to a parameter that accepts a sorting expression.
- Attempting to bind an ObjectDataSource to a DataTable or DataRow type in a VS DataSet. Remember that it is the TableAdapter type that exposes the methods for binding.
- Attempting to bind an ObjectDataSource to a TableAdapter type without first saving the DataSet.xsd file in the designer. You must save the file in order for the TableAdapter type to be available to the ObjectDataSource.

Summary

This chapter discussed the advantages of constructing an N-Tier application and took a detailed look at the different tiers created as part of an N-Tier application. It also covered some general design principles and then focused on the theme and variations of using the ObjectDataSource control in conjunction with the middle-tier components. Through the ObjectDataSource control, the data is made available for a data-bound control to display. To see the data, you used controls such as GridView and DropDownList.

You saw the steps involved in creating a data access logic layer component using the TableAdapter Wizard in Visual Studio's DataSet designer, as well as how to create the custom business logic layer components and implement sorting functionality in them.

14

XML and Other Hierarchical Data

Prior to this point in the book, you have worked with tabular data. In other words, the information could be organized in a series of rows, each of which had the same fields filled with data. In general, data up to now has been from relational databases. But there are other ways to organize data, and one that now pervades IT is hierarchical data. ASP.NET has a series of controls that make it both easy and logical to utilize hierarchical data. This chapter takes a look at some of those data source controls and how to use them from an ASP.NET Web form. It also explains the steps involved in using those data source controls in conjunction with data-bound controls such as a DropDownList, DataList, and so on for retrieving and displaying data from the database.

You will practice with the following Try It Out exercises in this chapter:

Try It Out	Topic
1	Display Navigation Structure of a Site
2	TreeView with Tightened Scope from XPath
3	Formatting TreeView
4	TreeView from XML and XSL
5	Handling Events in a TreeView Control
6	XML as Source for a ListBox and a GridView
7	XML as Source for a DataList Control
8	Using XPath to Display Data in a DataList Control
9	DataList Data-Bind with Nesting

What Is Hierarchical Data?

Before we talk about the hierarchical data, let us talk about the two different ways of storing data. There are two types of data:

- **Structured data**—This type of data is very rigid in that all records have the same fields. An example of structured data is a telephone book—every entry has a name, an address, and a telephone number. Relational databases are generally a better way to store highly structured data.
- **Semistructured data**—This type of data has some structure but is not rigidly structured. An example of semistructured data is a health record. For example, one patient might have a list of vaccinations, another might have height and weight, another might have a list of operations they have had. Semistructured data is difficult to store in a relational database because it means you have either many different tables (which means many joins and slow retrieval time) or a single table with many null columns. Semistructured data is very easy to store as hierarchical data.

Hierarchical data is categorized by a structure of relationships where each item is a child to, or member of, an item above it. At the top of the hierarchy is a single item that has no parent. There is a specific vocabulary for hierarchical data. Each item is called a *node*. The topmost node is named the *root*. Nodes that have a node below them are *parents* and all nodes except the root are *children*. As in families, a node can be both a parent and a child. Nodes with no children are called *leaf nodes*.

Types of Hierarchical Data

Some of the hierarchical data structures are as follows:

- **Folders**—The way folders are structured in a Windows file system denotes a hierarchical way of storing data.
- **XML**—XML documents are self-describing, meaning that the metadata required to qualify the data is actually contained in the XML document itself, providing a flexible way of handling XML data.
- **SiteMap**—SiteMap is nothing but an XML format that provides a consistent way of describing the contents of a Web site, including all the pages contained in that Web site. Although it is possible in ASP.NET 2.0 to store a SiteMap as something other than XML using a custom provider, this book only covers the XML implementation of SiteMap.
- **Menu system**—A menu system can also use an XML document as its input and displays the contents of the XML document in a hierarchical manner.

The next section details the support provided by ASP.NET in terms of handling hierarchical data.

ASP.NET 2.0 Hierarchical Data Controls

The architecture of controls for hierarchical data is very similar to the design of controls for tabular data. ASP.NET offers both hierarchical data source controls and hierarchical data-bound controls.

- ASP.NET hierarchical data source controls
    - XmlDataSource
    - SiteMapDataSource
- ASP.NET hierarchical data-bound controls
    - TreeView
    - Menu

Because of the flexibility and common object model in the ASP.NET data story, there are some situations where you can use a data-bound control that normally is for tabular data for hierarchical data. For example, an XML file holding the names of states can be used as the source for a list box. A GridView can display hierarchical data in a grid, but it tends to create very flat grids. The hierarchical data sources in ASP.NET implement a tabular interface that normal data-bound controls can bind against, so that in addition to using TreeView and Menu to bind to hierarchical data, you can also bind the tabular data-bound controls introduced in preceding chapters. As you can see later in this chapter, a new XML-based data-binding syntax also allows you to bind to hierarchical elements of a hierarchical data source in a templated data-bound control, such as DataList. Each of these applications of controls is discussed in the following sections.

XmlDataSource Control

The data controls supplied with ASP.NET support a variety of rich data-binding scenarios. By taking advantage of the new data source controls, you can bind to a data source without writing any code. One such control is `<asp:XmlDatasource>`. This control allows you to bind to XML data, which can come from a variety of sources, such as an external XML file, a DataSet object, and so on. Once the XML data is bound to the XmlDataSource control, this control can act as a source of data for other data-bound controls such as TreeView and Menu. For example, you can use the `<asp:XmlDataSource>` control to represent a hierarchical XML data source. The `<asp:XmlDataSource>` control can be bound to any of the data controls, including the following:

- `<asp:TreeView>`
- `<asp:GridView>`
- `<asp:DataList>`
- `<asp:DropDownList>`
- `<asp:Repeater>`

TreeView Control to Display Hierarchical Data

In this example, you will use the TreeView control to display hierarchical information about the site structure using the contents of the web.sitemap file. In the web.sitemap file, you specify the list of nodes that specifies the navigation structure of the site, which can be completely independent of the site folder layout or other structure. When a SiteMapDataSource is placed on the page, it will specifically look for a file with the name web.sitemap, by default. It will read the contents of the web.sitemap file and consume that information as a data source control.

Try It Out #1 — Display Navigation Structure of a Site

In this exercise, you will display information about books sold by Northwind on your page.

1. Start your page editor and navigate to `C:\Websites\BegAspNet2Db\ch14\`.
2. Add a page named `TO1.aspx` from the template Web Form. Change to Design view using the bottom tabs.
3. Add a web.sitemap file to the root of your site (C:\BegAspNet2Db) and modify it to look like the following (or copy from the download file):

```
<?xml version="1.0" encoding="utf-8" ?>
<siteMap>
<siteMapNode title="Default" description="Home" url="default.aspx" >
<siteMapNode title="Members" description="Members Home" url="members.aspx">
<siteMapNode title="My Account" description="My Account" url="MyAccount.aspx" />
          <siteMapNode title="Products and Services" description="Products and
Services" url="ProductsAndServices.aspx" />
     </siteMapNode>
     <siteMapNode title="Administration" description="Administration"
url="~/admin/default.aspx">
        <siteMapNode title="Customer" description="Customer Admin"
url="~/admin/customer/default.aspx" />
        <siteMapNode title="Products and Services" description="Products and
Services Admin" url="~/admin/productsAndServices/default.aspx" />
</siteMapNode>
</siteMapNode>
</siteMap>
```

4. Display the toolbox (Menu: View ⇨ toolbox or Ctrl+Alt+X) and expand the toolbox's Data panel.
5. Drag and drop a SiteMapDataSource onto your page.
6. Now drag a TreeView control onto your page. Select the TreeView control and click the top right small arrow to open the smart task panel. Click on the Choose Data Source drop-down menu and select the previously created SiteMapDataSource (named SiteMapDataSource1) as the source.
7. Your page should now appear as follows:

```
<%@ Page Language="VB" %>
<html>
<head>
  <title>TIO ch14 Treenode Sitemap</title>
</head>
<body>
 <h3>TIO 1 Demonstration of displaying information from a SiteMap
 </h3>
 <form id="form1" runat="server">
 <div>
   <asp:TreeView ID="TreeView1" Runat="server" DataSourceID="SiteMapDataSource1"
```

```
        ExpandDepth="2" ShowExpandCollapse="False" NodeIndent="10">
        <NodeStyle ChildNodesPadding="10" />
        <LevelStyles>
         <asp:TreeNodeStyle Font-Bold="true"/>
         <asp:TreeNodeStyle Font-Italic="true" />
         <asp:TreeNodeStyle Font-Size="x-small" ImageUrl="~/images/bullet.gif" />
        </LevelStyles>
      </asp:TreeView>
    </div>
    <div>
      <asp:SiteMapDataSource ID="SiteMapDataSource1" Runat="server"/>
    </div>
    </form>
  </body>
  </html>
```

8. Open your browser and view `C:\Websites\BegAspNet2Db\ch14\ TO1.aspx`. You will see a message in the browser indicating the value of the selected node.

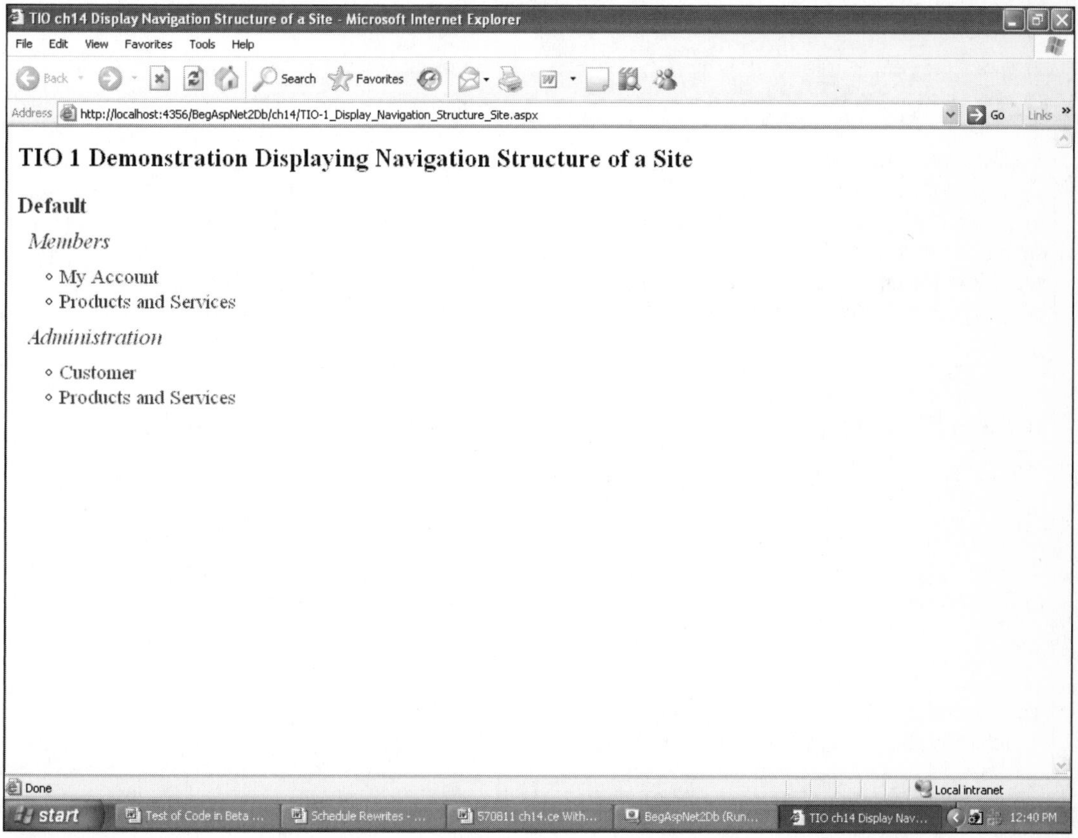

Figure 14-1

How It Works #1 — Display Navigation Structure of a Site

As previously mentioned, the SiteMapDataSource control acts as the data source control and reads all the information from the web.sitemap file. Once the information is available in a SiteMapDataSource control, you can then consume it from a data-bound control. In this example, you used the TreeView control as a data-bound control. You set the `DataSourceID` property of the TreeView control to the ID value of the SiteMapDataSource. As part of the TreeView declaration, you also used the asp:TreeNodeStyle elements to specify the node style for the individual nodes.

Display XML Data

Typically, you will want to modify the display of the XML to provide more meaningful information. The TreeView control exposes bindings that let you specify how each node is rendered. For example, you can create a binding for the bookstore element that states that it should be rendered using the static text, "Books." The TreeView also contains a number of built-in properties that let you easily customize its appearance. For example, you can set the `ImageSet` property to a specific value that will render with predefined graphics so that elements appear as folders.

XPath with XmlDataSource

XPath is a language designed to address specific parts of an XML document. An XPath pattern is a slash-separated list of child element names that describe a path through the XML document. It was designed to be used by both XSLT and XPointer. In addition, XPath provides basic functions for manipulating strings, numbers, and Booleans. In all XML documents, there must be a root element, which is represented by the slash (/) in XPath. In a standard XHTML document, the root element would be "html," so to match everything in the XHTML document, you would write the following:

```
/html
```

To match all the paragraphs in an XHTML document, you would write the following:

```
/html/body/p
```

`/html/body/p` would match all paragraphs within the body tag, but if there were paragraphs within a `div` tag or a `td` tag, these would be skipped. With XPath, you can specify all paragraph tags with two preceding slashes:

```
//p
```

This would match every paragraph tag in the XHTML document, no matter where it was. Or you could match only the paragraph tags that are inside a `div` tag, as follows:

```
//div/p
```

You can also use XPath to select multiple elements using the symbol *. To match every element that is within a `td` tag (such as `p`, `div`, and so on), you would write the following:

```
//td/*
```

But you can also use the asterisk to match the preceding path. For example, if you wanted to match every paragraph that was four levels in (such as `/html/body/div/p`), you would write the following:

```
/*/*/*/p
```

Attributes on a tag can be matched using XPath. You use the "at" symbol (@) to match an attribute. You can match the attribute named "class" in any tag in the document by using the following:

```
//@class
```

Or you can match the tag with a specific attribute using the following:

```
//p[@class]
```

Apart from matching the attribute, you can also match the contents of the attribute:

```
//p[@class='red']
```

This would match only those paragraphs with the attribute and value `class="red"`. Paragraphs with `class="blue"` would be skipped. The following Try It Out explores how to implement XPath expressions.

Try It Out #2 — TreeView with Tightened Scope from XPath

In this exercise, you will practice using XPath to filter data from an XML file.

1. Start your page editor and navigate to `C:\Websites\BegAspNet2Db\ch14\`.
2. Add a page named `TO2_TreeView_XML.aspx` from the template Web Form. Change to Design view using the bottom tabs.
3. Add the Bookstore.xml file to the App_Data folder by right-clicking on the Data folder and selecting Add Existing Item from the context menu. In the Add Existing Item dialog box, select the Bookstore.xml file.
4. Display the toolbox (Menu: View ➪ toolbox or Ctrl+Alt+X) and expand the Data panel of the toolbox. Drag an XmlDataSource onto your page.
5. Configure the XmlDataSource control in the same manner as shown in the previous examples.
6. Next to the Data File textbox, click the command button Browse and select `C:\Websites\BegAspNet2Db\App_Data\Bookstore.xml`.
7. In the XPath Expression textbox, type in the XPath expression `Bookstore/genre[@name='Fiction']/book`. Then click OK.

8. Go back to the toolbox and expand the toolbox's Standard panel.

9. Drag a TreeView control onto your page.

10. Select the TreeView control and click the top right small arrow to open the smart task panel. Click on the Choose Data Source drop-down menu and select the previously created XmlDataSource (named XmlDataSource1) as the source. Your page should now appear as follows:

```
<%@ Page Language="VB" %>
<html xmlns="http://www.w3.org/1999/xhtml" >
<head>
  <title>TIO 2 ch14 Using XPath Expressions</title>
</head>
<body>
  <h3>TIO 2 Applying XPath expression to filter the XML file contents</h3>
  <form runat="server">
   <div>
      <asp:TreeView ID="TreeView1" Runat="server" DataSourceID="XmlDataSource1">
      </asp:TreeView>
   </div>
   <div>
      <asp:XmlDataSource ID="XmlDataSource1" Runat="server"
        DataFile="~/App_Data/Bookstore.xml"
        XPath="Bookstore/genre[@name='Fiction']/book">
      </asp:XmlDataSource>
   </div>
  </form>
</body>
</html>
```

11. Open your browser and view `C:\Websites\BegAspNet2Db\ch14\TO2_TreeView_XML.aspx`.

How It Works #2 — TreeView with Tightened Scope from XPath

You have two controls on the page. The first, XmlDataSource, does all of the work, including reading the `Bookstore.xml` and applying the XPath expression to the contents of the XML file. The second, the TreeView, takes that data and displays that information on the page. To bind the TreeView to the XmlDataSource control, you need to set the `DataSourceID` property of the TreeView control to the ID of the XmlDataSource control. With the preceding few steps, you can see on your page a display of data from your XmlDataSource control.

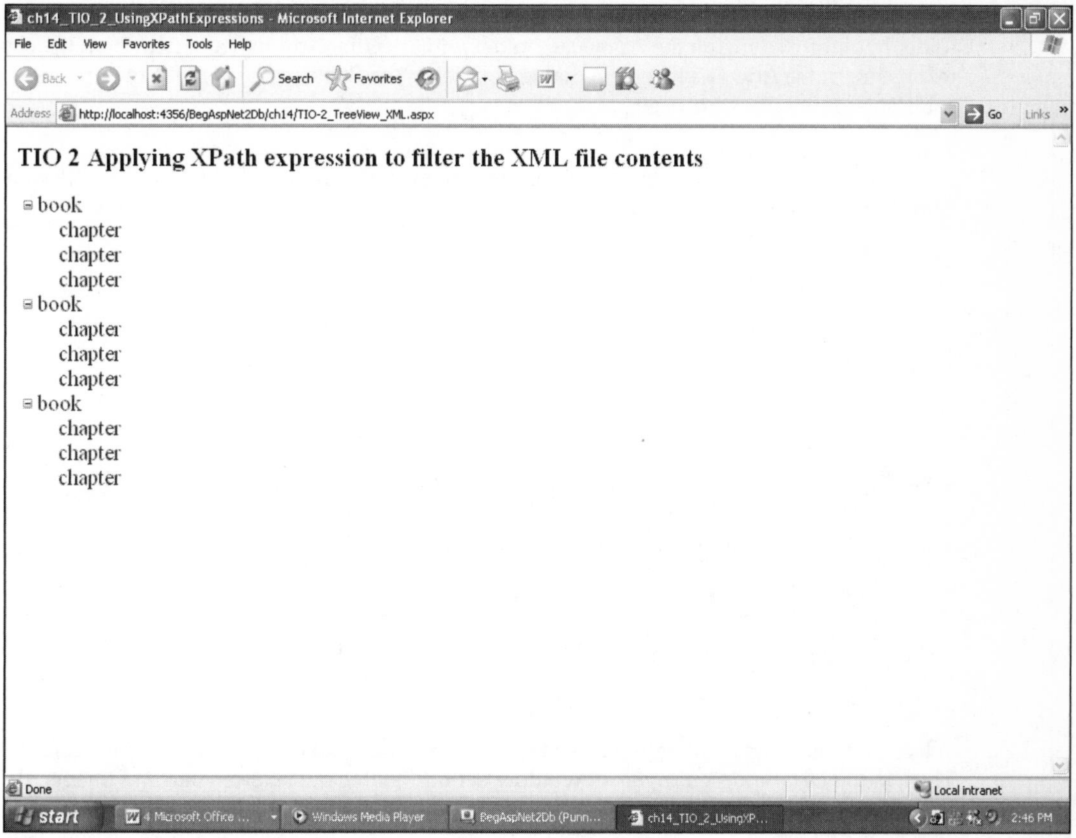

Figure 14-2

Formatting the TreeView

This section shows you how to add data-bindings to specify the data to display for the text and value of TreeNodes, in addition to styles of the nodes in the TreeView control. You will also see how to take advantage of the `ImageUrl` property of the nodes in the TreeView.

Try It Out #3 — Formatting TreeView

In this exercise, you will view the XML data using the XmlDataSource control and also handle events fired from the TreeView.

1. Start your page editor and navigate to `C:\Websites\BegAspNet2Db\ch14\`.
2. Add a page named `TO3_TreeView_XML.aspx` from the template Web Form. Change to Design view using the bottom tabs.
3. Display the toolbox (Menu: View ➪ toolbox or Ctrl+Alt+X) and expand the toolbox's Data panel. Drag an XmlDataSource onto your page.

4. If the Bookstore.xml file is not already present in the App_Data folder, add it to the App_Data folder by right-clicking on the App_Data folder and selecting Add Existing Item from the context menu. In the Add Existing Item dialog box, select the Bookstore.xml file. Now drag an XmlDataSource onto your page.

5. The control's smart task panel should appear automatically, but if not, select the new data source control and then click the top right small arrow to open the smart task panel. Click on Configure Data Source.

6. Next to the Data File textbox, click the command button Browse and select `C:\Websites\BegAspNet2Db\App_Data\Bookstore.xml`.

7. In the XPath Expression textbox, type in the XPath expression `Bookstore/genre[@name='Fiction']/book`. Then click OK.

8. Now go back to the toolbox and expand the toolbox's Standard panel.

9. Drag a TreeView control onto your page.

10. Select the TreeView control and click the top right small arrow to open the smart task panel. Click on the Choose Data Source drop-down menu and select the previously created XmlDataSource (named XmlDataSource1) as the source.

11. Select the TreeView control and click the top right small arrow to open the smart task panel. Click on Edit TreeNode DataBindings and ensure that the book node is selected in the Available Data Bindings tree. Then click the Add command button in the TreeView DataBindings Editor. In the DataBinding Properties window, set the TextField, DataMember, and ImageUrl properties to Title, book, and ~/Images/openbook.gif, respectively.

12. Select the chapter node in the Available Data Bindings tree and click the Add command button. Then, in the DataBinding Properties window, set the TextField, DataMember, and ImageUrl properties to name, chapter, and ~/Images/notepad.gif, respectively. Your page should now appear as follows:

```
<%@ Page Language="VB" %>
<html xmlns="http://www.w3.org/1999/xhtml" >
<head>
  <title>TIO ch14 Displaying information from an XmlDataSource</title>
</head>
<body>
  <h3>TIO 3 Demonstration of displaying information from an XmlDataSource
  </h3>
  <form id="form1" runat="server">
  <div>
    <asp:TreeView ID="TreeView1" Runat="server" DataSourceID="XmlDataSource1">
      <DataBindings>
        <asp:TreeNodeBinding ImageUrl="~/Images/openbook.gif" TextField="Title"
          DataMember="book"></asp:TreeNodeBinding>
        <asp:TreeNodeBinding ImageUrl="~/Images/notepad.gif" TextField="name"
          DataMember="chapter"></asp:TreeNodeBinding>
      </DataBindings>
    </asp:TreeView>
  </div>
  <div>
   <asp:XmlDataSource ID="XmlDataSource1" Runat="server"
     DataFile="~/App_Data/Bookstore.xml"
XPath="Bookstore/genre[@name='Fiction']/book">
```

```
      </asp:XmlDataSource>
    </div>
    </form>
  XPath="Bookstore/genre[@name='Fiction']/book"</body>
</html>
```

13. Open your browser and view `C:\Websites\BegAspNet2Db\ch14\TO3_TreeView_XML2.aspx`.

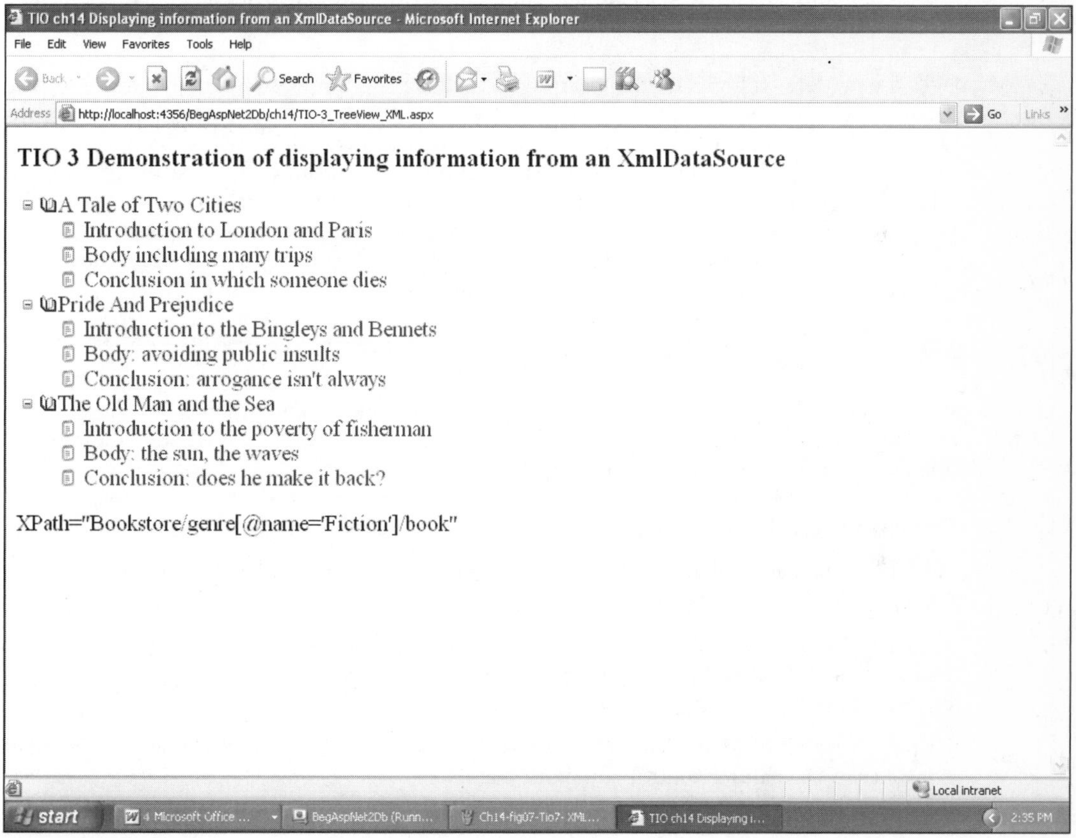

Figure 14-3

How It Works #3 — Formatting TreeView

You have two controls on the page. The first, XmlDataSource, does all of the work, including reading the `Bookstore.xml` and applying the XPath expression to the contents of the XML file. The second, the TreeView, takes that data and displays the information on the page. To bind the TreeView to the XmlDataSource control, you need to set the `DataSourceID` property of the TreeView control to the ID of the XmlDataSource control. Inside the TreeView declaration, you use the asp:TreeNodeBinding element to specify the DataMember that will be used to identify the data element to use from the XmlDataSource for display purposes. You also use the `ImageUrl` property to set the image that will be displayed right next to the node in the TreeView.

XSL Transformation with XML

XSLT is the most important part of the eXtensible Stylesheet Language (XSL) Standards. It is the part of XSL that is used to transform an XML document into another XML document, or another type of document that is recognized by a browser, such as HTML and XHTML. XSLT can also add new elements into the output file or remove elements. It can rearrange and sort elements, test and make decisions about which elements to display, and a lot more. A common way to describe the transformation process is to say that XSLT transforms an XML source tree into an XML result tree. XSL can also be used to define how an XML file should be displayed by transforming the XML file into a format that is recognizable to a browser.

HTML pages use predefined tags, and the meaning of each tag is well understood: `<p>` means a paragraph and `<h1>` means a header, and the browser knows how to display these pages. With XML you can use any tags you want, and the meaning of each tag is not automatically understood by the browser. `<table>` could mean an HTML table or maybe a piece of furniture. Because of the nature of XML, there is no standard way to display an XML document. So, to display XML documents, it is necessary to have a mechanism to describe how the document should be displayed. One of these mechanisms is XSL, which is the preferred style sheet language of XML. The following Try It Out demonstrates how to use XSL to format an XML document into another XML document.

Try It Out #4—TreeView from XML and XSL

In this exercise, you will apply XSL transformation on the XML data that is contained by the XmlDataSource control. Through the XSL transformation, you will convert the XML into a different format and then use that as a data source for the TreeView control.

1. Start your page editor and navigate to `C:\Websites\BegAspNet2Db\ch14\`.
2. Add a page named `TO4_TreeView_XML_Transform.aspx` from the template Web Form. Change to Design view using the bottom tabs.
3. Add the `Bookstore_Transform.xml` file to the Data folder by right-clicking on the App_Data folder and selecting Add Existing Item from the context menu. In the Add Existing Item dialog box, select the `Bookstore_Transform.xml` file.
4. Display the toolbox (Menu: View/toolbox or Ctrl+Alt+X) and expand the toolbox's Data panel. Drag an XmlDataSource control onto your page.
5. The control's smart task panel should appear automatically, but if not, select the new data source control and then click the top right small arrow to open the smart task panel. Click on Configure Data Source.
6. Right next to the Data File textbox, click the command button Browse and select `C:\Websites\BegAspNet2Db\App_Data\Bookstore_Transform.xml`.
7. In the XPath Expression textbox, type in the XPath expression `Bookstore/genre[@name='Fiction']/book`. Then click OK.
8. Go back to the toolbox and expand the toolbox's Standard panel.
9. Now add a file named Bookstore_Transform.xsl to the App_Data folder. The XSL file should appear as follows:

```
<xsl:stylesheet version="1.0" xmlns:xsl="http://www.w3.org/1999/XSL/Transform">
<xsl:template match="bookstore">
```

```
    <bookstore>
      <xsl:apply-templates select="genre"/>
    </bookstore>
  </xsl:template>
  <xsl:template match="genre">
    <genre>
      <xsl:attribute name="name">
        <xsl:value-of select="@name"/>
      </xsl:attribute>
      <xsl:apply-templates select="book"/>
    </genre>
  </xsl:template>
  <xsl:template match="book">
    <book>
      <xsl:attribute name="ISBN">
        <xsl:value-of select="@ISBN"/>
      </xsl:attribute>
      <xsl:attribute name="title">
        <xsl:value-of select="title"/>
      </xsl:attribute>
      <xsl:attribute name="price">
        <xsl:value-of select="price"/>
      </xsl:attribute>
      <xsl:apply-templates select="chapters/chapter" />
    </book>
  </xsl:template>
  <xsl:template match="chapter">
    <chapter>
      <xsl:attribute name="num">
        <xsl:value-of select="@num"/>
      </xsl:attribute>
      <xsl:attribute name="name">
        <xsl:value-of select="@name"/>
      </xsl:attribute>
      <xsl:apply-templates/>
    </chapter>
  </xsl:template>
  </xsl:stylesheet>
```

10. Now that you have created the XSL file, select the Properties window of the XmlDataSource control and set the value of the `TransformFile` property to the `Bookstore_Transform.xsl` file.

11. Drag a TreeView control onto your page.

12. Select the TreeView control and click the top right small arrow to open the smart task panel. Click on the Choose Data Source drop-down menu and select the previously created XmlDataSource (named XmlDataSource1) as the source. Your page should now appear as follows:

```
<%@ Page Language="VB" %>
<html xmlns="http://www.w3.org/1999/xhtml" >
<head>
    <title>TIO ch14 Applying XSL Transformation </title>
</head>
<body>
```

```
        <h3>TIO 4 Demonstration of applying XSL transformation on an XML data
       </h3>
        <form id="form1" runat="server">
        <div>
          <asp:TreeView ID="TreeView1" Runat="server"
                DataSourceID="XmlDataSource1" />
          <asp:XmlDataSource ID="XmlDataSource1" Runat="server"
            DataFile="~/App_Data/Bookstore_Transform.xml"
            TransformFile="~/App_Data/Bookstore_Transform.xsl" />
        </div>
        </form>
    </body>
    </html>
```

13. Open your browser and view `C:\Websites\BegAspNet2Db\ch14\TO4_TreeView_XMLTransform.aspx`.

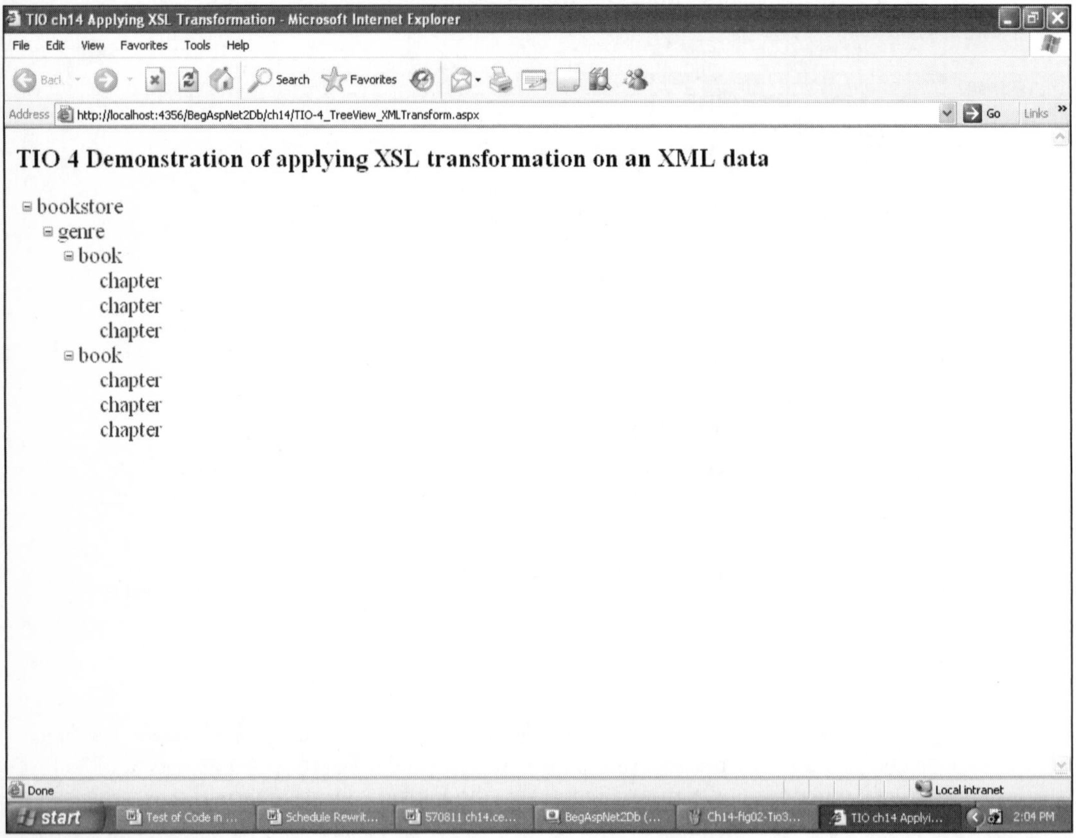

Figure 14-4

How It Works #4 — TreeView from XML and XSL

You have two controls on the page. The first, XmlDataSource, does all of the work, including reading the BookStore_Transform.xml and loading of XML contents into its memory. Instead of directly using the XML from the XmlDataSource control, you transform the XML into another format. This is accomplished using the `TransformFile` property. In this case, you set the value of the TransformFile property to `BookStore_Transform.xsl`. The second control, the TreeView, takes that data and displays that information on the page. To bind the TreeView to the XmlDataSource control, you need to set the `DataSourceID` property of the TreeView control to the ID of the XmlDataSource control.

Handling Events in a TreeView Control

So far, you have seen how to display information using a TreeView control. You also know how to use an XSL file for transforming the XML contents into another format before binding the TreeView to the XmlDataSource control. In this section, you will explore how to handle events generated from the TreeView control.

Try It Out #5 — Handling Events in a TreeView Control

In this exercise, you will display, on your page, metadata about the elements contained in the XML document.

1. Start your page editor and navigate to `C:\Websites\BegAspNet2Db\ch14\`.
2. Add a page named `TO2_TreeView_XML.aspx` from the template Web Form. Change to Design view using the bottom tabs.
3. Display the toolbox (Menu: View ➪ toolbox or Ctrl+Alt+X) and expand the toolbox's Data panel.
4. Drag an XmlDataSource onto your page.
5. The control's smart task panel should appear automatically, but if not, select the new data source control and then click the top right small arrow to open the smart task panel. Click on Configure Data Source.
6. Next to the Data File textbox, click the command button Browse and select `C:\Websites\BegAspNet2Db\App_Data\Bookstore.xml`.
7. In the XPath Expression textbox, type in the XPath expression `Bookstore/genre[@name='Fiction']/book`. Then click OK.
8. Go back to the toolbox and expand the toolbox's Standard panel.
9. Drag a TreeView control onto your page.
10. Select the TreeView control and click the top right small arrow to open the smart task panel. Click on the Choose Data Source drop-down menu and select the previously created XmlDataSource (named XmlDataSource1) as the source.

11. Add the `SelectedNodeChanged` event to the TreeView control. Inside this event, add code to display the value of the selected node. Your page should now appear as follows:

```
<%@ Page Language="VB" %>
<script runat="server">
    Sub TreeView1_SelectedNodeChanged(ByVal sender As Object, ByVal e As
         System.EventArgs)
         Response.Write("You Selected: " & TreeView1.SelectedNode.Value)
    End Sub
</script>

<html xmlns="http://www.w3.org/1999/xhtml" >
<head>
   <title>TIO #5 ch14 Handle TreeView events</title>
</head>
<body>
   <h3>TIO #5 Demonstration of displaying XML data and handling events in the
Treeview
   </h3>
    <form id="form1" runat="server">
    <div>
        <asp:TreeView ID="TreeView1" Runat="server" DataSourceID="XmlDataSource1"
            OnSelectedNodeChanged="TreeView1_SelectedNodeChanged">
            <DataBindings>
              <asp:TreeNodeBinding ImageUrl="~/Images/openbook.gif"
                 TextField="Title" DataMember="book"
                 ValueField="ISBN"></asp:TreeNodeBinding>
               <asp:TreeNodeBinding ImageUrl="~/Images/notepad.gif"
                 TextField="name" DataMember="chapter"></asp:TreeNodeBinding>
            </DataBindings>
        </asp:TreeView>
    </div>
    <div>
       <asp:XmlDataSource ID="XmlDataSource1" Runat="server"
           DataFile="~/App_Data/Bookstore.xml"
           XPath="Bookstore/genre[@name='Fiction']/book">
       </asp:XmlDataSource>
    </div>
    </form>
</body>
</html>
```

Alternatively, use the following script for the C# language.

```
<%@ Page Language="C#" %>
<script runat="server">
    void TreeView1_SelectedNodeChanged(object sender, EventArgs e)
        {
        Response.Write("You Selected: " + TreeView1.SelectedNode.Value);
        }
</script>
```

12. Open your browser and view `C:\Websites\BegAspNet2Db\ch14\ TO5_TreeView_XML_Select.aspx` and select one of the nodes in the TreeView. You will see a message in the browser indicating the value of the selected node.

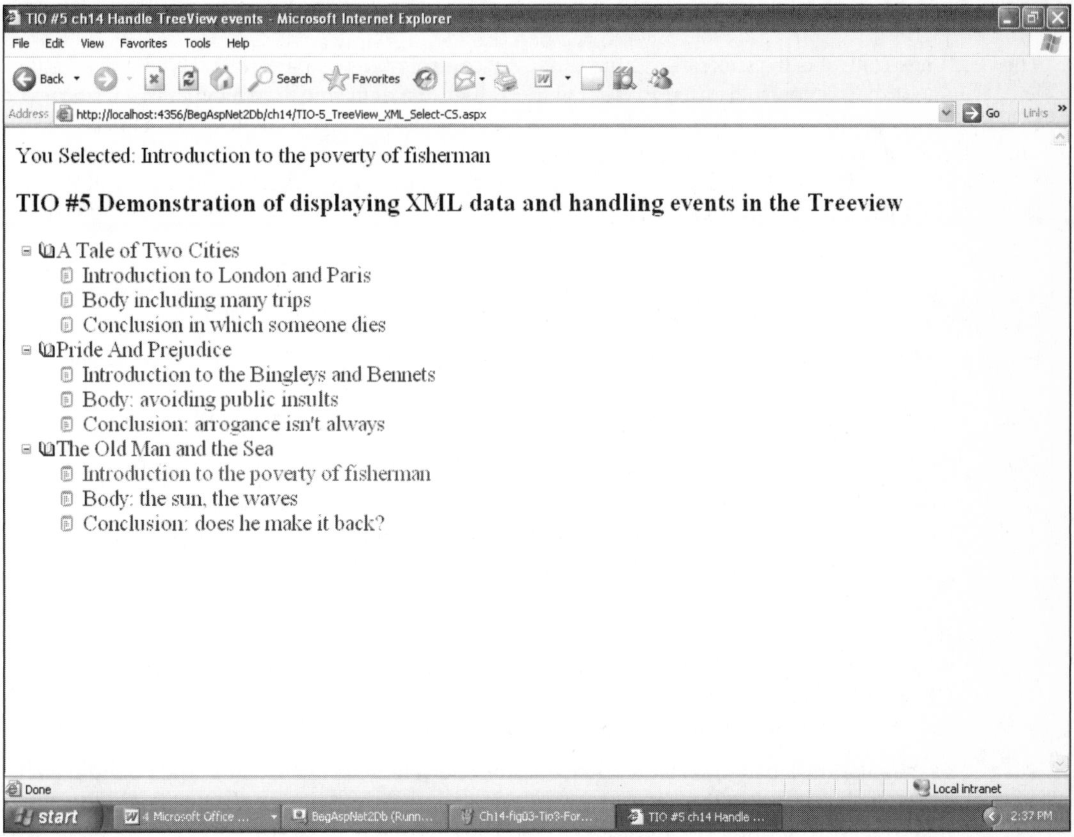

Figure 14-5

How It Works #5 — Handling Events in a TreeView Control

You have two controls on the page. The first, XmlDataSource, does all of the work, including reading the `Bookstore.xml` and applying the XPath expression to the contents of the XML file. The second, the TreeView, takes that data and displays the information on the page. To bind the TreeView to the XmlDataSource control, you need to set the `DataSourceID` property of the TreeView control to the ID of the XmlDataSource control. By using the ImageUrl property of the TreeNodeBinding element, you also set the `ImageUrl` property to be displayed right next to the node. In the `SelectedNodeChanged` event of the TreeView control, you also display the selected node information using the `SelectedNode` property that represents the currently selected node in the TreeView.

Hierarchical Data with Controls Other Than TreeView

Frequently, XML is the source of data, so you need a way to be able to display that XML data in other controls apart from the TreeView control. This section explores how to use XML data from data controls such as GridView, DropDownList, and so on.

XML and GridView

The GridView control is the successor to the DataGrid control that was part of ASP.NET 1.0. Like the DataGrid control, this control is used to display the values of a data source in a table. In a GridView control, each column represents a field, while each row represents a record. As you would expect, you can bind a GridView control to any data source controls, such as XmlDataSource, ObjectDataSource, and SqlDataSource, as well as any data source that implements the System.Collections.IEnumerable interface. The following Try It Out uses the XmlDataSource control as the data source for the GridView control.

Try It Out #6 — XML as Source for a ListBox and a GridView

In this exercise, you will use the XmlDataSource as the source for a GridView and a ListBox control.

1. Start your page editor and navigate to `C:\Websites\BegAspNet2Db\ch14\`.
2. Add a page named `TO6_GridView_XML.aspx` from the template Web Form. Change to Design view using the bottom tabs.
3. Configure the XmlDataSource control in the same manner as shown in the previous examples.
4. Go back to the toolbox and expand the toolbox's Standard panel.
5. Drag a GridView control onto your page.
6. Select the GridView control and click the top right small arrow to open the smart task panel. Click on the Choose Data Source drop-down menu and select the previously created XmlDataSource (named XmlDataSource1) as the source.
7. In the smart task panel, click on Edit Columns and select each field under the Bound Field node in the Available Fields TreeView and click the Add command button. This will add the three fields ISBN, Title, and Price to the Selected Fields TreeView that is displayed in the same screen.
8. Drag a ListBox control from the toolbox onto the Design view and click the top right small arrow to open the smart task panel. Click on Choose Data Source and select the previously created XmlDataSource1 as the data source. For the display field and the value fields, select Title and ISBN, respectively.
9. Your page should now appear as follows:

```
<%@ Page Language="VB" %>
<html xmlns="http://www.w3.org/1999/xhtml" >
<head>
    <title>TIO ch14 Display XML Data in a GridView</title>
</head>
<body>
   <h3>TIO 6 Demonstration of displaying XML data in a Gridview control
   </h3>
   <form id="form1" runat="server">
   <div>
      <asp:GridView ID="GridView1" Runat="server" DataSourceID="XmlDataSource1"
         AutoGenerateColumns="False">
         <Columns>
            <asp:BoundField HeaderText="ISBN" DataField="ISBN"
               SortExpression="ISBN"></asp:BoundField>
            <asp:BoundField HeaderText="Title" DataField="Title"
               SortExpression="Title"></asp:BoundField>
            <asp:BoundField HeaderText="Price" DataField="Price"
```

```
                SortExpression="Price"></asp:BoundField>
            </Columns>
        </asp:GridView>
      </div>
      <div>
        <asp:XmlDataSource ID="XmlDataSource1" Runat="server"
           DataFile="~/App_Data/Bookstore.xml"
           XPath="Bookstore/genre[@name='Fiction']/book">
        </asp:XmlDataSource> 
      </div>
      <div> </div>
      <div> </div>
      <div>
        <asp:ListBox ID="ListBox1" Runat="server" DataSourceID="XmlDataSource1"
           DataValueField="ISBN" DataTextField="Title" />
     </div>
     </form>
  </body>
  </html>
```

10. Open your browser, view `C:\Websites\BegAspNet2Db\ch14\ TO6_GridView_XML.aspx`, and select one of the nodes in the TreeView. You will see a message in the browser indicating the value of the selected node.

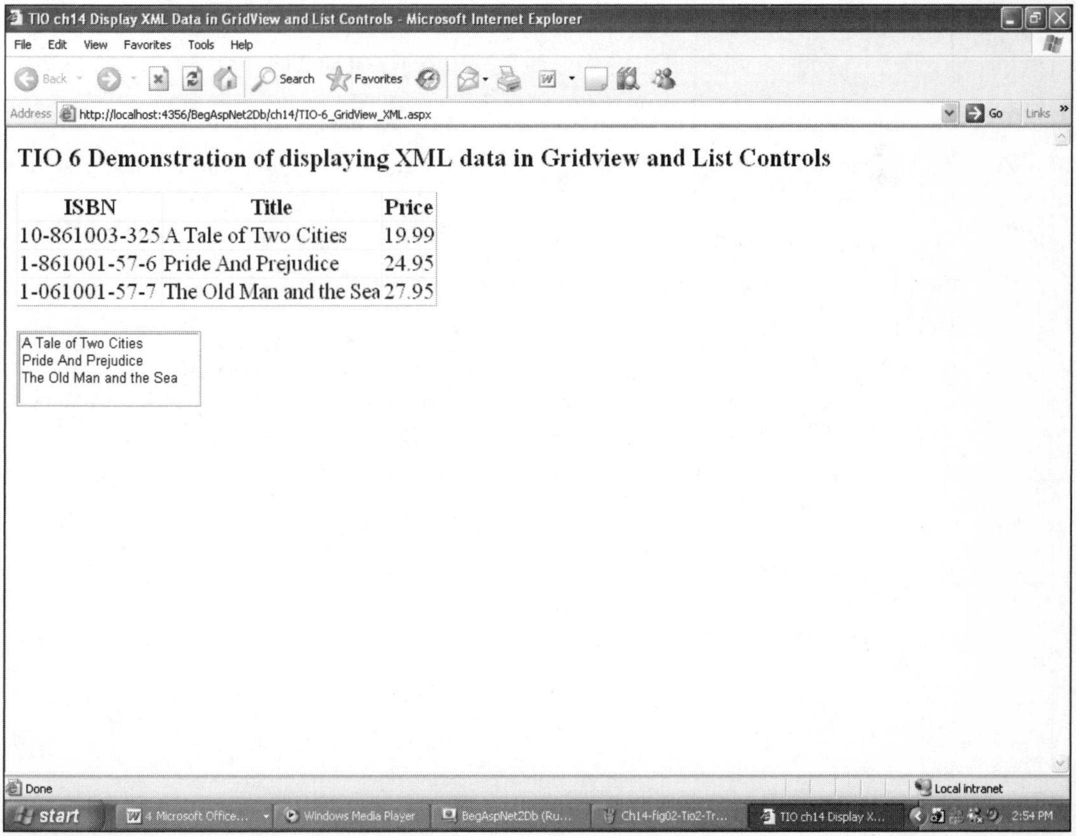

Figure 14-6

How It Works #6 — XML as Source for a ListBox and a GridView

You have the GridView control named GridView1, and its `DataSourceID` property is set to the ID of the XmlDataSource control. Once you have created that association, you can bind the individual fields in the XmlDataSource control to the columns in the GridView. As part of the columns declaration, you declared the following three columns: ISBN, Title, and Price. Along with the columns declaration, you also set the HeaderText, SortExpression, and DataField properties to appropriate values. That's all there is to displaying data in a GridView control using XmlDataSource as the data source. Similarly, the ListBox control is also bound to the XmlDataSource through the `DataSourceID` property. Apart from setting the `DataSourceID` property, you also set the `DataValueField` and `DataTextField` properties to appropriate values. Note that when binding hierarchical data to a tabular control, the bound data fields must be uniform for every XML element in the list. Unlike TreeView, which can bind to unstructured data (potentially having different fields for each element), tabular controls expect all fields to be the same for each data item.

Use XML Source with DataList

The DataList control is used to display a repeated list of items that are bound to the control. However, the DataList control adds a table around the data items by default. The DataList control may be bound to a database table, an XML file, or another list of items. The following Try It Out shows how to bind the XmlDataSource control to a DataList control.

Try It Out #7 — XML as Source for a DataList Control

In this exercise, you will use the XmlDataSource as the source for a DataList control.

1. Start your page editor and navigate to `C:\Websites\BegAspNet2Db\ch14\`.
2. Add a page named `TO7_DataList_XML.aspx` from the template Web Form. Change to Design view using the bottom tabs.
3. Configure the XmlDataSource control in the same manner as shown in the previous examples.
4. Now go back to the toolbox and expand the toolbox's Standard panel.
5. Drag a DataList control onto your page.
6. Select the DataList control and click the top right small arrow to open the smart task panel. Click on the Choose Data Source drop-down menu and select the previously created XmlDataSource (named XmlDataSource1) as the source. Your page should now appear as follows:

```
<%@ Page Language="VB" %>
<html xmlns="http://www.w3.org/1999/xhtml" >
<head>
  <title>TIO ch14 Display XML Data in a DataList</title>
</head>
```

```
<body>
  <h3>TIO 7 Demonstration of displaying XML data in a DataList control
  </h3>
  <form id="form1" runat="server">
  <div>
      
     <asp:DataList ID="DataList1" Runat="server" DataSourceID="XmlDataSource1">
       <ItemTemplate>
         ISBN:
         <asp:Label Text='<%# Eval("ISBN") %>' Runat="server" ID="ISBNLabel">
         </asp:Label><br />
         Title:
         <asp:Label Text='<%# Eval("Title") %>' Runat="server"
           ID="TitleLabel">
         </asp:Label><br/>
         Price:
         <asp:Label Text='<%# Eval("Price") %>' Runat="server"
           ID="PriceLabel">
         </asp:Label><br/><br />
       </ItemTemplate>
     </asp:DataList></div>
     <div> </div>
     <div>
       <asp:XmlDataSource ID="XmlDataSource1" Runat="server"
          DataFile="~/App_Data/Bookstore.xml"
          XPath="Bookstore/genre[@name='Fiction']/book">
       </asp:XmlDataSource> </div>
        <div> </div>
       <div></div>
  </form>
</body>
</html>
```

7. Open your browser and view `C:\Websites\BegAspNet2Db\ch14\TO7_DataList_XML.aspx`. You will see the data being displayed through the GridView.

How It Works #7 — XML as Source for a DataList Control

You have a DataList control named GridView1, and its `DataSourceID` property is set to the ID of the XmlDataSource control. In the DataList control, the ItemTemplate element is used to specify the data fields in the XmlDataSource control that will be displayed through the Label controls. As part of the label controls declaration, you use the Eval expression to identify the element in the XmlDataSource. To the Eval expression, you pass in the name of the data element as a parameter. Because your XmlDataSource contains elements such as ISBN, Title, and Price, you use them in the Eval expression.

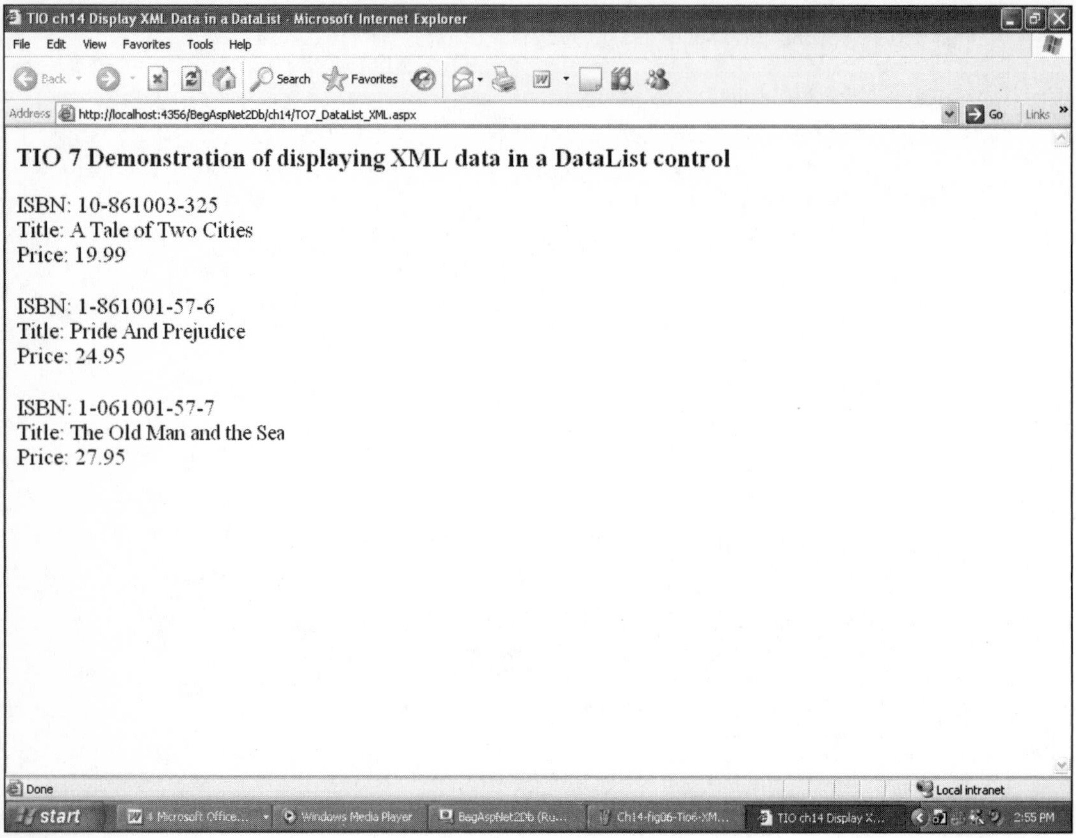

Figure 14-7

Use XPath to Display Data in a DataList Control

It is also possible to use XPath expressions inside the DataList control to display information from the XML elements contained in the XmlDataSource control. Note that whereas the Eval syntax used above would work for any data source, the XPath syntax is limited to only the XmlDataSource. The following Try It Out puts this approach into practice.

Try It Out #8—Using XPath to Display Data in a DataList Control

In this exercise, you will use XPath expressions to select the required data from the XmlDataSource control.

1. Start your page editor and navigate to `C:\Websites\BegAspNet2Db\ch14\`.
2. Add a page named `TO8_DataList_XML.aspx` from the template Web Form. Change to Design view using the bottom tabs.

3. Configure the XmlDataSource control in the same manner as shown in the previous examples.
4. Go back to the toolbox and expand the toolbox's Standard panel.
5. Drag a DataList control onto your page.
6. Select the DataList control and click the top right small arrow to open the smart task panel. Click on the Choose Data Source drop-down menu and select the previously created XmlDataSource (named XmlDataSource1) as the source. Then modify the ItemTemplate element in the DataList control by taking advantage of XPath expressions. After modification, your page should appear as follows:

```
<%@ Page Language="VB" %>
<html>
<head>
  <title>TIO ch14 Display XML Data in a DataList using XPath</title>
</head>
<body>
  <h3>TIO 8 Demonstration of displaying XML data in a DataList control using
   XPath Expressions
  </h3>
  <form runat="server">
   <h1>Bookstore: Fiction</h1>
   <asp:XmlDataSource id="MySource" runat="server"
DataFile="~/App_Data/Bookstore.xml"
     XPath="Bookstore/genre[@name='Fiction']/book" />
     <asp:DataList id="MyDataList" DataSourceId="MySource" runat="server">
       <ItemTemplate>
        <table>
          <tr>
            <td>
              <img src='<%# "../Images/" + XPath("@ISBN") + ".jpg"%>'>
            </td>
            <td>
              <h4><%# XPath("@Title") %></h4>
              <b>ISBN:</b> <%# XPath("@ISBN") %><br>
              <b>Price:</b> <%# XPath("@Price") %><br>
            </td>
          </tr>
        </table>
      </ItemTemplate>
    </asp:DataList>
  </form>
</body>
</html>
```

7. Open your browser and view `C:\Websites\BegAspNet2Db\ch14\TO8_DataList_XML.aspx`. You will see the data being displayed through the GridView.

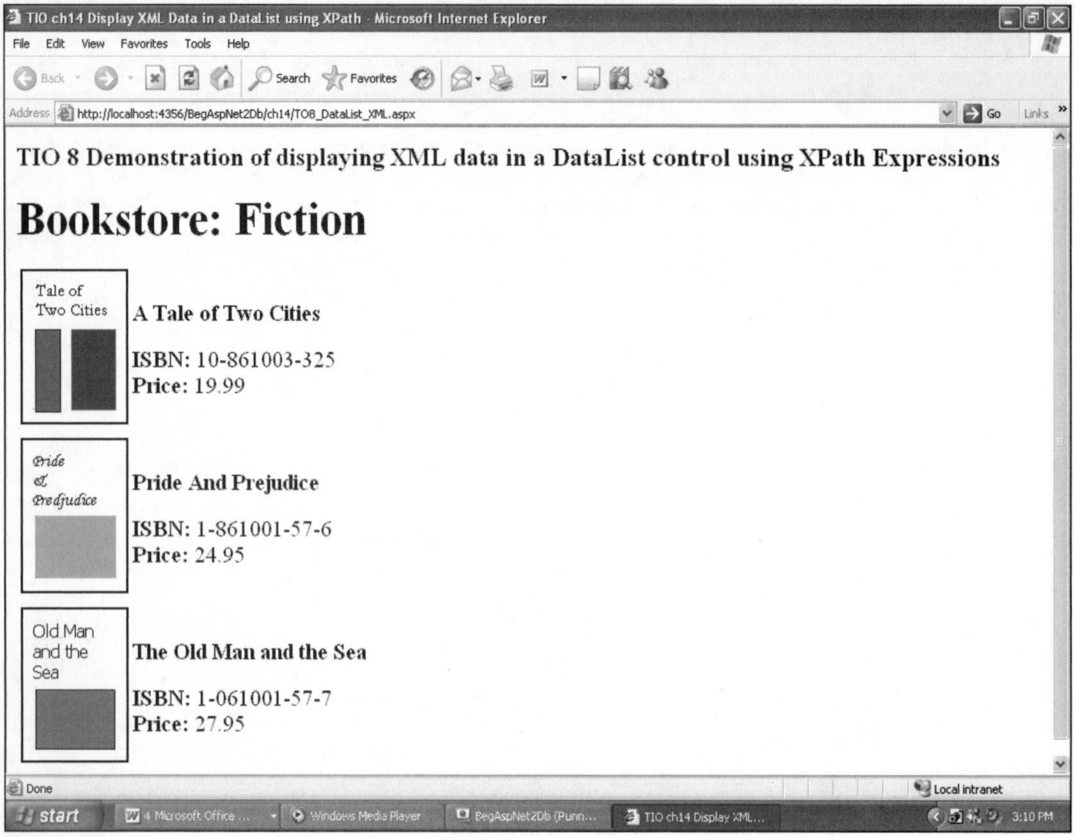

Figure 14-8

How It Works #8 — Using XPath to Display Data in a DataList Control

Similar to the previous example, you set the `DataSourceID` property of the DataList control to the ID of the XmlDataSource control. In the DataList control, the ItemTemplate element is used not only to specify the data fields in the XmlDataSource control but also to specify the formatting instructions. Because you want each XML element (named book) in the XmlDataSource to be displayed in a separate table, you specify an HTML table element and its corresponding TR and TD elements inside the ItemTemplate element. Because you also want to specify the cover page of each book, you use an HTML img element as part of the HTML declaration.

XML and DataList with Nesting

It is also possible for you to nest multiple DataList controls in a Web form. The following exercise explores how to construct a page that utilizes an XmlDataSource control and nested data lists.

Try It Out #9 — DataList Data-Bind with Nesting

In this exercise, you will use nested DataList controls to display information from the XmlDataSource.

1. Start your page editor and navigate to `C:\Websites\BegAspNet2Db\ch14\`.
2. Add a page named `TO9_DataList_XMLNested.aspx` from the template Web Form. Change to Design view using the bottom tabs.
3. Configure the XmlDataSource control in the same manner as shown in the previous examples.
4. Go back to the toolbox and expand the toolbox's Standard panel.
5. Drag a DataList control onto your page.
6. Select the DataList control and click the top right small arrow to open the smart task panel. Click on the Choose Data Source drop-down menu and select the previously created XmlDataSource (named XmlDataSource1) as the source. Then modify the ItemTemplate element in the DataList control to add XPath expressions as well as a DataList control. After modification, your page should appear as follows:

```
<%@ Page Language="VB" %>
<html>
<head>
    <title>TIO ch14 Display XML Data in a DataList with nesting</title>
</head>
<body>
  <h3>TIO 9 Demonstration of displaying XML data in a DataList control with nesting
  </h3>
  <form runat="server">
   <h1>Bookstore: Fiction</h1>
    <asp:XmlDataSource id="MySource" DataFile="~/App_Data/Bookstore.xml"
      XPath="Bookstore/genre[@name='Fiction']/book" runat="server"/>
      <asp:DataList id="DataList1" DataSourceId="MySource" runat="server">
      <ItemTemplate>
        <table>
          <tr>
           <td>
             <img src='<%# "../images/" + XPath("@ISBN") + ".jpg" %>'>
           </td>
           <td>
             <h4><%# XPath("@Title") %></h4>
             <b>ISBN:</b> <%# XPath("@ISBN") %><br>
             <b>Price:</b> <%# XPath("@Price") %><br>
           </td>
          </tr>
        </table>
         <asp:DataList id="DataList2" DataSource='<%# XPathSelect("chapter") %>'
           runat="server">
            <ItemTemplate>
              <br>
              <u>
                Chapter <%# XPath("@num") %>:
                <%# XPath("@name") %>
              </u>
              <br>
              <%# XPath(".") %>
```

```
            </ItemTemplate>
          </asp:DataList>
        </ItemTemplate>
      </asp:DataList>
    </form>
  </body>
  </html>
```

7. Open your browser and view `C:\Websites\BegAspNet2Db\ch14\TO9_DataList_XMLNested.aspx`. You will see the data being displayed through the GridView.

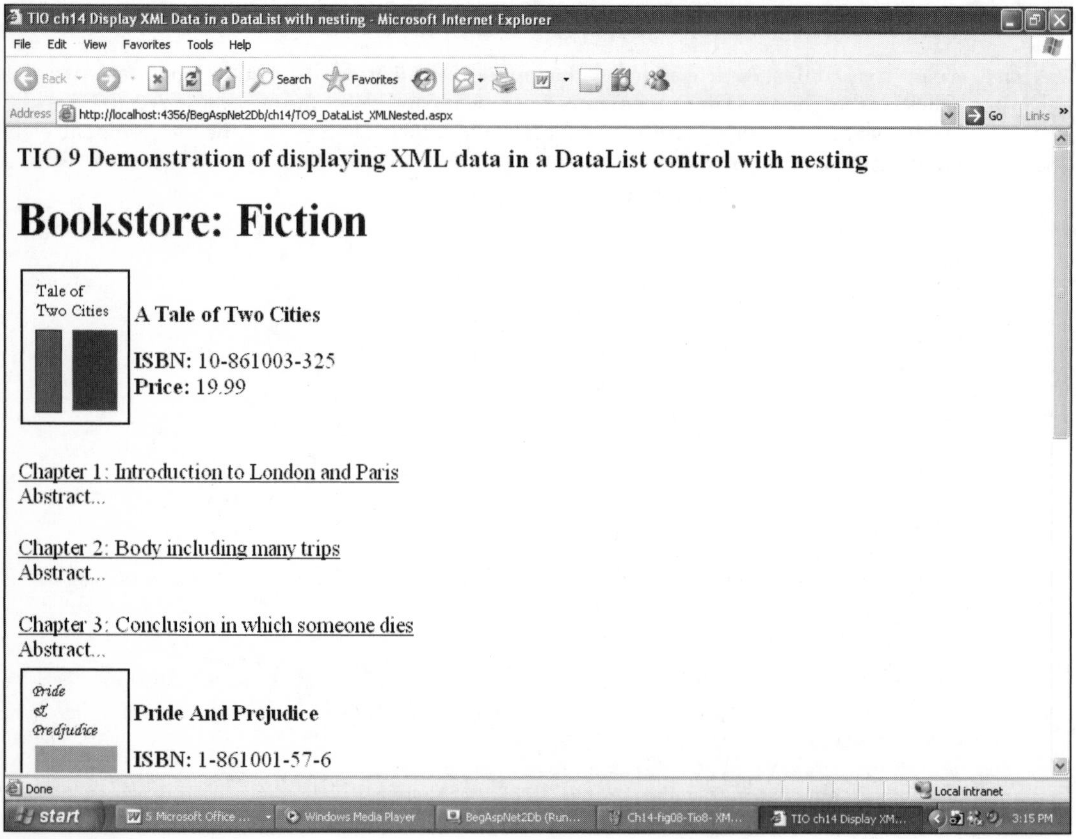

Figure 14-9

How It Works #9 — DataList Data-Bind with Nesting

Similar to the previous example, you set the `DataSourceID` property of the DataList control to the ID of the XmlDataSource control and add HTML elements inside the ItemTemplate element. The only difference in this example is that you add one more DataList control inside the ItemTemplate element. That DataList control uses the subset of the XML source from the XmlDataSource control. This subset is determined by the XPathSelect expression that is used in the `DataSource` property of the nested DataList control.

Common Mistakes with XmlDataSource Controls

The following mistakes are common when dealing with XmlDataSource controls:

- Using an incorrect name or path for the XML file. Recheck the exact name of the XML file and the path. To avoid errors in the pathnames, you can use the Browse button in the Configure Data Source Wizard to select the file names.
- Using incorrect permissions to access the XML file. You need to make sure that the Web application has permissions to access the XML file.
- Trying to use a data-bound control when there is no data source control. A data-bound control must have a source of data, that is, a data source control, specified by its `DataSourceID` property.
- Using an incorrect name or path for the XSL file. Recheck the exact name of the XSL file and the path. To avoid errors in the pathnames, you can use the Browse button in the Configure Data Source Wizard to select the file names.
- Errors in table or column names. This mistake usually arises when typing; it is less problematic when using the designer wizards or drag-and-drop in Visual Studio and Visual Web Designer.
- Attempting to bind a hierarchical data-bound control, such as TreeView or Menu, to a non-hierarchical data source, such as SqlDataSource or ObjectDataSource. Hierarchical data-bound controls must be bound to hierarchical data sources.
- Attempting to bind a tabular data-bound control, such as GridView or DropDownList, to unstructured hierarchical data. Tabular data-bound controls expect data fields to be the same for every data item in the data source.
- Attempting to use XPath data-binding syntax with a data source other than the XmlDataSource.
- Attempting to create a TreeView that does not follow the hierarchical structure of the underlying data. If you need to change the shape of the data to match the expected tree, use an XSLT Transform on an XmlDataSource before binding to TreeView.
- Attempting to bind to values of an XML hierarchy that are not exposed as attributes on the element node. Only XML attributes are bindable from XmlDataSource. To make non-attribute values bindable, use an XSLT transformation to reshape the data before binding to TreeView.
- Specifying duplicate URL properties in a `web.sitemap` file. Each siteMapNode must contain a unique URL in order to be valid.

Summary

This chapter discussed techniques of connecting an ASP.NET 2.0 Web page to XML-based data sources. It covered some general ideas and then focused on the theme and variations of using the XmlDataSource control to read from an XML file. The values in your XML file are then available for a data-bound control to display. To see the data, you used controls such as TreeView, GridView, and DataList.

You used the TreeView control to display the hierarchical XML data in a tree-based structure similar to the way Windows Explorer displays the folder hierarchy. The steps involved in applying an external XSL file to transform the contents of the XML file into another XML format were also covered.

Then you saw how to use the GridView control in conjunction with the XmlDataSource control to display information in the form of rows and columns. Later, you learned how to use the DataList control along with the XmlDataSource control to display the contents of the `Bookstore.xml` file. Finally, you saw how to implement nested DataList controls using an XmlDataSource as the data source.

15

Caching Data

Cache API in ASP.NET is one of the powerful features that can be immensely useful in increasing the performance of a Web application. The most dramatic way to improve the performance of a database-driven Web application is through caching. Retrieving data from a database is one of the slowest operations that you can perform in a Web site. If, however, you can cache the database data in memory, you can avoid accessing the database with every page request and dramatically increase your application's performance. This chapter discusses many of the new caching features in the ASP.NET Framework 2.0. You'll learn how caching support has been integrated into the new data source controls and how to configure and take advantage of SQL Cache Invalidation. Finally, you'll see how to enable partial-page caching using a new Substitution control that allows you to inject dynamic content into a cached page.

The following Try It Out exercises are presented as learning tools in this chapter:

Try It Out	Topic
1	Implementing a Page without Caching
2	Implementing a Time-Based Cache Technique
3	Implementing Cache with Parameters
4	Implementing Filtering Capability
5	Implementing SQL Cache Invalidation
6	Implementing Partial-Page Caching

Caching and Its Benefits

When clients access an ASP.NET page, there are basically two ways to provide them with the information they need:

- The ASP.NET page can obtain information from server resources, such as from data that has been persisted to a database.
- The ASP.NET page can obtain information from within the application.

Retrieving information from a resource outside the application will require more processing steps and will therefore require more time and resources on the server than if the information were obtained from within the application space. If the information that will be sent to the browser has already been prepared by a previous request, the application can retrieve that information faster if it has been stored in memory, somewhere along the request/response stream. This technique, known as caching, can be used to temporarily store page output or application data either on the client or on the server, which can then be reused to satisfy subsequent requests, avoiding the overhead of re-creating the same information.

When building enterprise-scale distributed applications, architects and developers are faced with many challenges. Caching mechanisms can be used to help you overcome some of these challenges:

- **Performance** — Caching techniques are commonly used to improve application performance by storing relevant data as close as possible to the data consumer, avoiding repetitive data creation, processing, and transportation. For example, storing data that does not change, such as a list of countries, in a cache can improve performance by minimizing data access operations and eliminating the need to re-create the same data for each request.
- **Scalability** — The same data, business functionality, and user interface fragments are often required by many users and processes in an application. If this information is processed for each request, valuable resources are wasted re-creating the same output. Instead, you can store the results in a cache and reuse them for each request. This improves the scalability of your application because, as the user base increases, the demand for server resources for these tasks remains constant. For example, in a Web application, the Web server is required to render the user interface for each user request. You can cache the rendered page in the ASP.NET output cache to be used for future requests, freeing resources to be used for other purposes. Caching data can also help scale the resources of your database server. By storing frequently used data in a cache, fewer database requests are made, meaning that more users can be served.
- **Availability** — Occasionally, the services that provide information to your application may be unavailable. By storing that data in another place, your application may be able to survive system failures such as network latency, Web service problems, or hardware failures. For example, each time a user requests information from your data store, you can return the information and also cache the results, updating the cache on each request. If the data store then becomes unavailable, you can still service requests using the cached data until the data store comes back online.

When to Use Caching

It is important to remember that caching isn't something you can just add to your application at any point in the development cycle; the application should be designed with caching in mind. This ensures that the cache can be used during the development of the application to help tune its performance, scalability, and availability. Now that you have seen the types of issues that caching can help avoid, look at the types of information that may be cached. This information is commonly called *state.* To successfully design an application that uses caching, you need to thoroughly understand the caching techniques ASP.NET provides, and you also need to be able to address questions such as the following:

- When and why should a custom cache be created?
- Which caching technique provides the best performance and scalability for a specific scenario and configuration?

- Which caching technology complies with the application's requirements for security, monitoring, and management?
- How can the cached data be kept up to date?

Before diving into caching technologies and techniques, it is important to have an understanding of state, because caching is merely a framework for state management.

Understanding State

Understanding the concept of state and its characteristics of lifetime and scope is important for making better decisions about whether to cache it. State refers to data, and the status or condition of that data, being used within a system at a certain point in time. The data may be permanently stored in a database, it may be held in memory for a short time while a user executes a certain function, or it may exist for some other defined length of time. It may be shared across a whole organization, it may be specific to an individual user, or it may be available to any grouping in between these extremes.

Understanding State Staleness

Cached state is a snapshot of the master state; therefore, its data is potentially stale (obsolete) as soon as it is retrieved by the consuming application. This is because the original data may have been changed by another process. Minimizing the staleness of data and the impact of staleness on your application is one of the tasks involved when caching state. State staleness is defined as the difference between the master state, from which the cached state was created, and the current version of the cached state. State can be defined in terms of the following:

- **Likelihood of changes** — Staleness might increase with time, because as time goes by, there is an increasing chance that other processes have updated the master data.
- **Relevancy of changes** — It is possible that master state changes will not have an adverse affect on the usability of a process. For example, changing a Web page style does not affect the business process operation itself. Depending on the use of the state within a system, staleness may or may not be an issue.

The following section details the various caching options available in ASP.NET 2.0.

Caching Options in ASP.NET 2.0

Storing frequently used data in memory is not a new concept for classic ASP developers. Classic ASP offers the Session and Application objects, which enable storing key/value pairs in memory. The Session object is used to store per-user data across multiple requests, and the Application object is used to store per-application data for use by requests from multiple users. ASP.NET introduces a new key/value pair object — the Cache object. The scope of the ASP.NET cache is the application domain; therefore, you cannot access it from other application domains or processes. The ASP.NET Cache object's life span is tied to the application, and the Cache object is re-created every time the application restarts, similar to the ASP Application object. The main difference between the Cache and Application objects is that the Cache object provides cache-specific features, such as dependencies and expiration policies.

ASP.NET provides a number of caching options that you can use in your applications.

- **Time-based** — You can specify the amount of time you want to cache the data. This type of caching can be specified using the OutputCache directive at the page level or at the control level such as when using an SqlDataSource control.
- **With parameters** — You can cache the output of a parameterized SQL query. Depending on the parameters passed to the SQL query, you will have multiple versions of query results stored in the cache object.
- **With filtering** — You apply filters on the cached result set and then display the filtered result set in your pages.
- **Data invalidation** — SQL Cache Invalidation is one of the most anticipated new features of the ASP.NET Framework 2.0. By taking advantage of SQL Cache Invalidation, you get all of the performance benefits of caching without the problem of stale data. SQL Cache Invalidation enables you to automatically update data in the cache whenever the data changes in the underlying database.
- **Partial page** — Page fragment caching involves the caching of a fragment of the page, as opposed to the entire page. This can be accomplished using Web user controls or using a Substitution control. This chapter looks at how to use Substitution control to accomplish this.

Before leveraging the caching features, take a look at a simple example of creating a data-driven ASP.NET page that displays information from the authors table in the Pubs database.

Displaying Data in ASP.NET

One of the biggest changes in the ASP.NET Framework 2.0 concerns how you access database data in an ASP.NET page. The ASP.NET Framework 2.0 includes a new set of controls, known collectively as the data source controls, which enable you to represent a data source such as a database or an XML file. In the ASP.NET Framework 1.0, you displayed database data with a control by binding the control to either a DataSet or a DataReader. In the ASP.NET Framework 2.0, you typically bind a control to a data source control instead. By taking advantage of the data source controls, you can build ASP.NET pages that display a database data without writing any code for accessing the database. When working with database data, you typically use one of the following three data source controls:

- **SqlDataSource** — Represents any SQL data source, such as a Microsoft SQL Server or an Oracle database.
- **AccessDataSource** — A specialized SqlDataSource control designed for working with a Microsoft Access database.
- **ObjectDataSource** — Represents a custom business object that acts as a data source.

For example, imagine that you need to display a list of authors' information from a database in a GridView control. The page explored in the following Try It Out and illustrated in Figure 15-1 shows how you can bind a GridView control to an SqlDataSource control.

Try It Out #1 — Implementing a Page without Caching

In this exercise, you will utilize the authors table in the Pubs database and display the authors' information in a GridView control by binding it directly to a SqlDataSource control. This example adds a custom TimeStamp column that updates each time the SQL query is executed, which will help to illustrate the benefits of caching in later examples.

1. Start your page editor and navigate to `C:\Websites\BegAspNet2Db\ch15\`.
2. Add a page named `TO1_NoCaching.aspx` from the template Web Form. Change to Design view using the bottom tabs.
3. Display the toolbox (Menu: View/toolbox or Ctrl+Alt+X) and expand the toolbox's Data panel.
4. Drag and drop an SqlDataSource control onto your page. Modify its declaration to look like the following:

```
<asp:SqlDataSource ID="SqlDataSource1" Runat="server" SelectCommand="SELECT
DatePart(second, GetDate()) As timestamp, * FROM [authors]"
ConnectionString="<%$ ConnectionStrings:LocalSqlPubs %>" />
```

5. Now drag and drop a GridView control onto the page. Select the GridView control and select Properties Window from the View menu. In the Properties window, set the AutoGenerateColumns, DataKeyNames, and DataSourceID properties to False, au_id, and SqlDataSource1, respectively.
6. Now add the required columns to the GridView control. After adding all the columns, your page should appear as follows:

```
<%@ Page Language="VB" %>
<html>
<head>
  <title>GridView with TimeStamp - No Caching</title>
</head>
<body>
  <form id="form1" runat="server">
    <asp:GridView ID="GridView1" Runat="server" DataSourceID="SqlDataSource1"
       DataKeyNames="au_id" AutoGenerateColumns="False">
       <Columns>
         <asp:BoundField ReadOnly="True" HeaderText="timestamp"
            DataField="timestamp" SortExpression="timestamp" />
         <asp:BoundField ReadOnly="True" HeaderText="au_id" DataField="au_id"
            SortExpression="au_id" />
         <asp:BoundField HeaderText="au_lname" DataField="au_lname"
            SortExpression="au_lname" />
         <asp:BoundField HeaderText="au_fname" DataField="au_fname"
            SortExpression="au_fname" />
         <asp:BoundField HeaderText="phone" DataField="phone"
            SortExpression="phone" />
         <asp:BoundField HeaderText="address" DataField="address"
            SortExpression="address" />
         <asp:BoundField HeaderText="city" DataField="city"
            SortExpression="city" />
         <asp:BoundField HeaderText="state" DataField="state"
            SortExpression="state" />
         <asp:BoundField HeaderText="zip" DataField="zip" SortExpression="zip" />
```

```
            <asp:CheckBoxField HeaderText="contract" SortExpression="contract"
               DataField="contract" />
         </Columns>
      </asp:GridView>
      <asp:SqlDataSource ID="SqlDataSource1" Runat="server" SelectCommand="SELECT
         DatePart(second, GetDate()) As timestamp, * FROM [authors]"
         ConnectionString="<%$ ConnectionStrings:LocalSqlPubs %>" />
   </form>
</body>
</html>
```

7. Open your browser and view `C:\Websites\BegAspNet2Db\ch15\ TO1_NoCaching.aspx`.

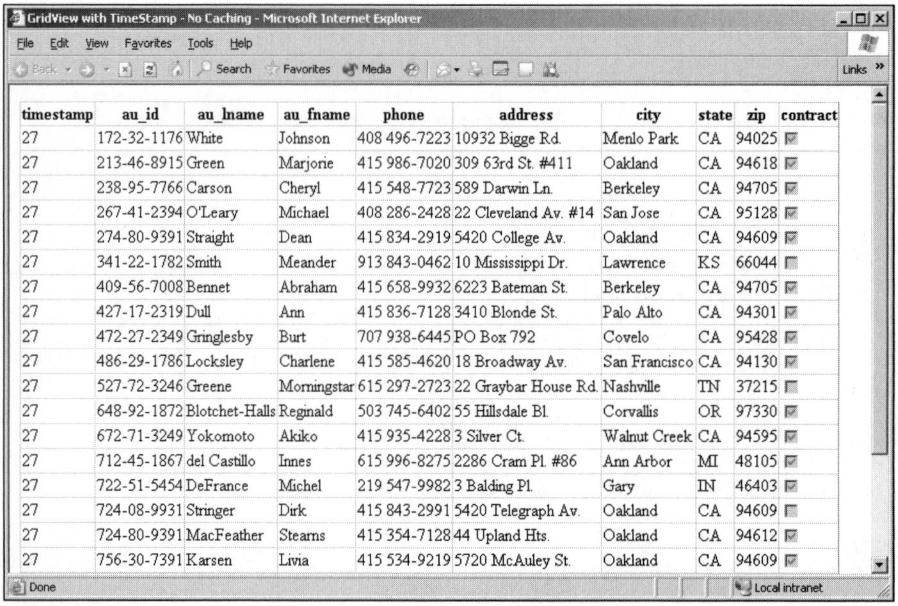

timestamp	au_id	au_lname	au_fname	phone	address	city	state	zip	contract
27	172-32-1176	White	Johnson	408 496-7223	10932 Bigge Rd.	Menlo Park	CA	94025	☑
27	213-46-8915	Green	Marjorie	415 986-7020	309 63rd St. #411	Oakland	CA	94618	☑
27	238-95-7766	Carson	Cheryl	415 548-7723	589 Darwin Ln.	Berkeley	CA	94705	☑
27	267-41-2394	O'Leary	Michael	408 286-2428	22 Cleveland Av. #14	San Jose	CA	95128	☑
27	274-80-9391	Straight	Dean	415 834-2919	5420 College Av.	Oakland	CA	94609	☑
27	341-22-1782	Smith	Meander	913 843-0462	10 Mississippi Dr.	Lawrence	KS	66044	☐
27	409-56-7008	Bennet	Abraham	415 658-9932	6223 Bateman St.	Berkeley	CA	94705	☑
27	427-17-2319	Dull	Ann	415 836-7128	3410 Blonde St.	Palo Alto	CA	94301	☑
27	472-27-2349	Gringlesby	Burt	707 938-6445	PO Box 792	Covelo	CA	95428	☑
27	486-29-1786	Locksley	Charlene	415 585-4620	18 Broadway Av.	San Francisco	CA	94130	☑
27	527-72-3246	Greene	Morningstar	615 297-2723	22 Graybar House Rd.	Nashville	TN	37215	☐
27	648-92-1872	Blotchet-Halls	Reginald	503 745-6402	55 Hillsdale Bl.	Corvallis	OR	97330	☑
27	672-71-3249	Yokomoto	Akiko	415 935-4228	3 Silver Ct.	Walnut Creek	CA	94595	☑
27	712-45-1867	del Castillo	Innes	615 996-8275	2286 Cram Pl. #86	Ann Arbor	MI	48105	☑
27	722-51-5454	DeFrance	Michel	219 547-9982	3 Balding Pl.	Gary	IN	46403	☑
27	724-08-9931	Stringer	Dirk	415 843-2991	5420 Telegraph Av.	Oakland	CA	94609	☐
27	724-80-9391	MacFeather	Stearns	415 354-7128	44 Upland Hts.	Oakland	CA	94612	☑
27	756-30-7391	Karsen	Livia	415 534-9219	5720 McAuley St.	Oakland	CA	94609	☑

Figure 15-1

How It Works #1 — Implementing a Page without Caching

In the preceding code, the Web.config file contains the connection strings required for connecting to the database. Once you have the connection string in the Web.config file, it can then be easily retrieved from within your Web page. In the ASP.NET page, you use the expression ConnectionStrings:LocalSqlPubs to retrieve the Pubs connection string contained in the connectionStrings element under the configuration element in the Web.config file.

In the ASP.NET page, notice that the SqlDataSource control is used to provide the connection string, and the SQL SELECT command is used for retrieving the records from the database. The GridView control is bound to the SqlDataSource control through its `DataSourceID` property.

Time-Based Caching

So far, you have seen how to create an ASP.NET page and take advantage of SqlDataSource control for displaying authors' information from the database. This section explains how to implement caching in conjunction with the SqlDataSource control.

The data source controls not only enable you to connect more easily to a database but also make it easier for you to cache database data. Simply by setting a couple of properties on the SqlDataSource control, you can automatically cache the data represented by a data source control in memory. For example, if you want to cache the Titles database table in memory for five minutes, you can declare a SqlDataSource control like this:

```
 <asp:SqlDataSource ID="SqlDataSource1" EnableCaching="true"  CacheDuration="300"
ConnectionString="Server=localhost;database=Pubs" SelectCommand="SELECT * FROM
Authors"   Runat="server" />
```

The following Try It Out explores implementing a time-based cache technique.

Try It Out #2 — Implementing a Time-Based Cache Technique

In this exercise, you will utilize the authors table in the Pubs database and cache the results of the SQL query for five seconds.

1. Start your page editor and navigate to `C:\Websites\BegAspNet2Db\ch15\`.
2. Add a page named `TO2_TimeBasedCaching.aspx` from the template Web Form. Change to Design view using the bottom tabs.
3. Display the toolbox (Menu: View/toolbox or Ctrl+Alt+X) and expand the toolbox's Data panel.
4. Drag and drop an SqlDataSource control onto your page. Modify its declaration to look like the following:

```
<asp:SqlDataSource ID="SqlDataSource1" Runat="server" SelectCommand="SELECT
DatePart(second, GetDate()) As timestamp, * FROM [authors]"
ConnectionString="<%$ ConnectionStrings:LocalSqlPubs %>" EnableCaching="True"
CacheDuration="5" />
```

5. Now drag and drop a GridView control onto the page. Select the GridView control and select Properties Window from the View menu. In the Properties window, set the AutoGenerateColumns, DataKeyNames, and DataSourceID properties to False, au_id, and SqlDataSource1, respectively.
6. Now add the required columns to the GridView control. After adding all the columns, your page should appear as follows:

```
<%@ Page Language="VB" %>
<html>
<head>
  <title>GridView with TimeStamp - No Caching</title>
</head>
<body>
    <h3>TIO #5 Demonstration of displaying XML data and handling events in the
Treeview</h3>
```

```
  <form id="form1" runat="server">
    <asp:GridView ID="GridView1" Runat="server" DataSourceID="SqlDataSource1"
       DataKeyNames="au_id" AutoGenerateColumns="False">
       <Columns>
         <asp:BoundField ReadOnly="True" HeaderText="timestamp"
            DataField="timestamp" SortExpression="timestamp" />
         <asp:BoundField ReadOnly="True" HeaderText="au_id" DataField="au_id"
            SortExpression="au_id" />
         <asp:BoundField HeaderText="au_lname" DataField="au_lname"
            SortExpression="au_lname" />
         <asp:BoundField HeaderText="au_fname" DataField="au_fname"
            SortExpression="au_fname" />
         <asp:BoundField HeaderText="phone" DataField="phone"
            SortExpression="phone" />
         <asp:BoundField HeaderText="address" DataField="address"
            SortExpression="address" />
         <asp:BoundField HeaderText="city" DataField="city"
            SortExpression="city" />
         <asp:BoundField HeaderText="state" DataField="state"
            SortExpression="state" />
         <asp:BoundField HeaderText="zip" DataField="zip" SortExpression="zip" />
         <asp:CheckBoxField HeaderText="contract" SortExpression="contract"
            DataField="contract" />
       </Columns>
    </asp:GridView>
    <asp:SqlDataSource ID="SqlDataSource1" Runat="server"
SelectCommand="SELECT DatePart(second, GetDate()) As timestamp, * FROM [authors]"
ConnectionString="<%$ ConnectionStrings:LocalSqlPubs %>"EnableCaching="True"
       CacheDuration="5"/>
  </form>
</body>
</html>
```

7. Open your browser and view `C:\Websites\BegAspNet2Db\ch15\ TO2_TimeBased Caching.aspx`.

How It Works #2 — Implementing a Time-Based Cache Technique

While declaring the SqlDataSource control, you set the `EnableCaching` property to true. When the `EnableCaching` property is set to true, the SqlDataSource will automatically cache the data retrieved by the SelectCommand. The `CacheDuration` property enables you to specify, in seconds, how long the data should be cached before it is refreshed from the database. By default, the SqlDataSource will cache data using an absolute expiration policy, meaning that the data will be refreshed after the number of specified seconds set in the `CacheDuration` property. You also have the option of enabling a sliding expiration policy. When the SqlDataSource is configured to use a sliding expiration policy, the data will not be dropped as long as it continues to be accessed within the specified CacheDuration. Employing a sliding expiration policy is useful when you have a large number of items that need to be cached, because this expiration policy enables you to keep only the most frequently accessed items in memory. In the preceding exercise, you cached the results of the SQL query for five seconds by setting the EnableCaching and CacheDuration attributes to True and 5, respectively.

Caching with Parameters

The following Try It Out shows you how to pass parameters to the SQL query specified in the `SelectCommand` property of the SqlDataSource control.

Try It Out #3 — Implementing Cache with Parameters

In this exercise, you will utilize the authors table in the Pubs database and cache the results of the parameterized SQL query for five seconds. This exercise is different from the previous one in that it uses a parameterized query whose results are cached by the SqlDataSource control.

1. Start your page editor and navigate to `C:\Websites\BegAspNet2Db\ch15\`.
2. Add a page named `TO3_CachingAndParameters.aspx` from the template Web Form. Change to Design view using the bottom tabs.
3. Display the toolbox (Menu: View/toolbox or Ctrl+Alt+X) and expand the toolbox's Data panel.
4. Drag and drop a DropDownList control onto your page and modify its declaration to look like the following:

```
<asp:DropDownList ID="DropDownList1" Runat="server" AutoPostBack="True">
  <asp:ListItem Value="CA" />
  <asp:ListItem Value="IN">IN</asp:ListItem>
  <asp:ListItem>UT</asp:ListItem>
</asp:DropDownList>
```

5. Drag and drop an SqlDataSource control onto your page. Modify its declaration to look like the following:

```
<asp:SqlDataSource ID="SqlDataSource1" Runat="server" SelectCommand="SELECT
DatePart(second, GetDate()) As timestamp, * FROM [authors]" where state = @state"
ConnectionString="<%$ ConnectionStrings:LocalSqlPubs %>" EnableCaching="True"
CacheDuration="10">
  <SelectParameters>
    <asp:ControlParameter Name="state" ControlID="DropDownList1"
       PropertyName="SelectedValue" />
  </SelectParameters>
</asp:SqlDataSource>
```

6. Now drag and drop a GridView control onto the page. Select the GridView control and select Properties Window from the View menu. In the Properties window, set the AutoGenerateColumns, DataKeyNames, and DataSourceID properties to False, au_id, and SqlDataSource1, respectively.
7. Now add the required columns to the GridView control. After adding all the columns, your page should appear as follows:

```
<%@ Page Language="VB" %>
<html>
<head>
  <title>Caching And Parameters</title>
</head>
<body>
<h3>Ch 15 TIO #3 Caching With Parameters</h3>
  <form id="form1" runat="server">
    <asp:DropDownList ID="DropDownList1" Runat="server" AutoPostBack="True">
```

```
      <asp:ListItem Value="CA" />
      <asp:ListItem Value="IN">IN</asp:ListItem>
      <asp:ListItem>UT</asp:ListItem>
    </asp:DropDownList>
    <br/><br/>
    <asp:GridView ID="GridView1" Runat="server" DataSourceID="SqlDataSource1"
       DataKeyNames="au_id" AutoGenerateColumns="False">
       <Columns>
         <asp:BoundField ReadOnly="True" HeaderText="timestamp"
            DataField="timestamp" SortExpression="timestamp" />
         <asp:BoundField ReadOnly="True" HeaderText="au_id" DataField="au_id"
            SortExpression="au_id" />
         <asp:BoundField HeaderText="au_lname" DataField="au_lname"
            SortExpression="au_lname" />
         <asp:BoundField HeaderText="au_fname" DataField="au_fname"
            SortExpression="au_fname" />
         <asp:BoundField HeaderText="phone" DataField="phone"
            SortExpression="phone" />
         <asp:BoundField HeaderText="address" DataField="address"
            SortExpression="address" />
         <asp:BoundField HeaderText="city" DataField="city"
            SortExpression="city" />
         <asp:BoundField HeaderText="state" DataField="state"
            SortExpression="state" />
         <asp:BoundField HeaderText="zip" DataField="zip" SortExpression="zip" />
         <asp:CheckBoxField HeaderText="contract" SortExpression="contract"
            DataField="contract" />
       </Columns>
    </asp:GridView>
    <asp:SqlDataSource ID="SqlDataSource1" Runat="server" SelectCommand="SELECT
       DatePart(second, GetDate()) As timestamp, * FROM [authors] where
       state = @state" ConnectionString="<%$ ConnectionStrings:LocalSqlPubs %>"
       EnableCaching="True" CacheDuration="10">
       <SelectParameters>
         <asp:ControlParameter Name="state" ControlID="DropDownList1"
           PropertyName="SelectedValue" />
       </SelectParameters>
    </asp:SqlDataSource>
  </form>
</body>
</html>
```

8. Open your browser and view `C:\Websites\BegAspNet2Db\ch15\TO3_CachingAndParameters.aspx`.

How It Works #3 — Implementing Cache with Parameters

The preceding code is similar to the previous example in that it also uses a SqlDataSource control as a data source control and a GridView control for display purposes. However, in this example, you have a DropDownList control that displays the list of states, and the authors GridView control displays the list of authors based on the selected state in the DropDownList control. This is accomplished in two steps. First, you specify a parameterized query in the `SelectCommand` property of the SqlDataSource control. Next, you supply the value of the @state parameter from the DropDownList control by setting the `ControlID` property of the asp:controlparameter (that is specified within the SqlDataSource control) to the ID of the DropDownList control.

One thing to note about this example is that each time a new item is selected for the DropDownList, a new copy of the cached data is created (the time stamp column updates). This is because the data source control stores a separate cache entry for each unique combination of parameters applied to the data source control. This prevents data for one set of parameters from being displayed for another set of parameters. While this is a perfectly valid use of the cache, it may sometimes result in more cache entries than is necessary. It is often useful to store only one copy of the unfiltered cached data and then use the parameters to filter over this cache entry dynamically in the data source. The following example demonstrates this technique.

Implementing Filtering Capability

At times, you may need to filter the resultset before displaying information that is contained within a data source control. To be able to do that, you need to use the `FilterExpression` property of the SqlDataSource control. This property makes it possible to set or get the filtering expression that is applied when the SQL query specified in the `SelectCommand` property is executed. The value supplied to this property is a string expression that is applied when the data is retrieved. The following exercise leverages the `FilterExpression` property to filter the authors resultset based on the selected state in the DropDownList control. The syntax used for the FilterExpression is the same syntax used for the `System.Data.DataSet.RowFilter` property. You can include parameters in the `FilterExpression`; these are specified with a format string substitution "{0}" like you've used in other format string properties. At runtime, the data source substitutes parameter values obtained from its FilterParameters collection for these placeholders in the FilterExpression. If the type of the parameter is a string or character type, be sure to enclose the parameter in single quotation marks, such as "field = '{0}'". Quotation marks are not needed if the parameter is a numeric type.

Try It Out #4 — Implementing Filtering Capability

In this exercise, you will utilize the authors table in the Pubs database and cache the results of the parameterized SQL query for five seconds. This exercise is different from the previous one in that it uses the `FilterExpression` property to pass in the appropriate value for a parameter in the FilterParameters collection.

1. Start your page editor and navigate to `C:\Websites\BegAspNet2Db\ch15\`.
2. Add a page named `TO4_FilteringCacheEntries.aspx` from the template Web Form. Change to Design view using the bottom tabs.
3. Display the toolbox (Menu: View/toolbox or Ctrl+Alt+X) and expand the toolbox's Data panel.
4. Drag and drop a DropDownList control onto your page and modify its declaration to look like the following:

```
<asp:DropDownList ID="DropDownList1" Runat="server" AutoPostBack="True">
  <asp:ListItem Value="CA" />
  <asp:ListItem Value="IN">IN</asp:ListItem>
  <asp:ListItem>UT</asp:ListItem>
</asp:DropDownList>
```

5. Drag and drop an SqlDataSource control onto your page. Modify its declaration to look like the following:

```
<asp:SqlDataSource ID="SqlDataSource1" Runat="server" SelectCommand="SELECT
DatePart(second, GetDate()) As timestamp, * FROM [authors]"
ConnectionString="<%$ ConnectionStrings:LocalSqlPubs %>" EnableCaching="True"
```

```
CacheDuration="10" FilterExpression="state='{0}'">
  <FilterParameters>
     <asp:ControlParameter Name="state" ControlID="DropDownList1"
       PropertyName="SelectedValue" />
  </FilterParameters>
</asp:SqlDataSource>
```

6. Drag and drop a GridView control onto the page. Select the GridView control and select Properties Window from the View menu. In the Properties window, set the AutoGenerateColumns, DataKeyNames, and DataSourceID properties to False, au_id, and SqlDataSource1, respectively.

7. Add the required columns to the GridView control. After adding all the columns, your page should appear as follows:

```
<%@ Page Language="VB" %>
<html>
<head>
  <title>Caching And Parameters</title>
</head>
<body>
<h3>Ch 15 TIO #4 Filtering Cache Entries</h3>
  <form id="form1" runat="server">
    <asp:DropDownList ID="DropDownList1" Runat="server" AutoPostBack="True">
      <asp:ListItem Value="CA" />
      <asp:ListItem Value="IN">IN</asp:ListItem>
      <asp:ListItem>UT</asp:ListItem>
    </asp:DropDownList>
    <br/><br/>
    <asp:GridView ID="GridView1" Runat="server" DataSourceID="SqlDataSource1"
       DataKeyNames="au_id" AutoGenerateColumns="False">
       <Columns>
         <asp:BoundField ReadOnly="True" HeaderText="timestamp"
            DataField="timestamp" SortExpression="timestamp" />
         <asp:BoundField ReadOnly="True" HeaderText="au_id" DataField="au_id"
            SortExpression="au_id" />
         <asp:BoundField HeaderText="au_lname" DataField="au_lname"
            SortExpression="au_lname" />
         <asp:BoundField HeaderText="au_fname" DataField="au_fname"
            SortExpression="au_fname" />
         <asp:BoundField HeaderText="phone" DataField="phone"
            SortExpression="phone" />
         <asp:BoundField HeaderText="address" DataField="address"
            SortExpression="address" />
         <asp:BoundField HeaderText="city" DataField="city"
            SortExpression="city" />
         <asp:BoundField HeaderText="state" DataField="state"
            SortExpression="state" />
         <asp:BoundField HeaderText="zip" DataField="zip" SortExpression="zip" />
         <asp:CheckBoxField HeaderText="contract" SortExpression="contract"
            DataField="contract" />
       </Columns>
    </asp:GridView>
```

```
        <asp:SqlDataSource ID="SqlDataSource1" Runat="server" SelectCommand="SELECT
           DatePart(second, GetDate()) As timestamp, * FROM [authors]"
           ConnectionString="<%$ ConnectionStrings:LocalSqlPubs %>"
           EnableCaching="True" CacheDuration="10" FilterExpression="state='{0}'">
           <FilterParameters>
              <asp:ControlParameter Name="state" ControlID="DropDownList1"
                PropertyName="SelectedValue" />
           </FilterParameters>
        </asp:SqlDataSource></form>
    </body>
    </html>
```

8. Open your browser and view `C:\Websites\BegAspNet2Db\ch15\TO4_FilteringCacheEntries, aspx`.

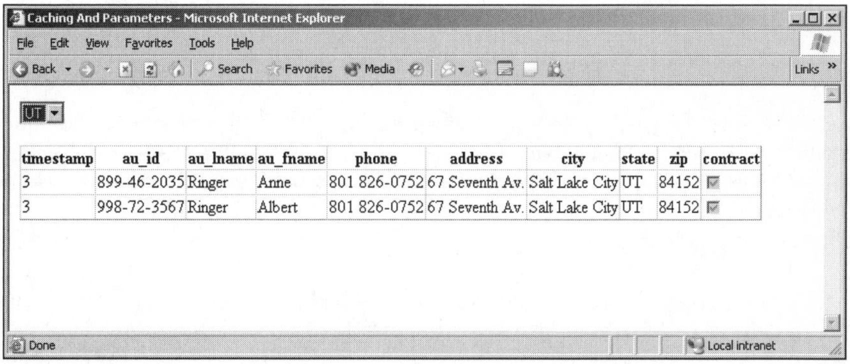

Figure 15-2

How It Works #4 — Implementing Filtering Capability

The preceding code demonstrates how to retrieve data from the authors table and filter it using a FilterExpression string. The FilterExpression of the SqlDataSource is applied any time the Select method is executed to retrieve data. In this example, the FilterExpression contains a placeholder for a filter parameter, which is '{0}' in this case. In addition, the filter parameter is a ControlParameter bound to the SelectedValue of the DropDownList control. Because the DropDownList control has its `AutoPostBack` property set to true, any change in the DropDownList selection causes the page to post information back to the server and causes the GridView to rebind to the data source control with the new filter.

Notice that when a new item is selected for the DropDownList in this example, the timestamp column does not update. This is because the unfiltered data is retrieved from the cache instead of going back to the database for each new parameter value. The parameter values are then applied to filter the cached data in memory using the FilterExpression/FilterParameters of the data source.

Note that the SqlDataSource control only supports filtering data when in DataSet mode. This property delegates to the `FilterExpression` property of the SqlDataSourceView that is associated with the SqlDataSource control.

SQL Cache Invalidation

The only drawback to caching is the problem of stale data. If you cache the contents of a database table in memory and the records in the underlying database table change, your Web application will display old, inaccurate data. For certain types of data, you might not care if the data being displayed is slightly out of date, but for other types of data, such as stock prices and auction bids, displaying data that is even slightly stale is unacceptable. The initial release of ASP.NET did not provide a good solution to this problem. When using ASP.NET 1.x, you just had to live with this tradeoff between performance and stale data. Fortunately, ASP.NET 2.0 includes a new feature called SQL Cache Invalidation that solves this very problem. To enable SQL Cache Invalidation, take the following steps:

- Add the caching element to the Web.config file and specify the polling time and the connection string information.
- Enable SQL Cache Invalidation at the database and table levels by using either the aspnet_regsql utility or the SqlCacheDependencyAdmin class.
- Specify the SqlCacheDependency attribute in the SqlDataSource control.

The next exercise shows an example of the Web.config file entries that need to be added to enable SQL Cache Invalidation. Then you need to enable the database and the table to support cache invalidation so that the data can be automatically removed from the cache when the data in the table changes. As previously mentioned, you can do that using either the aspnet_regsql utility or the SqlCacheDependencyAdmin class.

The aspnet_regsql tool enables you to configure SQL Cache Invalidation from the command line. The aspnet_regsql tool is located in your Windows\Microsoft.NET\Framework\[version] folder. You must use this tool by opening a command prompt and navigating to this folder. Behind the scenes, the aspnet_regsql tool uses the methods of the SqlCacheDependencyAdmin class to configure Microsoft SQL Server. If you prefer, you can use the methods of this class directly from within an ASP.NET page. The SqlCacheDependencyAdmin class has five important methods:

- **DisableNotifications** — Disables SQL Cache Invalidation for a particular database
- **DisableTableForNotifications** — Disables SQL Cache Invalidation for a particular table in a database
- **EnableNotifications** — Enables SQL Cache Invalidation for a particular database
- **EnableTableForNotifications** — Enables SQL Cache Invalidation for a particular table in a database
- **GetTablesEnabledForNotifications** — Returns a list of all tables enabled for SQL Cache Invalidation

Try It Out #5 — Implementing SQL Cache Invalidation

In this exercise, you will cache the authors table in the Pubs database using the SqlDataSource control. Through the SQL Cache Invalidation mechanism, you will invalidate or remove the item in the cache object when the data in the authors table changes.

1. Start your page editor and navigate to `C:\Websites\BegAspNet2Db\ch15\`.

2. For SQL Cache Invalidation to work, you must appropriate entries to the Web.config file. Open up the Web.config file and add the following element under the root configuration element:

```
<system.web>
   <caching>
      <sqlCacheDependency enabled="true" pollTime="1000">
        <databases>
          <add name="Pubs" connectionStringName="Pubs"/>
        </databases>
      </sqlCacheDependency>
   </caching>
</system.web>
```

3. Now that you have configured the Web.config file, you must configure the SQL Server to support cache invalidation. Open up the Visual Studio Command Prompt and navigate to the folder C:\Windows\Microsoft.NET\Framework\V2.0.40607. Because you are using the Pubs database, you need to execute the following command:

```
aspnet_regsql -E -d Pubs -ed
```

   In the preceding command, the `-E` option causes the aspnet_regsql tool to use integrated security when connecting to your database server. The `-d` option selects the Pubs database. Finally, the `-ed` option enables the database for SQL Cache Invalidation. When you execute this command, a new database table named AspNet_SqlCacheTablesForChangeNotification is added to the database. This table contains a list of all of the database tables that are enabled for SQL Cache Invalidation. The command also adds a set of stored procedures to the database.

4. After you enable a database for SQL Cache Invalidation, you must select the particular tables in the database that you want to enable for SQL Cache Invalidation. The following command enables the Titles database table:

```
   aspnet_regsql -E -d Pubs -t authors -et
```

   The `-t` option selects a database table. The `-et` option enables a database table for SQL Cache Invalidation. You can, of course, enable multiple tables by re-executing this command for each database table.

5. Now that you have completed the groundwork, add a page named `TO5_SqlCacheInvalidation.aspx` from the template Web Form. Change to Design view using the bottom tabs.

6. Display the toolbox (Menu: View/toolbox or Ctrl+Alt+X) and expand the toolbox's Data panel.

7. Drag and drop an SqlDataSource control onto your page. The control's smart task panel should appear automatically, but if not, select the new DropDownList control and then click the top right small arrow to open the smart task panel.

8. Drag and drop a DropDownList onto the page. The control's smart task panel should appear automatically, but if not, select the new DropDownList control and then click the top right small arrow to open the smart task panel. Click on the Configure Data Source hyperlink.

9. In the Choose a Connection dialog box, select Pubs as the data connection and click Next.

10. In the Configure Select Statement dialog box, select the Specify a Custom SQL Statement or Stored Procedure option and click Next.

11. In the Define Custom Statements or Stored Procedures dialog box, specify the SQL queries to use for Select, Update, Insert, and Delete operations. In the SELECT tab, specify the SQL as `"SELECT DatePart(second, GetDate()) As timestamp, * FROM [authors]"`.

12. For the UPDATE tab, specify `"UPDATE [authors] SET [au_lname] = @au_lname, [au_fname] = @au_fname, [phone] = @phone, [address] = @address, [city] = @city, [state] = @state, [zip] = @zip, [contract] = @contract WHERE [au_id] = @original_au_id"`.

13. In the INSERT tab, specify `"INSERT INTO [authors] ([au_id], [au_lname], [au_fname], [phone], [address], [city], [state], [zip], [contract]) VALUES (@au_id, @au_lname, @au_fname, @phone, @address, @city, @state, @zip, @contract) "`.

14. In the DELETE tab, specify `"DELETE FROM [authors] WHERE [au_id] = @original_au_id"` as the SQL statement. Then click Next.

15. In the Test Query dialog box, you can test the query to see if it executes properly. Click Finish.

16. Go back to the Design view and select the SqlDataSource1 control, and select Properties Window from the View menu. In the Properties window, set the EnableCaching and SqlCacheDependency properties to True and Pubs:authors, respectively. This value is case-sensitive, so be sure to type it exactly as it appears here, using the names configured by the aspnet_regsql utility in the previous steps.

17. Add a GridView control to the page and set its DataSourceID, DataKeyNames, and AutoGenerateColumns properties to SqlDataSource1, au_id, and False, respectively. Add the required columns to the GridView control. After modification, the page should appear as follows:

```
<%@ Page Language="VB" %>
<html>
<head>
   <title>SQL Cache Invalidation</title>
</head>
<body>
<h3>Ch 15 TIO #5 SQL Cache Invalidation</h3>
  <form id="form1" runat="server">
    <asp:GridView ID="GridView1" Runat="server" DataSourceID="SqlDataSource1"
      DataKeyNames="au_id" AutoGenerateColumns="False">
      <Columns>
        <asp:CommandField ShowEditButton="True" />
        <asp:BoundField ReadOnly="True" HeaderText="timestamp"
           DataField="timestamp" SortExpression="timestamp" />
        <asp:BoundField ReadOnly="True" HeaderText="au_id" DataField="au_id"
           SortExpression="au_id" />
        <asp:BoundField HeaderText="au_lname" DataField="au_lname"
           SortExpression="au_lname" />
        <asp:BoundField HeaderText="au_fname" DataField="au_fname"
           SortExpression="au_fname" />
        <asp:BoundField HeaderText="phone" DataField="phone"
           SortExpression="phone"/>
        <asp:BoundField HeaderText="address" DataField="address"
           SortExpression="address" />
```

```
          <asp:BoundField HeaderText="city" DataField="city" SortExpression="city" />
          <asp:BoundField HeaderText="state" DataField="state"
             SortExpression="state" />
          <asp:BoundField HeaderText="zip" DataField="zip" SortExpression="zip" />
          <asp:CheckBoxField HeaderText="contract" SortExpression="contract"
             DataField="contract" />
        </Columns>
      </asp:GridView>
      <asp:SqlDataSource ID="SqlDataSource1" Runat="server" SelectCommand="SELECT
         DatePart(second, GetDate()) As timestamp, * FROM [authors]"
         ConnectionString="<%$ ConnectionStrings:LocalSqlPubs %>"
EnableCaching="True"
         DeleteCommand="DELETE FROM [authors] WHERE [au_id] = @original_au_id"
         InsertCommand="INSERT INTO [authors] ([au_id], [au_lname], [au_fname],
         [phone], [address], [city], [state], [zip], [contract]) VALUES (@au_id,
         @au_lname, @au_fname, @phone, @address, @city, @state, @zip, @contract)"
         UpdateCommand="UPDATE [authors] SET [au_lname] = @au_lname, [au_fname] =
         @au_fname, [phone] = @phone, [address] = @address, [city] = @city, [state] =
         @state, [zip] = @zip, [contract] = @contract WHERE [au_id] =
         @original_au_id" SqlCacheDependency="Pubs:authors">
         <DeleteParameters>
           <asp:Parameter Name="original_au_id" />
         </DeleteParameters>
         <UpdateParameters>
           <asp:Parameter Type="String" Name="au_lname" />
           <asp:Parameter Type="String" Name="au_fname" />
           <asp:Parameter Type="String" Name="phone" />
           <asp:Parameter Type="String" Name="address" />
           <asp:Parameter Type="String" Name="city" />
           <asp:Parameter Type="String" Name="state" />
           <asp:Parameter Type="String" Name="zip" />
           <asp:Parameter Type="Boolean" Name="contract" />
           <asp:Parameter Name="original_au_id" />
         </UpdateParameters>
         <InsertParameters>
           <asp:Parameter Type="String" Name="au_id" />
           <asp:Parameter Type="String" Name="au_lname" />
           <asp:Parameter Type="String" Name="au_fname" />
           <asp:Parameter Type="String" Name="phone" />
           <asp:Parameter Type="String" Name="address" />
           <asp:Parameter Type="String" Name="city" />
           <asp:Parameter Type="String" Name="state" />
           <asp:Parameter Type="String" Name="zip" />
           <asp:Parameter Type="Boolean" Name="contract" />
         </InsertParameters>
      </asp:SqlDataSource>
    </form>
</body>
</html>
```

18. Open your browser and view `C:\Websites\BegAspNet2Db\ch15\TO5_SqlCacheInvalidation. aspx`.

How It Works #5 — Implementing SQL Cache Invalidation

In the preceding code, the SqlDataSource control is declared with both an EnableCaching attribute and an SqlCacheDependency attribute. The `SqlCacheDependency` property uses the same syntax as the OutputCache directive's SqlDependency attribute. You list the name of the database, followed by the name of the database table. SQL Cache Invalidation works only with Microsoft SQL Server version 7 and higher. You cannot use this feature with other databases such as Microsoft Access or Oracle.

Behind the scenes, SQL Cache Invalidation works by constantly polling the database to check for changes. Every so many milliseconds, the ASP.NET Framework checks whether there have been any updates to the database. If the ASP.NET Framework detects any changes, any items added to the cache that depend on the database are removed from the cache (they are invalidated).

Note that SQL Server 2005 (next version of SQL Server) supports a completely different method of SQL cache invalidation. In SQL Server 2005, you can configure it to notify your ASP.NET application whenever changes have been made to a database, a database table, or a database row. This means that the ASP.NET Framework does not need to constantly poll an SQL Server 2005 database for changes.

The Web.config file in the preceding code example contains two sections. The `<connectionStrings>` section is used to create a database connection string to the Pubs database. The caching section is used to configure the SQL Cache Invalidation polling. Within the `<databases>` subsection, you can list one or more databases that you want to poll for changes. In the preceding code, the database represented by the Pubs is polled once a minute (every 1,000 milliseconds). You can specify different polling intervals for different databases. The server must do a little bit of work every time the database is polled for changes. If you don't expect the data in the database to change very often, you can increase the polling interval.

When you run this page, notice that the timestamp does not change. This is because the CacheDuration is set to Infinite by default, which will cache the data indefinitely until the underlying data in the database changes. If you enable editing on the GridView in this example and edit a particular row, you will see that the timestamp column updates when the updated row is submitted. This is because the SqlCacheDependency expires the cache entry in response to the changed data and the data source goes back to the database to re-execute the command and refresh the data.

Caching Partial Pages

Page fragment caching involves the caching of a fragment of the page, as opposed to the entire page. Sometimes full-page output caching is not feasible — for example, when portions of the page need to be dynamically created for each user request. In such cases, it can be worthwhile to identify portions of the page or controls that do not often change and that take considerable time and server resources to create. After you identify these portions, you can wrap them in a Web Forms user control and cache the control so that these portions of the page don't need to be re-created each time. This was the only way you could implement page fragment caching prior to ASP.NET 2.0. With ASP.NET 2.0, there is a new control named Substitution control that allows you to inject dynamic content into a page. This process is called post-cache substitution and is made possible by the new Substitution control.

The Substitution control has one important property named `MethodName`, and this property is used to specify the method that will be invoked to provide the dynamic content. The method called by the Substitution control must be a Shared method. Furthermore, the method must have one parameter that represents the current HttpContext.

Try It Out #6 — Implementing Partial-Page Caching

In this exercise, you will utilize the Substitution control to implement partial-page caching.

1. Start your page editor and navigate to `C:\Websites\BegAspNet2Db\ch15\`.
2. Add a page named `TO6_PartialPageCaching.aspx` from the template Web Form. Change to Design view using the bottom tabs.
3. To the top of the page, add the OutputCache directive and modify it to look like the following:

```
<%@ OutputCache Duration="6000" VaryByParam="none" %>
```

4. Then add a server-side script block and add a method named GetRandomNumber that looks like the following:

```
<script runat="server">
  Shared Function GetRandomNumber(ByVal context As HttpContext) As String
    Dim randomNumber As Integer
    randomNumber = New System.Random().Next(1, 10000)
    Return randomNumber.ToString()
  End Function
</script>
```

Alternatively, use the following script in C#:

```
<%@ Page Language="C#" %>
<%@ OutputCache Duration="6000" VaryByParam="none" %>

    <script runat="server">
      static String GetRandomNumber(HttpContext context)
      {
            int randomNumber;
            randomNumber = new System.Random().Next(1, 10000);
            return randomNumber.ToString();
      }
    </script>
```

5. Display the toolbox (Menu: View/toolbox or Ctrl+Alt+X) and expand the toolbox's Standard panel.
6. Drag and drop a Substitution control onto your page. Ensure that the control is selected and select Properties Window from the View menu. In the Properties window, set the `MethodName` property to GetRandomNumber. This allows you to execute the GetRandomNumber method every time the page is requested, even though the entire page is cached.
7. After making all the changes, the page should appear as follows (VB version):

```
<%@ Page Language="VB" %>
<%@ OutputCache Duration="6000" VaryByParam="none" %>
<script runat="server">
  Shared Function GetRandomNumber(ByVal context As HttpContext) As String
     Dim randomNumber As Integer
     randomNumber = New System.Random().Next(1, 10000)
     Return randomNumber.ToString()
  End Function
</script>
```

```
<html>
<head>
  <title>Partial Page Caching using Substitution control</title>
</head>
<body>
<h3>Ch 15 TIO #6 Partial Page Caching Using Substitution Control VB version</h3>
  <form id="form1" runat="server">
   The random number generated is:
   <asp:Substitution ID="Substitution1" MethodName="GetRandomNumber"
      Runat="Server"/>
   <p>
   The current time is
   <%= DateTime.Now.ToString("t") %>. It never changes since the page is cached.
   </p>
  </form>
</body>
</html>
```

8. Open your browser and view `C:\Websites\BegAspNet2Db\ch15\TO6_PartialPageCaching.aspx`.

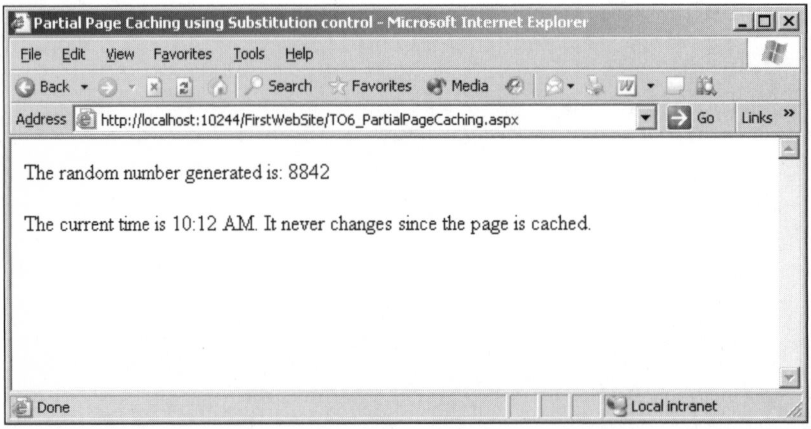

Figure 15-3

How It Works #6 — Implementing Partial-Page Caching

At the top of the page, the OutputCache directive is used to cache the contents of the page in memory. In the OutputCache directive, you set the Duration attribute to 6,000 milliseconds. The VaryByParam attribute indicates whether ASP.NET should take page parameters into consideration when caching. When VaryByParam is set to none, no parameters will be considered; all users will receive the same page no matter what additional parameters are supplied.

You set the MethodName attribute of the Substitution control to a method named GetRandomNumber, which simply returns a random number between 1 and 10,000. When you make a request for the page, you will find that the displayed current time always remains the same, whereas the portion of the page that is generated by the Substitution control keeps changing every time. In this case, it displays a random number between 1 and 10,000 every time someone requests the page.

Common Mistakes

The following is a list of common errors made while attempting to implement caching in ASP.NET 2.0:

- Using an incorrect connection string. Recheck the connection string specified in the Web.config file.
- Using an incorrect username or password. Make sure that the connection string contains the correct username and password.
- Trying to use a data-bound control when there is no data source control. A data-bound control must have a source of data, that is, a data source control, specified by its `DataSourceID` property.
- Trying to cache the output of a SqlDataSource control without setting the `EnableCaching` property. Before you can cache the output of a data source control such as SqlDataSource control, you need to set its `EnableCaching` property to `true`.
- Errors in table or column names. This mistake usually arises when typing; it is less problematic when using the designer wizards or drag-and-drop in Visual Studio and Visual Web Designer.
- Attempting to use Sql Cache Invalidation without first configuring the database and table using aspnet_regsql.exe.
- Typing an incorrect value for the `SqlCacheDependency` property of `SqlDataSource`. Note that this property is case-sensitive and must be typed exactly using the database and connection names specified when configuring them using aspnet_regsql.exe.
- Attempting to use Sql Cache Invalidation on an unsupported database server. SQL Cache Invalidation is only supported on Microsoft SQL Server version 7 or higher.

Summary

Caching has a dramatic impact on the performance of database-driven Web applications. You can use caching to store data that is consumed frequently by an application; you can also use it to store data that is expensive to create, obtain, or transform. There are three main benefits to implementing caching in your applications:

- Reduction of the amount of data that is transferred between processes and computers
- Reduction of the amount of data processing that occurs within the system
- Reduction of the number of disk access operations that occur

Fortunately, ASP.NET 2.0 includes a number of features that make it easier to take advantage of caching in your applications. The new data source controls include properties that facilitate caching database data in memory. By taking advantage of the data source controls, you can retrieve database data and cache the data without writing a single line of code. The support for SQL Cache Invalidation enables you to automatically reload database data in the cache whenever the data is modified in the underlying database. This feature provides you with all the performance benefits of caching, without the worries of stale data. Finally, the new Substitution control enables you to more easily mix dynamic content in a cached page.

16

Handling Events for Data Controls

Rounding out the book are a few ideas about writing your own code in event handlers. In the past, this was the primary tool to perform many tasks, but with ASP.NET 2.0 the need for writing events is greatly reduced. Nevertheless, writing custom code in events is unavoidable as an application becomes complex. This chapter explains the basics of creating events, including the general techniques. A specific explanation of page-level events and events to handle button clicks follows. Then you'll find sections on responding to events from lists and how to work with the events raised by data controls. Last is a look at the events raised when a page encounters an error.

You will practice the concepts presented in this chapter with the following Try It Out exercises:

Try It Out	Topic
1	Sample Event Handler
2	Event Code Locations
3	Custom Events for Buttons
4	List Selection and Page Events Handling
5	Data-Binding Events for GridView
6	Handling Error Events

A major goal of the ASP.NET 2.0 design team was to eliminate the need for this chapter. They have cataloged the most common Web scenarios that required code and built those functions into properties and methods of objects. You have seen this pattern in prior chapters for data source controls and data-bound controls. However, it is impossible for the ASP.NET team to cover every possibility. So the team has also included the capability to execute custom code that you write by using event handlers.

An event is an action like "Button1 has been clicked" or "The page has been loaded into memory." Events can have an *event handler*, which is a container for code to execute when the event occurs. Microsoft writes some code for event handlers; a page's designer also writes some. For example, Microsoft has written event handlers for its command buttons such as Update to gather values, put them in a parameters collection, append them to the data source control's Update statement, instantiate the appropriate ADO objects, and execute the command. Conversely, the designers can write their own custom code in an event handler.

Why not just use the Microsoft-provided event handlers? In most cases you can, particularly for the predictable tasks of binding data to controls. But as pages and sites become more complex, it is necessary to create customized code beyond what Microsoft could have anticipated anyone using. After all, they can't predict everything for everybody. However, always first look carefully for a built-in way to achieve objectives; writing custom event handlers should be undertaken only if needed.

Execution Control When an Event Is Triggered

When the user takes certain actions, an event is triggered. For example, when the user clicks on a button, that button's `Button_Click` event is triggered. In addition, there are some cases where steps taken by ASP.NET 2.0 itself triggers events, such as `Page_Load` or `Data_Bind`. Server-side controls such as `<asp:button...>` will have a property such as `OnClick`, which gets the event handler's name as a value to trigger when the button is clicked. The kinds of events supported for each control are listed in the control's property box after you click the lightning icon. Designers can write code in the event handler that will be executed at the time that particular event is triggered.

Custom event handlers are written in two steps. First, in the server-side control, declare which handler to use for the event. This is usually a standard name, for example, `Button1_Click`. Then the code is written into an event handler, which has the name designated in step 1.

Types of Events

When explaining events, it is useful to divide them into functional groups. There is no basis for this taxonomy in the ASP.NET 2.0 object model, but it helps in considering where to write code. The events are categorized as follows:

- **Events triggered by the page** — Page_Load, Page_PreRender, etc.
- **Events triggered by command buttons (command fields)** — Insert, update, delete, and select. These buttons are available in data-bound controls.
- **Events from custom buttons** — Buttons that trigger custom code. These buttons can be inside or outside of data-bound controls.
- **Events triggered by server-side controls** — A list select, for example.
- **Events that are triggered by data-binding** — DataBound and RowDataBound, for example.

- **Events raised by errors** — `Page_Error` and `Application_Error` events.
- **Custom events (not covered in this book)** — The designer creates a set of circumstances that triggers an event.

General Techniques for Writing Event Handlers

Event handlersare very similar to procedures that you may have studied in general books on ASP or a .NET-supported language. A procedure (or function) is called by another line of code. An event handler is automatically invoked by some action that the user performs (such as a button click) or in the life of the page (such as page load).

Event handlers are located within script tags. Script tags (sometimes called script blocks) can be located anywhere on the page but are usually after the `<%@Page%>` tag and before the `<html>`. Note that in the `@Page` tag there is a language designation. ASP.NET 2.0 supports many languages, but only one language per page. Within a single set of script tags can be any number of individual event handlers. Procedures and functions are typically located within the same script tags, as well; however, they will be designated by a simple name, whereas event handlers are typically designated in the form `Object_Event`.

Each language supports a basic syntax to begin and end an event handler. Visual Basic uses the `Sub` and `End Sub`, as follows:

```
Sub MyObject_Event (ByVal sender As Object, ByVal e As System.EventArgs)
    'Visual Basic Code goes here
End Sub
```

C# uses the keyword `void` along with braces. Note that the closing brace ends the handler; there is no need for an `END` statement because in C# the braces indicate the end.

```
void MyObject_Event(Object sender, EventArgs e)
{
    //C# Code goes here;
}
```

When you use VWD, the language framework is set up automatically for you in two steps. First, when you create the page, you select the language for scripts in the Add New Item dialog. Then, when you want to write code in a specific handler, you can select an object such as a button and in its Properties window, click on the lightning icon to see the list of available event handlers. A double-click on one of those will cause VWD to create the preceding event handler stub. Alternatively, you can just double-click on the control in Design view and you will be led to the default event (click for buttons; change in selected index for lists).

Try It Out #1 — Sample Event Handler

In this exercise, you will write a very basic event handler that displays the time in a label and changes the text on a button when the button is clicked. In addition, including some simple code will add a time-appropriate note to the time. Enter only one of the following options, Visual Basic or C#.

1. Create a new folder named `C:\BegAspNet2Db\ch16` and within the nascent folder a file named `TIO-01-DemoEvents-VB.aspx`. Select either Visual Basic or C# language, but turn off the "Place code in separate file" option.

2. Drag a label onto the page and name it `ShowTimeLabel`. Then drag a button and name it `GetTimeButton`.

3. Double-click on the button, and VWD will automatically create an event for the most common button event, a click. You will see the following for VB:

```
<%@ Page Language="VB" %>
<script runat="server">

    Sub GetTimeButton_Click(ByVal sender As Object, ByVal e As System.EventArgs)
    End Sub

</script>
<html>
<head><title>Ch-16-TIO--</title></head>
<body>
<h3>Chapter 16 TIO #  1 Demonstration of Basic Event Handler Syntax</h3>
<form runat=server>
  <asp:Button ID="GetTimeButton" Runat="server" Text="Button"
OnClick="GetTimeButton_Click" />
  <asp:Label ID="ShowTimeLabel" Runat="server" Text="Label"></asp:Label>
</form></body>
</html>
```

If your page language is C#, the setup from VWD will appear as follows:

```
<%@ Page Language="C#" %>
<script runat="server">
    void GetTimeButton_Click(object sender, EventArgs e)
    {

    }
</script>
```

4. Within this framework, add the following code, which will change the text shown in your label. Then change the text displayed on the button, and lastly add a time-sensitive message to the label. For VB coders, the statements follow:

```
<script runat="server">

    Sub GetTimeButton_Click(ByVal sender As Object, ByVal e As System.EventArgs)

        ShowTimeLabel.Text = "The date and time on the server is " & Now()
        sender.Text = "Click again to update"

        If Hour(Now()) > 12 Then
            ShowTimeLabel.Text += ". Good Afternoon"
        Else
            ShowTimeLabel.Text += ". Good Morning"
        End If

    End Sub

</script>
```

The same code in C# follows:

```
<%@ Page Language="C#" %>
<script runat="server">

void GetTimeButton_Click(object sender, EventArgs e)
{
    DateTime MyDateTime;
    ShowTimeLabel.Text = "The date and time on the server is " + DateTime.Now;

    ((Button)sender).Text = "Click to Update";

    if(DateTime.Now.Hour<12)
    {
        ShowTimeLabel.Text += ". Good morning.";
    }
else
    {
        ShowTimeLabel.Text += ". Good Afternoon";
    }
}
</script>
```

5. Save and open in your browser. Click the button to see how the texts change from the defaults to new messages.

How It Works #1 — Sample Event Handler

This demonstration gives you an overview of several topics that are discussed in detail later in this chapter. First, observe that when you are in the Design view of VWD and double-click on an object, VWD will switch to Source view and create the frame of a handler for the most common event for that control. For example, the default event for a button is a click event. Many kinds of events are discussed in this chapter. Second, observe the location of the event handler within a Sub. Also note the keywords in the argument of the event handler. The event handler is within the `<script>` tags.

By default, there are two arguments after the event handler name: `sender` and `e`. The first holds a reference to the object that invoked the event (such as the button that was clicked). The second holds a list of values that are sent by the object. These values vary depending on the kind of event. For example, in a `TreeView TreeNodeExpanded` event, it would include a reference to the node that was expanded. Observe that the term `ByVal` is used, which means that a copy of the original value is sent to the event handler. These arguments are discussed in detail later in the chapter.

In Visual Basic, your event handler will begin with `Sub`, the same as any VB procedure. Next comes the event handler name; by default, that will typically be in the form of the object name, underscore, and event name. Although you can name an event handler anything you want, following this simple convention will allow you to easily locate event handlers in your page. After the code, the event handler ends with the keywords `End Sub`. Within the code, you use a few simple VB statements, including assigning the label some text followed by the results of the function `Now()`. The second line changes the text on the radio button. You could have used `GetTimeButton.Text = "..."`, but by using `sender` you demonstrate the use of an argument that is discussed later in this chapter.

```
ShowTimeLabel.Text = "The date and time on the server is " & Now()
sender.Text = "Click again to update"
```

You then wrote some basic VB code that checks whether the current hour is less than 12 and, if yes, add a morning message to the label. Otherwise, it will add an afternoon message.

```
If Hour(Now()) > 12 Then
    ShowTimeLabel.Text += ". Good Afternoon"
Else
    ShowTimeLabel.Text += ". Good Morning"
End If
```

In C#, the syntax starts with the term `void` to signify a procedure or event handler. Because the name is of the form `MyObject_Event`, you know it is the latter. Because C# is more rigid, you must create a variable to hold the current time in the following bold line:

```
void GetTimeButton_Click(object sender, EventArgs e)
{
    DateTime MyDateTime;
```

Next, you put the boilerplate text into the label and follow it with the value returned from the `Now` property of the `DateTime` variable.

```
    ShowTimeLabel.Text = "The date and time on the server is " + DateTime.Now;
```

In C# you can also refer to the sender, but you must typecast it first (change the type of the data). This is done most simply as follows, where the `(Button)` will cast the sender object to a button:

```
    ((Button)sender).Text = "Click to Update";

if(DateTime.Now.Hour<12)
    {
        ShowTimeLabel.Text += ". Good morning.";
    }
else
    {
        ShowTimeLabel.Text += ". Good Afternoon";
    }
}
```

Now turn your attention to the server-side `<asp: button>` control in the body of the page. Notice how the button control has a property named `OnButton-Click`, as follows. This instructs the page to use that event handler when the button is clicked. ASP.NET allows you to specify an alternately named click handler, for example, if you wanted one handler to be triggered from several different buttons.

```
<asp:Button ID="GetTimeButton" Runat="server"
Text="Button"
 OnClick="GetTimeButton_Click" />
```

Transfer of Values When an Event Is Triggered

When an event is triggered, there is an automatic transfer of some information from controls (and the page in general) to the event handler. This data has been standardized into two parameters. The first is the name of the object that triggered the event, and the second is a set of values called *event arguments*.

Object Sender

The Object sender argument seems odd at first thought. After all, if you are handling an event named `MyButton_Click`, there should be no ambiguity about what object initiated the event handler; it was `MyButton`. But you may use the same event handler for several buttons or several lists. For example, in a library catalog, you may have three lists for title, subject, and author. The user is to pick from any of the three. In each case, a similar action will occur — information for a book will be retrieved and displayed. For all three, the same event handler (perhaps named `LookUp`) will be set as the `On_Click` value. The Object sender argument allows you to determine which list the user clicked and create the appropriate SQL statement.

Accessing the properties of the sender is not as easy to use as it might seem. It does not contain a simple string with the name of the sender, nor does it contain a strongly-typed reference to the control that fired the event. Rather it contains an object of the type of the sender, stored in an untyped Object variable. So the object can be a button, a list, and so on. Extracting a value is different when using Visual Basic and C#. In VB, the value of a property can be referred to in the standard `Object.Property` syntax. For example, the Object will have an `ID` property holding the name it was given in the server-side control properties. So to see the name (and two other properties) of the object that initiated the event handler, you would use the following code:

```
Label1.Text = SendingButton.ID
```

Conversely, you can affect the sender with the following:

```
SendingButton.Text = "My string"
```

> **VB lets you get away with not typecasting the Object; you do pay a performance penalty for late binding. It is always better coding practice, even in VB, to properly typecast variables before accessing their properties.**

But C# is more exacting in how it handles types. You must first cast the object; then you can read from or write to the values of the sender's properties. The following code example achieves the same objectives as the preceding VB code:

```
Button SendingButton = ((Button)sender);
Label1.Text=SendingButton.Text;
```

EventArgs

The event arguments are a set of values sent from the control to the event handler. They are specific for each kind of control. You can see the event arguments that are returned by looking in the object browser (`VWD Menu` ➪ `View` ➪ `ObjectBrowser`). For example, click through `System.Web` ➪ `UI.Webcontrols` ➪ `GridViewSelectEventArgs` and you will see the `NewSelectedIndex` argument. Instead, you can refer to the object and property directly (for example, `MyGridView.SelectedItem`). You will practice using event arguments in the Try It Out that deals with selections.

Location of Event Handlers

Event handlers, like other procedures, can be located in several places. The two basic divisions are code-inline and code-behind (that is, code inside the ASPX page file or code inside a separate class file associated to the ASPX page). Same page is easier to read and easier to transfer to the host because there is one file only. Separate code makes it easier to separate the user interface definition (controls and HTML) from the programming code (event handlers and other functions). Therefore, same page is generally used for simpler sites, hobbyist sites, or projects with just one programmer. Generally speaking, enterprise-level sites with separate teams for UI and logic will favor separate-page architecture.

An important traditional advantage of code separation was to precompile, and thus hide, the source code in the separate file. However, ASP.NET 2.0 can precompile entire sites with a command line utility named `aspnet_compiler`. In balance, code on page was easier because the designer or maintainer did not have to jump back and forth between pages. VWD also solves this problem by opening both the design and code-behind files and automatically jumping the view between them, as necessary.

So far, you have placed both server-side code as well as HTML object declarations on the same page.. The code can be located anywhere on the page, as long as it is within `<script>` tags. The code can also be broken up into several script blocks, and ASP.NET 2.0 will find the event handler regardless of its location on the page. By default, VWD will locate all on-page code in one block near the top of the page.

Code can also be located on a separate page named a CodeFile in a technique called "code-behind." The file is generally named with a `.aspx.vb` or `.aspx.cs` extension indicating its language (note the syntax of two periods to create a double extension). Start by declaring the partial class in the CodeFile, which could be named MyCodeFile.aspx.vb, as follows:

```
Imports Microsoft.VisualBasic
Partial Class MyPartialClass
     Inherits System.Web.UI.Page
     Protected Sub SeparatePageCodeButton_Click(ByVal sender As Object, ByVal e As
System.EventArgs)
        OutputLabel.Text = "From separate code page."
    End Sub
End Class
```

Then, in the ASPX page, you must indicate in the first tag which page holds the code using the three directives in the following code. Assuming the CodeFile page is named MyCodeFile.aspx.vb, you would start your ASPX page as follows:

```
<%@ Page Language="VB"
    AutoEventWireup="false"
    CodeFile="MyCodeFile.aspx.vb"
    Inherits="MyPartialClass"
    %>
```

Or, in C#, you would use the syntax that follows in the code-behind page which could be named MyCodeFile.aspx.cs.

```
public partial class MyPartialClass   : System.Web.UI.Page
{
```

```
        protected   void SeparatePageCodeButton_Click(object sender, EventArgs e)
        {
            OutputLabel.Text = "From separate code page.";
        }
    }
```

And in the ASPX page using C#, you would start with the following:

```
<%@ Page Language="C#"
 CodeFile="MyCodeFile.aspx.cs"  Inherits ="MyPartialClass" %>
```

Of course, VWD writes this automatically for you when you designate code in a separate page. AutoEventWireUp will connect all of the events of the ASPX page to their event handlers in the code-behind page. This eliminates the need to add specific reference to event handlers in the ASPX page. Note that if you AutoEventWireUp and you specify events within ASP controls, you will fire off the event twice. `CodeFile` designates the name of the file holding the code. By convention, that is the name of the ASPX file plus an extension indicating the language. The Inherits attribute indicates the partial class to use within the code file. Although it is possible to have one code file support several ASPX pages (each with its own partial class), most often each page has its own code file.

When VWD creates a new item in a folder, there is a check box option to locate code on a separate page. An alternate option is to place the code on the same page. Whichever option you choose, VWD will remember it for future new items. And, as you saw in the demonstration, VWD will autotype boilerplate code for the event handler. This assistance initiates in one of three ways:

- In Design view, you can double-click on a control and VWD will create the structure for and then jump to the default (most common) event handler.
- You can select a control, and in the Properties window, click on the lightning icon. This opens a list of events. Double-clicking on one will jump you to the appropriate handler in the source code.
- If you are in source code, you can select an item from the drop-down list in the top left of the code pane (right under the tab showing the name of the file) and then select an event from the drop-down at the top right of the pane.

There is actually a third, but fundamentally different, location for code. As discussed in Chapter 13, code can be placed in an object to be shared by all pages in the site, and the properties and methods of the object may be called from your pages. This was discussed in Chapter 13.

Try It Out #2 — Event Code Locations

In this exercise, you will see code in four locations: three places on the same page as the presentation controls and then one page where the code is in a separate file.

1. In the VWD solution explorer, right-click on your `ch16` folder and click on Add New Item. Double-check at the bottom that Place Code in Separate File is turned off, and then create a file from the Web Form template named `TIO-2-EventCodeLocations-SamePage.aspx`. Add a label named `OutputLabel` and three buttons named `TopCodeButton`, `MiddleCodeButton`, and `BottomCodeButton`. Set the buttons' `Text` property to be similar to their name.

2. When you double-click on the `TopCodeButton`, VWD will take you to the script tags at the top of the file and create a `TopCodeButton_Click` event. Add the following code:

```
<%@ Page Language="VB" %>
<script runat="server">
    Sub TopCodeButton_Click(ByVal sender As Object, ByVal e As System.EventArgs)
        OutputLabel.Text = "From code located at top of page"
    End Sub
</script>
```

3. To demonstrate that you can place a script tag in the middle of the page, add the following:

```
<html>
<head><title>Ch-16-TIO-02-CodeLocation-VB</title></head>
<body>
<h3>Chapter 16 TIO #02 Code Location- VB</h3>
    <p>
        Same Page - Visual Basic version</p>
  <form id="form1" runat="server">
      <asp:Button ID="TopCodeButton" Runat="server"
                Text="Top Code Button"
                OnClick="TopCodeButton_Click" />
      <br />
      <asp:Button ID="MiddleCodeButton" Runat="server"
                Text="Middle Code Button"
                OnClick="MiddleCodeButton_Click" />

<script runat="server">
    Sub MiddleCodeButton_Click(ByVal sender As Object, ByVal e As System.EventArgs)
        OutputLabel.Text = "From code in middle of page"
    End Sub
</script>

      <br />
      <asp:Button ID="BottomCodeButton" Runat="server"
                Text="Bottom Code Button"
                OnClick="BottomCodeButton_Click" />
      <br />
      <br />
      <asp:Label ID="OutputLabel" Runat="server"
                Text="Default Text"
                Width="398px"
                Height="39px" />
  </form>
</body>
</html>
```

4. Last on this page, create a script tag after the closing HTML tag and insert code for another event handler, as follows:

```
</body>
</html>
<script runat="server">
    Sub BottomCodeButton_Click(ByVal sender As Object, ByVal e As System.EventArgs)
        OutputLabel.Text = "From code located at bottom of page"
    End Sub
</script>
```

5. Alternatively, if you prefer C#, your page should appear as follows:

```
<%@ Page Language="C#" %>
<script runat="server">
    void TopCodeButton_Click(object sender, EventArgs e)
        {
        OutputLabel.Text = "From code located at top of page";
        }
</script>
<html>
<head><title>Ch-16-TIO-02-CodeLocation-CS</title></head>
<body>
<h3>Chapter 16 TIO #02 Code Location - CS</h3>
    <p>Same Page -  C# version</p>
  <form id="form1" runat="server">
      <asp:Button ID="TopCodeButton" Runat="server" Text="Top Code Button"
OnClick="TopCodeButton_Click" />
      <br />
      <asp:Button ID="MiddleCodeButton" Runat="server" Text="Middle Code Button"
OnClick="MiddleCodeButton_Click" />
<script runat="server">
    void MiddleCodeButton_Click(object sender, EventArgs e)
        {
        OutputLabel.Text = "From code located at top of page";
        }
</script>
      <br />
      <asp:Button ID="BottomCodeButton" Runat="server" Text="Bottom Code Button"
OnClick="BottomCodeButton_Click" /> <br />
      <br />
      <asp:Label ID="OutputLabel" Runat="server" Text="Default Text" Width="398px"
Height="39px"></asp:Label>
  </form>
</body>
</html>
<script runat="server">
    void BottomCodeButton_Click(object sender, EventArgs e)
        {
        OutputLabel.Text = "From code located at top of page";
        }
</script>
```

6. Save and run the page, noting that all three buttons work.

7. Now experiment with code on a separate page. Back in VWD's solution explorer, right-click on your `ch16` folder and click on Add New Item again. This time, turn on the option to Place Code in Separate File and then create a file from the Web Form template named `TIO-2-EventCodeLocations-SeparatePage-VB.aspx`. Add a single label and button and give them appropriate names, as follows. Double-click on the button to begin coding, and note that you are jumped to a new file page that holds only code. Add the following highlighted line:

```
Partial Class t3_aspx
    Sub SeparatePageCodeButton_Click(ByVal sender As Object, ByVal e As
System.EventArgs)
        OutputLabel.Text = "From separate code page."
    End Sub
End Class
```

8. If you prefer C#, select it in the New Item dialog box and double-click on the button to go to a C# code page. You will already see most of the following lines autotyped by VWD. Add the single highlighted line.

```
using System;
using System.Data;
using System.Configuration;
using System.Web;
using System.Web.Security;
using System.Web.UI;
using System.Web.UI.WebControls;
using System.Web.UI.WebControls.WebParts;
using System.Web.UI.HtmlControls;

public partial class TIO_2_EventCodeLocations_SeparatePage_CS_aspx
{
    protected void SeparatePageCodeButton_Click(object sender, EventArgs e)
    {
        OutputLabel.Text = "From separate code page.";
    }

}
```

9. Save and run the file in your browser, noting that code on a separate page works fine.

How It Works #2 — Event Code Locations

The first example simply demonstrates that a `<script>` tag with event handlers can be located anywhere on a page and still work. By default, VWD will place all of the event handlers after the `<%@page>` tag but before the `<html>` tag. This convention allows you and other maintainers of the code to see all of the event handlers right up front.

In the second example, you instructed VWD, in the Add New Item dialog, to place code in a separate page. The code file was automatically created by VWD with a name extension of the language. You open and jump into that page by double-clicking on the control that will invoke the handler. Alternatively, you can select a control and open all of its events in the Properties window using the lightning icon.

For both VB and C#, VWD autotypes several lines of code. You merely have to add the code specific to your goals using the proper syntax for the chosen language.

Command and Custom Button Events

Buttons on an ASPX page fire events that are handled by page-level event handlers, as demonstrated above. However, when a button is placed inside a data-bound control such as FormView or GridView, it is actually the FormView or GridView control that handles the event on the button's behalf. This may be handled automatically or may fire an event on the FormView or GridView that you can handle yourself. In any case, you are not handling the button's click event, but an event of the outer data-bound control. The button only has a simple `CommandName` property (and optional `CommandArgument` property) that indicates to the outer data-bound control the action to perform. We call this "event bubbling" in ASP.NET because the command is "bubbled" up from the button to the outer control. Consider the case where GridView has several edit buttons next to each row. You would not want to wire up a separate event handler for each of these buttons, since there may be many rows in the grid. Event bubbling allows you to handle a single GridView OnRowEditing event instead. You don't always need to handle the event, since the GridView will automatically perform some reasonable behavior in response to commands. Note that the commands that are handled automatically by the data-bound control can be different for each control. The GridView handles Select, Edit, New, Update, Insert, Delete, Cancel, and Page. You can also define your own command names and handle them yourself using the GridView's OnItemCommand event.

Using Events Raised by Command Buttons (Command Fields)

As discussed in the chapters on presenting and modifying data, command buttons can be divided into three general categories:

- **Selecting data** — Select
- **Modifying data** — Insert, New, Cancel, Update, Delete
- **Paging** — First, Last, Previous, Next, Number

A HyperLinkField doesn't render a link button like CommandField does. It simply renders a direct hyperlink tag to the browser (no postback required).

The first concept to understand is that all of the code needed for these buttons to perform their tasks is prewritten by Microsoft into the control. After all, this is the great advance in the data story for ASP.NET version 2.0: displaying and modifying data is now codeless for most scenarios. However, the designer can augment those behaviors at two points: before they perform their built-in behavior and after.

Before a command button's behavior is executed, ASP.NET 2.0 triggers an "ing" event: Inserting, Deleting, Selecting, and so on. This is an appropriate time to execute validation, typecasting, or other customized qualifying steps prior to the behavior executing. After a command button's behavior is complete, there is an "ed" event: Inserted, Deleted, Selected, and so on. This event is appropriate for checking on the success of the operation. Like other command buttons, paging controls have `PageIndexChanging` and `PageIndexChanged` events.

Using Events Raised by Buttons with Custom Behavior

The buttons we described above raise built-in events. But we can also create a button which raises a custom event, that is block of code written by the developer. For buttons with custom behavior, the designer must write all behavior, as expressed in the first few examples of this chapter where you put a button control on the page. The button was not in a data-bound control and thus could not be designated as a command button, such as Select or Insert. Instead, as the designer, you created all of the behavior in an event. One event is built into all buttons: click. Note that this is limited compared with Windows Forms or client-side code where the page exposes events such as `MouseOver` and `OnFocus`. If these more ephemeral events were handled by server-side code, the number of page refreshes (and thus round-trips) would become onerous.

Try It Out #3 — Custom Events for Buttons

This exercise looks at a GridView of products that displays both command buttons and custom buttons. The command buttons for Edit and Select review concepts of the chapters on modifying data. You will add to the GridView custom buttons for Buy and Sell that would set off the custom code for processing a transaction.

1. Create a new page named `TIO-3-EventsFromCommandButtons.aspx`, turning off the option to put code in a separate file.
2. Add a GridView that displays the products from Northwind and includes command fields for Edit and Select.
3. Open the smart task panel and select "Add two new columns"; set the field type to `CommandField` and check the Select and Edit/Update check boxes.
4. Similarly, add a new `ButtonField` by selecting "Add new columns" and then setting the `CommandName` and `Text` properties to `Buy` and `Buy`, respectively. Add another `ButtonField`, but this time, set the `CommandName` and `Text` properties to `Sell` and `Sell`, respectively.
5. Now add a `RowCommand` event handler to the GridView declaration by setting the `OnRowCommand` attribute of the GridView control to `GridView1_RowCommand`. The `RowCommand` event is raised when a button is clicked in the GridView control. The code for the RowCommand event handler as well as the entire page is as follows:

```
<%@ Page Language="VB" %>
<script runat="server">
    Sub GridView1_RowCommand(ByVal sender As Object, ByVal e As
System.Web.UI.WebControls.GridViewCommandEventArgs)
        Response.Write("Commmand Name: " & e.CommandName & "<br/>")
        Dim rowIndex As Integer = e.CommandArgument
        If e.CommandName = "Buy" Then
            Response.Write("You Bought: " & GridView1.DataKeys(rowIndex).Value)
        ElseIf e.CommandName = "Sell" Then
            Response.Write("You Sold: " & GridView1.DataKeys(rowIndex).Value)
        End If
    End Sub
</script>
<html>
<head><title>Ch-16-TIO-3-CustomButtons</title></head>
<body>
<h3>Chapter 16 TIO #3 Custom Buttons</h3>
  <form id="form1" runat="server">
      <asp:GridView ID="GridView1" Runat="server"
        DataSourceID="SqlDataSource1"
        OnRowCommand="GridView1_RowCommand"
        AutoGenerateColumns="False"
        DataKeyNames="ProductName">
          <Columns>
              <asp:CommandField ShowEditButton="true"
ShowSelectButton="true"></asp:CommandField>
              <asp:BoundField HeaderText="Product ID"
DataField="ProductID"></asp:BoundField>
              <asp:BoundField HeaderText="Product Name"
DataField="ProductName"></asp:BoundField>
              <asp:BoundField HeaderText="Unit Price" DataField="UnitPrice"
```

```
DataFormatString="{0:c}"></asp:BoundField>
              <asp:BoundField HeaderText="Units In Stock"
DataField="UnitsInStock"></asp:BoundField>
              <asp:BoundField HeaderText="Discontinued"
DataField="Discontinued"></asp:BoundField>
              <asp:ButtonField CommandName="Buy" Text="Buy"></asp:ButtonField>
              <asp:ButtonField CommandName="Sell" Text="Sell"></asp:ButtonField>
          </Columns>
      </asp:GridView>

      <asp:SqlDataSource ID="SqlDataSource1" Runat="server"
        ConnectionString="
           <%$ConnectionStrings:LocalSqlNorthwind%>"
          SelectCommand="select * from Products">
      </asp:SqlDataSource>
  </form>
</body>
</html>
```

How It Works #3 — Custom Events for Buttons

In this exercise, you used the `RowCommand` event to determine when the user has clicked the button in the GridView control. Using the `RowCommand` event, you can execute custom code whenever the click event in any of the button controls in the GridView occurs. One of the arguments to the `RowCommand` event handler is of type `GridViewCommandEventArgs`. This object exposes two important properties: `CommandName` and `CommandArgument`. The `CommandName` property allows you to identify the button that was clicked inside the GridView control, and the `CommandArgument` property provides you with an index of the clicked row. In the code, you used the combination of these properties to write out an appropriate message to the screen.

To retrieve the `ProductName` field value from the current row, you use the `DataKeys` collection of the GridView control. Note that as part of the GridView control declaration, the `DataKeyNames` attribute is set to the `ProductName` field.

List Selection and Page Events

Having covered generic event handling, you can begin to focus on events that are directly related to the topic of working with data on ASP.NET 2.0 pages. GridView and list controls both offer the ability to select one row or item. They also expose Selecting and Selected events. They pass their own identity for the sender and a set of event arguments, including the index of the selected record. However, to identify the user's choice, it is easier just to refer to the GridView or list control's `SelectedItemIndex` without using the `EventArgs`.

A series of events occurs when a page is prepared on the server to be sent to the browser: `Page_Init`, `Page_Load`, `Validation`, and finally `Page Unload`. These events are automatic for every page; they do not depend on any user action. In earlier versions of ASP.NET, data had to be bound at critical times during the page events. However, in ASP.NET 2.0, binding is handled automatically, lessening the degree to which you must know the page events.

The most commonly used event is the `Page_Load` event. You can use this event to perform operations such as setting default values for the controls or objects and so on. In particular, you can use a property called `IsPostBack` to determine whether the page is being visited for the first time (`IsPostBack = false`). For example, a page may have a label or GridView that should be visible only after the user has made an initial selection in the first rendering of the page.

Try It Out #4 — List Selection and Page Events Handling

This exercise demonstrates employment of a user selection in an event handler. The user will be able to select from a DropDownList, TreeView, or GridView.

1. Create a new page named `TIO-4-ListSelection.aspx` with the code on the same page.
2. Drag and drop a Label control onto the page and leave the ID of the control as `Label1`.
3. Drag and drop a list box and bind it to a hand-entered list of three states (use `CA`, `UT`, and `IN`).

```
<asp:DropDownList ID="DropDownList1" Runat="server"
   AutoPostBack="True"
   OnSelectedIndexChanged="DropDownList1_         SelectedIndexChanged">
  <asp:ListItem>CA</asp:ListItem>
  <asp:ListItem>IN</asp:ListItem>
  <asp:ListItem>UT</asp:ListItem>
</asp:DropDownList>
```

4. Next add a TreeView and hard-code a few layers, as follows:

```
<asp:TreeView ID="TreeView1" Runat="server"
OnSelectedNodeChanged="TreeView1_SelectedNodeChanged">
  <Nodes>
    <asp:TreeNode Value="Parent 1" Expanded="True" Text="Parent 1">
      <asp:TreeNode Value="Parent1.Leaf2" Text="Leaf 1" />
        <asp:TreeNode Value="Parent1.Leaf2" Text="Leaf 2" />
    </asp:TreeNode>
    <asp:TreeNode Value="Parent 2" Expanded="True" Text="Parent 2">
      <asp:TreeNode Value="Parent2.Leaf1" Text="Leaf 1" />
        <asp:TreeNode Value="Parent2.Leaf2" Text="Leaf 2" />
    </asp:TreeNode>
  </Nodes>
</asp:TreeView>
```

5. Add a GridView of the authors from the Pubs database, including just the ID number and last name. Enable selection for the GridView.

```
<asp:GridView ID="GridView1" Runat="server" DataSourceID="SqlDataSource1"
DataKeyNames="au_id"
  AutoGenerateColumns="False"
OnSelectedIndexChanged="GridView1_SelectedIndexChanged">
  <Columns>
    <asp:CommandField ShowSelectButton="True" />
    <asp:BoundField ReadOnly="True" HeaderText="au_id" DataField="au_id"
SortExpression="au_id" />
    <asp:BoundField HeaderText="au_lname" DataField="au_lname"
SortExpression="au_lname" />
  </Columns>
</asp:GridView>
<asp:SqlDataSource ID="SqlDataSource1" Runat="server"
```

```
      SelectCommand="SELECT * FROM [authors]"
            ConnectionString="
<%$ ConnectionStrings:LocalSqlPubs %>"
        />
```

6. Add the following three events to support clicks on each of the selectable data-bound controls:

```
<%@ Page Language="VB" %>
<script runat="server">

    Sub Page_Load(ByVal sender As Object, ByVal e As System.EventArgs)
        If (Not Page.IsPostBack) Then
            Label1.Text = "This text was set in the Page_Load event"
        End If
    End Sub

  Sub DropDownList1_SelectedIndexChanged(ByVal sender As Object, ByVal e As
System.EventArgs)
        Label1.Text = "You used the " & sender.ID
        Label1.Text += " to select " + DropDownList1.SelectedValue
    End Sub

  Sub TreeView1_SelectedNodeChanged(ByVal sender As Object, ByVal e As
System.EventArgs)
        Label1.Text = "You used the " & sender.ID
        Label1.Text += " to select " + TreeView1.SelectedNode.Value
  End Sub

    Sub GridView1_SelectedIndexChanged(ByVal sender As Object, ByVal e As
System.EventArgs)
        Label1.Text = "You used the " & sender.ID
        Label1.Text += " to select " & GridView1.SelectedValue
    End Sub
</script>
```

7. Alternatively, you can create a page using C# with a script section as follows:

```
<%@ Page Language="C#" %>
<script runat="server">
void DropDownList1_SelectedIndexChanged(Object sender, EventArgs e)
        {
        if(Page.IsPostBack)
            {
            Label1.Text = "You used the " + ((DropDownList)sender).ID;
            Label1.Text += " to select " + DropDownList1.SelectedValue;
            }
        }

void TreeView1_SelectedNodeChanged(Object sender, EventArgs e)
        {
        if(Page.IsPostBack)
            {
            Label1.Text = "You used the " + ((TreeView)sender).ID;
            Label1.Text += " to select " + TreeView1.SelectedValue;
            }
        }
```

```
void GridView1_SelectedIndexChanged(Object sender, EventArgs e)
        {
        if(Page.IsPostBack)
            {
            Label1.Text = "You used the " + ((GridView)sender).ID;
            Label1.Text += " to select " + GridView1.SelectedValue;
            }
        }
</script>
```

How It Works #4 — List Selection and Page Events Handling

In this example, you utilized the events of the controls to demonstrate event handling. Controls used in this example include DropDownList, TreeView, and GridView. Apart from these controls, you also used the `Page_Load` event to set the default text for the Label control. The `Text` property of the Label control is set for the first time only when the page is requested from the client browser. That code never gets executed after the initial load because of the `IsPostBack` property check. The `IsPostBack` property of the `Page` object returns `false` only when the page is requested for the first time. After that, it always returns `true`.

Similar to the `Page_Load` event, both the GridView and DropDownList controls expose the `SelectedIndexChanged` event that is fired whenever the selected index is changed in the page. You used those events to set the `Text` property of the Label control to the appropriate value. There is also a TreeView control in the page for which the `SelectedNodeChanged` event handler is implemented. Inside this event handler, you set the value of the selected node in the TreeView control.

Data Control Binding Events

When you data-bind a GridView control with a data source, there are two important events that get fired before the GridView is rendered. They are as follows:

- **`RowCreated`** — The `RowCreated` event is raised when each row in the GridView control is created. In this event handler, you can execute custom code, such as adding custom content to a row.
- **`RowDataBound`** — This event is raised when a data row is bound to data in the GridView control. You can use this event to modify the contents of a row when the row is bound to data.

Both of the preceding events are passed with a `GridViewRowEventArgs` object, which can be used to access the properties of the row being bound. To access a specific cell in the row, use the `Cells` property of the `GridViewRow` object. You can get access to the current `GridViewRow` object by invoking the `Row` property of the `GridViewRowEventArgs` object. It is also possible to determine the type of the current row (header row, data row, footer row, and so on) by examining the `RowType` property of the `GridViewRow` object.

Try It Out #5 — Data-Binding Events for GridView

In this exercise, you will understand how to use the `RowDataBound` event to modify the value of a field in the data source before it is displayed in a GridView control. For the purposes of this example, the Products table in the Northwind database is used. When displaying the products information, wherever the category ID is to be displayed, you will replace that with the category name by using code in the `RowDataBound` event handler.

1. Create a new page named `TIO-5-DataBindingEvents.aspx`. Add a SqlDataSource control and GridView that shows product ID, product name, and category ID fields from the Northwind Products table.
2. In the GridView declaration, add the `OnRowDataBound` attribute and set its value to an event handler method named `OnRowBound`.
3. Now add the code for the `OnRowBound` method to the top of the page, as shown:

```
<%@ Page Language="VB" %>
<script>
  Public Sub OnRowBound(ByVal sender As Object, ByVal e As GridViewRowEventArgs)
        If e.Row.RowType = DataControlRowType.DataRow Then
            e.Row.Cells.Item(2).BackColor = Drawing.Color.DarkGray
            Dim categoryName As String =  _
                GetCategoryName(CType(e.Row.Cells.Item(2).Text, Integer))
            e.Row.Cells.Item(2).Text = categoryName
        End If
  End Sub
</script>
```

4. Add within the `<script>` tags a server-side function named `GetCategoryName`. As the name suggests, this method is used to get the name of the category based on the supplied category ID. After adding the method, the page should appear as follows:

```
<%@ Page Language="VB" %>
<script runat="server">
    Public Sub OnRowBound(ByVal sender As Object, ByVal e As GridViewRowEventArgs)
                If e.Row.RowType = DataControlRowType.DataRow Then
             e.Row.Cells.Item(2).BackColor = Drawing.Color.DarkGray
             Dim categoryName As String = _
                GetCategoryName(CType(e.Row.Cells.Item(2).Text, Integer))
             e.Row.Cells.Item(2).Text = categoryName
        End If
    End Sub
    Function GetCategoryName(ByVal categoryID As Integer) As String
        Dim categoryName As String = ""
        Select Case categoryID
            Case 1
                categoryName = "Beverages"
            Case 2
                categoryName = "Condiments"
            Case 3
                categoryName = "Confections"
            Case 4
                categoryName = "Dairy Products"
            Case 5
                categoryName = "Grains/Cereals"
            Case 6
                categoryName = "Meat/Poultry"
            Case 7
                categoryName = "Produce"
            Case 8
                categoryName = "Seafood"
        End Select
        Return categoryName
```

```
    End Function
</script>
<html xmlns="http://www.w3.org/1999/xhtml" >
<head runat="server">
    <title>Ch-16-TIO-5-DataBinding Events</title>
</head>
<body>
    <form id="form1" runat="server">
    <div>
        <asp:GridView ID="GridView1" OnRowDataBound="OnRowBound" Runat="server"
            DataSourceID="SqlDataSource1" DataKeyNames="ProductID"
            AutoGenerateColumns="False">
            <Columns>
                <asp:BoundField ReadOnly="True" HeaderText="ProductID"
                    InsertVisible="False" DataField="ProductID"
                    SortExpression="ProductID"></asp:BoundField>
                <asp:BoundField HeaderText="ProductName" DataField="ProductName"
                    SortExpression="ProductName"></asp:BoundField>
                <asp:BoundField HeaderText="CategoryID" DataField="CategoryID"
                    SortExpression="CategoryID"></asp:BoundField>
            </Columns>
        </asp:GridView>
        <asp:SqlDataSource ID="SqlDataSource1" Runat="server" SelectCommand="SELECT
            [ProductName], [CategoryID], [ProductID] FROM [Products]"
            ConnectionString="<%$ ConnectionStrings:LocalSqlNorthwind %>">
        </asp:SqlDataSource>
    </div>
    </form>
</body>
</html>
```

How It Works #5 — Data-Binding Events for GridView

In this exercise, you created a GridView control that displayed information from the Products table in the Northwind database. While doing that, you also replaced the category ID with the category name from a custom function.

The GridView control declaration contains the event handler method for the `OnRowDataBound` event. Inside that method, you check to see whether the current row type is `DataRow`. If the row type is `DataRow`, you set the backcolor of the third cell (identified with the index of `2`) to dark gray. Then you retrieve the value of the category ID by using the `Text` property of the `GridViewRow` object. This category ID is sent as an argument to the `GetCategoryName` method. The `GetCategoryName` uses a `Select Case` statement to return the proper category name based on the category ID. Once the category name is obtained, it is displayed in the third cell, replacing the category ID.

General Error Events

Errors will occur in your applications. Even though you try to trap most errors using try-catch blocks, you usually don't cover every possible exception. What happens when an unhandled error occurs? Usually the user is shown the default error message produced by ASP.NET, which is not very intuitive for the normal user. Errors are a development fact, but you should strive to eliminate or handle them gracefully. With this in mind, there are three things about the error that you should know:

1. When an error occurs
2. Where it occurred
3. What the error is

ASP.NET provides an excellent approach that allows you to identify and track the errors as they occur. There are three places in ASP.NET where you can define what happens when an error occurs:

- **On the page itself** — This is done using the `Page_Error` event handler. Handling errors at this level is very simple. All you need to do is invoke the `Server.GetLastError` method to return the error. If you want to redirect to a specific page, simply call the `Response.Redirect` from this event handler. From within this event handler, you can also call the `Server.ClearError` to cancel the bubbling up of the error at any time so that the next level of error handler (which is the `Application_Error` event, in this case) is not invoked.
- **On the entire application** — This is done using the `Application_Error` event handler in the `global.asax` file. Logging the errors using the `Application_Error` event provides a centralized approach to handling errors. This event handler will be called only after the `Page_Error` event handler is called. Here also you can log the error message and redirect to another page.
- **In the customErrors section in the Web.config file** — This is the last line of defense, and the configurations specified in the `customErrors` section will come into play only after the `Page_Error` and `Application_Error` event handlers are called and only if they don't do a `Response.Redirect` or a `Server.ClearError`.

When you handle errors in the `Page_Error` or `Application_Error` events, you can get more information about the error using the `Server.GetLastError` method. The `GetLastError` method simply returns a reference to a generic `HttpException` object.

Try It Out #6 — Handling Error Events

The code in this exercise uses the previous example `TIO-5-DataBindingEvents.aspx` to demonstrate error handling. For the purposes of this demonstration, you intentionally generate an error by changing the table name in the `SelectCommand` attribute of the SqlDataSource control to an invalid value. For this error, you will employ different types of error handlers to catch the exception.

1. Make a copy of the `TIO-5-DataBindingEvents.aspx` page and rename it to `TIO-6-ErrorEvents-ver01.aspx`.
2. In the SqlDataSource declaration, modify the `SelectCommand` attribute by changing the table name in the SQL `SELECT` clause from `Products` to `NonExistentTable`. After modification, the declaration of the SqlDataSource control looks as follows:

```
<asp:SqlDataSource ID="SqlDataSource1" Runat="server" SelectCommand="SELECT
  [ProductName], [CategoryID], [ProductID] FROM [NonExistentTable]"
  ConnectionString="<%$ ConnectionStrings:LocalSqlNorthwind %>">
</asp:SqlDataSource>
```

3. Save the page as version 1 and view it in the browser. You will get an error message that says `Invalid object name 'NonExistentTable'`. In the same screen, you will also see other error attributes such as `Description`, `Exception Details`, `Source Error`, and `Stack Trace`. This user-unfriendly error message is caused because there is no event handler for handling errors.

4. Now add the `Page_Error` event to the server-side script block. The code for the `Page_Error` event is as follows:

```
Public Sub Page_Error(ByVal sender As Object, ByVal e As EventArgs)
    Response.Write("Error Message is : " & Server.GetLastError().Message)
    Server.ClearError()
End Sub
```

5. Now save the page as version 2 and view it in the browser. You will notice that the page displays the message `Error Message is : Invalid object name 'NonExistentTable'.` This message is caused by the `Response.Write` statement in the `Page_Error` event. Since the error message is cleared by the call to the `Server.ClearError` method, the exception is not propagated up through the call stack.

6. Now we will create a system to respond to any error in the application (Web site). On `TIO-6-ErrorEvents_ver02`, comment out the `Server.ClearError` line in the `Page_Error` event and save as version 3. Now the page will rely on any application-level handling of error events.

7. Check whether your application root has a `global.asax` file (it would be in `C:\Websites\BegAspNet2Db`). If the file exists, add the code line listed following this step. If the file does not exist, add an item to that folder of the type `Global Application Class` and with the name `global.asax`. Double-check that it is in `C:\Websites\BegAspNet2Db`. In the new ASAX page, find the `Application_Error` event and modify it as follows to redirect to a page that you will build shortly.

```
Sub Application_Error(ByVal sender As Object, ByVal e As EventArgs)
    Response.Redirect("~\ErrorPage.aspx")
End Sub
```

8. Add a new page named `ErrorPage.aspx` to the root of the Web site and modify the code in that page to look as follows:

```
<%@ Page Language="VB" %>
<html xmlns="http://www.w3.org/1999/xhtml" >
<head runat="server">
    <title>Error Page</title>
</head>
<body>
    <form id="form1" runat="server">
    <div>
        Error Page for entire application
    </div>
    </form>
</body>
</html>
```

9. Save the `ErrorPage.aspx` and then view the `ErrorEvents-ver03.aspx` in the browser. Since the `Server.ClearError` method is commented out in the `Page_Error` event, the control will be automatically transferred to the `Application_Error` event. In the `Application_Error` event, the control is transferred to the `ErrorPage.aspx` file by means of a `Response.Redirect` statement. This will ensure that any time an error occurs in the application, the users will be automatically redirected to the `ErrorPage.aspx` file.

10. When you are done with this exercise and have studied the How It Works, go back to the `global.asax` page and comment out the `Application_Error Response.Redirect` with a preceding single quote as follows. This will re-enable the default ASPX yellow troubleshooting page, which is more useful during your studies.

```
Sub Application_Error(ByVal sender As Object, ByVal e As EventArgs)
    ' Code that runs when an unhandled error occurs
    ' Response.Redirect("~\ErrorPage.aspx")
End Sub
```

How It Works #6 — Handling Error Events

In this exercise, you deliberately introduced an error by changing the table name in the `SelectCommand` attribute to an invalid value. That error was handled by providing the `Page_Error` event in the page script block. In the `Page_Error` event, a message describing the details of the error is displayed using the `Response.Write` statement. You also cleared the error by invoking the `Server.ClearError` method. This will ensure that the error is not propagated up through the call stack at the end of the `Page_Error` event.

Then you explored further by adding the `Application_Error` event to the `global.asax` file. The `Application_Error` event will be automatically invoked any time an error occurs anywhere in the application. Before you did that, you also uncommented the `Server.ClearError` method call in the `Page_Error` event. This is done to ensure that the error propagates up through the call stack to the `Application_Error` event. Then in the `Application_Error` event, the users are redirected to an error page by invoking the `Response.Redirect` statement.

Common Mistakes

Following are some mistakes commonly made in attempting to handle events for data controls:

- Failure to check Page.IsPostBack when you only want code to execute if the page is loaded for the first time.
- Attempting to directly handle the Click event of a command button inside a data-bound control. You should handle events of the outer data-bound control instead.
- Coding errors in the language for an event handler. Check the built-in help for your language to check proper syntax and conventions.
- Incorrect declaration of an event handler prototype, or using incorrect event arguments. Be sure to check the correct syntax of the event you want to handle.
- Attempting to refer to `EventArgs` properties that do not exist. Find the available event arguments in the object browser.
- Failing to typecast the arguments to an event handler.
- Incorrect understanding of the error propagation mechanism through the call stack. Page_Error fires first, then Application_Error, then custom error handlers defined in configuration.
- Failing to clear the current error (by calling the `Server.ClearError` method) while troubleshooting the error propagation mechanism.

Summary

This chapter explained how to write customized code to handle more advanced scenarios. However, recall that most common scenarios are handled automatically by ASP.NET version 2.0, including data-binding to controls and the concomitant instantiation of ADO objects. When you must use custom code, you have two steps: create an event handler within a script block and specify that handler in the server-side ASP.NET control. Custom event handlers reside within script blocks that can be anywhere on the same page or in a separate file.

Event handlers have the same basic syntax as procedures. They start, in VB or C#, with a `Sub` or `void` keyword, then contain statements, and end with `End Sub` or `}`. Following the name of the handler is an argument list with two parameters. First is the `sender`, which holds the ID of the object that invoked the event handler. In most cases, you know the `sender` independently of this argument and can refer to it directly (`Button1.MyProperty` as opposed to `Sender.MyProperty`). Second is an `EventArgs`, which holds various values depending on the type of control that evoked the handler. Again, you generally know the argument of interest and can refer to it directly as `MyControl.MyProperty` rather than `Sender.E.MyProperty`.

Buttons on the page will be one of two types. Command buttons (also called command fields) have a built-in behavior, such as Update, Edit, and Select. You can add code in event handlers, such as Updating and Updated, and so on. The "ing" executes prior to the built-in behavior, and the "ed" executes after the task is complete. Custom buttons have no built-in behavior and will only execute the code written by the designer in their event handler. GridView controls also provide various event handlers such as `RowCreated` and `RowDataBound` that you can use to customize or modify the data before it is rendered through the GridView control.

You can't debug a problem if you don't know that it exists. After you take your Web application live, you are no longer the only one who is using it (hopefully), so you need an effective plan to track errors when they occur while users are surfing your site. A great way to do this is to implement error handlers at different levels. One commonly used approach is to handle errors at the application level using the `Application_Error` event. This will allow you to consolidate the logging and notification parts of your exception handling in one convenient place.

Exercises

1. Describe how to induce VWD to automatically type for you the first and last lines of an event procedure.
2. Contrast events that end in "-ing" with events that end in "-ed."
3. What is the data type of the Object Sender in the arguments of an event handler?
4. List places where event handler code can be located.
5. Can you mix code languages on a single ASPX page?
6. Compare and contrast command buttons and custom buttons.
7. When a selection is made in a GridView or list control and you have written an event handler, how can you identify (from within the event handler) which item was selected?
8. Describe the steps to use a general error page for an entire application.

A

A Short and Practical Introduction to SQL Statements

Structured Query Language (SQL) is the most universal means to request data from a database. Almost every front-end can send a SQL statement to a data source and almost every database can understand a SQL command. This book focuses on Microsoft ASP.NET 2.0 pages sending SQL statements from the data source controls. The same statements can be sent from Visual Basic, C++, Oracle front ends, Cold Fusion, Access, and WebSphere. Because SQL is the near-universal language to request a set of data, you can learn one syntax and be able to operate in dozens of environments.

SQL is primarily a declarative language, not a procedural language. Consider an example of getting a set of all the orders placed by Acme Company. In a procedural language, you would write several lines of code to move to the first Order record and open it. Then you would write more lines of code that would check to see if the customer for that order was Acme. If yes, you would copy the record into the results set. Then, another line of code would move you to the next record and restart the checking process. SQL statements work differently. You create one statement that describes what you want back and send that to the data source. How the database management system gets the result set is of no interest to us; that is completely internal and proprietary to that software vendor. After a few hundred milliseconds, you get back the result set. Keeping this procedural versus declarative model in mind, you will send just a single SQL statement to the data source for most objectives.

Having noted that SQL is declarative, it is possible to write multiple lines of SQL statements into a structure called a stored procedure (SPROC) that can include procedural commands such as looping and conditionals. SPROCs are used in more complex scenarios, where the declarative nature of the language is augmented with some simple procedural flow.

SQL is a standard for a language, not a software product. You can type a SQL statement any place that can hold text; there is no need for a development environment or editor. Having said that, there are tools to help you build SQL statements. Perhaps the most well-known is the QueryBuilder in Access. Using this drag-and-drop interface, you can add fields, set criteria, and create alias names. If you click through View ➪ SQL, you can see how Access has converted the GUI into the text of a SQL statement. VWD will also build SQL statements for you. For example, when you drag and drop fields from the database explorer to the page, VWD writes SQL statements into several properties of the nascent data source control.

There is a consortium that sets the standards for SQL syntax, but many data source vendors have added various extensions to the language, and these are generally incompatible. Fortunately, these variations are minor, easy to learn, and not a factor for our basic discussion in this section. Microsoft uses a variation of the Data Manipulation Language (DML) called Transaction-SQL (T-SQL), which adds support for declared variables, transaction control, error handling, and row processing to the consortium's SQL functions. All of the statements in this presentation have been tested in Microsoft SQL Server Express (the lighter-weight version of the Yukon release of SQL Server).

The SQL consortium defines three broad areas of the language:

- The Data Definition Language (DDL) sets standards for SQL statements that create databases, tables, columns, and other elements of the schema.
- The Data Manipulation Language (DML) defines how to read and write to the data.
- The Data Control Language (DCL) outlines the statements for security schemes to determine who can perform what actions on the data.

This presentation only concerns the DML.

Try It Out #1 — SQL SELECT Statement Tester

This page allows you to test SQL SELECT statements against the Northwind database. Download the page from the book's Web site or type it as follows. On screen, the gray area gives you pre-typed SQL SELECT statements to try. The green area is where you can drag and drop a statement and run it. The yellow area is for results. You can find the page in the downloads. The source code follows, along with some variations in the following paragraphs.

```
<%@ Page Language="VB" %>
<!DOCTYPE html PUBLIC "-//W3C//DTD XHTML 1.1//EN"
"http://www.w3.org/TR/xhtml11/DTD/xhtml11.dtd">
<script runat="server">
    Sub Page_Load(ByVal sender As Object, ByVal e As System.EventArgs)
        SelectCommandInUse.Text = SqlDataSource1.SelectCommand
    End Sub

    Sub Button1_Click(ByVal sender As Object, ByVal e As System.EventArgs)
        SqlDataSource1.SelectCommand = SqlStatementNew.Text
        SelectCommandInUse.Text = SqlDataSource1.SelectCommand
        SqlStatementNew.Text = ""
    End Sub
</script>
<html xmlns="http://www.w3.org/1999/xhtml" >
<head runat="server">
```

```
    <title>Appendix: SQL Statements Introduction</title>
</head>
<body>
    <form id="form1" runat="server">
    <div>
        <h2>Appendix - A Short and Practical Introduction to SQL Statements </h2>
            <table>
                <tr>
                    <td style="width: 386px">
                        <h3> From Beginning ASP.NET 2.0 and Databases<br />
                            by John Kauffman       ISBN 0764570811</h3>
                    </td>
                    <td style="width: 459px">
                        <span style="color: #ff0033">
        This is a page for developer education and testing. In a deployed page
never use in
        a SQL Statement any text entered by users (danger of SQL injection attack).
Instead allow the
        users to select from a list or radio buttons.<br />
                        </span>
                    </td>
                </tr>
            </table>
        <span style="color: red">
        </span>
        <br />
        <table bordercolor="black">
            <tr>
                <td bgcolor="#ccffff" height="100" valign="top" style="width:
300px">
                    Enter (or drag and drop from gray region at right) a new SQL
statement
                    for the SelectCommand
                </td>
                <td bgcolor="#ccffff" style="width: 542px;" align="center"
height="100px" valign="top">
                    <asp:TextBox ID="SqlStatementNew" Runat="server" Width="384px"
Height="200px" TextMode="MultiLine" Rows="5"></asp:TextBox><br />
                    <br />
                    <asp:Button ID="Button1" Runat="server"
                        Text="Submit New statement"
                        OnClick="Button1_Click"
                        />
                    <br />
                </td>
                <td style="width: 700px" valign="top" align="left" rowspan="4"
bordercolor="black" bgcolor="silver">
                    Try these SQL statements for the Northwind database:<br />
                    <br />
                    <span style="font-family: Courier New">SELECT
FirstName,LastName FROM Employees
                    <br /><br />
                    SELECT EmployeeID FROM Employees
                    <br /><br />
                    SELECT EmployeeID,FirstName,LastName FROM Employees
                    <br /><br />
```

```
                    SELECT<br />  EmployeeID,   FirstName,
  LastName<br />    FROM Employees
                    <br /><br />
                    SELECT CategoryName,CategorySales FROM [Category Sales for
1997]
                    <br /><br />
                    SELECT * FROM Employees
                    <br /><br />
                    SELECT EmployeeID AS 'Associate Number', LastName FROM
Employees
                    <br /><br />
                    SELECT OrderID, RIGHT(OrderId,3)
                    AS 'ShortID' FROM Orders
                    SELECT OrderID, YEAR(OrderDate) FROM Orders
                    <br /><br />
                    SELECT OrderID, OrderDate, CustomerID FROM Orders WHERE
CustomerID = 'CHOPS'
                    <br /><br />
                    SELECT OrderID, OrderDate, CustomerID FROM Orders WHERE OrderID
&gt;= 10500
                    <br /><br />
                    SELECT OrderID, OrderDate, CustomerID FROM Orders WHERE
OrderDate='11/20/1997'
                    <br /><br />
                    SELECT OrderID, OrderDate, CustomerID FROM Orders WHERE
OrderDate BETWEEN '1/15/1998'
                    AND '1/31/1998'
                    <br /><br />
                    SELECT OrderID, OrderDate, CustomerID FROM Orders WHERE
YEAR(OrderDate)&lt;1998
                    <br /><br />
                    SELECT OrderID, OrderDate, CustomerID AS 'Client' FROM Orders
WHERE CustomerID = 'chops'
                    <br /><br />
                    ***Wrong Syntax:
                    <br />
                    SELECT OrderID, OrderDate, CustomerID AS 'Client' FROM Orders
WHERE Client = 'chops'
                    <br /><br />
                    SELECT CustomerID, CompanyName FROM Customers WHERE CompanyName
LIKE 'C%'
                    <br /><br />
                    SELECT CustomerID, OrderDate FROM Orders WHERE
CustomerID='CHOPS' AND YEAR(OrderDate)=1997
                    <br /><br />
                    SELECT CustomerID, OrderDate FROM Orders WHERE
CustomerID='CHOPS' OR YEAR(OrderDate)=1997
                    <br /><br />
                    SELECT OrderID, OrderDate FROM Orders WHERE NOT Year(OrderDate)
= 1997
                    <br /><br />
                    SELECT OrderID, OrderDate, CustomerID FROM Orders ORDER BY
CustomerID ASC
                    <br /><br />
```

```
                    SELECT OrderID, OrderDate, CustomerID FROM Orders ORDER BY
OrderDate DESC
                    <br /><br />
                    SELECT OrderID, OrderDate, CustomerID FROM Orders ORDER BY
CustomerID ASC, OrderDate
                    DESC
                    <br /><br />
                    SELECT DISTINCT Country FROM Customers SELECT TOP 10 ProductID,
UnitPrice FROM Products
                    <br /><br />
                    SELECT TOP 10 ProductID, UnitPrice FROM Products ORDER BY
UnitPrice DESC
                    </span>
                </td>
            </tr>
            <tr>
                <td bgcolor="#ffffcc" height="100px" valign="bottom" style="width:
300px">
                    <br />
                    SelectCommand<br />
                    in use below<br />
                </td>
                <td bgcolor="#ffffcc" style="width: 542px" bgcolor="yellow"
height="100px" valign="bottom">
                    <asp:Label ID="SelectCommandInUse" Runat="server"
                        Width="375px" Height="73px" ></asp:Label>
                </td>
            </tr>
            <tr>
                <td bgcolor="#ffffcc" valign="top" style="width: 300px">
                    <br />
                    Results:</td>
                <td bgcolor="#ffffcc" style="width: 542px" valign="top">
                    <br />

        <asp:GridView ID="GridView1" Runat="server" DataSourceID="SqlDataSource1">
        </asp:GridView>
                </td>
            </tr>
            <tr>
                <td valign="top" height="1000" style="width: 300px">
                </td>
                <td style="width: 542px" valign="top">
                </td>
                <td style="width: 700px" valign="top" align="left" rowspan="1">
                </td></tr>
        </table>
        <asp:SqlDataSource ID="SqlDataSource1" Runat="server"
        ConnectionString= "<%$ connectionStrings:LocalSqlNorthwind %>"
        SelectCommand = "SELECT OrderID,CustomerID,OrderDate FROM Orders">
        </asp:SqlDataSource>
    </div>    </form></body></html>
```

If you have not set up a connection string in the Web.config, as in Chapter 3 Exercise 2, you can use this code for the SqlDataSource:

```
<asp:SqlDataSource ID="SqlDataSource1" Runat="server"
ConnectionString= "Server=(local)\SQLExpress;
    Integrated Security=True;
    Database=Northwind;
    Persist Security Info=True"
providerName="System.Data.SqlClient"
SelectCommand = "SELECT OrderID,CustomerID,OrderDate FROM Orders">
```

Following is the script in C#:

```
<%@ Page Language="C#" %>
<!DOCTYPE html PUBLIC "-//W3C//DTD XHTML 1.1//EN"
"http://www.w3.org/TR/xhtml11/DTD/xhtml11.dtd">
<script runat="server">
    void Page_Load(Object sender, EventArgs e)
        {SelectCommandInUse.Text = SqlDataSource1.SelectCommand;
        }


    void Button1_Click(Object sender, EventArgs e)
        {SqlDataSource1.SelectCommand = SqlStatementNew.Text;
        SelectCommandInUse.Text = SqlDataSource1.SelectCommand;
        SqlStatementNew.Text = "";
        }
</script>
```

How It Works #1 — SQL SELECT Statement Tester

On the first load, the SqlDataSource uses the SELECT statement that is hard-coded in the page. The user can see the SQL Statement that was used in the yellow row and the results in the GridView at the bottom of the page. At the top of the page is a textbox in which you can type SQL statements. When the Submit New Statement button is clicked, the typed statement of the textbox SelectCommandNew is set as the new SelectCommand of the SqlDataSource, and the page is refreshed. In the download page is a column on the right with many more pre-typed SQL statements than the above code to speed your exploration of the syntax.

Note that ASP.NET 2.0 uses separate commands for reading (SELECT) and writing or deleting (INSERT, UPDATE, and DELETE). This page sends only the typed SQL statement to the `SELECT` command, so data modifying commands such as DELETE... will not work.

Overall Syntax

The syntax of a SQL statement is designed to be parallel to a spoken English request for data. Common nouns and verbs are used to make a sentence-like statement in plain text. To start, here are some simple rules for typing the statement. Examples (partial code) follow each rule.

- Generally, SQL statement keywords are in all uppercase, while names of database objects (fields, tables) are in mixed case.

```
SELECT FirstName,LastName FROM Employees
```

- Spaces must surround keywords in the statement.

```
SELECT EmployeeID FROM Employees
```

- An optional semicolon signifies the end of a SQL statement.

```
SELECT EmployeeID,FirstName,LastName FROM Employees;
```

- Lists of items are separated by commas (commas after spaces are optional).

```
SELECT EmployeeID,FirstName,LastName FROM Employees
SELECT EmployeeID, FirstName, LastName FROM Employees
```

- Extra returns, tabs, and spaces (collectively called white space) are ignored. They can be used liberally to make the statement more readable to the human eye.

```
SELECT
  EmployeeID, FirstName, LastName
         FROM Employees
```

- If there is any ambiguity about names of fields that are in more than one table, use the table name followed by a period and the field name.

```
SELECT Employees.EmployeeID, Orders.EmployeeID
```

Most applications require the entire statement to be in double quotes because it will be a string that is handed off to the data source. For example, the SelectCommand used in ASP.NET 2.0 requires the statement to be in double quotes. However, when entering a SQL statement into the textbox of a property window, you do not need the double quotes because VWD will add them for you.

Objects in the database, such as field names, table names, views, and stored procedures (SPROCs), can be referred to directly by name. They should not be in quotes. The database will find the correct object from the schema. However, if the object name contains a space, there must be a designation that sets off the entire name. Depending on the provider, place the space-containing object name in square brackets, [My Spacey Object Name], or in quotes, 'My Spacey Object Name'.

When presenting values, such as a string to be matched or a new number to be added to a field, SQL has three rules. Note that these apply to values such as "Abraham," not to object names such as a column FirstName.

- Literal strings are enclosed in single quotes, as are dates.

```
UPDATE FirstName VALUES('Abraham')
UPDATE DateBirth VALUES('01/01/2000')
```

- Numbers and Booleans do not need quotes.

```
UPDATE Price VALUES(2.34)
UPDATE Member VALUES(True)
```

- Values may be substituted from a parameters collection, in which case the syntax varies with the front end, provider, and database vendor. Some examples used in versions of ASP follow:

```
UPDATE Price VALUE(@PriceTextBox) WHERE ItemID=@DropDownListSelection)
INSERT INTO Authors (ID, Name, Address) VALUES (?, ?, ?)
```

> **For some providers, there is no naming of parameters; rather, they must appear in the correct order, and they are read into the argument from first to last.**

Retrieving Columns of Data

The basic command to retrieve data is SELECT, followed by the columns desired and then the keyword FROM and the name of the table.

```
SELECT EmployeeID, FirstName, LastName FROM Employees
```

Records can be retrieved from Views, Queries, or SPROCs in the same manner:

```
SELECT CategoryName,CategorySales FROM [Category Sales for 1997]
```

If an object's name has a space in it, enclose the entire name in brackets, as follows. Note that this particular example does not work for the Northwind sample database because these are not real field names.

```
SELECT [Order ID], [Order Date] FROM [Order Details]
```

If you want all of the columns, you can use the wildcard `*` instead of a list of columns.

```
SELECT * FROM Employees
```

You can create an alias, or renaming, of columns as follows. Then, in your front end, you must refer to the column by its alias.

```
SELECT EmployeeID AS 'Associate Number', LastName FROM Employees
```

Most databases support a set of functions that can be used to modify data in columns. Here is where you see large variability among vendors of databases because there is no mention of these functions in the SQL standards. Note that functions with the same name can have subtle differences between vendors. The following will return just the last three digits of the EmployeeID data from Microsoft products. The second example extracts the year data from the OrderDate field that contains time, day, month, and year.

```
SELECT OrderID, RIGHT(OrderId,3) AS 'ShortID' FROM Orders
SELECT OrderID, YEAR(OrderDate) FROM Orders
```

Limiting the Set of Records

Frequently, you won't want all of the possible records to be included in the answer set. A `WHERE` clause can be appended to the statement followed by an expression.

```
SELECT OrderID, OrderDate, CustomerID FROM Orders WHERE CustomerID =  'CHOPS'
SELECT OrderID, OrderDate, CustomerID FROM Orders WHERE OrderID >=  10500
SELECT OrderID, OrderDate, CustomerID FROM Orders WHERE OrderDate='11/20/1997'
```

SQL supports the `BETWEEN ... AND` keywords, as follows:

```
SELECT OrderID, OrderDate, CustomerID FROM Orders
  WHERE CustomerID BETWEEN '1/15/1998' AND '1/31/1998'
```

A function can be used in the `WHERE` clause:

```
SELECT OrderID, OrderDate, CustomerID FROM Orders WHERE YEAR(OrderDate)<1998
```

If a column is given an alias with `AS` and you use that column in a `WHERE` clause, you must refer to the column with its original name, not the alias.

```
SELECT OrderID, OrderDate, CustomerID AS 'Client' FROM Orders
  WHERE CustomerID = 'chops'

***Wrong Syntax (a common mistake):
SELECT OrderID, OrderDate, CustomerID AS 'Client' FROM Orders
  WHERE Client = 'chops'
```

SQL supports an option to match more than one target pattern in a string using `LIKE` and wildcard(s). The percent (`%`) wildcard represents any number of characters. The underscore (_) represents a single leading character. To see all of the customers whose names begin with the letter C, you would use the following:

```
SELECT CustomerID, CustomerName FROM Customers WHERE CustomerName LIKE 'C%'
```

Multiple expressions can be included in the `WHERE` clause using the logical operators `AND`, `OR`, and `NOT`. The following example gives only orders placed by the customer coded CHOPS during 1997.

```
SELECT CustomerCode, OrderDate FROM Orders
  WHERE CustomerID='CHOPS' AND YEAR(OrderDate)=1997
```

The following example gives all of the orders from CHOPS in all years, as well as all the orders placed (by everyone) in 1997:

```
SELECT CustomerCode, OrderDate FROM Orders
  WHERE CustomerID='CHOPS' OR YEAR(OrderDate)=1997
```

The `NOT` keyword reverses the result of a logical expression. A list of orders but without the orders of 1997 follows:

```
SELECT OrderID, OrderDate FROM Orders WHERE NOT Year(OrderDate) = 1997
```

Ordering the Records

The set of records is ordered. By default, it will be ordered by the primary key of the table. You can override the order by appending an `ORDER BY` clause (after the `WHERE` clause, if used) followed by `ASC` for ascending and `DESC` for descending.

```
SELECT OrderID, OrderDate, CustomerID FROM Orders ORDER BY CustomerID ASC
SELECT OrderID, OrderDate, CustomerID FROM Orders ORDER BY OrderDate DESC
```

A tie in the order is broken by specifying a second order column. The following example lists orders starting with the lowest CustomerID. For the records with the same CustomerID, the presentation is from latest to earliest.

```
SELECT OrderID, OrderDate, CustomerID FROM Orders
  ORDER BY CustomerID ASC, OrderDate DESC
```

Distinct and Top

You can eliminate repeats in a results set by using the `DISTINCT` keyword, as follows. This technique is particularly useful when making a data set of choices for a list to present to the user, such as states or customers.

```
SELECT DISTINCT Country FROM Customers
```

Another option is to limit the number of results in a set according to a criterion by using the `TOP` keyword. For example, the most expensive items can be obtained by the following:

```
SELECT TOP 10 ProductID, UnitPrice FROM Products
```

Although an `ORDER BY` clause is not required, it is generally used as in the following example:

```
SELECT TOP 10 ProductID, UnitPrice FROM Products ORDER BY UnitPrice DESC
```

Changing Data

SQL supports three basic commands for changing data. `INSERT INTO` adds a new record and can optionally stock its fields with data. The first example creates a record and fills it with data that is hard-coded. The second uses ASP.NET-specific syntax to create a new record and fills it with data that comes from a parameter collection. Note that the values list must be in the same order as the columns list.

```
INSERT INTO Employees (FirstName, LastName) VALUES ('Abraham','Lincoln')
INSERT INTO Employees (FirstName, LastName) VALUES (@FirstName,@LastName)
```

`UPDATE` changes values in an existing record. Be careful to include a `WHERE` clause that identifies the one record to change, as in the first line in the following example. If you want to update a value in all records where it appears, you can use the second syntax. The third replaces a value with a `NULL`. The fourth example shows updating all records in the table.

```
UPDATE Employees SET Country = 'America' WHERE LastName = 'Davalio'
UPDATE Employees SET Country = 'America' WHERE Country = 'USA'
UPDATE Employees SET Country = NULL WHERE Country = 'America'
UPDATE Employees SET Country = 'United Nations'
```

Keep in mind when inserting or updating that some fields may automatically be given values from the database, such as an automatic numbering for the ID field. Trying to add or change a value for an ID field generally throws an error.

`DELETE` removes an entire record. The first case, rarely used, eliminates all records from a table. The second, more common, case eliminates only one record, assuming that the ID field is unique (a primary key). The third example eliminates a group of records. Use caution when experimenting with these statements; make a copy of your database for testing purposes to try these commands.

```
DELETE FROM Orders
DELETE FROM Orders WHERE OrderID = 10500
DELETE FROM Orders WHERE Year(OrderDate) = 1997
```

As with updating, constraints and built-in behavior may prevent you from carrying out a `DELETE`. If you are trying to delete a record that is a foreign key for another table, you will likely invoke an error. For example, deleting the customer CHOPS would leave all of their orders in limbo, no longer connected to a customer.

Joins

Last, we will cover a very basic example of returning a set of records that display values from more than one table via relationships. If you want a results set of all the orders and you want to show both the order date (from the Orders table) and the customer's telephone number (from the Customers table) you have a problem because they are in two different tables. The solution is to use a join, as in the following example:

```
SELECT Orders.OrderDate, Customers.Phone
  FROM Customers INNER JOIN Orders
         ON Customers.CustomerID = Orders.CustomerID
```

Joins have many permutations, which can become wickedly tricky. Read a SQL textbook to understand the `INNER JOIN` and `OUTER JOIN`.

SQL Injections

Beware of a major problem with using SQL statements. Strenuously avoid allowing typing from a user to go into a SQL statement. Instead, require the user to make a selection from a populated control such as a list or set of radio buttons and then use the ASP.NET 2.0 parameter features to substitute the value into the SQL statement.

The problem derives from the fact that a second SQL statement can be added to a SQL statement and they will both be executed. So, if your page has a statement such as `Select * From Customers WHERE X`, you might (erroneously) set up your page to allow the user to type a string in a textbox and substitute that for X in the code. But a user could type something like `Acme;Delete FROM Orders`. The `Acme` would complete your intended SQL statement; however, the semicolon indicates that a new SQL statement will be coming, which means your database would get the statement `Delete FROM Orders`.

B

Exercise Answers

Chapter 1

Exercise 1

What is the basic pattern for showing data on an ASP.NET 2.0 page?

Exercise 1 solution

Use two controls: a data source control to connect to the data and a data-bound control to display the data on the page.

Exercise 2

Name several types of data sources that ASP.NET 2.0 supports.

Exercise 2 solution

SQL Server, Oracle, Access, XML files, any other OLEDB-enabled data source, and so on.

Exercise 3

Name several ways that ASP.NET 2.0 can display data.

Exercise 3 solution

Grid (GridView), list of values for one record (DetailsView), tree (TreeView), list boxes.

Exercise 4

What is the difference between the .NET Framework 2.0 and ASP.NET 2.0?

Exercise 4 solution

The framework is a set of standards for development of many types of software, including applications that run on the desktop without connection to the Internet. ASP.NET 2.0 is a technology to write Web-based applications. ASP.NET 2.0 subscribes to the standards of the .NET Framework as a whole and thus can communicate efficiently with other .NET-standardized software.

Exercise 5

Make some observations comparing SQL Server, MSDE, and SSE.

Exercise 5 solution

SQL Server is the full-scale database management software from Microsoft. MSDE and SSE are for local use by hobbyists or developers. Both MSDE and SSE have limited capabilities and are not designed to support public deployed Web sites. MSDE is based on SQL Server 2000 while SSE derives from the SQL Server Yukon version.

Chapter 2

Exercise 1

Describe the difference between the terms Access, JET, and MDB file.

Exercise 1 solution

Access is an application that can store data, receive and display data, and support development of a user interface.

JET is the core of Access that stores and serves up data.

MDB is a file format for holding data and user interfaces such as forms and reports.

Exercise 2

What two basic ASP.NET 2.0 server-side controls are required to display data from an MDB file?

Exercise 2 solution

- AccessDataSourceControl
- A data-bound control such as the GridView

Exercise 3

Explain the advantage of using syntax a instead of syntax b, which follow.

a. `C:\Websites\MySite\app_Data\MyFile.mdb`

b. `~\app_Data\MyFile.mdb`

Exercise 3 solution

The second syntax is relative to the root of the Web site. When the Web site is deployed from your development to your production Web server, there will be no need to change the reference. In the first code sample, a deployment to a host that uses a drive named D would require a change in your source code.

Exercise 4

List disadvantages to using Access as a source of data for Web sites.

Exercise 4 solution

- Access cannot handle many simultaneous users.
- Access uses a slow procedure for preventing simultaneous changes.
- Access is less secure.
- Many hosts will not allow Access to be run on a Web server.
- The Access model for handling parameters makes coding more difficult.

Exercise 5

If you want to write more sophisticated SelectCommands, what language should you study?

Exercise 5 solution

Structured Query Language (SQL).

Exercise 6

When handling an Access connection failure, you will use objects with three names. Fill in the following table:

Purpose	Object Name
Connection with the MDB file	
Transfer arguments to the event handler	
Hold the exceptions raised by the connection	

Exercise 6 solution

Purpose	Object Name
Connection with the MDB file	AccessDataSourceControl
Transfer arguments to the event handler	SqlDataSourceStatusEventArgs
Hold the exceptions raised by the connection	System.Data.OleDb.OleDbException

Chapter 3

Exercise 1

List differences in the connection string for AccessDataSource and SqlDataSource.

Exercise 1 solution

Access data is held in a file, so the connections string identifies the file. SQL holds information in a database, so the name of the database is identified.

Access MDB file will be in a path using Windows file syntax, whereas SQL will be on a server and instance.

Exercise 2

What is the difference between SQL Server, MSDE, and SSE?

Exercise 2 solution

SQL Server is designed for full-scale deployment. SSE is designed for development or for local and lightweight uses. MSDE is an older form of SSE: SSE is based on the upcoming Yukon version, while MSDE is based on SQL 2000.

Exercise 3

What is the syntax to refer to an SSE instance on your local machine?

Exercise 3 solution

```
Server = (local)\SQLExpress
```

Exercise 4

What are the benefits of storing the connection string in the Web.config file?

Exercise 4 solution

A connection string holds sensitive information, including the name of a server, name of a database, user ID, and password. By storing the connection string in the Web.config file, that information is further hidden from the user. In addition, information in the Web.config can be encrypted.

Exercise 5

What event is of interest when detecting and responding to a connection failure?

Exercise 5 solution

The OnSelected event of the data source control.

Exercise 6

What arguments are of interest when detecting and responding to a connection failure?

Exercise 6 solution

`e,exception` identifies if there was a failure of any sort. If the `e.exception` equals a `System.Data.SQlClient.SqlException`, you know it was a connection failure.

Chapter 4

Exercise 1

Describe the major differences between connecting to an unsecured MDB file and a password-protected MDB file.

Exercise 1 solution

When connecting to an MDB without security, we use the AccessDataSource. If there is a password, we use the SqlDataSource so that we can pass the credentials.

Exercise 2

Name the two files specified in a connection string to an MDB with user-level security.

Exercise 2 solution

One file name (`.MDB`) is the database and the other file (`.MDV`) is the workgroup file that contains the security information.

Exercise 3

When setting up a MySQL, you are asked for the initial catalog. What does that mean in MySQL terminology?

Exercise 3 solution

Catalog in general SQL terms translates to database in MySQL.

Exercise 4

Why didn't we specify a provider in Chapter 3 when connecting to Microsoft SQL Server?

Exercise 4 solution

The provider for Microsoft SQL Server is the default and thus does not have to be stated in the code.

Exercise 5

Which data source is used to connect to MySQL and Oracle?

Exercise 5 solution

SqlDataSource with a non-default provider.

Exercise 6

In earlier versions of ASP, it was necessary to instantiate ADO objects. Why is this not necessary in ASP.NET 2.0?

Exercise 6 solution

The smart data controls (data source controls and data-bound controls) automatically instantiate ADO objects as needed and with the proper properties.

Exercise 7

What additional piece of software must be obtained to connect to a MySQL database?

Exercise 7 solution

A MySQL driver. Currently, a driver is available for an ODBC connection. Expect one or more third-party OLEDB managed code providers to be available soon.

Exercise 8

Contrast the `Password` property of the connection string when used with an Access database password security scheme and an Access workgroup security scheme.

Exercise 8 solution

When used with an Access database password security scheme, the `Password` property means the password for the entire database. When used with an Access Workgroup security scheme, the `Password` property refers to the user's specific password.

Chapter 6

Exercise 1

Compare and contrast the term *header* as used in the GridView and the DetailsView controls.

Exercise 1 solution

For both controls, the heading is a set of one cell per field that normally shows the name of the field. The difference is in the physical location of the heading. GridView has the heading as the first row, running horizontally across the top of the GridView. DetailsView places the heading as the first column, running vertically down the left side of the DetailsView control.

Exercise 2

State the precedence of formatting in different tags and files.

Exercise 2 solution

The top-level GridView CSS setting is the least precedent and a column/field `ItemStyle` property takes precedence over all others:

```
GridView CssClass < GridView Style property < RowStyle CssClass < RowStyle property
< Column/Field ItemStyle CssClass < Column/Field ItemStyle property
```

When alternate display of rows is invoked (editing or selecting), the precedence becomes the following:

```
RowStyle < AlternatingRowStyle < SelectedRowStyle < EditRowStyle or InsertRowStyle
```

Exercise 3

Describe the difference between the terms *borders* and *gridlines*.

Exercise 3 solution

Borders refers to the single rectangle around the entire GridView or DetailsView control. *Gridlines* refers to the internal lines that separate the cells; they can be modified in two ways.

Exercise 4

Describe the three systems for defining a color in data-bound controls.

Exercise 4 solution

- RGB uses three hexadecimal values for Red, Green, and Blue in the format RRGGBB. RGB colors are a logical selection for desktops but do not always translate well to the Web.
- WWW palette of about 150 colors that have been recognized and named by the WWW Consortium. They should be available in every modern Web browser.
- System will display a color that depends on the user's Windows settings with a scheme defining a color for each part of a window, as set by each Windows user.

Exercise 5

Describe the difference between cell spacing and cell padding.

Exercise 5 solution

Cell spacing is the distance between the borders of cells. It is spacing between cells. Cell padding is an empty space between the inner edge of a cell and its contents. It is a distance within cells.

Exercise 6

Write the proper syntax for a dotted cell border.

Exercise 6 solution

```
GridView1.BorderStyle = BorderStyle.Dotted
```

Exercise 7

Write the two syntaxes for setting a property for a style.

Exercise 7 solution

Option 1:

```
<asp:GridView ID="GridView1" Runat="server">
   <Columns>
   <HeaderStyle
           Font-Bold="true">
   </HeaderStyle>
   </Columns>
</asp:GridView>
```

Option 2:

```
     <asp:GridView ID="GridView1"
HeaderStyle-Font-Bold="true">
     </ asp:GridView>
```

Exercise 8

In what situation will the EmptyDataRowStyle be applied to a data-bound control?

Exercise 8 solution

EmptyDataRowStyle will be applied when there is a set of (no rows) returned by the data source control. The single EmptyDataRowStyle will be used instead of all the other styles that would have been used if there had been row(s) returned.

Exercise 9

Why does the DetailsView control have an InsertRow style but the GridView lacks that style?

Exercise 9 solution

Because the GridView is not a control for inserting new records. That task is only available in the DetailsView.

Chapter 7

Exercise 1

What is necessary to enable paging in a GridView control?

Exercise 1 solution

A data source that supports paging and `GridView.AllowPaging=true`.

Exercise 2

What two event arguments are useful when creating custom sort expressions?

Exercise 2 solution

`e.SortExpression` and `e.SortDirection`.

Exercise 3

Describe the syntax of the `SortExpression` property.

Exercise 3 solution

Field name followed by ASC or DESC, then a comma. Repeat the pattern for a tie-breaking field. For example, to sort on last name with first name as a tie-breaker, you would use the following syntax:

```
LastName ASC,FirstName ASC
```

Exercise 4

Name the interfaces that enable the user to navigate through pages in a GridView or DetailsView control.

Exercise 4 solution

Numeric, First/Last, and Next/Previous.

Exercise 5

Where in the Properties window do you set the kind of paging links shown (First/Last, Numeric, and so on)?

Exercise 5 solution

Select the GridView. Look in Properties Windows ➪ Paging ➪ Mode.

Exercise 6

Describe how a user might be misled about which record is currently selected.

Exercise 6 solution

A selection is made, and then a sort is performed. The selected style will remain on the same line of the GridView, even though after the sort there is a new record on that line.

Chapter 9

Exercise 1

In a data source control SelectCommand `WHERE` clause, what is the difference between `Xxx` and `@Xxx`?

Exercise 1 solution

`Xxx` refers to the name of the field in the database. `@Xxx` refers to a variable that holds a value filled by the `<Parameters>` tag. The value in the parameter would come from a querystring (forwarded by the requesting page), a control on the page, or another source.

Exercise 2

Write the syntax to include the value `567` in the MemberID field in a URL that calls a page named `MemberProfile.aspx` at the `MyYachtClub.org` site.

Exercise 2 solution

```
http://MyYachtClub.Org\MemberProfile.aspx?MemberID=567
```

Exercise 3

Continuing from Question 2, on the page `MemberProfile.aspx`, write the code for a SqlDataSource control to show information for only the member ID passed from the URL.

Exercise 3 solution

```
<asp:SqlDataSource ID="SqlDataSource1" Runat="server">
    ConnectionString=" ... "
    SelectCommand="SELECT * FROM [Members] WHERE MemberID = @MemberID"
  <SelectParameters>
```

```
            <asp:QueryStringParameter Name="MemberID"
                QueryStringField="MemberID" />
        </SelectParameters>
    </asp:SqlDataSource>
```

Exercise 4

What is the default property for binding to a `ControlParameter` for a DropDownList and a GridView?

Exercise 4 solution

DropDownList–`SelectedValue` (not `Text`).

GridView–`SelectedValue`, which is the first field in the list of the `DataKeyNames` property.

Exercise 5

When populating a DropDownList from a SQL statement, how can you avoid multiple listings of the same value (for example, multiple `PA`s when four authors are from Pennsylvania)?

Exercise 5 solution

Use the `DISTINCT` keyword in the data source SelectCommand, as follows:

```
SELECT DISTINCT [state] FROM [authors]
```

Exercise 6

How can you display in a DropDownList a combination of items from hard coding and from a data source control?

Exercise 6 solution

In the DropDownList control, add the hard coded items with `<Items>` tags and set `AppendDataBoundITems = true`.

Exercise 7

How does an ASP.NET 2.0 data source `ControlParameter` handle values that are an empty string?

Exercise 7 solution

It converts them to a `NULL`.

Exercise 8

How does a data source control react to a `ControlParameter` containing a `NULL` value?

Exercise 8 solution

The data source control will not execute SelectCommands that contain a `NULL`. This behavior can be reversed with the data source control property `CancelSelectOnNullParameter=false`.

Exercise 9

The GridView control was designed to display values for many records. What controls are designed to show values for only one record at a time?

Exercise 9 solution

DetailsView control and FormView control.

Exercise 10

Describe the difference between a GridView's `DataNavigateUrlField` and `DataNavigateUrlFormatString` properties.

Exercise 10 solution

`DataNavigateUrlField` holds the URL for that record's link (however, see the next two questions for a special case).

`DataNavigateUrlFormatString` allows the value of the `DataNavigateUrlField` to be formatted with characters such as a leading `http:` or a trailing querystring.

Exercise 11

How is the value from the `DataNavigateUrlField` put into the `DataNavigateUrlFormatString`?

Exercise 11 solution

In the `DataNavigateUrlFormatString`, refer to the value of the `DataNavigateUrlField` with a {0}, as in the following:

```
DataNavigateUrlFields="MyIdField"
DataNavigateUrlFormatString=http://www.{0}.com
```

Exercise 12

How are the `DataNavigateUrlField` and `DataNavigateUrlFormatString` properties set when a GridView is calling for details of one record on another page?

Exercise 12 solution

`DataNavigateUrlField` holds an ID value for the selected record, which comes from the `GridView.SelectedField` property.

`DataNavigateUrlFormatString` holds the name of the target page (same for all records) with an appended "?ID={0}" to add the value from the `DataNavigateUrlField`.

Chapter 10

Exercise 1

Describe the differences between a bound field and a templated field.

Exercise 1 solution

A bound field shows the value in one field of the `SELECT` statement, with few layout options.

A template field is a space into which the designer can add one or more bound fields and arrange them as desired.

Exercise 2

Which controls can contain a templated field?

Exercise 2 solution

GridView, DetailsView, DataList, Repeater, and FormView.

Exercise 3

Which controls can and cannot create new records?

Exercise 3 solution

DetailsView and FormView can create new records. GridViewcannot create new records.

Exercise 4

What is the fundamental difference between DetailsView and FormView?

Exercise 4 solution

DetailsView provides some pre-formatting and default layout of all fields provided by the data source control.

FormView is a blank template in which the designer builds a presentation.

Exercise 5

Which two data-bound controls covered in this chapter are holdovers from earlier versions of ASP.NET and thus are not written in fully managed code?

Exercise 5 solution

DataList and Repeater. Whenever possible in ASP.NET 2.0 pages, switch to using the fully managed code controls: GridView, DetailsView, or FormView.

Exercise 6

Does ASP.NET 2.0 support HTML tables within a template? Explain.

Exercise 6 solution

Yes. VWD offers a useful interface to create HTML tables by using Menu: Layout ➪ Insert Table.

Exercise 7

Once a column is added to a GridView as a bound type, can it be converted to a template?

Exercise 7 solution

Yes. In the smart task panel, click edit columns, select the bound column and click on "Convert this field into a Templated Field."

Exercise 8

What is the main difference between the DataList and Repeater controls?

Exercise 8 solution

The DataList control puts each record in a cell of an overall HTML table. This permits formatting, such as repeat direction and number of columns. The Repeater control does not use an overall HTML table. (However, both allow HTML tables inside each item template.)

Chapter 11

Exercise 1

What is the difference between the SQL terms `UPDATE` and `INSERT INTO`?

Exercise 1 solution

`UPDATE` changes values in an existing record. `INSERT INTO` creates a new record and, optionally, adds values to the nascent record.

Exercise 2

What is the difference between the commands New and Edit?

Exercise 2 solution

New performs an `INSERT INTO` to create a new record (optionally filling values into its fields). Edit performs an `UPDATE` to change values in an existing record.

Exercise 3

How do you configure a GridView to create a new record?

Exercise 3 solution

GridView does not support adding a new record. Instead, use a hyperlink to a DetailsView that can perform an `INSERT INTO`.

Exercise 4

How does a command field know which command to execute?

Exercise 4 solution

It will include one of the Show properties, such as ShowEditButton or ShowDeleteButton.

Exercise 5

What is the purpose of a `DataKeyName` property in a data-bound control?

Exercise 5 solution

It allows updates to a Primary Key field by holding the old value of the field and using that in the `WHERE` clause of the `UPDATE` statement.

Exercise 6

What is the difference between a command field and a command column?

Exercise 6 solution

They function the same. CommandFields are used by GridViews with its vertical arrangement of fields. CommandColumn is used by DetailsView with its horizontal alignment of fields.

Exercise 7

Values that a user types into a textbox will always be of the data type string. How can a typed value be changed to a number for a numeric field?

Exercise 7 solution

In the `DataSource.ControlParameter` for that field, set the type to one of the numeric types. ASP.NET 2.0 will then perform the conversion if it is possible.

Exercise 8

What property adds the capacity to delete records to a DetailsView control?

Exercise 8 solution

In the DetailsView's data source control, add a DeleteCommand that is a proper SQL `DELETE` statement (almost always including a `WHERE` clause, so you only delete one record). Ensure that the DataKeyNames in the DetailsView includes the Primary key field that is used in the `WHERE` clause of the data source's `DELETE` command. Then, in the DetailsView, add a CommandField with its `ShowDeleteButton=True`.

Chapter 16

Exercise 1

Describe how to induce VWD to automatically type for you the first and last lines of an event procedure.

Exercise 1 solution

In Design view, double-click on the control and VWD will automatically create the opening and closing lines of code for the default event. This works very well for a button.

In Source view, drop down the list of controls at the top of the code window and select the control. Then drop down the events window at the top right of the code window and select the event. VWD will automatically create the opening and closing lines of code for the default event.

Exercise 2

Contrast events that end in "-ing" with events that end in "-ed."

Exercise 2 solution

Events that end in "-ing" are triggered before the name of the event. Events that end in "-ed" are triggered after the named event. For example, the `MyControl.Initializing` event occurs, then ASP.NET 2.0 initializes MyControl, then `the MyControl.Initialized` events occur.

Exercise 3

What is the data type of the Object Sender in the arguments of an event handler?

Exercise 3 solution

It is not a string containing the name of the sending object. Rather, it is an object of the type of the sender. If the sender is a button, the sender object in the event handler argument is of the data type button.

Exercise 4

List places where event handler code can be located.

Exercise 4 solution

- Option 1—On the same page as the controls, located anywhere on the page.
- Option 2—On a separate page which holds only code.

Exercise 5

Can you mix code languages on a single ASPX page?

Exercise 5 solution

No.

Exercise 6

Compare and contrast command buttons and custom buttons.

Exercise 6 solution

Both accept a user click and trigger events. Command buttons are provided by ASP.NET 2.0 and are only of a few types: New, Delete, Select, and so on. Custom buttons are provided by the user and can be for any purpose. When a command button is clicked, it invokes a built-in method of the data-bound control; the designer does not write code. When a custom button is clicked, ASP.NET 2.0 will trigger whatever procedure has been written by the designer.

Exercise 7

When a selection is made in a GridView or list control and you have written an event handler, how can you identify (from within the event handler) which item was selected?

Exercise 7 solution

```
MyControl.SelectedValue
```

Exercise 8

Describe the steps to use a general error page for an entire application.

Exercise 8 solution

1. Create the general error page and store it in the root of the Web application.
2. Create or open the `global.asax` file in the root of the Web application. Within that file, add to the `Application_Error` event a `Response.Redirect` to your general error page. *(Do not use a `Page_Error` event on each page of the site. Errors will automatically be forwarded to the `global.asax` and handled by its `Application_Error` event.)*

Index

D

F

G

L

M